THE JOURNALS OF JOSIAH GORGAS
1857–1878

The Journals of Josiah Gorgas 1857–1878

EDITED BY

Sarah Woolfolk Wiggins

WITH A FOREWORD BY

Frank E. Vandiver

THE UNIVERSITY OF ALABAMA PRESS
Tuscaloosa and London

Copyright © 1995
The University of Alabama Press
Tuscaloosa, Alabama 35487–0380
All rights reserved
Manufactured in the United States of America

Designed by Paula C. Dennis

∞

The paper on which this book is printed meets the minimum requirements of
American National Standard for Information Science-Permanence of Paper for
Printed Library Materials, ANSI Z39.48–1984.

Library of Congress Cataloging-in-Publication Data

Gorgas, Josiah, 1818–1883.
    The journals of Josiah Gorgas, 1857–1878 / edited by Sarah Woolfolk Wiggins ;
with a foreword by Frank E. Vandiver.
        p.   cm.
    Includes bibliographical references and index.
    ISBN 0-8173-0770-2 (alk. paper)
    1. Gorgas, Josiah, 1818–1883—Diaries. 2. United States—History—Civil War,
1861–1865—Personal narratives, Confederate. 3. Alabama—History—Civil War,
1861–1865. 4. Reconstruction—Alabama. 5. Generals—Confederate States of
America—Diaries.
I. Wiggins, Sarah Woolfolk, 1934–   . II. Title.
E467.1.G68A3   1995
973.7'82—dc20
[B]   94-21651

British Library Cataloguing-in-Publication Data available

For
Henrietta

Contents

Antebellum
January 1857–March 1861

Civil War
June 1862–May 1865

Illustrations

Maps

Photographs

Foreword

FRANK E. VANDIVER

Josiah Gorgas's journals rank among the better sources in southern history. Most famous as a soldier in the "Old Army" and later in the Confederate Army, Gorgas had an unusual career in the United States Ordnance Department, as Chief of Confederate Ordnance, and after the war in business and higher education. Well educated and widely read, Gorgas had a lively outlook on his world. A Pennsylvanian, he married Amelia Gayle, daughter of one of Alabama's governors, and began a lifetime devotion to her and the South she loved.

Sarah Woolfolk Wiggins has done much more than present a well-edited version of Gorgas's diaries and journals; she has interpreted them in full Gorgas family context and in the perspective of the times they cover. She offers biographical sketches of family members and friends. Her devoted efforts give point and meaning to Gorgas's lengthy recollections of a life that spanned sixty-five busy years, 1818–1883; years filled with travel, duty, war, and an especially touching family life. Wiggins informs with the sort of editorial notes expected of a careful scholar, but she enlightens with wide knowledge of American and southern history.

She sees, for instance, the importance of social networking in the Old and New South and uses the Gorgas family closeness to illustrate the value of "connexions." She sees, too, the significance of Gorgas's careful record keeping for an unusual sweep of history. Careful to preserve the fullness of the Gorgas tale, Wiggins is at pains to present as complete a book as possible, with the result that Josiah Gorgas speaks for himself in his clear, unpuffed prose. His opinions are crisp, his eye sharp, his prejudices fairly typical for his era and presented without apology.

His journals have long intrigued me. In the 1940s I became interested in writing a biography of General Gorgas. While working on the Confederate Ordnance records in the National Archives in Washington, D.C., I made the acquaintance of Mrs. Aileen Gorgas Wrightson, daughter of Josiah's son, William Crawford Gorgas, one of yellow fever's conquerors. She sent me to Tuscaloosa, Alabama, to meet her three surviving aunts—Mary Gayle ("Mamie") Gorgas, Christine Amelia ("Minnie") Gorgas Palfrey, and Maria Bayne ("Ria") Gorgas. By the time I reached Tuscaloosa in 1945, "Mamie" was dead, but "Minnie" and "Ria" were full of life. Little old ladies they were, but not tennis shoe types. Witty, charming, zealous teasers, they took me in with some skepticism. As I look back on the wonderful three weeks I spent with them, I realize that for the first week they were testing me and having much fun.

Accustomed to having all kinds of visitors coming to ask about their world-famous brother, they were excited to have someone interested in their father, whom they revered. They plied me with various decoctions—ice cream and sherry, ice cream and tomatoes (!), and an occasional luncheon—talked eagerly about my proposed biography of the general, and showed me absolutely nothing. I kept asking if they had papers, especially a copy of Josiah's rumored diary that I desperately wanted to see. They turned away the questions always with vague uncertainties. After a week, I almost gave up—my nerves and digestion rebelled.

My favorite, "Ria," finally burst out laughing at one lunch as I must have looked stricken when another experimental menu came my way. "That's enough," she said. "Go and look at the trunk at the top of the stairs." I do not remember how I got to the trunk, but it seemed magical when I reached it—an old-fashioned round-top, time worn and a little battered, it promised every treasure I imagined. When I opened it, I noticed that someone had carefully filed documents in manila folders—the first folder contained letters from General Lee to Gorgas about ordnance needs of the Army of Northern Virginia. I was looking into a true treasure chest. The trove continued. I took out layer after layer of letters from President Jefferson Davis, from most of the various Confederate army commanders, from ordnance officers in the field, from arsenals and armories and laboratories, from Confederate agents in England, Bermuda, Nassau, Cuba. If I had not hoped so hard for the diaries I would have wallowed in riches beyond belief—but I was dejected as I stared at the empty trunk. Not a single volume of Gorgas's diaries was in it.

As I was beginning to put the documents back, I noticed a scrap of paper that seemed caught in a crack; I pulled on it and up came the trunk's false bottom. There, spread out neatly were the journals—safe, sound, and real. The ladies were as elated as I was, and they heartily approved of my proposal to publish the Civil War sections.

Always, for me, the Gorgas House on the campus of The University of

Alabama will be a kind of Camelot, a dream place where I fell in love with two wonderful ladies and into the world of the Civil War.

Enter that world now, some of the world before the war, and the harsh world of Reconstruction through the eyes and words of Josiah Gorgas—an unusually observant, passionate man, a "galvanized Rebel" who deserves rank among the true geniuses of American logistics.

Introduction

Josiah Gorgas (1818–1883) was a soldier, ordnance administrator, industrialist, educator, and always a husband and father. When he began his journals on January 1, 1857, his stated intent was to instruct his children, especially his eldest son, William Crawford. "Such a record from the hand of my father," he wrote, "would command my reverence and affection. May this not be unworthy of theirs." In addition to transmitting values to his children, Josiah subconsciously maintained the journals as a matter of self-discipline. Each year on his birthday, July 1, Josiah weighed his accomplishments for the past year and usually compared his current position with that on July 1 in previous decades. Ever the professional soldier, his journals gave him the information with which to assess his progress almost as if he were evaluating himself for a promotion.

Maintained between 1857 and mid-1878, the journals reflect Josiah's economic successes and failures, detail the course of the South through the Civil War, and describe the ordeal of Reconstruction in the South. Few journals cover such a sweep of the history of antebellum, Civil War, and Reconstruction America. An added dimension of the journals is their view of Victorian family life as Josiah explored his feelings about aspects of parental responsibilities.

After Josiah met Amelia Gayle, the woman who became his wife, the focus of his life shifted. He adopted the South as his own. Five years after his marriage he described what had happened to him: "The South has, indeed, . . . wooed and won me. Its blandishments have stolen my senses, and I am its willing victim."[1] A Pennsylvania Yankee now married to a daughter of a former Alabama governor, Josiah recognized that he had been absorbed by the world of his wife, and he reveled in that sweet surrender. His marriage permitted the son of a poor farmer to be received into a class of southern society that he could have reached on his own only with great difficulty. His conversion to become an adopted son of the South ultimately led him to resign his commission in the U.S. Army and to cast his lot with the southern Confederacy.

This absorption into Amelia's family also led to an estrangement from his own family. While Josiah's journals are peopled with his wife's family, references to his own family are infrequent, and among the voluminous Gorgas family papers only one letter from them after 1861 survives.[2] After the war Josiah sought refuge with Amelia's relatives in the South, not his own in the North, recognizing that his own family was "bitter" against all "rebels." This estrangement was severe and lifelong after he allied with the Confederacy, and he accepted it with total resignation: "I do not," he wrote, "look for good feeling from northern friends or relatives."[3]

Josiah was the ultimate patriarch, obsessed with his responsibility for the financial and moral well-being of his wife and children. The antebellum and postwar journals reflect his deep involvement in the day-to-day activities of his children and his great pride in them. Although the wartime journals focus primarily on the demands of the Confederate Ordnance Department, even here Josiah regularly described his activities with his children—introducing them to Confederate generals, taking walks, going swimming, attending church, nursing the sick.[4] He was never a father so absorbed in his profession as to ignore his children, and his utter devotion to Amelia is touching. He considered that his life dated only from the time of his marriage.[5]

If Josiah's integration into southern society was complete, his desire to put down permanent roots in the region was intense. Wherever the family lived before or after the war, Josiah planted a garden and fruit trees and set about landscaping the adjacent grounds.[6] After his marriage he fell under the spell of the southern ideal of the country gentleman as he wistfully dreamed of buying a southern plantation and living amidst servants. He grieved whenever reassignment uprooted his family and expressed envy of one who had been able to live and die in the haunts of his childhood.

Journal entries are particularly numerous for the year 1865. Separated from his family and thrashing about for a new profession with which to support them, Josiah had unusual leisure to record his thoughts on many subjects. The journals in this period provide an especially full picture of the frustrations, turmoil, and adjustments of the first year of Reconstruction in Alabama. His acquiescence to Confederate defeat was total as he worried about the possibility of arrest or exile; he did not glorify or boast about a "Lost Cause." "It is best for us now to turn the other cheek," he wrote to Amelia.[7]

The antebellum Gorgas household reflected a comfortable, but not lavish, lifestyle. That world contrasted sharply with the family's gradual descent into genteel poverty after the Civil War, a result of Josiah's careers as a manager of a failing ironworks and as a harassed teacher in a school verging on bankruptcy. The harsh eyes of the world judged Josiah to be a success as a soldier and a failure as a civilian. Like so many other southern families fallen on hard times, all the Gorgases had left after 1865 was pride in the family's past. As Josiah agonized over the possibility of failure in his parental responsibilities, his family attempted to boost his morale by emphasizing his earlier successes.[8] From such reminiscences as these grew the South's nostalgia and veneration of the "Lost Cause."

The Gorgas family was the archetype of southern families of their time and class as the household became headquarters for an extended family. The children's nurse became like a devoted maiden aunt, remaining with the family until her death. Amelia's widowed stepmother (with four children) regularly came and went and taught the Gorgas children as well as her own. One of Amelia's brothers, mentally shattered in the war and helpless thereafter, was supported financially by two brothers-in-law and nursed by his stepmother and Amelia. Another brother, a Confederate sailor twice imprisoned and weakened in health, considered the Gorgas household his home until his marriage. The oldest sister, an antebellum widow, coped poorly with life and repeatedly sought help from Amelia and Josiah. Another sister, widowed in the last weeks of the war, moved in with the family of Amelia and later with that of another sister. The youngest sister, the wife of a wealthy New Orleans attorney, enjoyed wealth and leisure that she generously attempted to share with her less fortunate siblings. Still, she and her husband and their eight children made the Gorgas home their headquarters for months at a time. The Gayle sisters and stepmother regularly named their offspring for each other, swapped children, kept house together, and took in unmarried or widowed relatives. Gayle family members almost constantly resided with the Gorgases. At one point the household numbered twenty-three, "besides servants."[9] If ever there was a movable feast, it was Josiah's table, whether in Richmond, Brierfield, Sewanee, or Tuscaloosa. Few months during the life of the Gorgas marriage saw Amelia and Josiah living alone with their children, almost never after 1865. In the spring of 1866 Amelia jokingly predicted that they would "be obliged" to construct "a log cabin in the yard . . . for our numerous visitors."[10]

Josiah's racial views were those pervasive among educated nineteenth-century Americans, North and South. Paternalistic and patronizing, his views never changed before, during, or after the war. Before and after the war he referred to blacks as "darkies,"[11] and in 1857 he commented with consternation in his journal about whites in Maine entertaining Frederick Douglass. Despite his belief in black inferiority Josiah was ready to enlist slaves into the Confederate service with the promise of freedom as the South's fortunes sank late in the war. In the postwar era race relations seemed to Josiah so dreadful as to be a "gigantic dream." He considered blacks to be such infants in intelligence and morality that they soon would disappear before "the moral & intellectual superiority of the white."[12] He was appalled that suffrage was extended to blacks, that blacks and whites sat together in the Alabama constitutional convention, that the legislature listened to prayers by a black chaplain.

A broad streak of fatalism runs throughout the journals. Josiah viewed the war in its early stages as an event where God was on the side of the Confederacy. As the Confederacy's fortunes waned, he wondered if God had abandoned the South, and at the surrender he accepted the outcome as the judgment of God. "Providence seems to have utterly abandoned us to our enemies, and we have nothing to do but submit."[13] His fatalism extended to his efforts to provide for his family during Reconstruction. Only faintly cognizant of the larger economic circumstances that doomed the Brierfield Iron Works he saw failure again as the will of God. Perhaps that fatalism made it easier for him to acknowledge that after the war all his hopes had "burned to ashes in my mouth."[14]

Josiah ultimately succumbed in 1883 to the effects of a series of strokes. The first symptoms had appeared in 1862,[15] and over the years he suffered increasing pain until he experienced a major paralytic stroke in 1879. The mixture of opiates and other medicinal prescriptions made him very depressed and at times near suicidal. The medical combinations were enough to overwhelm the strongest physical constitution.

The journals bluntly assess the abilities of Josiah's contemporaries whether Confederate political or military leaders or business associates or Episcopal bishops. He poured out his frustrations at his own failures in the ironmaking business, at the unrealistic expectations for Sewanee held by the leaders of the Episcopal Church, at his uncontrollable pain and depression. His journals provided the one place where he could release the furies of his personal despair without depressing his beloved Amelia.

The originals of Josiah's journals are now located in the Gorgas Family Papers in the Hoole Special Collections Library, The University of Alabama, Tuscaloosa, Alabama. The eighteen volumes of the journals physically reflect that they were composed during years of war and peace. The books are either 4½" × 7½" or 8½" × 8½" and are written in ink and pencil. Entries range from one line to several pages and vary in frequency. Sometimes lapses of months occur between entries, and in some instances

Josiah summarizes his activities during the time when he made no entries. The quality of paper and ink vary, and the journals, except for the post-1865 volume, are in remarkably readable condition. However, some pages in the volume beginning in 1866 are quite fragile where repairs with scotch tape have been attempted. In many places the tape has deteriorated and become either sticky or brittle. Numerous pages are loose from their spine and are fraying around their edges.

More serious damage has occurred where portions of the journals were defaced in a large, dark, looping scrawl. The information in the defaced sections is most often one of three types: blunt but perceptive assessments of Confederate leaders, reflections of Josiah's depressed mental state, or observations about family members. An unidentified person has attempted to reconstruct some of the defaced passages, writing between the defaced lines of the journals. Some of these inserted transcriptions misread the original.

The identity of the person or persons responsible for defacing the journals is unclear. Evidence suggests two possibilities. Clues within collections of Gorgas and Gayle family papers suggest one individual, but an interview with a librarian suggests another. While Josiah's eldest son, William Crawford, was stationed in the Panama Canal Zone as chief sanitary officer, typed transcriptions of the journals were begun, probably by a secretary but certainly by someone unfamiliar with Gorgas family names and the South in general. Family correspondence reflects that volumes of the journals went to Panama, and typed copies were mailed in installments to the Gorgas siblings. This process continued after the eldest son became U.S. Surgeon General in 1914, and the family in Tuscaloosa received copies from wherever he was stationed at the moment, for example, Washington, D.C., and Caracas, Venezuela.[16] In the days before the advent of Xerox machines copies of the transcriptions subsequently were retyped and distributed to the families of Amelia's sisters. Inaccuracies have crept into the various typescripts donated by members of the Gayle and Gorgas families to several libraries and archives. The Gorgas Family Papers in the Hoole Special Collections Library contain two different typed transcriptions of the complete journals, 1857–1878. The Alabama Department of Archives and History, Montgomery, has a carbon copy of a transcription for the period from July 1863 through December 1865. Other complete carbon copies are located in the William Crawford Gorgas Papers, Manuscript Division, Library of Congress, Washington, D.C., and in the Josiah Gorgas Papers, Southern Historical Collection, University of North Carolina, Chapel Hill, North Carolina.

Comparisons of handwritings and inks and determination of access to particular copies of the journals suggest information to identify the person who feared future generations might think less of Josiah for his perceptive

Sample of a defaced page from the Journals (Courtesy of Hoole Special Collections, University of Alabama, Tuscaloosa, Alabama)

honesty and his reflections of self-doubt. All of Josiah's children consistently expressed great pride in their father's gutsy confrontations with adversity. William Crawford, especially, was very philosophical in his letters to his sisters about the fleeting nature of fame and was deeply sympathetic toward his father's mental and physical anguish.[17] At the time when the cult of the "Lost Cause" grew strong in the Depression-era South much of the Gorgas material was in the hands of the daughter of

William Crawford and Marie Gorgas. All of the defaced copies of the Gorgas journals—originals and typed transcriptions—were at some time in her possession, or she had access to them in Tuscaloosa in the Gorgas home. The ink and the pen of the defacing scrawl closely resemble those appearing in her handwriting.

Other clues come from examination of the journal of Josiah's mother-in-law, Sarah Haynsworth Gayle. The original of this journal (1827–1835), located in the Hoole Special Collections Library, has been defaced in the same fashion as have the Gorgas journals, and, even worse, words and lines have been cut from the Gayle journal. The original of the Gayle journal was at one time with the Gorgas manuscripts in the Gorgas home in Tuscaloosa. Additional clues exist in the microfilm of a handwritten copy of parts of the Gayle journal in the Bayne-Gayle Papers at the Southern Historical Collection. Marie Gorgas, wife of William Crawford Gorgas, copied by hand portions of the Gayle journal in 1901 while she and her husband were stationed in Ecuador. The same defacing appears on this copy in the same style with the same ink as mars the Gorgas journals. That copy appears to have been in the hands of only William Crawford and Marie Gorgas and their daughter; the latter permitted the University of North Carolina Library to microfilm that copy, which has since disappeared.[18]

Discussions with a thirty-five-year veteran of the Hoole Special Collections Library suggest another person who may have been responsible for defacing the Gorgas journals. After the Gorgas papers were donated to the university library, one of Josiah's descendants came regularly to the library and read through the Gayle and Gorgas journals. She was seen applying scotch tape to mend the Gorgas and Gayle journals and otherwise "fussing" with both journals. This librarian always has presumed that this lady defaced both journals, although the librarian cannot recall actually witnessing such action.

Reproduced in this edition are the eighteen volumes that Josiah himself called his journals. In his last months as chancellor of The University of the South at Sewanee, Tennessee, Josiah also maintained a daybook that he termed a "Diary of the School – Win[ter] Term 1877" between August 1877 and July 1878. Only one entry for this period appears in his journal. Apparently, Josiah and his family never considered this daybook as part of his journals, and this daybook is unlike the journals in any way. The daybook entries are only one or two lines in length, contain no personal reflections, and list who visited Sewanee, wrote to Josiah, skipped chapel, or left school. Individuals are mentioned only by their last initial. Josiah's growing difficulties with the Sewanee board of trustees are totally absent from this daybook. Because this document differs so greatly from Josiah's journals and because he and his descendants clearly did not consider it a part of his journals any more than they did his personal account book (with which the daybook apparently always has been filed), the contents of this calendar-daybook are not included with Josiah's journals.

Although someone defaced portions of the journals, apparently no censorship has been attempted by removing pages. Many pages of the last volume (1866–1878) have separated from their binding, but all of the pages are intact except for that page containing the journal's final entry. The eldest Gorgas daughter, Jessie, copied her father's last entry. This entry appears after Josiah's last surviving notation, in her hand, signed, enclosed in quotation marks, and incorrectly dated. The contents of this entry "sound" as if Josiah had written it, and the information is typical of entries made on earlier birthdays: reflections on his family and personal evaluation of his own progress in life combined with comments on current events. This last page, as one of those loose in the journal, probably became damaged almost to illegibility, and Jessie copied its contents, dated it incorrectly, and added it to the journal. This entry is included here as part of Josiah's journals.

The Gorgas manuscripts remained in the hands of the family in the Gorgas home until 1958. At that time the Gorgas descendants, Aileen Gorgas Wrightson (William Crawford's daughter), Minna Palfrey Tait and Jessie Palfrey Leake (daughters of Josiah's daughter Minnie), and Gene Palfrey Ellis and William Gorgas Palfrey (grandchildren of Minnie Gorgas Palfrey), gave the items then located in the Gorgas House—correspondence, original journals, typed transcriptions, Bibles belonging to both the Gayle and Gorgas families—to The University of Alabama, where they now remain as the Gorgas Family Papers. Subsequently, family members have augmented the university's Gorgas holdings with additional gifts. Wrightson donated a voluminous collection of materials relative to her father that comprise the William Crawford Gorgas Papers at The University of Alabama, and she transferred to The University of Alabama items earlier given to the Smithsonian Institution. George Tait (grandson of Minnie Gorgas Palfrey) has contributed Gorgas manuscripts to the Gorgas Family Papers, and Mary Adams Hughes has added the journal and the scrapbooks of her grandmother Sarah Gayle Crawford (Amelia's older sister) and the correspondence of her grandparents as the Sarah Gayle and William B. Crawford Papers to the university's holdings. Other manuscript collections are cited in the bibliography of manuscript sources.

After Josiah's journals were transcribed in the early twentieth century, the originals apparently were returned to the Gorgas family papers stored in the family home in Tuscaloosa. They lay forgotten until the explorations in the 1940s of Frank Vandiver, then a young history student. Vandiver subsequently edited and published the Civil War portions of the journals, omitting the defaced passages.[19] Although the Gorgas family papers remain a rich manuscript resource, the treasure trove found by Vandiver with the journals has vanished.

A reading of the entire eighteen volumes of Josiah's journals, rather than just those familiar ones of the war years, adds new dimensions to our understanding of a man usually known only as a military figure. As a conscientious father Josiah provides through his journals an unusual perspective on nineteenth-century southern family life. His journals also broaden our knowledge of Reconstruction as seen from the very personal perspective of a participant.

Above all else, the journals dramatize a quality about the South that escapes so many historians who write about the region. Southerners rely on social and family networks—what southerners call "connexions"—to make their world function. On the surface the twists and turns of Josiah's life and careers may appear to be luck or accidents of fate. Closer examination, however, reveals that an old acquaintance or some hidden network of relationships is the key to understanding the course of events. These relationships are visible from study of the Gorgas manuscript collections and are detailed in the sketches in the biographical directory that follows the text of the journals. For example, from these sketches one learns that Francis Strother Lyon of Demopolis had been a prominent member of the Alabama House of Representatives when Amelia's father was Alabama governor. The two men also were close friends. Thus, it was not by accident that Gorgas and Lyon, who had been only casual wartime acquaintances, embarked together after the war on a business venture when Josiah resided in Alabama not far from Lyon's home in Demopolis. Nor is it surprising that Secretary of War John B. Floyd intervened in Josiah's army assignments after they had traveled together between Philadelphia and Baltimore in 1858 when one learns from Josiah and Amelia's correspondence that Floyd had been a college classmate of the husband of Amelia's older sister, Sarah. And certainly, in 1865 Amelia and her sister Maria did not arbitrarily choose to refugee to rural Maryland where neither personally knew anyone. But the reason for their choice becomes clear from the memoirs of one of Maria's sons who explained that they were welcomed by the generous hospitality of the elderly father of the Yale roommate of Maria's husband, T. L. Bayne. Historians generally have not seen the importance and power of personal "connexions" in southern life.[20] Those who would understand the South—whether family, village, town, or city—must unravel those invisible webs of southern relationships. Josiah's journals and the family's correspondence drive home the reality that public and private life in the nineteenth-century South turned on "who you knew."

Notes

1. Josiah Gorgas and John Hillhouse, "Epistolary Gossipings of Travel, and Its Reminiscences," *Russell's Magazine*, V (May 1859), 134.

2. [Christine Gorgas Zerbe] to [Mary Gayle Gorgas], September 2, 1884, Gorgas Family Papers, Hoole Special Collections Library, The University of Alabama, Tuscaloosa, Ala. (hereafter cited as GFP).

3. Josiah Gorgas Journals, April 13, 1868, ibid.

4. For a discussion of Josiah as a father see Sarah Woolfolk Wiggins, "A Victorian Father: Josiah Gorgas and His Family," in *In Joy and In Sorrow: Women, Family, and Marriage in the Victorian South, 1830–1900,* ed. by Carol Bleser (New York: Oxford University Press, 1991), 239–40.

5. JG to AG, July 1, [1858], GFP. Many letters in the Gorgas Family Papers are undated; others have missing day, month, or year, which are supplied in these notes in brackets. Numerous undated letters can be placed in a particular year, especially 1858. Formerly, individual letters could be identified by a folder and an item number. Recently, Hoole Special Collections Library has reorganized this collection, removing all identification from each item. The result is that a dozen letters may exist for one year that can be cited only as [year], such as [1858].

6. Ibid., [1858], February 23, 1866, September 30, 1878, no month 27, 1878.

7. AG to JG, June 26, [1865], JG to AG, June 14, July 19, July no day, August 14, 20, September 4, 1865, February 15, 1866, ibid.

8. See [AG to JG], [1865], ibid.

9. Gorgas Journals, September 8, 1867.

10. AG to JG, March 18, [1866], GFP.

11. JG to AG, [July 1858], September 26, 1878, ibid.

12. Gorgas Journals, September 25, 29, October 2, 6, 1864, June 15, 1865, January 13, 1867.

13. JG to AG, May 11, 1865, GFP.

14. Gorgas Journals, June 30, 1867.

15. JG to AG, [1862], GFP.

16. See, for example, WCG to AG, October 3, 1912, from the Canal Zone: "Father mentions in his journal"; WCG to Mary Gorgas, October 27, 1912, from the Canal Zone: "I send you as a birthday present a copy of fathers journal"; WCG to Richard Gorgas, September 5, 1916, from Caracas, Venezuela: "I enclose you another installment of the diary"; Jessie Gorgas to WCG, September 30, 1916: "The family is enjoying reading the diary," William Crawford Gorgas Papers, Hoole Special Collections Library, The University of Alabama, Tuscaloosa, Ala.

17. See Sarah Woolfolk Wiggins, "Introduction," John M. Gibson, *Physician to the World: The Life of General William C. Gorgas* (1950, reprint ed., Tuscaloosa: University of Alabama Press, 1989), xx.

18. The Bayne-Gayle Papers, Southern Historical Collection, University of North Carolina, Chapel Hill, N.C., also contain typed transcriptions of Sarah Gayle's journal, in addition to the handwritten copy on microfilm. Another typed transcription of the Gayle journal is located in the Thomas Bayne Denègre Papers, Tulane University Library, New Orleans, La.

19. Frank E. Vandiver, ed., *The Civil War Diary of Josiah Gorgas* (University, Ala.: University of Alabama Press, 1947).

20. A rare exception to this statement is Daniel E. Sutherland, *The Confederate Carpetbaggers* (Baton Rouge: Louisiana State University Press, 1988).

Acknowledgments

Without the encouragement of the descendants of John Gayle this project could not have been undertaken. Gene Palfrey Ellis of Atlanta, Georgia, and Dr. William Gorgas Palfrey of Baton Rouge, Louisiana (descendants of Josiah and Amelia Gorgas), gave me permission to work with the Gorgas manuscripts, provided me with photographs, genealogical information, and family stories, and became my friends. Two New Orleans cousins of Gene and Will also have been encouraging. George Denègre (descendant of Maria Bayne) and Dr. David Aiken (descendant of Mary Aiken) have sent me photographs, books, genealogical tables, Xerox copies of manuscripts, typescripts, and articles. Mr. Denègre alerted me to family material in archives and libraries across the country that I did not know existed and contacted surviving Gayle descendants for family information. Dr. Aiken has secured accurate information for me from gravestones in New Orleans cemeteries. To this day I am acquainted with these two gentlemen only by mail and by phone. To a total stranger these four busy people have been incredibly generous with their time and information. In them the southern tradition of graciousness continues. Amelia and her sisters would be very proud.

The staffs of various libraries and archives have been most helpful: Manuscript Division, Library of Congress, Washington, D.C.; Manuscript Department, Perkins Library, Duke University, Durham, North Carolina; National Library of Medicine, National Institutes of Health, Bethesda, Maryland; University of the South Archives, Sewanee, Tennessee; Special Collections, Tulane University Library, New Orleans, Louisiana; Southern Historical Collection, University of North Carolina, Chapel Hill, North Carolina. The staff of the Hoole Special Collections

Library, The University of Alabama, Tuscaloosa, Alabama, has provided me with more than a place to work. Patiently, Joyce Lamont, Gunetta Rich, Clark Center, Patricia Jones, and Jerry Oldshue have answered my questions, located information, and otherwise assisted me far beyond what one expects of a library staff; they have brought me food and given me a typewriter at especially frantic stages of this work. Their knowledge and concern have been invaluable. Maggie Sudduth, docent of the Gorgas House, has assisted me in securing photographs.

Two grants moved this project forward at critical periods. A grant from the National Endowment for the Humanities in the summer 1989 permitted me to research the collections at the Southern Historical Collection, University of North Carolina, Chapel Hill, and at Duke University, Durham, North Carolina. A grant from the National Historical Publications and Records Commission released me from teaching and provided assistance in the preparation of Josiah's journals for publication. I am indebted particularly for the encouragement and knowledge of Mary Giunta of the NHPRC staff who guided me in grant writing and in focusing on the essentials of the project. Richard Sheldon of the NHPRC staff also led me to a better understanding of what comprises a documentary edition through the NHPRC editing seminar at the University of Wisconsin. The guidance of Mary and Dick and the support of the NHPRC grant pushed my work to a conclusion. Timothy Connelly, another of the NHPRC staff, unearthed information in the National Archives that I alone could not have located. Without the support of the NHPRC the project would not now be complete.

Thomas E. Jeffrey of the Thomas Edison Papers, Rutgers University, New Brunswick, New Jersey, and Beverly Palmer of Pomona College, Claremont, California, have advised me about editing principles at the NHPRC seminar and ever afterward. They assisted me to focus on what was peculiar about Josiah's journals, gave me options and examples, and pushed me to confront and to solve my own problems. As good teachers, they made me think.

John Duffy of the University of Maryland has given me the benefit of his extensive knowledge of nineteenth-century medicine. He has discussed the medical treatments prescribed for Josiah, explaining what these medicines were as well as their side effects.

Craig Remington of The University of Alabama Cartographic Laboratory has converted my lists and scribbles into clear and precise maps.

Professor Frank Vandiver, director of Mosher Institute for Defense Studies, Texas A&M University, College Station, Texas, encouraged me to undertake publication of all of Josiah's journals. The copyright on his edition of the Civil War journals has lapsed, and his other responsibilities prevent him from returning to the Gorgas material.

Two secretaries have typed and retyped this manuscript. Pamela

Franklin first typed the journals onto a word processor from a frightful copy, and Betty Wedgeworth added the countless additions. Ruth Smith Truss and Jason J. Battles have researched details and proofread for many hours. Their precision has spared me many mechanical problems. David Fischer has carefully prepared the index.

The University of Alabama has provided a sabbatical leave and a reduced teaching load to facilitate completion of this project. The university also has provided in-kind support to match assistance from the NHPRC.

My daughter Henrietta, a teenager when this project began and now a twenty-something, has listened patiently as I read aloud Josiah's letters and journals, while she took care of her own needs. Her toleration of my absorption in the Gorgas world has been remarkable. That she did not overchoose her parents' career is a telling commentary on growing up in an academic household.

The Gorgas family and its cousins in a very real sense have become an extension of my own. It is through their assistance that Josiah can speak to future generations.

Editorial Policy

The intent of a published edition of the journals of Josiah Gorgas is to allow the author to speak for himself to readers through a literal and readable text. The text has been transcribed exactly as it was written. Editorial intervention is minimized and appears in brackets in the text to replace footnotes located inconveniently at the end of a book. The editor has divided the journal text into antebellum, Civil War, and Reconstruction units and, within those divisions, created chapters.

Individuals important in Josiah's life are identified in a biographical directory. This group includes members of Josiah's family, Amelia's numerous relatives, and close friends and business associates of the Gorgas family. Military figures readily identifiable in general reference works are not included in the directory. Biographical entries include nicknames because so many of the children of Amelia and her sisters bore the same name and nickname. Birth and death dates are supplied if these could be found. A genealogical chart for the Gayle family and the Gorgas children also is included.

Persons are identified in the text by full name, if possible, when they are first mentioned. On the first occasion where names are misspelled, corrections follow in brackets. Corrections are repeated where confusion might occur. Bibliographies of sources consulted for annotation and for the biographical directory are included at the end of the edition. Readers should consult especially the bibliography of manuscript sources to locate additional biographical information.

On the first occasion where geographical names are misspelled, corrections follow in brackets. Maps accompany the text to aid the reader in following the movements and directions that Josiah describes.

Josiah was remarkably consistent and legible in his writing, regularly discussing the same topics and maintaining the same format over a period of twenty years. His handwriting clearly reflects his deteriorating health during the 1870s. Josiah repeatedly misspelled the same words, and these have not been emended. The occasional variations in his spellings follow the journals.

Antiquated or idiosyncratic spellings as well as misspelled words in the journals include

> accouchment - accouchement
> aids - aides
> alledged - alleged
> arthmetic - arithmetic
> beeves - beefs
> Blakeley - Blakely guns
> botts - bots
> cemetry - cemetery
> defence - defense
> defenceless - defenseless
> descendents - descendants
> despatch - dispatch
> egg-nogg - eggnog
> fillibuster - filibuster
> Freedman's Bureau - Freedmen's Bureau
> handkerchef - handkerchief
> harrassed - harassed
> indorse - endorse
> intrenchments - entrenchments
> moveable - movable
> negros - Negroes
> per cent - percent
> potatos - potatoes
> principal - principle
> protegee - protégé
> retailing - retelling
> schrapnel - shrapnel
> sett - set
> staid - stayed
> straitened - straightened
> visier - vizier
> weazle - weasel
> zince - zinc

Josiah's punctuation is excellent and appears in this edition as his own as the editor has been able to determine it. No alterations are made.

Instances where he capitalized words in mid-sentence have been allowed to stand. At first glance Josiah's periods at the end of sentences often resemble dashes, especially in the Civil War volumes. However, careful examination with a magnifying glass in a bright light reveals that some periods written in ink have bled through the cheap paper; others are smeared. What appear to be genuine dashes are infrequent, and the editor's transcription reproduces these as em dashes. Josiah occasionally left a space in his journals. For clarity for the reader these blanks are identified as [space]. His word combinations appear in various forms, sometimes as one word or as two words or as a hyphenated word. In this edition these words appear as Josiah wrote them, and they are not included in the list of idiosyncratic spellings. Where Josiah drew a line, a line appears in this edition. Josiah sometimes corrected earlier entries by inserting an asterisk in the text and placing a note at the bottom of the page. These insertions appear as Josiah wrote them.

Josiah's paragraphing is quite regular except in passages written in pocket-sized books during the Civil War. In an effort to conserve writing space in these smaller volumes he left a slight gap between sentences where he began a new subject. The editor has treated these breaks as she believes Josiah intended them, as opening a new paragraph.

Listed here are the conventions used in preparation of the text:

[ ]	to enclose editorial interventions
[??]	to enclose illegible word
< >	to enclose defaced material restored by editor
[[ ]]	to denote Josiah's use of brackets
( )	to denote Josiah's parentheses
_____	to denote Josiah's underscore
—	to denote Josiah's dashes

The date for each journal entry appears in boldface type to enable readers to identify easily the date of any entry. The most irregular aspect of Josiah's journals is his dateline for each entry. Sometimes he gives the day and month, and the editor has supplied the year enclosed in brackets. Often he gives the day of the month, and the editor has supplied month and year in brackets. Where only the day of the week appears in the journals, the editor has supplied the day, month, and year, again in brackets. Occasionally, Josiah wrote two entries on the same day. Those entries are dated as he wrote them.

No section of the journals is omitted, and defaced passages have been restored through a simple process. The editor placed the defaced page on a piece of glass with a bright light under the glass. A piece of yellow mylar was placed on top of the defaced manuscript page, and using a magnifying glass the editor separated the journals' words from the defacing scrawl. The resulting transcriptions disagree with the handwritten efforts to restore between the journals' lines portions of the defaced material and with the inaccurate typescripts that escaped defacing. Copies of two diagrams that appear in the text have been reproduced and appear where Josiah included them in his journals.

The editor has considered the journals' relationship to Josiah's other papers and believes that his journals can stand alone rather than be included with an edition of his letters. In fact, if an edition of Josiah's correspondence is ever undertaken, it should be a collection of the letters and journals of members of Amelia's family over a period of one hundred years and three generations.

Family of Josiah and Amelia Gorgas

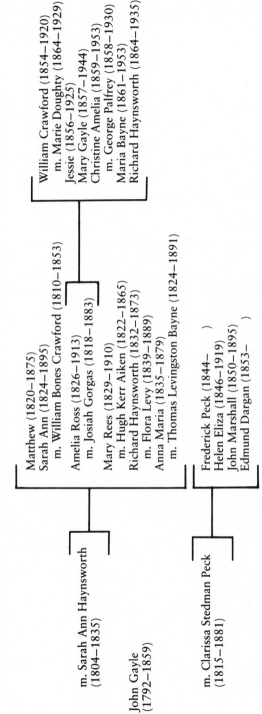

Prologue

Josiah Gorgas was born on July 1, 1818, in Running Pumps, Pennsylvania, the son of Joseph Gorgas and Sophia Atkinson. As the tenth child of a struggling clockmaker-mechanic-farmer, Josiah did not know the ease of a privileged childhood. Instead, the older children early assumed family responsibilities and contributed to the family's well-being. The family moved soon after Josiah's birth, first to Fishing Creek near Harrisburg, and then to Myerstown. Here Josiah grew up with little formal education except for a few years when his father was financially able to send the boy away to school.[1]

At eighteen Josiah moved into the household of his older sister Elizabeth and her husband Daniel Chapman in Lyons, New York. After an apprenticeship with a newspaper Josiah began reading law in the office of the local congressman, Graham Chapin. The young man's abilities and thirst for an education that his family could not afford led the congressman to nominate Josiah for an appointment to West Point.

In July 1837 Josiah became a West Point cadet and prepared himself for a career as a professional soldier. Here his education not only trained him in military subjects but also introduced him to cultural interests to which he would return with pleasure throughout the remainder of his life. Along with a heavy dose of mathematics during his first year at the academy Josiah took a course in French. Regularly as an adult, he retreated to the pleasure and discipline of reading and translating works written in that language. The junior year curriculum at West Point introduced Josiah to science and philosophy and to one of his great loves—landscape painting.[2] Throughout the remainder of his life Josiah painted contemporary scenes in watercolor or maintained a sketchbook or drew in the margins of his journals. Ranking sixth in his class of fifty-two at West Point, he chose the Ordnance Corps as his branch of service when he graduated in June 1841.

Josiah's first assignment was quite a plum for a young brevet second lieutenant: assistant ordnance officer at Watervliet Arsenal near Troy, New York. His older brother Solomon, a successful businessman, lived nearby in Philadelphia, and the two brothers enjoyed the cultural opportunities readily available to them.[3]

His next assignment—to Detroit Arsenal—was located in the cultural desert of the Northwest. This assignment was mercifully brief, and Josiah maneuvered himself back to Watervliet by January 1844.

Soon Josiah learned that a former classmate, John Hillhouse, planned a European tour, and despite his own limited financial resources Josiah determined to join his friend. As Josiah prepared for this trip of a lifetime in 1845, his youthful eagerness led him to commit a faux pas that proved costly in making long-lasting enemies among influential government officials. That the War Department had authorized his trip for six months to study foreign ordnance was not enough: Josiah wrote the U.S. Secretary of State requesting letters of introduction to several U.S. embassy officials in Europe. When he was refused, he wrote a second letter (apparently a rather blunt one) that eventually circulated to the War Department. These efforts made long-term enemies for him in both the State Department and War Department.

Oblivious to the seriousness of the damage of his efforts, Josiah sailed with Hillhouse to England in May 1845 and toured England, Scotland, and Ireland, where he visited art galleries at every opportunity. By the end of June Josiah was maneuvering for an extension to his leave from the War Department, and a friend in the department secured such for him despite the lingering effects of his earlier injudicious letters. During the summer of 1845 Josiah traveled through Holland, Germany, Austria, and Italy and in the fall through Switzerland, Italy, Greece, and Turkey, ending the tour in Paris in early 1846. Here Josiah indulged his artistic interests to the fullest while he sandwiched into his schedule visits to French military institutions. He left for home in early April and at the end of May 1846 resumed his responsibilities at Watervliet Arsenal.[4]

Fighting along the Mexican border had begun when Josiah returned from Europe, and he sought an assignment there. The desired opportunity came in late 1846 when he was assigned to assist in preparations of a siege train for artillery for General Winfield Scott's campaign in Mexico. As he wrote to his mother, he "could not desire any better employment" than what lay before him, for he had to make his "own way in the world, and as I have chosen the sword I must live by it."[5] Josiah embarked in January 1847 for Vera Cruz, where he played a vital role in erecting the army batteries that contributed to the fall of the city.

With Vera Cruz secure, Scott quickly moved the U.S. Army inland and out of the unhealthy city. Josiah accompanied the army as far as Cerro Gordo before he was ordered back to Vera Cruz to ensure dependable management of ordnance for Scott's army as it moved farther inland. Living in a city in ruins, Josiah found the simple matters of storage of ordnance and its transportation maddeningly difficult. In June 1847 a dreaded outbreak of yellow fever struck the city, and Josiah suffered a mild case while hundreds of other soldiers died.

Bored with his duty in Vera Cruz out of the war action, Josiah requested a reassignment in June 1847. However, other than one unsuccessful foray against Mexican guerrillas he saw no further military action. Although too late to participate in the major attacks on Mexico City, Josiah still wanted to see the area. His long anticipated replacement at Vera Cruz arrived in early February 1848, and Josiah headed to the interior where he was assigned again to monotonous administrative duties similar to his responsibilities in Vera Cruz. Fighting had ceased by the time he reached Mexico City. His efforts to transfer to other duty failed, and he remained with the battery until the army evacuated and sailed home in July 1848. His service in the Mexican War did produce a promotion to first lieutenant in March 1847 but not the exciting military activity that Josiah had expected.[6]

Once in the United States, Gorgas was assigned briefly to Champlain Arsenal, Vergennes, Vermont, to put in order the accounts of that arsenal's deceased commander. This task completed by mid-December, he returned to Watervliet Arsenal. In this period he was frustrated as the War Department overlooked him in granting brevets to officers who had served with distinction in the Mexican War. This oversight perhaps was the result of lingering effects of those letters written immediately before his European trip in 1845.

In 1851 he held brief assignments at New York Arsenal on Governor's Island, Pittsburgh Arsenal, and Fort Monroe Arsenal before he was dispatched to Mount Vernon Arsenal north of Mobile, Alabama, in June 1853. Josiah found the oppressive heat of the Gulf South unbearable and immediately began repeated requests for reassignment. These requests stopped in the fall of 1853 when a major yellow fever epidemic struck nearby Mobile.

The location of Mount Vernon Arsenal atop a significant elevation north of Mobile made the area a traditional retreat from that city's periodic fever epidemics. In late summer of 1853 refugees from Mobile fled inland to escape this record outbreak, and among these was Amelia Gayle, the sister of the arsenal surgeon, Dr. Matt Gayle, bringing the children of one of their sisters. Each afternoon Amelia read aloud to the children on the porch of her brother's quarters, and Josiah always maintained that he fell in love with Amelia's voice before he met her. A whirlwind courtship led to their marriage on December 29, 1853. It was a genuine love match.

The daughter of a former Alabama governor, Amelia devoted herself to creating a domestic haven, a retreat, from the hectic professional world of her husband. Her success led Josiah to comment that there was "no peace or happiness away from" Amelia,[7] and when necessity separated him from his wife, he hung on receipt of her letters.[8] "Will there never be an electric telegraph between two hearts that yearn for each other which will annihilate distance?"[9] Theirs was a companionate marriage, a genuine partnership in which each respected and encouraged the other. They were best friends. This happy marriage led to devoted fatherhood for Josiah when the couple's first child was born on October 3, 1854, and named William Crawford for Amelia's late brother-in-law.

Josiah's command at Mount Vernon Arsenal included responsibilities for the condition of installations at nearby Pensacola, Florida, and throughout 1854, 1855, and early 1856 he worked to upgrade their condition as well as that of the arsenal. The ordnance chief in Washington grudgingly authorized minimum repairs. These efforts so improved the forts that Federal forces held them against Confederate efforts to seize them when the Civil War began.

In May 1856, a few weeks after the birth of a daughter, Jessie, Josiah was ordered to command Kennebec Arsenal in Augusta, Maine, but the family's move north did not occur until mid-July despite Josiah's renewed anxiety to escape the oppressive southern summer heat. Once settled in Augusta Josiah again found an army installation in need of major and expensive repairs. By this time Josiah's growing maturity, perhaps tempered by his happy domestic life, led him to deal diplomatically with his superiors as he requested and secured funds for improvements. As Josiah began his journal in 1857, he was at peace with himself and his profession, secure in the comfort of a domestic haven, enjoying the pleasures of marriage and fatherhood. He had some fears of the imminent disruption of the Union, but he did not anticipate civil war and the destruction of his tranquil personal lifestyle.

Notes

1. Introduction, Solomon Atkinson Gorgas Diary (1850–1851), microfilm typescript, Bayne-Gayle Papers, Southern Historical Collection, University of North Carolina, Chapel Hill, N.C. This prologue relies heavily on Mary Tabb Johnston, *Amelia Gayle Gorgas: A Biography* (University, Ala.: University of Alabama Press, 1978), 22–36, and Frank E. Vandiver, *Ploughshares into Swords: Josiah Gorgas and Confederate Ordnance* (Austin: University of Texas Press, 1952), 3–54.

2. Examples of his watercolor paintings survive. One large watercolor is located in the William Crawford Gorgas Papers, Manuscript Division, Library of Congress, Washington, D.C. A dozen small ones are framed in the Gorgas Home in Tuscaloosa. His sketchbook is in Gorgas Family Papers.

3. JG to Solomon Gorgas, August 7, 1842, GFP.

4. Josiah Gorgas European travel journal (1845–1846), ibid. A decade later Josiah and his travel companion wrote a series of essays about this trip. The essays were published as "Epistolary Gossipings of Travel, and Its Reminiscences," *Russell's Magazine,* V, VI (Charleston, 1859–1860).

5. JG to Sophia Atkinson Gorgas, December 13, 1846, GFP.

6. Josiah Gorgas Mexican War journal (1846), ibid.

7. JG to AG, August 1 [1858], ibid.

8. Ibid., [1858], [1862], July 29, 1865, [June 28, 1858].

9. Ibid., [1858].

Antebellum
January 1857–March 1861

Josiah Gorgas as captain, U.S. Army, 1855–1861 (Courtesy of the Gorgas Home, University of Alabama, Tuscaloosa, Alabama)

I

*"Her affectionate companionship is
sufficient for me"*

Janry 1st 1857   The journal begun this day is dedicated to my children and is devoted to their gratification and instruction. Such a record from the hand of my father would command my reverence and affection. May this not be unworthy of theirs.

Some friends dined with us to-day, & the evening passed cheerfully and happily. Minnie [Amelia] and I were alone together after 8 o'clock, alone but not lonely. Her affectionate companionship is sufficient for me in all times and places. Willie and Jessie were brought to the table at dessert and behaved very well. Willie seemed particularly devoted to the jelly his mother had made, at dinner; and afterwards listened with absorbed attention to the singing of Mrs. Cushing and Miss Child. The weather is not all cold, the thermometer standing at about 20° during the day time.

Jany 4th [1857]   Last evening I read [William H.] Prescott's history of Philip the Second [*History of the Reign of Philip the Second*] aloud. The easy fluency of the style and the clearness of the narrative lend to its pages the interest of a Romance. The evening before I read aloud Mr. [Lewis] Cass' [of Mich.] speech in the Senate in defence of the President's message, & in deprecation of the Slavery agitation at the north. This will perhaps be his last session in the Councils of the nation, the success of the Black Republican party (supporters of [John C.] Fremont [of Mo.]) in Michigan bringing in a new man. This fact gives the greater weight to what he says, and his warnings have the warmth of conviction. The death of Mr. [John M.] Clayton [of Del.] and the retirement of Mr. Cass will deprive the Senate of the last of those illustrious men, the compeers of

Webster Clay & Calhoun. The antecedents of the men who now chiefly compose that body give no weight to that hitherto august body. Most of them have no reputation beyond the narrow precincts of their own States; and the repute of such as are known like [William H.] Seward [of N.Y.], [John P.] Hale [of N.H.] and [Charles] Sumner [of Mass.] is rather a notoriety than an honor. Minnie is reading "Margaret" an obscure book written by a deceased clergyman, Mr. [Sylvester] Judd, late resident here, where his widow still lives. It has been illustrated with the best & most vigorous etchings yet produced in this country, by [F. O. C.] Darley [the famous illustrator]. The book is, she says, hardly worthy the drawings. It contains however some vigorous pictures of "Down East" country life & has been praised in various quarters. It was written some years ago.

Jany 12th, [1857]   On Thursday (8th) we went over to witness the inauguration of Govr. [Hannibal] Hamlin, the new "Black Republican" Govr. [of Me.]. The ceremony consists simply of administering the oath to support the constitution of the State. It is administered by the Speaker of the Senate. No one wore any insignia except the Adjt. Genl. who wore a uniform (undress). The Message delivered afterward by the Govr. he read from the Speaker's Desk. It was not quite as rabid and ultra as his stump speeches were; but he declared the South to be a Despotism and as such "aggressive," and if we did not oppose its encroachments our descendents would be Slaves & would deserve to be. The debates in Congress show pretty conclusively that the agitation on the subject of Slavery is to be continued at the north. It is in fact the only point on which a great unanimity of sentiment can be produced at the north, & political schemers will therefore continue to make use of it. It will not for a while however it is to be hoped affect the perpetuity of the Union. Something will interpose to reunite the national feeling; but an eventual separation appears but too inevitable.

On Friday we went to hear a Mr. Wellets, from Philadelphia lecture. His subject was "Home," and was very cleverly handled & very much to the entertainment of the audience. These lectures serve the places of popular amusements, and are frequently very entertaining. It is an institution somewhat peculiar to New England.

Yesterday (Sunday) was a very stormy day and kept us in doors. I had a sore on my hand to which Minnie applied poultices during the day. It is a great pleasure to be waited on by one we love, slightly selfish in its nature no doubt.

We sometimes speak with regret of our late home at Mount Vernon [Ala.]. The manner & habits of the people are so uncongenial here that one cannot help sighing after the frankness of southern manners. Then the balmy climate of the South cannot but make one wish the vigorous northern winters were somewhat shorter. Nature is as were walled up from us here during six months in the year. The "merry jingle" of the sleigh bells is but a sorry compensation for the rustle of leaves, the voice of birds, and the beauty & odor of flowers.

On Saturday (10th) we took a sleigh ride with the whole family nurse Anne [Kavanaugh] included. Baby [Jessie] & Willie enjoyed it famously. To-day is again a beautiful sunshiny day, if the thermometer did not stand at Zero this morning. We had a merry company on Saturday Evening, Mr. & Mrs. Gilman & Mr. Custer, & a game of whist at which Mr. Gilman was very amusing. Whist is one of the very best schools for acquiring command over one's temper. A well bred man shows to the best advantage at this game, where exhibitions of impatience & querulousness are not uncommon, but not the less out of place. Good nature is the best contribution a man or woman can make to society. It is really more valuable, because rarer, than talent or learning; and it can only be acquired by constant effort at self-command. Better, far better, be silent than say an ill-natured word.

Wednesday, Jany 28 [1857]   We have just passed thro' the coldest weather that has been known for many years. The thermometer fell to 36° below zero at our north window. With the help of good fires in the furnaces we were enabled to keep quite comfortable. Yesterday was a lucky day for us. We received letters from Mobile [where several members of his wife's family resided] and from [Amelia's younger brother] Dick, who has just arrived with his good ship at Genoa. I also learned of the passage thro' the House of the bill for increasing the pay of the Army Officers. There is no doubt of the action on it in the Senate. The chief matter of interest at Washington is the inquiry going on as to alledged corruption among the M.C.'s [members of Congress]. The charge was made by the correspondent of the [New York] "Times," Mr. [James W.] Simonton, in general terms. Notice was taken of it in the House, but no action would have been had on it, because it was merely newspaper report, had not Mr. [Robert T.] Paine [Representative] of N. C. said there was too much truth in the charge, as he knew. Mr. Simonton refuses to give up the names of the members who he says approached him to obtain pay for them for their votes on certain measures. He is in custody & a bill has passed the Senate to compel persons under heavy penalties to answer in these cases.

Poor little Jessie has been quite sick, with teething no doubt, and has kept her mother up for several nights, until she is very much worn out. I am such a poor nurse that I cannot relieve her much, and Anne (the nurse) good as she is, cannot manage the little ones. Willie is delighted with a new table which serves also to support his chair at [the] table. He is very bright, quite grave & tolerably mischievous & troublesome. Yesterday as I was reading a paragraph aloud to his mother while he was playing near, he, without interrupting his avocations, followed my reading & caught very accurately the principal words.

Now that our finances will be abundant for our wants Minnie & myself begin to talk of buying a plantation when we shall have grown rich. I think she would be quite happy if she could see herself 12 or 15 years hence the mistress of a hundred bales of cotton per annum and 40 or 50 ebony faces, whom she would make happy. She has eminently the faculty of making dependents contented, & would I dare say spoil every darkey about her, for the use of any one but herself. The weather has become very moderate again & we propose taking a family sleigh ride today. The mercury stood at 35° above yesterday & at 24° this morning.

Friday, Feby 6, [1857]   The mantle of snow with which the Earth has been draped has been gradually thickened by almost daily accessions, until the recollection of the green earth beneath is almost lost. The sleighing is not good on account of the superabundance of snow on the roads which causes it to wear into <u>pitch holes</u>. A succession of these pitch holes gives you the sensation of riding over waves in a small boat.

Some days ago we went to see in the evening some very good tableaux, at a public hall in Augusta. Many of them were taken from Darling's [Darley's] illustrations of "Margaret," the book heretofore referred to. The good citizens seemed to be very much entertained & there was a renewal of the exhibition on the following day. A bill has just passed in the House of Reps. to increase the pay of Officers of the Army by the addition of $20 per month pay & 10 cts additional for the commutation of the ration. It is just, much needed and will doubtless become a law. The mails are so retarded by the storms of snow that we get little news. The subject that attracts chief attention is the murder of Dr. [Harvey] Burdell in N. York. The inauguration [of Democrat James Buchanan as U.S. president] approaching also gives something to talk about. The sudden death of [S.C. congressman] Preston S. Brooks, from croup, has excited great sympathy in friend & foe. The remarks in the Senate & House on the announcement of his death from Mr. [R. M. T.] Hunter [senator from Va.], Mr. [Thomas L.] Clingman [congressman from N.C.] & others, were very touching, & vividly portrayed the manly traits of this man, so hated by the Republicans; & held up by them since his chastisement [in 1856] of Sumner, as a monster of wickedness.

Feby 11 [1857]   Last night we went to hear the lecture of [the pastor of the Plymouth Church in N.Y.,] Rev. Henry Ward Beecher, familiarly called "Rifle Beecher," from his recommending contributions of rifles to the free State Kansas emigrants. His subject was "the commonwealth," in which he taught the insidious doctrines of the "higher law," as advocated by the Abolitionists. The house was crowded, & the audience sympathetic. He is a man somewhat below the middle height with a bilious face, & long hair, eyes very prominent. His illustrations are the best part of his oratory & are sometimes exceedingly striking. As for example the comparison of governments in which a privileged class exists, to a stalk of wheat. The nobility is the wheat head, to which all the sustenance goes; the straw is the middling class that sustains the nobility, & the roots &c are the common people who furnish the vitality to all above, while themselves groveling in the earth, "and are ploughed in for a fresh crop." Mr. Gilman dined with us before the lecture & went with us.

I had a letter from Mr. [Thomas Hart] Benton [former U.S. senator from Mo.] telling me that I would perhaps be sent to West Point to take charge of a new branch of instruction, designated as "Instruction in Ordnance & the Science of Gunnery." Were the place South of Mason & Dixon's line I might incline to go there; as it is I have no special desire to go there to turn teacher. Govr. & Mrs. Hamlin returned yesterday our call. He talks like the rest of the great men at Washington, & wished to know whether he had ever seen either of us at W., because of course he was introduced to so many persons at W. that he could not pretend to retain a recollection of, &c, &c. Mrs. H. is young & pretty, being the second Mrs. H. We propose to invite them to dinner with a few others, & Minnie declares it shall be a handsome dinner but vows she will not give it until she feels secure of the passage of the bill increasing my pay. A prudent resolution but I would not risk much on its being kept, especially as the dinner bill will not cost an overwhelming sum. A party was given last week at a Mr. [Joseph H.] Williams (speaker of the [Me.] Senate) & Minnie would I think like to have gone; but as they had not called here at all until two days before the party & as Mr. W.[illiams] is an arrant black republican, a species of man I detest, we sent a regret & luckily stayed at home, luckily because both the children have very bad colds, & Willie was threatened with the croup during the evening. In Congress they are discussing the bill to assist the laying of the Atlantic Submarine cable, the proposed reduction of the Tariff, and minor matters. From all sides we hear of the intense cold weather prevailing. Near Columbia, Tenn. 7 persons white & black were frozen to death. The telegraph brings the news of a great freshet at Troy & Albany, the greatest ever known. The investigation into the murder of Dr. Burdell in New York (a dentist) continues without elucidation as to who were the murderers. The deed must have been committed about 11 o'clock in a house full of inmates, & in a very public street (Bond) a few steps out of Broadway. The weather has again become cold, & the mercury, from 46° above Saturday, stands now at 13° below, a great change. We sigh for the sunny days at Mt. Vernon, & cannot help thinking how we should be taking daily rides with the children in that mild climate.

March 6th, [1857]   Yesterday we received the news of the inauguration of President Buchanan. His inaugural address is brief and to the point. He expresses his conviction that his election evinced the devotion of the people to the constitution and the union, hopes that agitation on the subject of slavery will cease, deprecates corruption in the government, which flows in a great measure from the superabundance of money in the treasury, is satisfied with the limited reduction of the Tariff just made, believes in that sort of "squatter sovereignty" which is exercised at the formation of a State constitution, recommends the expenditure of surplus funds for increase of the navy, believes in a strict construction of the constitution, but thinks a military road to California one of the measures necessary for the common defense, & that in our foreign policy non-interference should guide us, except where self-preservation requires action, and that territory may be acquired consonant with honor & justice without just cause of complaint to other nations. Mr. Cass, Secy of State, Mr. [Howell] Cobb [of Ga.], Treasury, [John B.] Floyd of Virginia, War, Jacob Thompson of Miss., Secy. Interior, [Isaac] Toucey, of Conn, Navy, are said to be the Cabinet.* Yesterday evening Minnie & I went to a fancy ball of children. Finding nothing to amuse me I walked back & read the paper, returning to the ball at 10, no refreshments except such as we purchased, which consisted of a bowl of whitish liquid with 3 or 4 oysters in it under the name of stewed oysters. Our dinner to Govr & Mrs. Hamlin, spoken of before passed off very pleasantly & we formed a pleasant impression of both the Govr. & his wife. He has now resigned his place & resumed his seat as Senator for six years. I met his successor, Mr. Williams at dinner at Mr. Gilmans. He is not a man of the world I should judge. Having had my attention directed to him when I first came here as an active "black republican," I had a rooted antipathy to the man, which I find it difficult to overcome. We were however quite civil to each other & he took pains to apologize for not making my acquaintance before. Our pay has been increased by the Congress just dissolved, greatly to the gratification of the recipients & I believe everybody concedes the justice of the augmentation. It increases my income by about $650 per annum, & we begin already to speculate on the possibility of buying a plantation & 40 or 50 slaves, to settle down upon when we get old. Minnie's heart yearns for the darkies & she is prepared to spoil any number of them by indulgence. The weather is stormy, snowy, sunshiny & blowy by turns. Thermometer sometimes near zero & then up to 40 or 50.

March 17, [1857]   Jessie is just one year old to-day, & nice plump lovely little thing that gives us great pleasure. We are blessed with fine

---

*Cabinet corrected next page.

children certainly. The climate, rude as it is, seems to agree with them. Yesterday, Mamma, Willie, Jessie & nurse took a ride together in the sleigh, after "Old Ben" an excellent trusty old horse. A few days ago we were edified by the presence amongst us of Mr. Geo. Vandenhof, an excellent actor, who gave three public readings, one of which Hamlet is his famous character. As he is a gentleman we had him to supper & afterward to dinner. He is very fine looking & very agreeable. It is amusing to witness the eagerness with which the Yankee girls flocked to get introduced to him. One not very young lady, whom Minnie invited to see him, simperingly told him that "she had been waiting for seven long years to thank him for the pleasure he had given her," at some previous time in Boston. Poor girls! they have no husbands and no chance of getting any, & are sprouting all over with sentiment, which a few children to take care of would have absorbed. All the young men leave here to seek their fortunes elsewhere, in Iowa, California, Sandwich Islands &c. We heard yesterday of the serious illness of Maria's [Amelia's youngest sister] little girl "Mamie." She was convalescent however before the letter left. The sleighing is still so-so, & on the river excellent. To-day is sunshiny & windy. Three members of Congress, [Orsamus B.] Matteson, [William A.] Gilbert & [Francis S.] Edwards, all from N. York, were designated for expulsion by the Investigating Committee & resigned their Seats. A fourth, [William W.] Welch from Conn. was exonerated by the vote of the House. The Cabinet of Mr. Buchanan consists of Cass of Mich. State, Cobb of Ga. Treasury, Floyd, Va. War, Toucey of Conn., Navy, Thompson, Miss. Interior, [Aaron V.] Brown, Tenn. P.M. General, & [Jeremiah] Black of Pa. Atty Genl. Considerable sensation has been created by the decision of the Supreme Court in the Dred Scott case. The principal points decided were, 1st That a negro could not be a citizen within the meaning of the constitution of the U.S. 2d That the mere residence in a free State does not prevent the slave from resuming his condition of slavery on his return to it; & 3d That the principles of the Ordinance of '87 excluding slavery from the Territories N.W. of the Ohio were unconstitutional. This ought & it is to be hoped will be a final disposition of this vexed question, which has heretofore assumed such a threatening aspect.

April 6th, [1857]   The snow has at last nearly disappeared. It lurks only in the hollows & in shady places. It is raining now & the snow even in these sheltered places will finally disappear. Four months of snow and ice is too much, & I already look to the next winter with something like dread. The ice moved out of the River opposite to us about the 1st, but it is probably not yet clear below, nor has the ice come down from above the dam.

We were edified ten days ago by the presence of the notorious Fred[erick] Douglass, a mulatto, of very good parts and appearance, who delivered a lecture. He was entertained by a white man, a bookseller named Fenno, & the Govr. of the State & others of the principal citizens met him at tea! It is almost incredible. The lecture was I hear condemnatory of the decision of the Dred Scott case.

We have been entertaining an old comrade of mine, Captain [Robert A.] Wainwright, who stayed with us four days. He is a very handsome, gentlemanly person & Minnie was highly pleased with him. But alas! his wife, proud as she is of him, has his 'skeleton in the closet'; & it is his belief in spiritualism. I was somewhat shocked at the extent of his infatuation. He believes firmly that he is constantly surrounded by the spirits of his father & friends, & holds converse with Napoleon, Washington & minor celebrities. A beautiful female spirit, a stranger tho' to him in this world, or in the body as the spiritual term is, forms a very interesting and frequent member of his tableaux! The feats performed by these mediums, as the agents between the spirits & this mundane sphere, are called, are certainly inexplicable. The answers are most commonly given by raps, three raps being affirmative and one rap negative, in answer to questions. At other times these mediums write in a very wonderful manner, from dictations of the spirit, & without volition of their own. These writings are as often from right to left as in the natural way, at other times alternately backward & forward or to the right & to the left.

April 24, [1857]   A snow storm is going on out doors as I write! I hope it will be of short continuance. We have just planted peas & a few other vegetables, while at the South last year we were already enjoying them on our table at this time. This spring weather is very trying, & Minnie I think feels it sensibly. Willie went out this morning playing in the garden & his temper improves as he goes out-doors more, not that he is ill-tempered, but confinement to the house worries him.

I have lately been at Boston visiting Capt. Wainwright, & have seen some of the wonders performed by the media above alluded to. A good sized table weighing full forty pounds was made to rise at least a foot from the floor & come towards me. This lifting of the table was frequently repeated. The lower part of the table was wholly open to observation & there was no chance for imposition. The names of my mother, & father & of various of my friends were correctly spelled out by means of an alphabet & the raps. There was no chance for fraud or collusion, these people being utter strangers to me as I to them, & Capt. W. knowing nothing of my family. It is all very curious but hardly spiritual. I like a saying attributed to [Dominique Françoîs Jean] Arago [the French physicist], which occurs to me in this connexion "He is a rash man who asserts, outside of the realm of the pure mathematics, that there is anything impossible."

June 7th [1857]   Spring is at last upon us & in great beauty, yet the weather is still quite cool, cool enough for overcoats & shawls. The transition from bleak bare hills to the luxuriant growth of spring is very sudden and striking.

Willie was delighted yesterday at the receipt of a Donkey which his Uncle Dick brings him from Sicily. It is very tame & gentle & will be a great plaything for him. It is Sunday & I ought to have gone to church, the bells for which are now ringing reproachfully, but I did not feel like it, a poor excuse I fear. In consequence of my defection, Minnie is also at home. If we were members we should feel ourselves compelled to attend more regularly, and after all it is a good thing to have a day set apart for something besides making money, or doing work, something a little more intellectual, if not religious. I do not however like to go day after day and make professions which do not come wholly from the heart, and which are but too frequently accompanied by a yawn. How many hundreds of times have I gone over the service of the Episcopal Church, and yet I cannot repeat twenty consecutive words in it, beyond the Lord's prayer! Yet it is better to attend church regularly even if we do not join in the services. I have often there heard words which made me think, & not infrequently made me for the time being a better man. If we but listen to an earnest, honest man in the pulpit we are not wasting our time. This at least we can do without that feeling of self-doubting, which strikes me when I join in a service which is but too often to me only words, words, words, most unprofitably spoken. We should be careful not to trifle with our own sincerity, that is to assume the outward token of sincerity when we are not in earnest.

The recent death of the venerable Senator [Andrew] Butler of S.C. and the return of Gen. [William] Walker from Nicaragua are the most noted events of the last month. I trust the failure of Walker & the execution of Col. [Henry A.] Crabbe [Crabb] & some fifty of his followers (in Sonora) [Province in Mexico] will check these buccaneering expeditions, which are a stain on our national character.

June 8th, [1857]   Frost last night. There will be little fruit & poor crops this year it is predicted. The cool wet weather is unfavorable. Mamma, Willie, Jessie, Nurse & I took a long drive yesterday afternoon, after our span. We visited Togas a small mineral spring with a very poor looking boarding house pitched in among the rocks close by it. People are found however who stay there it seems. I have never seen so rocky a country half so populous. Great boulders conceal the whole face of the earth. Thro' the crevices a scanty herbage forces its way to the light of day. How habitable spots are "cleaned up" is to me an enigma.

June 9th, [1857]   Beautiful sunshiny morning. We went over last evening to meet Dick, but he did not come. He will be here this evening. I am engaged in excavating behind the river wall, preparatory to taking a part of it down, & in building a new brick kitchen; which latter will I doubt not add very materially to our own comfort & that of our successors. Jessie & Willie [are] out in the sunshine.

June 17th, [1857]   Dick arrived on the 10th, preceded a few days by the advent of a remarkably small & pretty Donkey, a present to Willie. He brought several other presents, one an oil copy of the [Beatrice] "Cenci" [by Italian baroque painter Guido Reni]. Nothing remarkable has occurred recently in the world outside of us. The most ominous feature of the times is the mustering of a large force to march to Utah. This may or may not be the beginning of a bloody warfare. If the Mormons are the fanatical adherents of [Brigham] Young they are said by some to be, they will resist our troops. Some say however that there are internal broils which will dissipate their strength.

June 22d, [1857]   Continued rains for the past two weeks. I rose at five this morning & hope to have the resolution to be less of a laggard in this respect hereafter. At 39 (nearly) one ought to be impressed with the value of time. Dick left us this morning, but will return in a short time to see us, before he sails again.

June 30th, [1857]   We have had a few pleasantly warm days, but the evenings are always cool & require blankets for comfortable night quarters. We drive out quite regularly every afternoon with our nice "span" of horses, and bright harness. The little ones enjoy the daily excursion very much, & Minnie requires regular exercise in her present situation. [Amelia was pregnant with her third child.] A dreadful accident has happened in the burning of a steamer on the Montreal & Quebec route, by which several hundred lives were lost, all nearly Scotch emigrants. Govr. [Alfred] Cummings [Cumming] is appointed to Utah, and 2500 men will escort & sustain him. Tomorrow is my 39th birth-day, a day for the beginning of several needful reforms, especially in the matter of rising in the mornings. Minnie and I are reading Dickens' last [most recent] novel "Little Dorrit," and find it but poor entertainment, a great falling off from those books which gave him fame.

July 12th, [1857]   I have entered my fortieth year; & if the curve of life has an apex, I must be considered to have entered its downward branch. The patriotic Fourth of July passed here very quietly. We fired the prescribed Salutes, & had a good exhibition of fireworks in the evening, the grounds full of people. We have been startled by two occurrences: the burning of a steamer between Quebec and Montreal by which about 250 lives were lost, and the death of Govr. [William L.] Marcy [of N.Y.], the Secy of State of Mr. [Franklin] Pierce's administration. He died very suddenly at Ballston, N.Y. of disease of the heart. He was buried with elaborate military honor at Albany, Ex-Presidents Pierce and [Martin] Van Buren being present. The military preparations for the Utah expedition are going on, the forces being assembled at Fort Leavenworth. Gen. [William S.] Harney will command it. Dick left us suddenly on Friday morning last, so suddenly as to spoil a trip we had made up, to go to the White Mountains. I have written to him to day. God speed his new voyage.

Septr 20th, [1857]   Pretty constant occupation has diverted my attention from this Journal. I have been much engaged in putting up a new kitchen to the quarters here, & in superintending the relaying of a heavy wall opposite to the river wharf. Since my last entry I have visited various points on the seaboard, Belfast, Castine, Wiscasset & Hunnewell's Point, & have been delighted with the scenery on this coast. It is bold, rocky & picturesque in the extreme, abounding with deep bays & rocky inlets. It is worth a visit to Castine to see its pretty bay [Penobscot]. I was sent to these various points, to inspect the old fortifications & examine their sites, probably with reference to the sale of the latter.

The summer has proved a very cold one, justifying the description of the climate of Nova Scotia, where there is "nine months of winter and three months of cold weather."

We have been visited by various of our friends, among the rest my brother Solomon & his daughter Nellie & my sister Sarah [Gorgas Dorsheimer]. I had not seen them for five or six years.

To-day we are again alone, enjoying our now comfortable quarters, & the wood fire which the cool weather makes very agreeable.

The news of the loss of the Central America steamer from Aspenwall to N. York, with 500 of her crew & passengers reached us the 18th. It is the most fearful catastrophe of the kind that has happened within my memory.

Decr 13, [1857]   Since my last entry a daughter [Mamie] has been born to us. She is a nice plump looking little pet. Will she live to look over these pages which here record the opening of her book of life? Heaven grant it. She was born on the 28th of October (1857) and was christened by [the Rev.] Mr. [William E.] Armitage the Episcopal clergyman [at St. Marks Church], together with "Jessie," on the 20th of Novr. Her aunt Mrs. [Mary Gayle] Aiken is her godmother, & she is named after her "Mary Gayle." Willie is delighted at the acquisition, which he persists in calling "Rose," having heard me call it "the last rose of summer." The loss of life on the "Central America" [on September 17] proved less by a half than at first supposed. Capt. [W.] Herndon, an officer of the Navy, her commander, was lost with her, & his death caused marked regret thro'out the country. A total prostration of the business of the country has occurred & still continues. It began with the failure of the "Ohio Life and Trust Co." and has swept away everybody with it. The oldest firms have gone down with it. One good effect has been produced in the lowering of the price of all articles of consumption full 30 per cent. The monetary difficulties are not confined to this country, but extend all over Europe.

We are daily hoping for orders to Charleston. Amelia & Mary settled their housekeeping arrangements between them long ago, & it will be a real grief to both of them if we are not sent there. I am so pestered with the character of servants here that I shall be very glad to get to the darkies again.

Congress assembled on the first Monday (7th) and have had warm debates already on the Kansas question. The indications at present are the Senator [Stephen A.] Douglass [Douglas of Ill.] will quit the democratic party, & the schism may be very detrimental to it. He seems however thus far to stand alone. The purity of his purposes is pretty generally questioned. Mr. Buchanan does not think it necessary to repudiate the action of the Constitutional Convention because it did not direct the entire constitution it has framed to the direct vote of the people. Instead of this they submit only the Slavery part of it. On this point Douglass differs.

We have no sleighing yet of any consequence tho' the weather is pretty cold. Willie has been out a long time this morning sliding down hill on his sled. It is called coasting, & the amusement extends to people of all sizes & ages.

Fears are entertained as to the situation of the troops sent out to Utah. Col. [Albert Sidney] Johnston, Cavalry, commands them. At the last advices there seemed to be no doubt that the Mormons intended active hostilities.

Decr 18, [1857]   It is raining to-day, when the latitude & the season demand snow. The rain is very heavy. Babies all very well. Minnie has turned assiduous nurse. We have now but one girl beside the cook, and have nobody to wait at table. Willie has a printed pocket kerchief & is "as proud as Punch" as his mother says. No news stirring in the papers. Stirring debates are going on in Congress on the Kansas question. Mr. Douglass has introduced what is called an enabling bill, to let the people of Kansas, as I understand it, vote for a new convention. In fact to begin de novo, I suppose. I see nothing to be gained by it. I am inclined to think that the administration will lose ground on this question. News received from Dick, that he is appointed pro. tem consul at Montevideo. He wants much to get the appointment. I at once wrote to Mr. Cass, presuming on a slight former acquaintance with little expectation however of doing any good. The salary is only $1000; but he is allowed to transact business.

Feby 9, [1858]   The topics which most agitate the country now and furnish paragraphs to the press, are first, Kansas and the LeCompton Constitution. 2d, The Utah expedition & 3d, The arrest and return of Walker & his fillibuster followers on their maraud into Nicaragua. The latter has nearly ceased to excite remark. Its history was briefly this. Walker sailed from N. Orleans with about 200 troops whom he succeeded, from the inertness or caution of Capt. Chatard [Commander Frederick Chatard of the U.S.S. *Saratoga*], in landing without interruption on Punta Arenas [Areas]. Here he organized a camp and waited for reinforcements, in the mean time detaching Col. [Frank] Anderson, with forty or fifty men to go up the river (San Juan) & capture the lake steamers & other boats. Anderson succeeded & fortified himself at the head of the river. In the mean time Com.[modore Hiram] Paulding appeared in the harbor & disapproving of the want of action of the commander of the Saratoga he landed a sufficient force, captured all Walker's force no resistance being made, and transferred it to the vessels of war, sending them back to Norfolk. A force was also sent up for Anderson who was also captured & bro't to the United States. So ended that expedition. The ultras of the South are of course heavily indignant with Com.[modore] P. & the administration. The Utah force consists of some 1600 men under Col. Johnston, at the last accounts safely housed or tented at Fort Bridger over one hundred miles from Salt Lake City. Apprehension was at first felt for their safety; but this has ceased and the only anxiety now is to get reinforcements to them in time in the spring, in case the Mormons don't evacuate. But the adoption of the "Lecompton Constitution" is the event on which now all eyes are turned with breathless interest. The South blusters over the prospect of its defeat & threatens disunion. The administration supports the coming in of the State under this constitution, whilst the great part of its supporters are loud against it. A fight took place during a night session last week between Mr. [Galusha] Grow of Pa. and Mr. [Laurence] Keitt of S. C. The latter [was] insulted they say. No great harm done as yet. Since I have written in this journal four great personages have passed off the stage, [Count Johann Joseph] Radetzky, the old Austrian marshal, Rachel [b. Elisa Felix], the celebrated French tragedienne, Rerchea Pasha, the Turkish visier, & Gen. [Henry] Havelock whose great fame is of recent Indian origin. Rachel leaves two natural children, one the grandson of Napoleon, its father Count [Andre] Walenski, being the natural son of Napoleon, and also leaves a large fortune. The babies are all doing well. Mary is growing fat & fast. Willie is devoted to "coasting" on his sled whenever the weather permits. He frightened me on Saturday by starting at the top of the hill and going down full speed. I feared he might acquire such an impetus as to send him over the wall into the river, and threw off my cloak to head him off. He stopped himself however or rather the sled did, for he is too little to guide himself, & I got a twinge of rheumatics in return for my parental anxiety. Jessie is growing sweeter every day, and more troublesome. Poor Mamma! what a time she has of it. The winter continues very mild, no lower temp. than − 1°, yet. It is snowing now with very little on the ground. <We fear greatly for poor Maria, who is again in the family way. She suffered so dreadfully at her last confinement, in which the child was destroyed.>

Feby 12, [1858]   It is very cold & stormy to-day, the mercury below zero, the coldest day of the winter thus far. I have been translating from the French a very good memoir of Pompey. Its pendant, Moreau, follows. I have been sorry to-day to hear how poor are some of the men whom I employ in the laboratory. One poor young fellow earns four and a half dollars a week & pays four of it for board for himself & wife. They are newly married & don't know how to save money. Bitter experience must be their teacher.

Feby 26th, [1858]   No harm came of the quarrel & consequent row in the House. Mr. K.[eitt] made a full apology, but has no recollection of being knocked down by Grow as asserted by the letter writers. He is a good deal laughed at by the opposition press, because his friends assert that he "stumbled & fell." Two officers, graduates of West Point, had a rencontre in a barbers shop, & went to Bladensburgh to exchange shots. The papers say that Williams (Dragoons) received Bell's (cavalry, Beall?) ball thro' the head & then fired into the snow, when the matter was made up. Messers. [John] Bell & Johnston [Andrew Johnson], Senators from Tenn, also exchanged high words. There seems to be an angry cloud hanging over Washington. James B. Clay, son of Henry Clay, & Mr. [William] Cullom, clerk of the last House [of Representatives, 34th Congress], also had a fisticuff & "went out," but Mr. Clay withdrawing his challenge, Mr. Cullom apologized & so that matter ended. The great steamer, the Leviathan, has at last been launched. Louis Napoleon's life was attempted in January, as he was going to the opera. The missiles used were explosive pear-shaped shells, arranged with percussion caps. A hundred or more persons were killed & wounded. One or two horses killed, the Emperor slightly grazed &c. The empress being enceinte [pregnant] fears were entertained for her, but fainting appears to have been the only result. The marriage of the English Princess Royal [Victoria, eldest daughter of Queen Victoria] to the Prince [Frederick] of Prussia fills the newspapers.

Willie is out with his rubber "boots," and enjoys the fine sunshiny day, "baby" [Mamie] has gone to be shown to a town lady who hopes to have one of her own before long. I have felt very downcast for a few days past, & can assign no good reason for it. Can these fits of gloom result from any physical derangement? I am translating "Commentaries of Napoleon" by [Victor-Jules] LeVasseur. Very good military reading and instructive.

March 15, [1858]   The snow still lies deep but to-day has been a genial day. I have finished re-reading the life of [Benjamin] Franklin [edited by Jared] (Sparks) which I have not read for 25 years. I remember there used to be a small "life," chiefly his autobiography at my father's which I read a dozen times, with great admiration for the subject. It is doubtless a valuable book to put into the hands of <u>most</u> children; yet I do not like the character of Franklin as much as I once did. There is throughout his life too much of the sense of worldly success. Nearly all his maxims relate to success in life, & many of his precepts in fact most of them are too deeply tinctured with policy. It is not a brave, open and generous nature that lies open before us in these pages and stirs us with sympathy for its struggles, & with admiration for its success. But a correct, disciplined, self-restrained, persevering, able and patriotic citizen whom we are reading of, patriotic, not from deep & boundless enthusiasm, like [Patrick] Henry, [Alexander] Hamilton and many others, but thro' consistency with the general tenor of his democratic life, thro' his position & associations. Tho' a cheerful & even genial man his character has not risen but rather sunk in my estimation from a re-perusal of it. Yet it seems almost ungenerous to say anything of this sort against a man to whom we owe so much.

Went to a ball at the Stanley House on Friday night (12th) and stayed until after 12. Much dancing, in which I participated but once. Tried to dance the "contra" dance & failed, not knowing the figure. Jessie is quite ill to-day with cold & derangement of the stomach. Must go and see her.

Mch 16, [1858]   Jessie is better to-day, nearly well. Willie was very uneasy last night with his cold, kicked out lustily, of which I his bed-fellow had the benefit. Am reading [Aaron] Burr's Journal. It is very trifling. [His daughter] Theodosia's letters in it are all that is graceful & winning. It has been thawing yesterday and to day with the thermometer above 40°. It is rather early to hope to get rid permanently of the snow; and it is so disheartening to wake up and find a fresh deposit a foot deep, that I had rather see it go off more gradually. I went to town this morning to find some little presents for the people "at home," but could not get anything fit to send. [We] shall have to fall back on trifles.

[March] 17, [1858]   To-day is Jessie's birth-day. Two years old. She has a troublesome cold & is cross enough. <u>Mamma</u> is busy making up her box for "home." Heard again from Col. [James W.] Ripley of the probability of our being ordered to Charleston. I don't know whether to like the idea or dislike it. It is thawing <u>hard</u>. Mr. Gilman here in the evening, an enormous eater.

April 9th, [1858]   The weather is somewhat springlike, the river is open, and yesterday the boats began to run on it. We have all had disagreeable influenza. Baby especially suffered from it, & <u>Mamma</u> quite sick for a day or two. Had a few gentlemen to dinner yesterday on a fine young turkey of last September's brood. Played whist in the Evey until near ten. Heard yesterday of the supposed suicide of Mr. Richards, Mr. Gardiners soninlaw, temporary insanity.

[April] 10th, [1858]   Rain last night which I hope will hasten the abstraction of frost from the ground, and thaw out the <u>water pipes</u> now frozen up, and threatening to cause a deficit in our supply of water. Mr. Benton reported dead in the House, but the report was premature. He is very near his end however. He continues to work on his "Abridgement" [*An Abridgement of the Debates of Congress from 1789 to 1856*], dictating in a whisper to his daughter Mrs. Jones who bends over him, & repeats the sentences to her husband. This is certainly to die "in harness." He objects to any notice of his death being taken by Congress, as he always opposed such things himself (meaning in reference to <u>outsiders</u>). Is this virtue or affectation? One cannot fathom the souls of men and women, and perhaps they cannot themselves. All getting the better of the influenza. Read to Amelia last evening the story of "Ashburn Rectory," [by H. Parr in *Littell's Living Age*] very good.

[April] 12th, [1858]   Yesterday (Sunday) we went to church in the morning. Willie with us, behaved very well, & only fell off the bench once. To-day is a beautiful and spring-like day, & Willie and Jessie are playing out of doors, well-clad and with rubbers on. I have been walking about the grounds meditating improvements, a great pleasure to me. The Lecompton Constitution with [Sen. John J.] Crittenden's amendment passed the House by a majority of 8, 120 to 112, the fullest vote ever given perhaps in any great legislative body. Great efforts will be made by the administration to modify this vote, which is a signal defeat of it. Believing that the administration is in the wrong I don't regret its defeat. Mr. Benton died on Saturday (10th).

[April] 16th, [1858]   Nothing new has occurred except that the Administration has experienced a slight success on the Kansas business, the house having agreed to a committee of conference by the casting vote of the Speaker, 108 to 108. Those of the administration who returned to their allegiance & produced this result are branded as "traitors" to the black republicans. Weather pleasant, roads muddy.

April 24th, [1858]   Returned from Boston on the 21st, found here 3 or 4 inches of snow. It has however all disappeared, but it is still too cold & wet to plant anything in our gardens. Children all well. Jessie had yesterday a little black spot like a dark mole picked out of her forehead, without wincing in the least, tho' it must have hurt her a good deal. Mamma has a sore throat the effect of this bad climate. Engaged in writing out what seems to me curious views on "forces," which may be called the "Metaphysics of Forces." I do not know yet whether there is anything in them. Translating also an Italian novel, the "Nun of Monza" on which I make but slow progress, as I do it to study the language.

April 29th, [1858]   A severe snow storm set in on Sunday (25th) & continued until yesterday. It has now become pleasant again. Nothing new has happened. Willie is somewhat indisposed & feverish & took a dose of calomel & rhubarb like a little hero this morning. Amelia is distressed at the prospect of losing her faithful nurse (Anne Kavanaugh) who has to join her brother in Por[t]land. Engaged yesterday in drawing out a plan of an Army "Mutual Insurance Company," which would I think be a good thing. An accident which might have been serious happened to Mamma last evening. While driving home from a neighbor with Dr. Briggs about 9½ o'clock in the evening the axle of the carriage broke; fortunately the horse "Old Ben" was quiet & the only evil to her and the Dr. was to be obliged to walk home over half a mile. Kansas bill not yet passed, & nothing doing in Congress.

April 30th, [1858]   Weather continues pleasant with cold winds. Willie is quite ill. We had the utmost difficulty in administering a dose of oil to him, the poor little fellow clenched his teeth firmly and for a time defied all our efforts. Seeing me however look about the room for something to insert between his teeth he "gave in," and took it like a man. Mr. [William] English's Kansas bill is likely to be defeated. Extracts are given of the reply of Mr. Cass to Lord [Francis] Napier [British ambassador to the U.S.] urging the increase of our squadron on the African coast. It is declined & the "right of search" doctrine as exercised by the English cruisers sharply criticized.

May 9th, [1858]   Willie has been very ill with a typhoid fever and has suffered a good deal of pain, chiefly about his head, and the muscles of the neck. He is now without fever, but his neck still very stiff. His fretfulness taxes his mother's patience to the utmost. On Monday evey (3d) [I] received orders to go to Charleston, for which we are now preparing. It is rather late in the season to go to so warm a climate. Yet we both anticipate the change with pleasure. We shall go as soon as Willie's condition permits.

II

*"My great regret is the wandering life
we are obliged to lead"*

[May] 19th, [1858]   On the eve of departure for Charleston, but Mamma too ill to go this morning. We are staying in nice rooms at the "Stanley House" [in Augusta]. I am to go to C. alone & return after the family in a couple of months. Mrs. G goes with me if well enough tomorrow as far as Boston, & then returns after a visit there to Augusta.

Monday, June 1st, [1858]   Charleston Arsenal. Came up & took possession of my Post. Capt [Charles P.] Kingsbury leaves on Thursday. I left Augusta, wife and babies with a heavy heart on Monday May 24th. Stopped over night in Boston. Saw Mrs. [Marion C.] Dexter [an old friend of Amelia] for an hour. Went on to Albany on Tuesday, stayed with Mrs. Barnard, ran up in the morning to see my friend John Hillhouse [former classmate and European traveling companion, 1845–1846], dined with him, visited the Arsenal after dinner, returned to Albany, took boat down the river at 8 P.M, ran about N. Y. all day (a very rainy day), took cars Wednesday evey for Washington, arrived early in the morning, stayed until Saturday evening. Took boat at 7 P.M, arrived at Richmond, by R.R. at 4 Sunday morning. Went to church there with little edification, took cars 3 P.M. for Wilmington, which reached at 5 A.M., left W at 6½ (boat 6.) & reached Charleston at 6½ P.M. Stopped at Mills House. Saw Gen. [Hugh] Aiken & Mary. Dick came on Wednesday. (The fare from N. Y. to Charleston is just $27.50).

Thursday, June 3d, [1858]   Moved up here, it is delightfully cool & shady, mosquitoes pretty numerous but not very annoying. No worse than at Mt. Vernon, if as bad.

Tuesday, June 8, [1858]   Dick left for Boston, by steamer to N. Y. on Saturday. Saw him on board & wished myself heartily in his place, for then I should have seen wife & babies in a few days. This separation is very irksome, & the 7 or 8 weeks yet to be passed alone afford but a dreary perspective.

Wednesday, June 16, [1858]   It is cool & pleasant, a northeast wind blowing. Had a letter from Amelia this morning, all well, & babies doing well. Willie dreamed of his Papa & woke up saying how lonesome he was without his Papa. Jessie too asks her Mamma to write Papa what a good girl she is. The other day her Mamma stepped to the nursery & found Miss Jessie busily engaged ironing a handkerchef which she had suddenly thrown over some forbidden nuts on the approach of her Mamma. "I iron Willies handkerchef smooth, and dont eat nuts, Mamma" she said, busily working away! Poor Dick sails in a few days for South America, instead of coming back here for a time as we had hoped. He has made an excellent arrangement with Durham & Co. Boston, he becomes their agent in Buenos Ayres and receives ⅓d profits. Good luck go with him! He is a fine-hearted fellow & will I hope succeed. Congress adjourned on Monday. The President pronounces the Utah war closed, & congratulates Congress on it! Merely because the Mormons have allowed Gov Cumming to enter on his functions as Governor! But the Mormons still persist that the troops shall not enter. I doubt the sagacity of this pseudo-submission. I doubt whether any good comes of it. It is announced in the British Parliament that if the report of outrages on American ships by British cruisers proves correct ample explanations will be made, which I think dispels that little speck of war. All our preparations dwindle down to 5 additional steam sloops of war!

Sunday, June 27th, [1858]   I am but an indifferent church-goer, and prefer staying at home to read and write. Were I lucky enough to hear a preacher occasionally whose sermon gave me something to think about, I should doubtless attend worship oftener. The religious principal is however not very strong in me. Hope to get a letter from my darling wife to-day. She writes at least every alternate day. I am so anxious about her and my babies that I wait impatiently for every letter. I know they all miss me very much. Suppose that they were all lost to me, as has happened to men before now, what would become of the remainder of my life! It is a thought which, like that of annihilation, the mind refuses to contemplate. Dear ones! the church-bells are now ringing to them as they are to me.

We are looking daily for news of the telegraphic squadron which left Liverpool on the 10th. We shall probably hear the result in two or three days at fartherest. The chances of failure are very great. The strain which the cable can bear is so little above what it is obliged to bear that the slightest accident will cause rupture. Great dexterity in the manipulation of the paying out apparatus seems to be necessary, and will be probably be [*sic*] acquired after repeated failures.

The Mormon troubles still look ominous, despite the proclamation of the President that these people had returned to their obedience. I, for one, don't believe it.

To-morrow there will be a great celebration here, on the laying of the corner stone of the Calhoun Monument.

. The British government disavows the outrages committed on our vessels in the vicinity of Cuba. France is arming, what does it mean? The English are very uneasy over it. There has been a great eruption of Vesuvius, without material damage as yet.

July 1st, 1858   I to-day enter on my forty-first year having been born in 1818, near the city of Lancaster in Pennsylvania. We celebrate the day over a bottle of champagne, nothing more. Next to no libations at all are moderate libations. This I mean to impress on Willie. Would that there were some way of impressing others with the truth we have ourselves acquired by hard experience. But outside of mathematics, & some of the physical sciences, there is no such thing as impressing conviction on the mind of another. If Willie inherits my own constitution, abstinence from excess in eating & drinking, more especially the former, is indispensable to his happiness. I am now convinced that the want of good spirits, as it is termed, which has followed me all my life, especially the earlier portions of my manhood, was due to over-eating. Of late years I have been much more cautious & have felt better & more buoyant, but I believe that permanent injury has been done to my constitution. Heavy suppers may appear to some not to be injurious to themselves. Ninety-nine times out of a hundred this is a self-delusion. However good the action of the stomach may appear to be, its tone is gradually impaired.

July 14th, [1858]   I have been much annoyed and very indignant at the refusal of a leave of absence for sixty days which I have asked for the purpose of bringing my wife & babies to Old Point Comfort. Having had no leave of absence for six years, none since my marriage, I am mortified at such want of consideration. I have not yet expressed it to the Colonel [H. K. Craig, Chief of Ordnance] but shall probably do so after a fuller digesting of the matter, & some others I have in my mind. Letters from Minnie tell me that the babies are all very well, & that she herself is gaining strength. The weather is very wet, the rains having been very heavy for four or five days past. To-day there are rumors of fever in town, always an alarming cry. Hugh & Mary [Aiken] left for Mobile yesterday morning, the latter to be at the accouchment of Maria [Bayne], the event of which we shall await with great anxiety, her last having been so disastrous. Played billiards yesterday for 3 or 4 hours with Dr. [John L.] Dawson [a Charleston physician].

July 25, [1858]   The last few weeks have been quite rainy, & sufficiently pleasant in temperature. The mosquitoes are my worst annoyance. Have rec'd leave of absence for 10 days! & am to wait for that until an Ordnance Sergt can come hither from Fort Myers Fla. Heaven knows when that will be. This is "asking for bread & receiving a stone" with a vengeance. The latest news refers to the failure to lay the telegraph cable. Three successive attempts were made about the close of June. In the last 140 miles wire laid out of the Niagara. The other ship (Agamemnon) not yet heard from. Dined day before yesterday at Mr. Aikens, played billiards yesterday with Dr. D.[awson]. We play about every two weeks! Went yesterday to see the pictures of the Art Union, a small collection in every sense.

Wednesday, January 19, 1859   I resume the entries in my journal which were interrupted by my leaving this Post on the 7th of August last on a leave of absence for twenty days. I went by steamer to N. York, had a rough passage, & renewed my oft-repeated determination never to travel by sea where there is a good land route; not that I got sea-sick, but it is altogether an unpleasant life & verifies Dr. Johnson's sagacity when he described being at sea, as living in a prison with the privilege of being drowned.

I reached Augusta, Me. on Wednesday following the Saturday on which I left from here, and found all well and Mamma looking better than when I left her. It was a joyful meeting after nearly three months' absence. We left there, bag & baggage, with the regrets and good wishes of all our kind neighbors, about the 20th or 22d of Augst & traveling slowly southward, stopping at Saratoga, Albany, N. York, Philadelphia & Baltimore, reached our destination at Old Point Comfort on the 27th. Here I heard definite news of the fatal prevalence of yellow fever in Charleston. I had very fortunately traveled from Baltimore with the Secretary of War, Mr. Floyd, & he finding that my leave expired in a few days first gave a verbal extension of it & next placed me on temporary duty at O[ld] P[oint Comfort, Va.].

We took rooms at the hotel, paying about $100 per month for my whole family, for the first seven weeks of our stay; and then the hotel being quite empty we took quarters within the Fort, & hiring furniture from the hotel, had our meals served by an old mulatto, at $50. per month. There we lived without much discomfort, indeed with considerable comfort at an expense about one half of our hotel bill.

During our stay at the Hotel we made the acquaintance of some very pleasant people, among others Mr. Dudley Mann [future Confederate diplomat in 1861], Mr. [J. D. B.] DeBow [editor of *DeBow's Review*] &

Govr & Mrs. Floyd, &c. For the first week the hotel was quite gay; there was a band and dancing every night, but it was the end of the season. Our table was made up of military people, Gen. [Winfield] Scott & his staff, Govr Floyd, Capt [William] Maynadier [of the U.S. Ordnance Office] et al.

I was kept tolerably occupied on Ordnance duties, among other things, devised an elevating apparatus for the 10in. Columbiad Carriage, which was desired.

One day in attempting to raise a 6pd brass gun by the breach, it slipped forward on the skid under the muzzle, & catching my left hand under the knob of the cascable & the rear iron skid, mashed it severely. I suffered great pain for a short time, which the application of Dally's Magical Pain Extractor seemed to relieve at once, yet I have no faith in nostrums of any sort. The wrist continues weak.

Mamma amused herself with the society of officers & their wives, & lived happily, despite bare floors & a scanty larder. Willie & Jessie were delighted with their big playgrounds, & strolled on the beach picking up shells, &c. & Anne (nurse) was entirely contented, & would have been glad to have stopped there. [Anne had returned to the Gorgas household earlier that summer.]

About the 10th of November we were advised that the advent of frost here made it quite safe to come on, so we packed our numerous trunks, stuffed our carpet bags, & with babies, baggage, & a vigorous lunch said good bye to our Old Point friends, not a few of whom accompanied us to the wharf, & turned our faces homeward! We rested at Norfolk the first night, the second at Wilmington, & without accident reached here the evening of the third day, Novr 17th. A blazing coal fire & a good supper made us comfortable in our new home, which looked very inviting.

Since then nothing material has happened to us. We took babies to the circus one day soon after coming here, to their great amusement. The elephants were the chief performers & were certainly wonderful. Among other things they stood all fours on the head of a barrel, and afterwards on their heads on it.

Christmas day they were made happy with presents, Willie receiving a set of gardening implements & Jessie dolls &c.

Our family comprises Hugh [Aiken], Mary [his wife], Milly Crawford [daughter of Amelia's older sister, Sarah], Mamma & myself. Yesterday we dined at Mrs. J. Aiken's. A very nice dinner for twelve.

The chief event that has stirred the world since my last entry was the laying of the telegraphic cable early in August. Messages were transmitted, but it soon became useless.

Wednesday, Feby 9 [1859]   Willie and Mamie have both been ill, the latter quite ill with teething. Willie has the jaundice, and for some days was quite yellow with it. They are both pretty well recovered as one may observe by their appetites, tho' Willie still looks hollow-eyed. Nothing ever seems to hurt Jessie, who is tough as a pine knot. She is very roguish too. Yesterday her mother came into my offce in my absence and found Miss Jessie seated high up on my desk, with a stick of liquorice (Nicolas she calls it) with which she was bedaubing her face, after vain efforts to cut off a portion as she had seen me do it, using a shagreen instrument case & a broken knife which I always use for the same purpose. On the floor were the sawdust contents of the spittoon & Willies spade in various picturesque heaps. Mamie grows in beauty, but is very backward in learning to walk.

An event happened at the close of the last year which created great excitement north and South. It was the landing of a cargo of Slaves on Jekyl[l] island on the coast of Georgia, by the sloop Wanderer. It is said that over 300 were landed. How so many could be stowed on so small a vessel, she is only a yacht, is indeed curious.

Cuba, the revenue, postage & a Pacific Rail-road seem to occupy the attention of Congress. The latter is however considered dormant for this session. A bill has also been reported for a retired list in the Army, of which little is to be hoped at this Congress. We shall I hope have it before many years. It is raining furiously to-day. I began this Journal by mentioning that I was reading Prescotts Phillip II [Philip II]; just two years after I have to record the death of that distinguished historian, in the 62d year of his age.

Sunday, Feby 13, [1859] The day is charming and I have been loitering about the grounds all morning, now carrying Mame, now looking at Willie and a playmate carrying and placing sods with considerable skill, as they yesterday saw the workmen do. But my chief occupation was to devise how I am to build a little aquarium, say 12 by 20 in one portion of the garden. I am always devising improvements, which are unfortunately not ever carried out (might say fortunately for Uncle Sam's purse). Mamma and I went to the races on Thursday of last week, and saw some excellent running. I wished to go yesterday (an extra or match race) to take Willie, who would have been vastly amused, but it rained hard until some time after mid-day. Despite the rain the race came off and was a very exciting one. I have not before seen a race since I was a bit of a boy, say 30 years ago.

The horizon of foreign politics still looks threatening and a war in which Austria and France would be the principals and the theatre Italy is still forboded, and has its effect upon the commercial world. Nothing of exciting interest seems to occupy Congress, who are discussing a bill to place thirty millions of dollars at the disposal of the President with a view to the acquisition of Cuba. A revision of the Tariff with a view to increase the revenue up to the standard of expenditures is also urged. The administration urges specific duties.

Thursday, Feby 17, [1859]   Oregon has just been admitted to the Union, making the whole no. of states now 32. Her senators are [Joseph] Lane and [Delazon] Smith. The increase in the tariff for the purpose of revenue chiefly occupies Congress. [Senator Lyman] Trumbull of Ill. proposes to reduce the current expenses of the Govt to 50,000,000, but does not indicate where the paring down is to be done. An Army board on retrenchment in the Quartermaster Dept. is ordered at Washington. Grumble as they may, however, over the expenses of the Govt., additional revenue must be raised or the debt increased. The weather still continues delightful and the mercury to-day stood near 70°. I drove out to-day with Mamma & Mrs. [A. W.] Waldron & her son to Magnolia Cemetery. [Mr. Waldron was a wholesale clothier.] They are from Buffalo & came with a letter from Mr. [Philip] D[orsheimer, husband of Josiah's sister, Sarah]. Mame is just beginning to stand alone & will I hope walk very soon now. Her successor is treading close on her heels. [The next Gorgas daughter would be born in June.] Mary & Hugh are both sick to-day.

March 9th, [1859]   Spring is fast advancing; and the grass is turning green and roses are blooming on all sides. Mame is at last using her little legs in the way intended by nature, & runs about at will. Willie was barberized yesterday for the third time in his brief life. A shocking affair occurred at Washington Sunday on the 27th ult. Mr. [Daniel] Sickles, rep. from N. Y. shot P. Barton Key in the street, for adultery with his wife. Mrs. S. made a full confession to her husband. After this confession K. made signals at the house with his hdkf, on seeing which Mr. S. was wrought up to such frenzy that he pursued K. at once and fired three shots of his revolver into him. The affair has of course created the greatest excitement not only in W. but thro'out the country. Mrs. S. was the daughter of Bagioli a well known music teacher in N. Y, is very pretty, very young, & now very penitent. She has commiseration if not sympathy; but few venture to blame the act of Mr. S.

March 20, [1859]   Sunday, and a very lovely day. The last two days have been quite cold, for this latitude. Nothing new has occurred to shock the world, save perhaps the burning of the "Princess" (explosion of boilers) [on the Mississippi River] near Baton Rouge by which many lives [200] were lost. But such occurrences are so common on the western waters as to excite little but casual expressions of horror, and then are forgotten. A few days ago, I was surprised by the visit of an old friend (Capt. G. W. Smith) whom I have not seen for nearly ten years. He was on his way to Havana on account of his health & had his wife with him.

He resigned from the Army to enlist in the affairs of Cuba, & was a prominent actor in the secret proceedings which he says, had their sole centre in Cuba, & of which Gen. [John A.] Quitman was the organ in this country. The world continues to look on with a sort of dread, at the preparations made by Austria & France; and the "Italian Question," as it is called, is not yet solved. What that question is precisely it would be difficult to state. It is probable however that France desires to diminish the influence of Austria in Italy, and perhaps favors the growth of Sardinia with a view of building up an Italian power. Mr. [Joseph] Holt [of Ky.] succeeds P.M. General [Aaron V.] Brown lately deceased. Poor Willie has been afflicted with toothache and swelling of the cheek. He is very good and obedient. <He seems a curious brother of Jessie who is up to all sorts of mischief. Her 3rd birth day came on the 17th, & I took her down town to purchase a doll with which she is greatly delighted.> A curious thing happened in the barn-yard last week. Some eggs which I tho't rotten were thrown into the manure pile. Three or four days afterwards, the men heard a chirping underneath the surface, & on opening out the surface found a little chicken just creeping out of its shell, & as he expressed it "whistling" lustily. It is alive & hearty now.

March 25th [1859]   Poor little Mame had to submit to-day to vaccination. She looked very gravely at the Doctor with her large eyes until he punctured the skin and hurt her, and then she began to cry as if her little heart would break, the big tears raining down on her cheeks.

    <Mamma says Jessie is the alarm of her life, and feels it worries her to exasperation.> I spent yesterday at Sullivan's Island to see the inauguration of the Court Martial on Dr. [Bernard M.] Byrne [a surgeon at Fort Moultrie]. A soldier only was tried; & then the court adjourned for the arrival of Col. [W. H. J.] Walker. [Byrne was accused of neglect of duty during the 1858 yellow fever epidemic.] I lunched with a pleasant party of citizens, Mr. [A. R.] Taft's & Mr. Brice's families, & made myself I hear agreeable. [Taft was a Charleston commission merchant.] Prospects of peace again brighten & cotton has gone up still more—it is ruling at about 13cts. We have rain almost every day, a great hinderance to outdoor work.

April 3d, [1859]   The commercial community was startled on the 1st of April by the news of commencement of hostilities between Sardinia and Austria. The report proved premature, and was for a time regarded as an April fool, but subsequent despatches indicate a decided leaning toward war. Business people are somewhat timid in consequence. I dined on the evening of the 1st with the "Charleston Light Dragoons," an excellent supper. Col. [Charles A.] May was present and responded to the toast to the Army (a duty I performed on the 22d of Feby. to my great discomfort). Other army officers were present. On Wednesday evening last we gave a supper to a number of gentlemen, chiefly officers, which passed off very pleasantly. The secret of digesting late meals and not feeling too greatly their effects next day, lies in these three rules: indulge in them as seldom as possible, eat little, and drink little. Then you will wake up next morning without headache. We had a letter from Dick yesterday. He is exercising the functions of his consulate at Montevideo, entertaining a great many officers of the Paraguay expedition, and as he says spending all he makes. His letter shows him to be sufficiently homesick, poor fellow. The court martial on Byrne is still in session. [Byrne was acquitted after proving that he had been ill and his wife dangerously ill at the time that he was absent from duty.] One of the most fearful events happened about carnival time at [the Gulf of] Taganrog on the Sea of Azof [Azov, an arm of the Black Sea]. About three thousand of the inhabitants were out on the ice hauling the nets, & the afternoon being beautiful there were many women & children. A wind came off shore & detached the ice blowing the multitude out to sea, where all save one old man went down!

April 15th, [1859]   The war question has become quite quiet, in consequence of a proposition for a Congress, which appears to be acceded to by the four great Powers. Sardinia it would seem has nothing to say in this Congress tho' the party chiefly interested. The Sickles trial (for the killing of Key) is progressing. To-days paper contains the confession of Mrs. Sickles detailing her criminality with Key. It is a sad exhibition of humanity. Public sympathy sets decidedly in favor of Sickles who will doubtless be entirely acquitted. [Sickles was acquitted on the grounds of temporary insanity, the first use in the United States of this defense.]

The recognition of the Juares government in Mexico, seems to be decided, & holds out some hope for a more permanent government for that misgoverned country. The settlement of our difficulty with Paraguay is announced, and our fleet may return from their excursion into the waters of the Panama.

Babies are feeling the warm weather which has suddenly come upon us, both Jessie & Mame are unwell. Milly [daughter of Amelia's sister, Sarah] left us yesterday morning for Mobile, all sorry to see her go. I am having a little donkey cart made for them to ride in from which I hope they will derive pleasure & exercise. I spent the 13th at the Island (Fort Moultrie) to hear the defence of Dr. Byrne, read by his counsel (Gen. [William E.] Martin). After we had several lunches, and champagne. Sold my horse Tom day before yesterday, & felt regret at parting from him, having bro't him with me from Kennebec Arsenal.

May 24th, [1859]   We have had a visit from Dr. & Mrs. [Daniel] Chapman [Josiah's sister, Eliza, and her husband]. They stayed nearly two weeks, the latter was very feeble from illness & sea-sickness. War has at last commenced between France & Sardinia on the one side, and Austria on the other. The latter began the war by crossing the Ticino [River] on the afternoon of the 29th of April. Babies have been suffering from colds, but are now recovered. The weather has been quite cool for the season, & we are promised a comfortable summer in which expectation I hope we may not be disappointed. A week ago we had the news of the death of [Baron F. H. A. von] Humboldt who died May 6th, 90 years (nearly) old. He was born in 1769 with [Napoleon] Bonaparte, [French naturalist George] Cuvier, [Arthur Wellesley, Duke of] Wellington, [former president] John Q. Adams, Mehemet Ali [Mohammed Al Pasha, founder of dynasty that ruled Egypt until 1952], &c. In the May number of "Russell's Magazine" published in Charleston began the publication of Letters entitled "Epistolary Touchings of Travel &c" ["Epistolary Gossipings of Travel and its Reminiscences"] written by my friend John Hillhouse & myself. There will be 22 letters. I place little stress on their literary merit, but "what is writ is writ," & as the editor desires to publish we are quite willing to contribute them, for the sake of preserving them in printed form.

June 4th, [1859]   This afternoon at 2 P.M. baby Minnie was born, a wee black-headed plump thing. A long and sunny life to her.

June 17th, [1859]   On the 20th of May the battle of Montebello was fought between the French & Sardinians, on one side & the Austrians on the other. The latter attacked with superior forces, but retreated eventually having suffered heavy losses. The Austrians have now withdrawn behind the Ticino. Como has been taken it is said by Garibaldi. I was occupied most of yesterday superintending cleaning of a large cistern which we did not finish until after 9 o'clock in the evening. We have had no rain for a month and everything is parched up. The clouds constantly threaten rain & yesterday there was a smart shower for 10 minutes, but not rain enough even to lay the dust.

July 4th, [1859]   The 'popping' about us gives undoubted evidence to any but the deaf of the return of another anniversary of Independence. I have passed another birthday & have entered my 42d year. It is hardly possible to realize that I am no longer a young man. The baby [Minnie] is "coming out." Her Mamma hesitates whether to call her after herself (as I wish) or after Mrs. Dexter (Marion) or Mrs. Bell (Adelaide) [two of Amelia's friends]. As they are all good names, which is what I bargain for, I await her decision without impatience. [Amelia named the child Christine Amelia.] We have heard of the battle of Magenta, the details of which I have written down separately, of the affair of Palestro, which preceded it, & of that at Malignano which followed it. The battle of Magenta took place on the afternoon of June 4th the day of our baby's birth.

Oct 28th, [1859]   We have been spending the summer, since the 3d of August, at Sullivan's Island in the house next (west) of the Fort. It has passed away pleasantly to ourselves and healthfully to the children. Poor little <u>Minnie</u> began wasting away after the entry above, & but for a black wet nurse we got for her no doubt would have died. The nurse came about the 26th of July, & by the time we went to the island the little thing was already better, and in a month after was hardly recognizable. She is now as plump and lovely a little body as need be. There is nothing like the natural food for babies, tho' we have reared three successfully by hand.

It is <u>Mame</u>'s birth-day. She is two years old. She has just been struggling thro' cutting her back teeth, & has been looking delicate for six weeks past. A little cousin [John] Gayle Aiken [son of Hugh and Mary Aiken] was born here (Charleston Arsenal) on Sunday morning the 16th inst. Great rejoicing over it. It is indeed a boon to its mother, whose heart has been dead to almost every joy since the death of her little girl [Nannie] over two years ago. On the 21st of July died [Amelia's father] Govr [John] Gayle at Mobile. A dispatch told us of it the next day. Amelia was overcome with grief & wept as if her heart would break. We had constantly promised ourselves the gratification of a visit to him this fall—too late. At a meeting of the bar ample justice was done to his memory, and the press of Mobile had various obituary notices of his life & Services. He had filled the offices in succession of Representative to the State legislature, Judge of Circuit Court, Governor of the State for two terms 4 years (from 1833 to 1837) [1831 to 1835], member of Congress '47 & '48, and finally U.S. District Judge, when he died. He was a man beloved and respected by all who came in contact with him; a pure, conscientious, upright man whose memory deserves to be cherished & his life imitated by his descendants.

The war between France & Sardinia & Austria was closed by the peace of Villafranca early in July. A conference has since been held at Zurich to settle definitively the terms of peace which include the cession of Lombardy to Sardinia.

Among the deaths of great people within the past two months are [I. K.] Brunel & [Robert] Stephenson, the [British] Engineers.

Decr 5th, [1859]   A few days ago Washington Irving died aged 76. He was buried at Tarrytown in the old churchyard where lay his father & mother. His has been a singularly enviable lot in life; to be born & reared in that beautiful country on the Hudson, to be surrounded by affluence, to render famous the scenes among which he lived, to be honored by his country & countrymen, to mingle with the world enough to know it, & to be known, to be always lauded & never detracted, to live in health to the limit of man's life, & then to die & be buried in the haunts he had always known, mourned by all, & loved by many, such seems to us a life allotted to few. I met him nearly fourteen years ago, in Paris at Mr. King's. He did not look old then, but yet much older than the portraits I had been accustomed to look at.

For the past six weeks the country has rung with the name of John Brown an old Kansas marauder, who with seventeen white followers possessed himself of the buildings at Harper's Ferry, & after holding them a day was seized by U.S. marines sent from Washington, losing seventeen killed (all the whites with him but one). He was hung last Friday, Decr 2d. His object was to free slaves & his course enlisted the sympathies of northern fanatics. Prayers were offered up in many places for him on Friday. Four of those with him (2 blacks) will be executed on the 16th unless pardoned, which is not likely.

We have a most unusual season. To-day I picked figs growing in the open air; but we are wishing for cool weather. Mamma received a box to-day from N. Orleans full of pretty things for the children from their Aunt Maria. It was a real ovation to them.

Jany 23d, 1860   A new year in this Journal. No startling events occupy the interval since my last entry. John Brown and his fellow marauders were executed according to their sentences without attempt at rescue, tho' not without attempt at escape by [John E.] Cook & Coppic [Barclay Coppoc], the night before their execution. They reached the top of the jail wall, but being discovered by the sentry were fired at, & returned to their cells. One would think they would have jumped & taken the death they were sure of the next day. Congress assembled as usual on the last Monday in Decr & is still without a Speaker. The Black Republicans nominate [John] Sherman [of Ohio] who indorsed [Hinton R.] Helper's book with about forty others, & now they will not leave him because of that indorsement, since such abandonment in order to nominate a more acceptable man would be a condemnation of all the other indorsers. Were the Democrats, South American, and Anti-Lecompton Demos. to unite they could elect, but that seems impossible.

Feby 7, [1860]   The House of Reps. was at last organized on the 1st of Feby by the election of [William] Pennington (Rep.) of New Jersey, Mr. [George] Briggs of N. Y. (Anti-L. Dem.) voting for him. It is sufficient triumph over the Republicans to have forced them to abandon Sherman, & then consign the Helper-ites to condemnation. We are to have Capt. & Mrs. [John] Gibbon to dinner to day. Capt. G. has just published a "Manual" of Artillery. The weather is dark and rainy. Mamma is not feeling very well. She has enflamed her eyes, sewing on a black dress.

Babies very well, & Minnie as small as a weazle. She is lively enough however & dotes on her black "Mamma."

March 28, [1860]   The loss of the steamer Hibernian [*Hungarian*] from Galway to Liverpool on the rocks off Newfoundland, every soul perishing is the saddest event that has occurred of late. Not a living being to tell the tale. The total of human beings on board is not accurately known, somewhere over 100 & under 200. <Jessie's brother bro't her a new doll, greatly to her delight but she gives her Mamma a great deal of trouble.> Mame is a great favorite with her uncle & auntie & promises to be pretty. We had their pictures taken together for their Auntie Sarah [Gayle Crawford]. Of family news the most astounding is the birth of twins (boys) [Edward B. and Thomas L.] in [Thomas L.] Bayne's family. As they [Thomas L.] B[ayne] & M[aria] are both delighted I wish them all manner of joy. Mr. B. is anxious to have plenty of children. This month has been very chilly except the first week. We had green peas from the garden ten days ago, & a few days ago I saw a strawberry nearly ripe.

March 29, [1860]   No news of importance yesterday. Had two young ladies (Mess. Adgen) to dinner on a splendid wild turkey which alas! proved too gamey for the ladies. We hear of the bombardment of Vera Cruz by [Miguel] Miramon. I feel an interest in the old town having lived there nearly a year, & having thrown bombs into it myself. The morning begins beautifully. It is clear & pleasant. Th. 46.

April 3d, [1860]   On the 1st a violent hail storm occurred which did some damage in the vicinity of the city. A fearful homicide was committed on the afternoon of the 31st, a man lately an enlisted man here was shot dead without any warning & without any known hostility on the part of the murderer. The latter belongs to a very good family here, Burckmyer, who are wealthy [commission merchants in Charleston]. Last night Mamma & I spent at Mrs. Taft's, a tea party. Several young ladies played, & the evening passed off agreeably. I abstained from much eating or drinking & feel very well for it. The protest of Presdt Buchanan against the action of the House in appointing a committee to investigate whether his government has influenced elections &c. is warm & spirited. It took the House by surprise. The report of Capt. Turner [of the *Saratoga*] on the capture of the two steamers before Vera Cruz seems satisfactory. The weather is charming this morning. Engaged in putting up water works for a fountain. I am to-day & yesterday beginning to abstain altogether from Alcoholic drinks, which I have heretofore used as often as once a day, sometimes two or three times as occasion presented. I believe their use to be idle if not injurious, and I trust if Willie ever reads this he will ponder over my example, and imitate it at an earlier period of his life. The occasional use of stimulants should be so regulated as to place the longest possible interval between those occasions. Alcohol has its uses, but its abuses are so prominent that the proper use of it vanishes out of sight. I have almost entirely abandoned the use of cigars, of which I was never a devotee, but I am fond of wines, & shall probably continue a moderate use of them, rather to avoid singularity perhaps than because I am fond of them. Let Willie beware of hearty dinners. Let him as I try to keep in sight that excellent rule, never to eat so much as to feel that you have a stomach. Perhaps more discomfort arises from eating heavily than from over-drinking, in the aggregate.

April 8th [1860]   (Easter Sunday). Mamma passed a restless night with baby & sleeps late this morning. There is no news abroad of stirring interest. In caucus Mr. Clingman (N. C.) exchanged blows with another member. Reconciliation &c, no harm done. A Mr. [Albert G.] Jenkins of Va. called Mr. [John F.] Farnsworth of Ill. a "liar" & Mr. F. said in reply "he couldn't descend to a cesspool to throw filth with blackguards." Congress earns the epithet of "bear-garden" it constantly receives. Manners and decency are forgotten.

April 16, [1860]   The day before yesterday Mame swallowed a cent, one of the new kind. As it was nickel chiefly, no serious results followed. The Doctor prescribed a plentiful meal, & a few hours after a dose of oil. Her mother gave the oil yesterday morning & the cent passed in the food, with slight pain. A week ago she swallowed a pin of which nothing has been heard. She has a morbid craving after unhealthy substances. The warmth of the weather (86°) has stimulated vegetation & I day before yesterday (14th) brot in a dozen strawberries for Mamma. We shall soon have plenty of them, of fine size, from some plants set out in November of the Peabody kind. I have set out a variety of fruit trees, pear, apricot, nectarine, peach & fig trees, binder grape roots, all of which are thriving. Am occupying myself in erecting a fountain in the grounds, & a windmill to pump up the water for it.

April 23d, [1860]   To-day the Dem. Convention meets here. It is a warm time for the members in all respects. There is a vast deal of excitement on all hands. The friends of Douglass are very sanguine of his success. My old friend Col. [Rufus L.] Baker arrived on Friday, & Major [John J.] Peck, & G. W. Smith on Saturday. Mamma is much chagrined at the non arrival of Mr. Bell. He sent us a despatch on Saturday at the last moment that he could not come. The opening of the Charleston and Savannah R. R. to the Sav. River was celebrated on Saturday, when the first train passed over.

April 25th, [1860]   Went to see the Democratic Convention yesterday. It is sufficiently boisterous. The President (Hon. Caleb Cushing [of Mass.]) has trouble enough to keep order, tho' a man of commanding ability, & great experience. To-day the debate on the "Platform" as it is called, or the principles which are to guide the party in the contest for the Presidency, are to begin. We have now two more added to our guests— the Messers Nelson of this State, & our table numbers <u>nine</u>. It is believed that if Mr. Douglass is nominated the Gulf States have arranged to leave the Convention. Then "farewell contest." A happy issue will however I dare say be found to all their political antagonisms.

May 6, [1860]   The great Convention adjourned on Thursday the 3d to meet again in Baltimore on the 18th of June. The majority of the Southern States headed by Alabama had previously withdrawn, and organized separately. Mr. [William Lowndes] Yancey of Alabama was the chief spirit of the seceders. Mr. [James A.] Bayard (Senator) of Delaware was their President. On Thursday night we heard him deliver a speech of over an hour at the theatre where the convention (seceding) sat. He appeared to be quite tipsy. We have had two weeks of excitement, & feel quite quiet with the reaction. Mamma looks very thin, & I fear has too many calls on her strength. Yesterday a box came from Mrs. Bell, with beautiful things for the children & Mamma, but chiefly for Willie; and a very pretty photograph of two of her children. Poor little Minnie continues to look delicate. (I omitted to mention that Minnie (<u>Amelia</u> <u>Christine</u>) was baptized with her little cousin [Gayle Aiken] sometime early in April, at the church of the Holy Communion by [the] Rev. Mr. [A. Toomer] Porter). The weather has been quite cool for the past ten days.

June 3d, [1860]   I had information yesterday that I was to be ordered to Frankford, near Phila.; to-day the order came. It is agreeable to me to be assigned to the command of a post so much more important than this but I find this constant breaking of fresh ties more & more disagreeable. I do not want Willie to take or retain a commission in the army. My great regret is the wandering life we are obliged to lead. This will be already the fifth post we have occupied since our marriage. I dislike to part with things, especially <u>growing</u> things, which I have collected about me, and I continually fancy how happy I could be with a spot of earth which I could call my own, which I could plant & improve, where the same things would constantly be about me, where I could live & die, & where some of my children might live & die after me.

Abraham (or Abram) Lincoln of Illinois was nominated candidate for President by the black Republican convention at Chicago. Poor Seward [N.Y. senator who had sought the Republican presidential nomination]! No less than three cargoes of slaves have been captured and bro't into Key West within a month past. The death of Wm. C. Preston [former U.S. senator from S.C.] the distinguished orator occurred at Columbia about ten days ago. He was the grandson of Patrick Henry. He has been infirm for years past, too infirm to mix in public life; but in his day he was the equal of Clay, Webster, Calhoun, [George] McDuffie [representative and senator from S.C.], & all that race of intellectual giants. The weather is unusually cool & pleasant, with days somewhat warm but cool nights.

June 14, [1860] A few days after my last entry I received intimation from a friend at Washington that I would be ordered to Frankford Arsenal, near Philadelphia; & on Sunday [[on writing this far I observe that I have already noted my anticipated transfer]] I find, on further information that I was removed to make way for my successor, a Mil. Store Keeper, named [Frederick C.] Humphreys, for whom a better post than his own (Apalachicola [Fla.]) was asked of the Secretary by Senator [David L.] Yulee [of Fla.]. The Colonel it seems stated that a Capt. was wanted at Fort Leavenworth, which would just chime in with the desired vacancy here. So I was recommended to go to Leavenworth. The Secretary [of War Floyd] knowing me, made a slight change by ordering [Maj. P. V.] Hagner there, & giving me Frankford for which I thank Mr. Secy Floyd. As Maynadier says Our Colonel "aimed at a crow, and shot his neighbor's sow." Mamma & I go to the island this morning (6½ A.M.)

July 1st 1860 To-day I enter upon my forty-third year. May it bring forth better fruit than the past tho. I have not been absolutely idle. The result is however disproportioned to the expenditure of time. What have I done since my last birth-day? I have read little except current literature & not much of that & I have written some papers for Russell's Magazine (letters). I have however made water to flow where it did not, having built up a fountain & constructed a windmill to supply it, & I have planted trees. Besides I have constructed a gun carriage, & contrived some shells, which have at least kept my tho'ts employed. Of the carriage I expect some results, the shells, of which a few were tried at Old Point will probably never be heard of again. We have many things to be thankful for in this past year of my life, especially in the preservation of our little Minnie, whose existence was but a precarious one a year ago. It is a very hot day to-day, the mercury standing at 83° at 7 A.M. & it is now 92° & rising. Yesterday it rose to 94°. In a few days we shall be on our way to Frankford Arsenal. The vessel on which we were to go having put back for repairs is laid up, & the journey must be done by land, no trifle in this hot weather. It will not be so long as the one we took just 4 years ago from Mobile to Augusta, Me. On Tuesday we attended the funeral of Mrs. Barnwell Rhett (he is the editor of the [Charleston] Mercury). She died very suddenly the day before, suddenly tho' after an illness of some weeks of typhoid fever. She was a schoolfriend of Mamma and her unexpected death has greatly distressed her.

Frankford Arsenal. Aug 7, [1860]   On the 9th of July in the evening
we bade good-bye to Charleston Arsenal, a pretty post which we left with
regret, and took the cars for Winnsboro, S. C. where we were to stop a
day to see the Aiken family. Riding all night we reached Columbia early
in the morning, and took a drive about the city, whilst waiting for the
cars to take us to W. We looked at the capitol a beautiful structure in
progress, at Columbia College, an ancient seat of learning, where Judge
Gayle was educated, & Hugh graduated, at the cemetery, the mil. School,
&c. The streets are wide, & were very dusty. Shade trees give a rural
aspect to the town, which stands on a level space. At 11 we reached W. &
stopped until the following evening, in the hottest weather I think I ever
felt. It is a small town in the cotton growing region, with a rather pretty
country about it. Mr. [David] A[iken] (senior) [Hugh's father] has I think
6 plantations, varying in size from 2 to 6000 acres, & has about 300
negros. He is of course very wealthy. At 6 P.M. on the 11th we parted
from our friends (Hugh & Mary with Gayle having come up from
Charleston with us) & passing thro' Charlotte, Raleigh & Weldon took
the Steamer at Portsmouth for Baltimore. The weather was now cool
enough for an outer garment, & it rained smartly as we passed Old Point.
The rain compelled Willie & me to change our rooms during the night,
the deck overhead proving leaky. We left Baltimore at 8 & reached here
at noon of the 13th, without accident & without encountering much
fatigue by the way. Mr. [Thomas J.] Treadwell met us at the Depot with a
wagon in which Mamma & the children rode out, & Lt. T. & myself
took the horse cars. No event more considerable than the arrival of the
Great Eastern Steamer has occurred. She attracts much attention & has
visited Cape May & Old Point & is now at Annapolis where the Presdt
(Mr. Buchanan) goes to see her. The visit of the Prince of Wales to
Canada excites attention. Yesterday we heard of the death of little Eddy
one of Maria's twin boys. It was I think over four months old, or about
that. Dr. [Daniel] Chapman is quite ill, & my Sister Eliza (Mrs. C) is &
has been much out of health.

Frankford Arsenal March 31st [1861]   Stirring events have taken
place since my last entry into this journal. On the 17th of December,
rather more than a month after the election of Abraham Lincoln, as
President, on a ticket purely sectional, the convention of the State of
South Carolina, passed its Ordinance of Secession, & was followed at
short intervals by Alabama, Georgia, Florida, Mississippi, Louisiana &
Texas. A government was organized at Montgomery Ala. & Jefferson
Davis [of Miss.] elected Presdt & Alex.[ander] H. Stephens [of Ga.] Vice
Presdt of this provisional organization for one year.
      On the night of the 26th of December Major [Robert H.] Anderson
who was stationed at Fort Moultrie with two companies, passed his

troops over to Fort Sumter an act which created great excitement thro'out the South, & was much lauded in the North. Soon after the troops were also thrown into Fort Pickens [at Pensacola, Fla.] so that these two points became the advanced posts of the contending parties. Both were soon surrounded by overwhelming forces, and it is daily expected that Fort S. will be evacuated.

Formidable works have been thrown up about it, & the provisions of the garrison are nearly exhausted. A weak effort was made to throw troops & provisions into it; & a steamer, the Star of the West, entering the harbor for that purpose was fired into, fortunately without bloodshed, & compelled to turn about. Major Anderson having no knowledge of the errand of the vessel did not attempt to protect her by returning the fire of the batteries.

An Army being organized at the South a commission was offered to me in it. I declined then, but being much urged by my own sympathies & likings, & importuned by my Southern friends, I sent in my resignation on the 27th, to take the effect on the 3d of April. I might have passed the summer here on account of your mother's health, but that I was ordered away from here (very wrongfully) & so I thought I might as well make one move of it & go where I should ultimately have to go, I doubt not. We leave here on Wednesday the 3d of April for Charleston where I shall leave all the family, & proceed myself to Montgomery, to report to the Secy of War (L. P. Walker [of Ala.]). These removals are always days of sadness to me.

Civil War
June 1862–May 1865

Josiah Gorgas as chief of Confederate Ordnance Bureau (Courtesy of Hoole Special Collections, University of Alabama, Tuscaloosa, Alabama)

III

*"Brilliant hopes which centered in
the possession of Richmond"*

Richmond Va. June 12th 1862   Since the last entry in this Journal I
have passed the most eventful period of my life. Days appear like weeks,
& the last day above entered confounds itself with my early life.

On the 7th of April [1861] I reached Montgomery [Ala.] and on the
8th took charge of the [Confederate] Ordnance Bureau, being assigned to
duty as Chief of Ordnance. On the 1st of June [1861] the government
established itself here [Richmond] as being nearer the scene of its most
active duties. On the 10th of June was fought the 1st battle of the war, at
Bethel, near Yorktown. The Yankees were signally defeated with heavy
loss, while ours was only one man killed. The artillery did excellent
service, Gen. [John B.] Magruder commanded our troops. A short time
before this a man by the name of [James T.] Jackson, killed [Col. E.
Elmer] Ellsworth, Col of [11th N.Y.] Zouaves, for entering his home, &
attempting to haul down the Confederate flag on his home in Alexandria.
Jackson was of course instantly butchered. His devotion had an electric
effect, & was looked on as a happy omen of the spirit of the war.

About the middle of July, we suffered a reverse in western Virginia.
Gen. [Robert S.] Garnett [[a classmate]] was killed and about four hundred of our men captured. This little success achieved with overwhelming
numbers was the sole foundation of [Gen. George B.] McClellan's elevation to command subsequently.

On the 21st of July (Sunday) was fought the decisive battle of Manassas or Bull run. It was preceded by a creditable affair on the 18th. The
battle was fought by the united forces of [Gen. Joseph E.] Johnston bro't
from Winchester, & of [Gen. P. G. T.] Beauregard, the latter having
made the disposition of the troops, before Johnston arrived. [Gen. Irwin]

McDowell commanded the Yankees. The odds were very heavily against us, about 25,000 to 45 or 50,000. We routed the enemy completely capturing twenty-eight pieces of artillery, and a large number of small arms, & stores of various kinds. Unfortunately the victory was not followed up, or Washington would have fallen into our hands without further contest.

About this time we heard of the victory at Springfield Mo. which resulted in the death of [Gen. Nathaniel] Lyon (my classmate & roommate [at West Point]) and the retreat of his forces. Lyon was one of the most valuable of their Generals, being a man of more than average ability, and of unswerving purpose. He would have been the general of the abolition school. He was a man of cruel disposition—who would never forego an advantage over an enemy. He was the grandson [great nephew] of Col. [Thomas] Knowlton, an officer of the revolution, from Connecticut. His ability was shown at West Point, chiefly in mathematics. He could not acquire languages, chemistry, or anything in which memory played a part.

Garnett, mentioned above, was a dashing man, & ambitious. He would have played a good part, & made an active enterprizing General. His death was a loss. His capacity was very moderate as a scholar, but he had studied men and manners. He was the nephew of R. M. T. Hunter, of Va. [Confederate Secretary of State, 1861–1862.]

[[I omitted to mention in its proper place that the bombardment of Fort Sumter, which began the war, took place on the 12th [of April] (Friday). This began the war. Lincoln immediately called out 75,000 men, whereupon Virginia seceded, accompanied by Arkansas and Tennessee.]]

Up to this time and until the affair in Missouri, where we captured over a thousand prisoners, our success was uniform. In October our reverses began with the capture of Hatteras [N.C.]. Port Royal [S.C.] followed at no long interval, and early in this year, Roanoke Island, a sad blunder, where we lost 2500 prisoners. Then came Crittendens disaster on the upper Cumberland,* relieved however soon after by our success at Belmont opposite Columbus, Ky. But the chief of our reverses was the fall of Fort Donelson [on the Cumberland River] and the capture of its entire garrison & the army then about 7000 men. Thus with the loss of Fort Henry [on the Tennessee River], a week before opened the Cumberland and Tennessee to the gunboats of the enemy, and lost to us the State of Tennessee. Johnston fell back from Nashville to the line of the Memphis and Charleston R.Road, & the boats of the enemy ascended at once to Florence in Alabama, the River being very full. <This was the

---

*Mill Spring

great mistake of the War. Ten thousand men would have converted Donelson from an overwhelming disaster to a victory—and 18000 men were literally doing nothing under Gen. [Braxton] Bragg at Pensacola and Mobile. If [Gen. U. S.] Grant had been beaten at Donelson as he might easily have been with proper disposition of troops, the tide would have been rolled back into Kentucky. Our President is unfortunately no military genius, & could not see the relative value of position. Pensacola was nothing compared to Donelson.>

The Missourians under [Gen. Earl] Van Dorn fought about this time a bloody combat at Pea Ridge [in Ark.] in which [Gen. Ben] McCulloch & [Gen. James] McIntosh were killed. It was indecisive but by no means discreditable to us.

On the 6th of April (Sunday) [Gen. Albert Sidney] Johnston attacked Grant at Shiloh, on the Tennessee, where he had effected a landing & established himself. The forces were not very unequal, Grant having five heavy divisions of which four were engaged. He was drawn completely from his camps, back to the river under the fire of his boats, & darkness found him completely defeated, our troops being every where in possession of their camps. During the night the advance of [Gen. Don Carlos] Buell's column arrived, on the other side of the river, & began crossing. The fight was renewed next day, & our troops gradually forced back again, without confusion however. Unfortunately Johnston fell on Sunday at about 2½ P.M. and Beauregard [was] left in command. Had Johnston continued in command it is possible that his genius & energy would have crushed Grant before night brot darkness & Buell to his rescue. The loss was heavy on both sides, neither party in this contest appears to pay much regard to truth, & especially in the statement of losses must accounts be read with caution. Our loss was probably 5000**, while the enemy lost a few thousand more.

After the fall of Fort Donelson our forces evacuated the lines they had held since last summer at Manassas. All the Potomac was abandoned, & our troops fell back, first to the Rappahannock, and very soon were transferred to Yorktown, whither McClellan had transferred his force. The lines at Yorktown were held until some time in April when the Army fell back to Richmond. On the retreat was fought the bloody combat of Williamsburg, of which we had the best.

The abandonment of Yorktown & the Peninsula it is said necessitated the evacuation of Norfolk and with it came the destruction of the [Confederate ironclad] Merrimac which had produced such terror in the Yankee Navy.

About the 10th of March she attacked the whole Federal Squadron in

---

**more probably 12,000, while the enemy lost perhaps 15,000, and 3700 prisoners

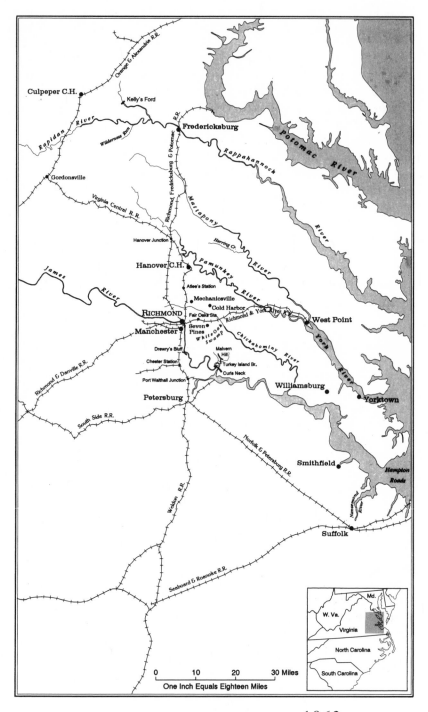

THE PENINSULA CAMPAIGN, 1862

Hampton Roads. With her iron prow she ran into and sank the Cumberland, in five minutes. She then attacked & destroyed the Congress, both of them frigates of the largest class. An iron clad vessel called the Monitor armed with two heavy guns in a revolving tower, which had just come down from New-York, interposed & saved the whole fleet from destruction. Com. [Flag Officer Franklin] Buchanan the commander of the Merrimac was wounded.

No one event of the war, not even the disaster of Ft. Donelson created such a profound sensation as the destruction of this noble ship. It was intended to bring her up the James River as far as her draught would permit, after the evacuation of Norfolk. For this purpose she was lightened by throwing her coal overboard; but after all had been taken out she could not pass the bar at the mouth of James River. She was now in a condition nearly defenceless. Her iron sheathing had come up to the water line & even above it—& her fuel was gone—nothing was left but to blow her up which was done with 36,000 lbs of powder on board. It was indeed a fearful blunder, and one which came very near being fatal to us. There was nothing now to prevent the gunboats from reaching Richmond. The battery at Drury's bluff [Drewry's Bluff] had but three guns mounted—the obstructions were wholly incomplete, & the enemy could have made their way right up to this city. Fortunately they waited until a week after her destruction before making the attempt. The obstructions were completed, & when they did make the attempt on the 17th of May they were signally defeated. It was the turning point in our fortunes.

McClellan having crossed a portion of his troops over the Chickahominy, Johnston attacked the Divisions which had crossed on Saturday the 31st of May [the battle of Seven Pines]. The enemy was driven back out of his camps, eight or ten pieces of artillery captured, several standards & about four hundred prisoners, not without severe loss. The commander in chief was seriously wounded, Gen. [James J.] Pettigrew wounded & a prisoner—Gen. [Robert Hopkins] Hatton killed, & many field officers killed & wounded. Our loss was about 5000 in killed & wounded—that of the enemy perhaps greater, as they confess about that many. The fight was renewed on Sunday morning, but the enemy had been re-inforced, & the attack was abandoned. The fight was therefore indecisive. It was however a heavy check to the enemy. One of his Divisions was entirely destroyed—that of Gen. [Silas] Casey. The enemy is now building bridges over the Chickahominy—consolidating his position & making some advance along the [Richmond &] York River R.R.

Sunday June 15, [1862]   Gen. Stewart [J. E. B. Stuart] has just come in from a brilliant foray against the enemys communications. He started from Hanover [Court House]—went round their rear—destroyed two transports in the Pamunkey [River]—cut up several trains, & brot in about 150 prisoners and 200 to 300 mules—without any loss.

About the lst of June & last of May Gen. [Thomas J.] Jackson succeeded in completely routing Gen. [N. P.] Banks in the [Shenandoah] valley, & driving him across the Potomac. He has since retired up the valley, followed by [Gen. John C.] Fremont & by [Gen. James] Shields, whom he has separately met & driven back with loss. In a skirmish [near Harrisonburg, Va.] a week ago Gen. [Turner] Ashby, a distinguished cavalry officer rather of the partizan kind, fell, greatly lamented. The loss of the enemy in these operations in the Valley has been very great. 3000 prisoners were taken, & a large amount of army stores, medicines, &c.

Monday, [June] 16, [1862]   Some skirmishing took place yesterday, & at one time a Regiment of the enemy was in our toils, but a very heavy storm came on and prevented the capture. A Capt. & seven or eight prisoners only were taken. The enemy is said to be pressing into East Tennessee, being relieved from the pressure on their front by the retreat of Beauregard from Corinth. It is a point of weakness to us there, where there is so much union sentiment. A little fight has taken place at Secessionville, on James Island near Charleston, [S.C.] the enemy attacking and being repulsed, with the loss of forty prisoners. Jackson saved himself from capture the other day by great presence of mind. He had crossed a bridge over the Shenandoah, with a couple of aids & ridden to a hill at some distance. Coming back he found the bridge in possession of the enemy & a piece of artillery on it. He rode up to it at once, at full speed, & ordered it to be placed in a different position. They took him for one of their own officers & immediately limbered up, & moved off. He put spurs to his horse & rode over. His aids were taken, but subsequently re-captured.

Wednesday [June] 18, [1862]   The reconnaissance made by Stuart which resulted so brilliantly was ordered by [Gen. Robert E.] Lee, commander in chief. He should have credit for the orders. I have seen the President to-day. He appears very much discontented with Beauregards movements at Corinth. They are certainly inexplicable.

Friday, [June 20, 1862]   No results yet. A heavy skirmish took place on Wednesday, with some loss on both sides, how much on that of the enemy is not known—about 60 killed & wounded on our side. Exaggeration is so much indulged in by both sides that it is difficult to find the exact truth. <The Yankees are probably the greatest liars, but we are not much behind them.> Much speculation is still indulged in as to the course of England & France, in this war. How much evil they could have spared to their own people & to us, had they acknowledged our independence after the battle of Manassas, when they could very properly have done so. I trust a new era is about to dawn upon us in the defence of our cities; & that no more will fall like N. Orleans & Memphis until they are captured by land forces. <The evacuation of N. Orleans by [Gen. Mansfield] Lovell is a shameful chapter in our history. He should have insisted on the defence of the city & asked for 48 hours to remove the women & children.>

Sunday 22d June, [1862]   Preparations are evidently being made for a general action. Jackson with I hope 20,000 men is coming down from Gordonsville to fall on McClellan's right, I presume, while another attack is being made in front, by our forces here. Another Sunday will see us either victors, & defiant, or beaten & humiliated. Your*** mother and all the children except yourself are at Greensboro' N. C.—you at Winsboro S. C. All the little girls & baby Ria have measles, after having had them as we supposed last winter. [Maria Bayne Gorgas had been born August 4, 1861, in Charleston, S.C.]

Tuesday, June 24, [1862]   There is very little firing along the lines. The battle may take place to-morrow or next day or the next or ten days hence, but probably cannot be long delayed. I think it may take place Thursday. A train leaves to-morrow morning for Hanover, where Gen. Jackson may be. It will carry ammunition which he needs, & therefore he will not be ready to-morrow morning. I fear if there is much delay Fremont and McDowell may unite & fall upon Jackson before he can attack the right of McClellan's army. Poor little Ria is still very ill, according to her mothers letter of Sunday. I am very anxious about her. She has measles & is teething.

Friday, June 27, [1862]   The great battle is now going on [the Seven Days battles, June 26–July 1]. It opened yesterday on our left, at about 5 P.M., perhaps earlier, and continued until 9½ P.M. At 4 this morning the fire was resumed. It is now 7 A.M. & going on with vigor.

Saturday, [June 28, 1862]   Yesterday the enemy were driven from their positions at Powhite Creek after a desperate & bloody conflict. The ground is still covered with their dead. In one field there are 40 or 50 of the Zouaves lying. They are being buried in trenches. Just before I got out to-day two Regiments of [Robert A.] Toombs' brigade had charged on a battery of the enemy on this side of the Chickahominy, below New Bridge & were repulsed with heavy loss. It is said they took the battery but were unsupported & could not hold it. I have had a long & severe ride to the battle field of yesterday & back.

***Willie

Tuesday, [July 1, 1862] The enemy left his positions on the north bank of the Chickahominy, & massed his troops on the South Side. On Sunday morning he began to abandon his position on the South side, & took up his retreat for the James River about Curls Neck or Dutch Gap. [Gen. Benjamin] <Huger was negligent & permitted him to get away unperceived.> A vigorous pursuit was made at once by [Gen. James] Longstreet, [Gen. D. H.] Hills, & Magruders Divisions—Jackson covering the Chickahominy behind McClellan and pressing on the left. There was a good deal of fighting on Sunday, and a very heavy battle on Monday, the enemy showing a determined front. To-day has been the severest battle, tho' not so critical as that of Friday. The enemy took post on or near the junction of the Quaker & Darbytown Road, & with his artillery mowed down our troops. Our loss was very severe. He withdrew toward the close of the fight, & during the night continued his retreat. I rode out & was within a mile of the field during the heat of the battle. The firing was very heavy. My ride of nearly 30 miles, between 4½ & 11, was fatiguing.

Friday, July 4, [1862] There has been no more serious fighting since Tuesday. The enemy has reached the river and is resting under cover of his gunboats below Turkey Island. He is committing ravages on the crops & stock of the vicinity. Whether there will be anything more done to molest him I know not. Prisoners are coming in daily. We have about 5000 I suppose, & two generals [Gen. George A.] McCall & [Gen. John F.] Reynolds, the latter of my class.

July 8, 1862 The enemy has attained a comparatively safe position without much further loss. The word "Safe" in this connexion tells the full extent of his late reverses forcibly enough, & indicates the nature of our success. From a bold and threatening attitude he has been reduced to one which is characterized as safe—that is the first tho't connected with it. He has been driven from Mechanicsville along the north bank of the Chickahominy, below New bridge, across the Chickahominy & thro' the marshes & thickets of White Oak Swamp to the James River, at Herring Creek where he now lies under cover of his gun-boats. Where are now the brilliant hopes which centered in the possession of Richmond. McClellan was certain to be in Richmond. There was no doubt about it. He was 6 miles off then. Now he is 25 miles away having lost in the meantime not less than 25 to 30 thousand men, 40 to 50 pieces of artillery, an immense amount of stores, wagons, & camp equipage of all sort. We have about 5000 well prisoners & 2000 wounded ones including two General officers.

The papers (one of them at least) grumble that McClellan has "slipped thro' our fingers." We should have gladly compromised for such a "Situation" two weeks ago.

Mamma writes from Greensboro, that Ria is still ailing, poor little baby. The summer will go hard with her and I long for the cool days of October. The last three days have been intolerably hot, & I have been by no means well. I have practiced abstinence however and shall soon get right again. I impress this important fact on Willie that with his constitution a few days fasting is worth all the medicine in the world. Whenever I feel ill I diet, & have thus avoided the use of medicine almost entirely. I have found a half grain of blue mass, without anything else a very good corrective in warm weather. Sluggishness of the liver seems inherent in my organization, at least I cannot endure warm climates with impunity.

July 27, [1862]   I returned from Greensboro after an absence of a week, on Wednesday. I found all well except Ria who was very ailing, and her poor little face looked pinched and had a fixed expression of suffering. Mamma writes that she is now however improving. I found them in a fine large building—a Methodist College [Greensborough Female College]—with 40 or 50 refugees. The surroundings are very attractive, and the air very salubrious. It stands on the outskirts of the little town which has about 1500 inhabitants. On my way down I stopped at Edenburgh to visit our lead smelting works there, under charge of Dr. Piggott. To this point I rode in the conductor's car on a trunk with Senator [James L.] Orr of S. C. So full were the cars with wounded soldiers & their friends that we could not get seats. The railroads are badly conducted and it is impossible to get along with any degree of comfort. Baggage is no longer taken care of, & travelers must do the best they can. The great struggle in which we are engaged disorganizes every thing, which is not energetically supervised.

This month has been signalized by the defence of Vicksburgh, under Gen. Van Dorn, and by the operations of Cols. [John Hunt] Morgan and [Nathan Bedford] Forrest in Central Kentucky. Vicksburgh has been bombarded, heavily, without much injury, and the enemy has been foiled, by its determined occupation. He cannot get command of the Mississippi, & has withdrawn his forces. All his work to get command of the River is therefore lost. Morgan & Forrest have taken and held various towns & cities about Frankfort & Lexington, & have burnt bridges on the road between Lexington & Louisville.

Jackson's command has been sent up the road toward Fredericksburgh & Gordonsville to hold [Gen. John] Pope in check & to defeat him if he attempts to move southward. The day is beautiful, & the air pleasant. It is Sunday & I attended church this morning. I omitted to state that Mamma and I were baptized and confirmed on the same day (Tuesday May 6, 1862). President Davis and one other person were the only others confirmed, the confirmation being held by the bishop for him. Rev. Mr. [Charles] Minnegerode baptized us in St. Paul's [Episcopal] church [in

Richmond]. My mind has since turned oftener toward religious tho'ts, & I trust I shall benefit by thus linking myself to the visible church.

The death of Gen. [David E.] Twiggs occurred about the middle of this month, at an advanced age. Bragg has succeeded Beauregard in the command of the Army in Miss. & is now moving on Chattanooga by way of Mobile. He will I believe be able to drive Buell back & perhaps redeem Tennessee, if not Kentucky.

Aug 3d, [1862]   Troops have been moved in large numbers up to reinforce Jackson at Gordonsville. News of a battle are expected from there and from Chattanooga, where our troops are now face to face with the enemy—Bragg at C. & Jackson at Gordonsville. Buell opposes Bragg & Pope, Jackson. Pope is morally worthless, Jackson is a just and upright man, & in earnest. Providence will help the righteous man who puts his shoulder to the wheel. Between Bragg & Buell there is little to choose on the score of morality. Both are like the common run of humanity. On Thursday night our siege & field guns attacked the transports of the enemy in [the] James River at Coggins Point after midnight. What damage was done does not appear. Night attacks are seldom worth the trouble they give.

Mamma writes that she remains at Greensboro as Ria is so much better.

Aug 8, [1862]   News were received yesterday of heavy fighting at Baton Rouge. Gen. [John C.] Breckinridge attacked the enemy and drove them toward the River until stopped by the Arsenal (which was probably fortified). His own loss severe. Gen. [Charles] Clark of Miss. mortally wounded. [Clark actually suffered only a shattered hip.] Gen. B had withdrawn his troops, to renew the attack in half an hour. Three or four thousand of our prisoners arrived yesterday under the system of exchange among them Gens. [Simon B.] Buckner & [Lloyd] Tilghman. The former was kept in close confinement for 4½ months.

Aug 9, [1862]   Three Divisions (at least) marched down to Malvern Hill on Wednesday to confront 20,000 of the enemy. The troops lay in front of the enemy all night expecting to attack in the morning. But with the morning the Yankees had vanished & our troops marched back. A bulletin says that we have captured [Gen. George W.] Morgan's forces at Cumberland Gap—too good to be true. This Morgan came to West Pt just as I graduated—then a full grown man, & it was said having already fought with the Texans against Mexico. He stayed there but a few months (or less). I next saw him as Col. of a regiment in Mexico. I shall be glad to meet him a third time as a prisoner. No further news from Breckinridge, & it is feared that he was roughly handled at Baton Rouge.

An unpleasant rumor says the Arkansas (ram) had to be blown up, her machinery having given out, & she became unmanageable.

Gen. Stewart [Stuart] sent in over 100 prisoners, & about the same number were taken at Malvern Hill. The weather is the hottest I have yet felt here. [[The destruction of the Arkansas is confirmed. Her machinery became deranged on her passage down the river. She was run ashore for repairs & while in this situation was attacked by the enemy's fleet.]]

Aug 11, [1862]   Troops moved yesterday to join Jackson, who it is said captured a General & other officers. As an order has been issued that in consequence of Gen. Pope's conduct toward citizens, the officers of his army shall not be entitled to be considered prisoners of war, the capture of officers is looked to with peculiar interest. The brilliant passage of the Arkansas thro' the enemy's fleet three weeks ago, destroying several of them made us hope much of her. Had she lived N. Orleans might have been re-taken. With her dies all hope of re-conquering the Mississippi. Yesterday & Saturday were the hottest days I have felt here. In the afternoon a thunder shower cooled the air & laid the dust.

Aug 14, [1862]   Gen. Lee has gone to take command of the army near Gordonsville, which now contains the greater part of the troops, Longstreets Corps having been sent up. It will be necessary to drive the enemy out of Virginia before he can get his new levies into the field, which are to amount to 600,000 (six hundred thousand) men, viz: 300,000 militia called out for nine months, & 300,000 volunteers. If the volunteers are not forthcoming by the 15th of August then a draft is to be made. As great tendency has been shown to avoid duty, an order has been promulgated permitting no one to go abroad. If we can but hold our own for the next nine months of which I have no doubt, all will end well.

Aug 16, [1862]   From oppressive heat the weather has turned pleasantly cool. Gen Lee called yesterday for the Division of Gen. Anderson, (R.H.) and announced his intention to push forward beyond the Rapidan [River]. The telegram was from Gordonsville. Mr. Lincoln would not receive the proclamation or order of the President, ordering that Pope's officers should not be treated as prisoners of war, in consequence of Pope's infamous orders holding citizens responsible for the shooting of his men by guerillas, or rangers. Lincoln says it is an insult to his government. McClellan says that he is ordered by the commander in chief to say that the war will be conducted on their side according to the usages of civilized warfare. What a coming down for McClellan to be obliged to confess himself Second, who was so late the Napoleon, the idol of the people, & the army. Mamma writes that she is very comfortable and that the children are all well. She has not heard again from Willie who has the whooping cough very lightly.

Aug 20, [1862]   McClellan has crossed the lower Chickahominy & moved over to the Pamunky [Pamunkey] to place himself in supporting distance of [Gen. Ambrose] Burnside at Fredericksburg, eventually, no doubt. <It seems to me our troops are very inert to allow him to make this movement without being harrassed.> The battle of Cedar Mtn [west of Culpeper] fought on Saturday the 9th was very creditable to our troops. The enemy confess to great loss. Pope as usual issues a lying despatch claiming the success, tho' in faint terms. Our troops under Jackson made the attack, on Banks' corps, which was very roughly handled. Congress met on Monday & seems inclined to vigorous measures. Our expenses have thus far been under $350,000,000, which is wonderful considering that we have had for a year between 3 & 4 hundred thousand men in the field.

Sept 7, [1862]   Great battles were fought on the 28th 29th & 30th on the old battle grounds about Bull Run. The enemy were repulsed on the first two days & defeated on the last. We have taken 30 or 40 pieces of arty, a great many small arms, & more than 7000 prisoners. The loss of the enemy is vastly greater than ours. On the 30th the enemy also suffered a signal defeat at Richmond in Kentucky, by Gen. [Edmund] Kirby Smith. 3 or 4 thousand prisoners were taken. Great hopes are entertained of the campaign in Kentucky. I fear the result of the far advance of our troops toward Washington, unless the campaign can be prosecuted into Maryland, & the troops subsisted there. The acquisition of arms in these battles will be very important to us. Hugh & Mr. Bayne [husbands of two of Amelia's sisters] came here last week. The latter stays with me. Hugh came to get his command of Partizan Rangers mustered in. Mamma still stays at Greensboro, but will soon go to Winsboro & thence return here, not to leave again I trust until the capital is moved from here further south. Baby Ria is getting as fat as a little pig again, after her summer of illness.

Septr 14, [18]62   Our army has crossed over into Maryland and is now I hope at Harrisburgh and on its way to Philadelphia. We shall have to fight one more great battle to defeat that army now at & about Washington, & then the enemy will be completely prostrate at our feet. God grant us this victory not for vengeance but for peace. Let us trust in Him. In Kentucky Gen. Kirby Smith is probably on the bank of the Ohio. I trust Cincinnati is ours or will be soon. Our forces in Kentucky & in Maryland are sufficient to overwhelm the foe & now is the time for audacity. Uncle Tom now Capt. Bayne went to Winsboro on Friday & takes Mamma & all the children along with him from Greensboro. In three weeks now I shall be a joyful man on seeing them all back around me. I saw Gen. [Gideon] Pillow on Friday & looking very well. He has lost property by the Yankees to the amt of $700,000. Yesterday morning

I was called before the Committee on Ord. Stores (of the [Confederate] House [of Representatives]). Mr. [Charles M.] Conrad [of La.] is Chairman. My Dept. is in a very satisfactory condition, & the committee were well pleased with my account of affairs.

Sept 21, [1862]   Last Sunday our army captured Harpers Ferry with 11,000 prisoners and a large amount of stores. From 600 to 1000 negroes were recaptured. Yesterday the people were disturbed by the accounts of a Philadelphia paper of the 18th, rec'd by flag of truce, to the effect that on the day before Harpers Ferry had been retaken Jackson and Longstreet killed and 40,000 of our Army killed and captured! As we have a messenger with the flags who left there on Wednesday we may safely pronounce it a <u>canard</u>. Will the fruits of our victories be peace? That is the vital question. On Tuesday it is known that there was heavy fighting in which McClellan's army was driven back, but no details are known, except the death of Gen. [Samuel] Garland of Lynchburgh. Our army was massed at [space] west of Fredrick city [Frederick, Md.] on Wednesday. It is doubtless safe, and with Harper's Ferry in our hands we have a reliable base in case of disaster.

No late news from Kentucky except that the Kentuckians are rallying to us.

Oct 4, [1862]   Our army is not far from Winchester. After the heavy battles of Sunday & Wednesday (Sept. 17) it withdrew to the Virginia side of the Potomac carrying with it nearly all its wounded and all of its baggage and stores. Longstreets division lost an ammn train before the battle which was the chief loss of material sustained. Four pieces of artillery were lost on Thursday from the Corps of Artillery. We heard that [Hugh Aiken's brother] Col. Wyatt Aiken of the 7th S.C. was mortally wounded, but it turned out otherwise & he is recovering tho' shot thro the breast, the ball entering near the left nipple & coming out under the shoulder blade. Some apprehensions are entertained lest the enemy may make a dash on Richmond. We could not muster above 12,000 men at the very utmost for its defence. The yellow fever is making some ravages at Wilmington, for the first time for forty years. This must be due to the vessels running the blockade from the West Indies. Lincoln has issued his proclamation liberating the slaves in all rebellious states after the 1st of Jany next. It is a document only to be noticed as showing the drift of opinion in the northern gov. It is opposed by many there. Mamma is still at Winsboro, S.C. A bill has just passed both houses making the chief of ordnance a Brig. Genl. I shall hail the day which returns me to my grade of Lt. Col, and peace. <u>Capt. Bayne</u> is on duty with me and relieves me more than I conceived possible. The best indication of the times at the North is that gold has gone up to 123, a very ominous feature in their currency. With us gold is 210 & even more, but it affects us very little because we buy scarcely anything abroad. It affects their trade vastly. And now everybody is buying gold, & it will entirely disappear, & there will be but little left to pay for their importations. Trade will be ruined, & chaos will follow, unless the war ceases.

Oct 17, [1862]   We are now anxiously expecting news from Kentucky, where Gen Bragg has encountered the forces under Buell, with doubtful result. The news from our side is that we have captured guns and prisoners, & achieved a decided success—but no one is satisfied of its authenticity. Two weeks ago to-day our forces attacked the enemy under Gen. [William S.] Rosecrans at Corinth and were defeated. Gen Van Dorn was evidently out generaled—allowing himself to be drawn into a trap, & getting his forces very much cut up. [Gen. Sterling] Price commanded the Missouri & other troops. The full details of the disaster are not yet known but we have lost prisoners, arms & artillery. It is a mournful result, risked without an object. The proclamation of Lincoln, freeing all slaves in disloyal states after the 1st of January next encounters marked opposition at the north, & is denounced by the democrats generally.

Mamma is still at Winsboro, with all the children, and will not return until the first of next month.

Bayne & myself spent an evening at the President's last week. He was very much depressed at the news from Corinth, & said we have been out generaled. Mrs. Davis was very talkative and inquired particularly about Mamma & said when we next fled from Richmond they would go to Raleigh (where she had gone last May) together. She is a lady of great good sense & of much more than ordinary cultivation. <She lacks refinement of manner, perhaps, but impresses me favorably whenever I meet her.>

IV

"The Confederacy totters to its destruction"

March 20, 1863   The five months which have elapsed since my last entry have been fruitful in military events. I regret that I have not entered them as they occurred and can now only glance back over them. The battle of Perryville closed the brilliant successes of the Kentucky campaign, by a drawn fight in which we captured artillery, and inflicted heavy loss on the enemy. Bragg however effected the object he had in view viz: the withdrawal of the supplies he had captured. The military results of this campaign were the capture of about 10,000 prisoners, eight or ten thousand small arms, several batteries of Artillery, and large supplies of cloth and bacon for the army. Bragg's forces were now thrown on the road to Nashville and our pickets approached within a few miles of the city. On the approach of Rosecrans our army fell back and took up a position a few miles in advance of Murfreesboro'—awaiting an attack. Finding the enemy indisposed to an attack, Bragg threw himself vigorously on the enemy's right and drove it back up his centre inflicting heavy loss and capturing 3000 prisoners and 27 pieces of artillery. This was on the last day of the old year 1862. Had the fight stood thus we should have had unchecked triumph. Unfortunately Breckinridge attacked the centre and left of the enemy on the 2nd of January and met with a bloody repulse, losing full 3000 men of his division and 2 pieces of artillery. After this Bragg fell back slowly to Tullahoma where he now is. The battle of Murfreesboro was fought with undoubtedly greatly inferior force, our army numbering less than 35,000 men. Rosecrans had probably 50,000 and over. This great battle closed the campaign in middle Tennessee. A series of brilliant cavalry dashes under [Gen. Joseph] Wheeler and Forrest have however characterized the winter months.

These have resulted in the capture of a great number of wagons, horses, &c and the destruction of many more. Among other exploits Wheeler attacked the transports of the enemy below Nashville at Cumberland Shoals and sunk one, and destroyed several with all their stores. The enemy has thus been constantly harrassed and a great deal crippled. About the first of this month Van Dorn attacked and captured five regiments at Thompson's Station on the Columbia road taking some 2500 prisoners and killing and wounding many.

In North Mississippi Van Dorn pounced on the rear of Grant's army at Holly Springs some time in December, & besides taking many prisoners destroyed stores to the amount of it is said $10,000,000. which is perhaps an exaggeration.

At Vicksburgh the enemy attacked vigorously on the Yazoo [River] and were repulsed with heavy [[Decr 29]] slaughter. Several gunboats, the Queen of the West and the Indianola, both iron-clads, having passed the batteries at V. were captured by our enterprizing infantry. The Queen of the West was used in the capture of the Indianola, which vessel was sunk in 9 feet of water & still lies there.

About the 8th or 10th of this month the fleet of [Adm. David] Farragut from N. Orleans attacked Port Hudson and were repulsed with the loss of the Mississippi burned by one of our shells, and several of the larger sloops of war crippled.

The Port of Galveston was also cleared of the enemy by a daring attack on his ships, with cotton clad steamers, which resulted in the capture of the "Harriet Lane" after severe loss on board. Sabine Pass was soon after cleared out and then the coast of Texas delivered of the enemy, and the Port of Galveston declared open—a declaration which no one will heed. Thus the fortune of war in the West has been largely in our favor, despite the capture of Arkansas Post on the Arkansas, with about 3000 prisoners, by the land and naval forces of the enemy.

A few days after the achievement at Galveston Com. [Duncan M.] Ingraham sallied out of Charleston with the two iron clads under his command. He ran into the "Mercedita" cut a hole into her and fired a Seven inch rifle shot thro her boilers. She surrendered, her crew was paroled, but eventually escaped as the iron-clad had to follow other game. Other of the enemy's vessels were also injured & the whole blockading fleet temporarily dispersed. The Port of Charleston was declared open but this too is disregarded, both by the enemy and by neutrals.

On the Rappahannock the enemy under Gen. Burnside crossed the river at Fredericksburgh and on the second day afterwards, Decr 13, attacked our troops in position, under Gen. Lee. Jackson commanded our right wing and Longstreet our left. The attack was repulsed with great slaughter, and with little loss on our side—the loss being about 3000 to 10,000. Gens [Thomas R. R.] Cobb & [Maxcy] Gregg were killed on our side. Our Cavalry forces have been quite active, but with less signal successes than those achieved in Tennessee. After the defeat of Burnside, Gen. [Joseph] Hooker was placed in command, and much is expected of him by the Yankees.

On Wednesday the 18th a cavalry force said to be [Gen. William] Averell's division, crossed at Kellys Ford about twenty miles above Fredericksburgh, & drove in our pickets. They were handsomely defeated by the brigade of cavalry of Gen. Fitzhugh Lee, & the battery of artillery attached to the brigade. Major [John] Pelham of Alabama a very young and promising officer was killed by a random shot. Major [J. W.] Puller of Va was also killed.

Saturday March 21, [1863]   [Gen. John] Hood's Division which was ordered up on the report of the fight at Kelly's Ford has returned to its position near Petersburgh. They marched back thro' a terrible snow storm. Our armies are increasing in size, & will I hope be in good condition for the coming campaign.

A fearful accident occurred at our Laboratory here on Friday the 13th of March, by which 69 were killed and wounded of whom 62 were females chiefly girls & children. Only four were killed outright, burnt from the burns received in the burning of their clothes the number of dead will probably reach 50. It is terrible to think of—that so much suffering should arise from causes possibly within our control. The accident was caused by the ignition of a friction primer in the hands of a grown girl by the name of Mary Ryan. She lived three or four days, & gave a clear account of the circumstances. The primer stuck on the varnishing board and she struck the board three times very hard on the table to drive out the primer. She says she was immediately blown up to the ceiling and on coming down was again blown up. Cartridges were being broken up temporarily in the same room, where many operators were sent temporarily on account of repairs in the shop they usually worked in. The deaths are due chiefly to the burning of their clothes.

Mamma has been untiring in aiding visiting & relieving these poor sufferers, & has fatigued herself very much. She has done an infinite deal of good to these poor people.

Congress has for the past three weeks been engaged in secret session exclusively on the currency and tax bill—the former is too elaborate I fear i.e. not simple enough, the latter is not yet announced. On these two measures will greatly depend the life of our young nation, as appears very evidently.

[March] 23d, [1863]   I spent an hour with the President at his office yesterday. He is at present evidently wholly devoted to the defence of the Mississippi, and thinks and talks of little else. I went to get some instructions as to sending ordnance West of the Miss. but he continually directed the conversation to the Miss. He read a long telegram from [Gen. John] Pemberton, relating chiefly to the movements of the enemy, & expressing confidence in his ability to maintain the defence of the river. There is nothing special relative to the war, the conviction is fixing itself in the public mind that the end is not yet. The devastation the enemy commits is distressing. Gen. [Edward] Sparrow of La. Chairman of the Mil. Com. of the Senate read to me a few evenings ago an extract from a northern paper describing the present condition of his once beautiful place on Lake Providence, on the West bank of the Miss. above Vicksburgh. It has been the head quarters of [Gen. John] McArthur's Division of Yankees. Fences and outhouses are torn down for fuel, shrubbery destroyed—gardens & walks ruined—houses defaced and furniture dragged out & scattered about the camp. The family & servants have been removed. As the Yankee writer says, the place will shortly be restored to a wilderness. This is of course a faint picture of the actual state of ruin in this and many similar cases.

March 25, [1863] Congress has it is said matured the tax bill & acted on it but it is not yet announced. Every one prays that it may be one adequate to sustain the war and remedy the deplorable state of the currency. Gold is now at nearly five to one—provisions in proportion. Flour is $30 a barrel here & twice and three times that price elsewhere. The difficulties of transportation add to the scarcity. We now pay $3 per lb for butter $2 for eggs. A turkey costs $15. Beef is 1.50 per lb. Common domestic is $2 a yard. Calicos are unobtainable. Of course in this state of things many colossal fortunes will be made. It is currently believed that the enterprizing firm of John Frazer & Co at Charleston have already made nine millions of dollars by importations. The manufacturing & business firm of the Crenshaw's [large blockade-running business] here are making out of woolen factories & flour contracts many hundreds of thousands monthly. But we salaried officers who do the work of the war are pinched. My pay will actually not purchase 1000 dollars worth in ordinary times.

March 28, [1863] We heard yesterday of a fresh attempt by the enemy to pass our batteries at Vicksburgh. Two boats attempted it—one was sunk with (probably) all on board—the other was apparently disabled & laid up at the mouth of the famous canal under cover of the batteries there.

Fast day [proclaimed by President Davis] was observed yesterday, by going to church; but in my department work was carried on—laborare est orare [to work is to pray]. It will not do to omit anything now. We must both pray and work.

March 31, [1863] The month goes out cooly but with a gleam of sunshine after a rainy morning. There is nothing of special interest. Pemberton telegraphs from Vicksburgh that the vessel sunk by our batteries a week ago was the Lancaster, & the crippled one lying at the lower mouth of the canal is the Monitor No. 2, built at St. Louis. The tax bill does not seem to find general favor, and the remedy for our financial evils does not yet appear to be found.

April 2d, [1863]   There is a report said to be true that D. H. Hill had entered Washington N.C. after a bloody combat, capturing a large number of negros. It lacks confirmation like many of our rumors. We also hear that our people made a successful dash at Ponchatoula (La.) and took a good deal of property. I met Gen. Hood in the street yesterday and asked him to come to dinner. His division had just been ordered below Petersburgh. It has been committing depredations in and about Manchester.

Mamma entertained a few friends last evening, among them Mr. [Ethelbert] Barksdale, M.C. from Miss.—Gen. [Francis A.] Shoup, who has been fighting under [Gen. Thomas C.] Hindman in Arkansas. He told me a good deal about affairs in that Dept. It is a lamentable record of bad management and of failures of the four considerable actions in Ark. & Miss. [Mo.] viz—Springfield, (where Lyon was killed), Lexington, [Mo.] where the Yankee Col. [James A.] Mulligan & all his command were captured, Pea ridge or Elkhorn, and Prairie Grove, the first two were accidental victories, & the last two disastrous retreats, if not positive defeats. Major [Isaac] St. John my chief of the Nitre & Mining Bureau, Lt [John] Ellicott of that Bureau, & Mrs. Guild [wife of Dr. Lafayette Guild, Lee's medical director], made up the guests. Beef has now risen to $1.50 per lb & Bacon to 1.60. Butter is 3½ to 4 dollars. Eggs are $3, &c.

April 3d, [1863]   Yesterday a crowd of women assembled on the public square and marching thence down Main [Street] sacked several shoe, grocery and other stores. Their pretence was bread; but their motive really was license. Few of them have really felt want. The President went down amongst them and said a few words to them telling them that the course they were pursuing was the one most likely to bring scarcity of food on the city. They soon separated and some food was distributed. It was a real women's riot, but as yet there is really little cause for one—there is scarcity, but little want. Laborers earn 2½ to three dollars per day, and women and children can earn 1½ to 2½. With such wages and flour at even $30 they cannot starve. I spent an hour with the President yesterday, talking over various matters especially the establishment of furnaces and a foundry on [the] Trinity River in Texas. He understands the geography and resources of the country very well. He spoke of the high prices, and said that large as his salary appeared and altho' he lived just as he did as a Senator in Washington, he found it took all of it to defray his expenses. No war news. Our vessel the Cornubia arrived at Wilmington on Wednesday bringing 5200 arms and other stores. Spent the evening at Mrs. [Mary] Jones on 6th St. Mr. J. thinks the women ought to have been fired on—and augers badly of the effect of their conduct on the markets. The weather was very fine yesterday, & promises well this morning.

Apl 4, [1863]   It is said to-day that the gunboats at Charleston have come up into Stono river, which bodes a land attack I suppose. The enemy seems to have failed in his design of getting to the rear of Vicksburgh by Yazoo pass. The bread riot demonstration has not been renewed. It is denounced on all hands. There were few or no sufferers in the crowd. It is snowing furiously as I write at 10 P.M.

April 6, [1863]   Nothing decisive has occurred at any of the threatened points. Gen. [Henry Hopkins] Sibley has captured a gunboat the [space] in the Atchafalaya [River] with all on board. Beyond the Rappahannock Capt. [John S.] Mosby has again captured a party of the enemy, it is said. These accounts must be taken with allowance on both sides. I find that our officers are nearly as prone to exaggeration as the enemy. From Mobile the only accounts relate to dissipations of officers and society—an ungrateful picture to dwell on. From Florida it is said the Yankees have retired from Jacksonville with their negro regiments. The enemy at Charleston was said to be on the Stono threatening a land attack.

April 7, [1863]   The next bulletin from Charleston is the great object of interest. Yesterday the enemy appeared off the bar with "24 wooden ships, the Ironsides and six monitors—two monitors seem to be inside the bar—24 wooden vessels off Goat Island—fleet moving about all night." Perhaps the attack will develop itself to-day. Mosby['s] success is a fact attested by the presence of the prisoners. The party was sent out to capture him! Meal is $16 per bushel yet there is no positive scarcity. I cannot fathom this state of things. I suppose the fear of scarcity combined with the plethora of money induces people to lay up a stock, & thus they enhance the prices of provisions. Mr. [J.] Bujac & Mr. [J. M.] Seixas refugees from N. Orleans spent the evening. The former owned a large foundry & machine shop, and amused me, for he is no grumbler, with his narration of his flight from the city, with such of his machinery as he could get off. The enemys gunboat entered the dock he left about 20 minutes after his departure with his goods & chattels. He had some 1700 tons of iron, which would be of great value to us.

April 10, [1863]   On Tuesday the 7th at 3 P.M. nine iron clads attacked Fort Sumter, at distances of about 900 to 1000 yds. After two to three hours firing they retired, one of them, the Keokuk so damaged that she has sunk on the beach off Morris' Island. She is by no means the most powerfully armed, but was well clad with iron. She is 159½ feet long, has two fixed turrets, is turtle, or oval backed, & has two eleven inch guns. She is manoeuvred with two independent screws. Was provided by Whitney. In South western Kentucky [Gen. John] Pegram has met with a check, having been driven back with loss from Somerset by forces under the Yankee General [Quincy] Gil[l]more (an old acquaintance). It is now well established that the enemy is retiring from Vicksburgh. Gold is again going up with great rapidity in N. York. As it rises & falls with their prospects it is [an] esteemed & excellent barometer of their feelings on the war.

April 12th, [1863]   The damage inflicted on Fort Sumter by the enemy's artillery without being serious is not to be despised. The Fort was struck about 34 times. Some of the indentations measure 60in dia & 25in in depth, which in the parts between the tiers, where the wall is recessed for the gun, & is only 5 feet thick would soon make the casemate untenable. At a point where the hits are right over each other the wall may be said to be shaken. If thirty odd shots produce this effect what may not be expected from 1000—an amount readily fired from 8 boats in 10 hours. I have hopes that the covering of the lower tiers of guns by sand bags, laid 8 feet thick, as directed by Col. [Jeremy F.] Gilmer, will greatly aid the resistance. I believe however that a determined attack might be successful. The boats came up one at a time to the distance of 900 to 1200 yd, fired, & then gave place to another, so that only 80 shots were fired at the Fort in the two and a half hours fighting. A gunboat was sunk on Wednesday in the Coosaw river below Charleston by field artillery. No special news elsewhere. The taking of the $15,000,000 Conf. loan in London is perhaps the most significant expression of foreign views yet given. It is undoubtedly the forerunner of recognition. It was subscribed at 90, & rose immediately to 5 pr ct premium. Of course the delivery of cotton, on which the loan is based, depends entirely on our ability to bring the war to a successful close; and the avidity with which the loan is taken up shows that this is a foregone conclusion among capitalists the most cautious, & sensitive portion of the thinking public.

Dr. [William A. W.] Spotswood [the surgeon in charge of the Confederate Naval Bureau of Medicine and Surgery] & his son George spent the evening with us, & Mrs. West Robinson came in to see me on business connected with a protegee of hers, whom the officers of his company wished to force back into the ranks. He is a clerk at the Arsenal. The conscription is rigidly enforced, & stragglers are pretty generally bro't back to their companies. System is being established in this vast army of 400,000 men, & it is getting to be manageable. Thursday evening we spent at Mrs. [Mary] Jones, a beautiful and a very good woman who took charge of all our children when Mamma was supposed to be lying at the point of death with scarlet fever, the last week of December '61. It was a winter of trial & sickness to me & mine. All the children had scarlet fever, & Jessie & Mamie were very ill. I had a slight attack of pneumonia while Mamma was convalescing.

Thursday, April 16, [18]63   We have rumors to-day that Suffolk has been taken by Gen. Longstreet with a large number of prisoners. A Yankee general is said to be slain. I doubt the story. Last week Gen. [Henry A.] Wise with about 1200 men marched to Williamsburgh, and sending troops to the rear succeeded in inflicting some damage on the enemy, in destroying stores wagons, & horses. No great results are ever hoped for when Wise heads any force, & therefore this little success is accepted in place of all promises. Wheeler is said to have again destroyed a gunboat on the Cumberland. He is very energetic & successful. He is a Major General tho scarcely 23 years old. No further news of the iron clads at Charleston, which have left the harbor. The Keokuk is stated by northern accounts to have been hit over 100 times, of which 90 were near the water line. Mamma, Bayne & I have just returned from spending the evening at Gen. [George W.] Randolph's, late Secy of War, where we drank good punch, ate some nice cheese, and met Mrs. Harrison (of Brandon) and Mr. [George] Davis, Senator from N. C.

Tuesday April 21, [1863]   All rumors about operations at Suffolk were exaggerated. The object of the advance was simply to cover the country and draw supplies from it. That being accomplished our troops will probably fall back. D. H. Hill is still before Washington N. C. and has alarmed the enemy for the safety of [Gen. John K.] Foster. Did they know Hill as well as we do they would be little alarmed. He can never achieve a success, tho' he might I suppose blunder upon one, as other short witted people do. Five or six more boats have lately run past Vicksburgh, so that there is now a fleet of eight under Farragut between Port Hudson & V. What their object is remains to be seen—probably marauding up the Red River.

The attack on Charleston seems to have been a confessed failure, & abandoned as such. The monitors were it would seem more seriously damaged than was at first supposed. No movement yet on the Rappahannock. The President has been quite ill for some days back. Prices of provisions are coming down people say, tho' they are still so high as to be nearly inaccessible. Beef has returned to $1.

Sunday April 26, [1863]   No serious military event since my last entry. [D. H.] Hill has fallen back from Washington, but no great hopes were indulged of his success. So far as can be learned Longstreet still blockades Suffolk. His forces have contrived to lose a battery of five pieces (Capt. [R. M.] Stribling's) among which are three Napoleons quite fresh from the foundry. The Yankees crossed the Nansemond [River] below where the battery was placed and came up in rear of it—about 150 prisoners were made. They were marched thro Suffolk, and were cheered by the women, who they say are not subdued tho' overpowered for the present. More gunboats and batteries have succeeded in passing Vicksburgh, and joining Farragut. With the heavy guns in position which are now on the way there, I hope the river will be of little use to them. [Gen. Richard] Taylor we hear is retreating from Opelousas & that part of Louisiana it is feared is to be given up to the enemy, including our Salt works at Berwick. Our affairs west of the Miss. have never prospered, probably because nearly all our means and attention were concentrated on the great theatres East. Perhaps the energy & ability of Kirby Smith will be felt before long in that department. Troops have been sent from Mobile into Tenn. where active operations are soon anticipated. The enemy abandoned Pensacola, burning & plundering several of the houses, about the middle of March, & confines himself in that quarter to Warrington. It has doubtless become necessary for them to concentrate detachments in order to keep up their main armies. Their nine months and two years men are to go home about the 1st of May, which doubtless weakens their force very materially. It is even doubtful whether they will be in force for aggressive operations before fall. This will be so far favorable that it will enable us to gather our troops without interruption. As food is a material question this will be an important feature in the operations of this year.

Thursday April 30, [1863]   The news from the Southwest is discouraging. Taylor has been forced back & has abandoned nearly all of Louisiana. The Salt works are in the hands of the enemy and are destroyed. Alexandria if not now, will soon be in the hands of the enemy. Our troops have fallen back to Nachitoches [Natchitoches]. The enemy are reported to have crossed below Fredericksburg on Tuesday, on pontoon bridges, at Deep Run. This was the same place at which they crossed before. A heavy rain set in yesterday afternoon, & will doubtless delay the enemy. Two vessels, the Merrimac, & the R. E. Lee (Giraffe) have come in from Bermuda with stores for us. These vessels are running immediately under charge of the Ordnance Dept. The first has 3. 170 pd Blakeley guns—the second 6000 small arms, & 8 rifle pieces of good calibre.

May 2d, [1863]   Troops have crossed in considerable numbers at Deep Run & there has been some fighting. It is now said however that the main crossing is far up above Kelly's Ford—the point where the fight took place a month or more ago between the cavalry of the enemy and Gen. Fitzhugh Lee's brigade. Longstreet's corps is now moving up, & will be in position in two days, or a part of it. This is all that is needed to insure the defeat of the enemy's plans—two Divisions Hoods and [Gen.

George] Picketts being down near Suffolk. The boats at Vicksburgh seem now to pass the batteries with comparative impunity. Lee's force as I see by his return of arms comprises about 50,000 infantry. The artillery & cavalry will carry it up to about 60,000 (or 62,000) not over. With Longstreet's two absent divisions, he will have nearly 80,000 effective men. Bragg had about the same number (60,000) but has been reinforced from Mobile & must have nearly 70,000 men.

Bayne went to Winsboro yesterday, his little girl being ill. I miss him very much in the office, & Mamma wants his pleasant company at home. He is always cheerful, an admirable constitution, unfortunately not my own.

May 3d, [1863]   There is no reliable news as to the operations yesterday, on Gen. Lee's front. Rumors are rife and of course favorable, representing for example that Jackson had captured a brigade. Another report not so favorable is that the Yankees are continuing their course.

In the evening we rec'd definite news of a Yankee cavalry raid which throws the whole city in violent commotion. A large cavalry force struck the central road at Louisa C[ourt] H[ouse]. Having torn up the track it crossed & divided, one part continuing South toward the canal at Columbia, the other turning to the left, struck the Fredericksburgh road at Ashland, and captured a train of sick & wounded. Burning the cars, depot &c & tearing up a part of the track, the force, or a part of it came down the Brooke turnpike to within about four miles of the city. When this was known the utmost consternation prevailed in the city. All our troops had been sent off to Lee, & there were no guards in the batteries about the city. People were in utter despair & even the Comng General declared "we were ruined." Imagination already depicted the Yankee cavalry dashing through the streets. Citizens (May 4) turned out with all sorts of arms, & mustered on the public square. Senators & Cabinet officers fell into the ranks, & were marshalled to the batteries under direction of Gen. Randolph. The Yankees came no further however; but crossed over to the Central, & finally to the York River Road & were last heard of some ten miles off making for the Peninsula. The party which struck for the Canal at Columbia where there is an aqueduct were overtaken by Fitzhugh Lee's Cavalry & driven back with some loss. So happily ends the cavalry attack on Richmond. People were frightened and indignant, at such Yankee impudence.

May 5, [1863]   As the excitement of yesterday was dying away with the receding Yankees the city was cheered with the news of another great victory achieved by Lee over the forces of Hooker. It is announced by him in a despatch brot by courier as follows "To President Davis: To-day Gen. Jackson penetrated to the rear of the enemy and drove him from all his positions, from the Wilderness to within one mile of Chancellorsville.

He was engaged at the same time in front by two of Longstreet's divisions. Many prisoners were taken, & the enemy's loss in killed and wounded is large. This morning the battle will be renewed. He was dislodged from all his positions around Chancellorsville & driven back towards the Rappahannock over which he is now retreating. We have again to thank Almighty God for a great victory. I regret to state that Gen. [Elisha F.] Paxton was killed, Gen. Jackson severely and Gen. [Harry] Heth & A. P. Hill slightly wounded. —R. E. Lee—Comdg"

The weather is beautiful and it is hoped may enable us to profit by the victory. Longstreet's other two Divisions are passing thro, & ought to be with Lee to-morrow, as the track at Ashland is said to be very little injured.

May 6, [1863]   There are few details of the general engagement which took place near Chancellorsville on Saturday the 2d. Jackson has lost his left arm and was shot thro the right hand. There is a general sadness even over this mutilation of the hero. He is however they say doing well. The enemy appears to have recrossed the Rappahannock defeated but not routed and may again advance. We have not the genius to achieve decisive victories it appears; and it is probably a problem not often solved except with the concurrence of fortunate incidents, that a large army is defeated & routed by a very inferior one. The news from Ala. & Ga. is that 1600 cavalry or mounted infantry were captured on the 1st [3rd] near Rome Ga. [Commanded by Col. Abel D. Streight, U.S. troops attempted to cut railroads supplying Confederates in Chattanooga (April 19–May 3). General N. B. Forrest captured the U.S. troops, who were mounted on mules.] This is the force which made the raid into Miss at Meridian. From the Miss. we hear that [Gen. John S.] Bowen has fallen back from Grand Gulf, before overpowering forces.

May 8, [1863]   The news comes in slowly from the late battlefields. The loss is heavy on both sides—that of the Yankees perhaps unprecedented in this war. Our own is placed at eight or ten thousand. The enemy has recrossed the Rappahannock without further serious loss. It is deplorable that all our sacrifices of life, and all our successes lead to no decisive result. Is this owing to our inferior numbers, or to want of solidity in the commands, or finally, to want of genius in our commanders? The weather turned quite cold yesterday morning, & fires are again very comfortable. The cavalry of the enemy are reported by Gen. Lee to have probably recrossed the Rappahannock.

May 9, [1863]   The worst news received yesterday was the death of Van Dorn at Spring Hill, Tenn. on the 7th. He appears to have been killed in a rencontre. This and the wounding of Jackson are serious losses. The wounded are arriving & being sent off to other points.

Mamma went to the hospital last evening, & stayed some hours assisting the poor fellows. It is a pity she cannot spare more time from her household duties to spend in these cares, as she is a very apt nurse. The day is beautiful tho the air is chilly. The Yankees appear to have formed the design of sending cavalry into our agricultural districts to destroy crops, implements &c. It is stated that Kirby Smith has reached Alexandria [La.] with re-inforcements, and that he will be able to drive the Yankees back to Berwick.

May 10, Sunday [1863]   The morning is balmy & beautiful. We have yet no news of the effect of Hooker's defeat [at Chancellorsville] on the Yankees. It is said that Lincoln has ordered another draft of 500,000 men. No doubt that the war will go on until at least the close of his administration. How many more lives must be sacrificed to the vindictiveness of a few unprincipled men! for there is no doubt that with the division of sentiment existing at the North the administration could shape its policy either for peace or for war. Yesterday some three or four thousand prisoners came down. It is tho't we have captured about 6000 & lost 1000—with 11 pieces of artillery and lost eight, and have gained ten or twelve thousand small arms. There are besides some 1500 to 2000 wounded captured. On the whole the victory grows in magnitude each day—a peculiarity of Lee's victories. There is no further news from Vicksburgh or the Mississippi. In Tennessee there seems to be no immediate inclination for active operations.

May 13, [1863]   On Sunday evening we heard of the death of our great warrior Jackson. He died about 3 o'clock of that day, of pneumonia, aggravated by causing himself to be bathed about the chest with cold water. Yesterday the body was carried in procession from the Governor's house to the Capitol, & lay in state during the day. To-day it is taken to Lexington [Va.] where it is to be buried. I took Willie and Jessie to look at his face. The crowd nearly crushed us. Mamie had to be satisfied with a peep at the door where the coffin lay, in the room used for the house of Representatives, below the library. There is no news of interest from the Mississippi, now the point most critical to us. It is believed however that Smith has beaten the enemy & driven him back to Opelousas. It requires some energetic genius to restore affairs in that quarter.

May 14, [1863]   It was said yesterday that the enemy was landing in force at West Point—in what force was not known. There is of course a demonstration on Lee's communications. Our losses at the great battles of the Wilderness, are perhaps heavier than we anticipated. We have lost no doubt over two thousand prisoners, & ten pieces of artillery, while our killed & wounded will I fear exceed ten thousand. On the other hand we have captured eleven pieces, & perhaps, six thousand prisoners, kill-ing & wounding fifteen thousand, thus making a total of twenty-one thousand, against our twelve or thirteen thousand. Had we not lost Jackson; all would be well, but that loss would more than counterbalance a victory ten times as decisive.

Sunday May 17, [1863]   The enemy has penetrated from Grand Gulf [La.] to Jackson Miss. & our troops in that vicinity are said to have fallen back to Canton, on the R.R. north of Jackson. The enemy's force is estimated at thirty thousand, but I cannot persuade myself that they would venture so far from their base with so large a force. It would be difficult to subsist them. I dare say ten or 12 thousand would cover their numbers. I trust Gen Johnston will yet send them back staggering, & that Vicksburgh will be maintained. The news is here to-day, that [Clement] Vallandingham [prominent Midwestern opponent of the war], for his bold speech against the Government of Lincoln, has been banished to the dry Tortugas.

May 20, [1863]   On the 15th Grant attacked Pemberton near Ed-wards Depot, and after a severe fight our troops fell back beyond the Big Black [River]. Johnston has eleven thousand men, and if he can but unite with P. all will go well. But affairs there are in a very critical condition. As Vicksburgh has provisions for two months, I trust no disaster need be feared. The enemy has evacuated Jackson after destroying a good deal of property, and communication with Jackson is restored.

May 21, [1863]   Grant appears to have out generaled us, & is now said to have invested Vicksburgh. If Johnston can bring about a junction of our forces, he will be able to fall on Grant with 25,000 men, which with the garrison of Vicksburgh ought to be able to give him a disas-terous defeat and restore our command of the Mississippi. As V. has at least two months provisions there is good reason for hope that this effort of Grant's may prove his ruin.

Mamma amuses us often with accounts of the queer things that hap-pen to her at the hospital whither she goes every day, at the corner of 7th & Cary Sts. One man asked her to smoke his pipe until he could get ready for it, the pipe being filled & the bit paper in the attendant's hands. Willie really distressed me to-day by striking Mamie on the nose so as to make it bleed because she had his marbles, & some were lost. We spent a half hour at the Presidents last evening. He is recovering but looks feeble still—has had fever and a cough.

May 23d, Saturday [1863]   Pemberton was I fear badly beaten near the Big Black [River], and lost a good deal of artillery. He was of course greatly outnumbered. It is probable that Grant has fully forty-thousand. Vicksburgh is reported to be closely invested. I fear it has not munitions enough for a long fight. It has not been possible to give them over perhaps 150 rounds per man. However, they have the means of making cartridges for themselves. I spent the evening yesterday at the hospitable table of Mr. Haxall on Main St. He gave us the largest variety of excellent wines I have ever seen. Gen [Richard S.] Ewell was there with some dozen gentlemen.

Troops have been moving Southward, since yesterday morning, doubtless for the West.

May 25, [1863]   The news is to-day that the enemy has been repulsed at Vicksburgh. I trust it may prove true. Should we be driven from the Mississippi it would have an important influence on the duration of the war. There is a painful rumor to-day that the outer lines of Vicksburgh have been forced and 50 cannon captured. It comes from the Yankees & is not believed. Gen Johnston telegraphs for large quantity of field ammunition, & for percussion caps. There is great anxiety about affairs there. The people of Richmond are laughed at for their continually gloomy countenances. Officers from the field say they see more long visages here than any where else. It must be recollected that every blow struck at any point vibrates here; & we listen to and feel here every rumor of ill luck or of distress occurring in any part of the country.

May 26, [1863]   No later news from V. Hopes and fears alternate, but hope predominates. It cannot be that this strong city will fall an easy prey to a land attack. If it had a few thousand more defenders I should feel more easy. The weather since Sunday has turned quite cool, & it is chilly enough for fires.

May 28, [1863]   A dispatch from a citizen at Vicksburg published this morning, assures us that "all is well" & that "V. holds out bravely." The Yankee papers publish it captive; but I trust they are too fast for the truth, and that it never will catch up with them. Vallandingham, the Yankee opponent of his administration, is sent to the South, and has been left in front of Bragg's lines. This is of course done to discredit his influence at home. The device is too shallow. He will I suppose be permitted to pass thro', & go to England or Canada. All "registered" enemies have been sent out of N. Orleans, with nothing save what they could carry, & ten days' provisions. All who had relatives in the Conf. Army seem also to have been sent. It is reported that the number which have reached Pascagoula [Miss.] is four to five thousand.

May 30, [1863]   The public anxiety was relieved yesterday by a despatch from Gen. Johnston to the effect that Vicksburg held its own manfully, & that a large number of the enemy had been killed and wounded. So great was the stench from unburied dead Yankees that Pemberton was burning tar barrels for disinfectants.

June 1, [1863] No satisfactory news yet from V. It is to be hoped that Johnston will soon move upon Grant. The public will never forgive Johnston if he allows the city to fall without an effort to relieve it. He has probably near thirty-thousand men now. The weather is very fine, but unless we can have rain soon our crops will suffer sadly, & without good crops what will become of us? It is indeed a sad and critical time to the Confederacy.

June 3d, [1863] A despatch to the Associated Press states that Grant summoned Pemberton to surrender and gave him three days. Pemberton replied that he did not require three minutes, that he would fight to the last, whereupon Grant attacked and lost very heavily. It is difficult to get reliable news. We know only generally that Pemberton was beaten on Bakers Creek [Champion's Hill]—on Saturday the 16th—that he lost largely in artillery—that a part of his force was cut off from him—that he retreated and abandoned his works on the Yazoo—that he was attacked in his lines repeatedly and has signally repulsed every attack; & that in the battle of Saturday a portion of our troops behaved very badly, said to be Georgians. All the available force of the enemy appears to be concentrated on this one effort, and there is no disposition to attack at any other point. Lee will probably not let them alone however on the Rappahannock. Mr. [John E.] Ward, late Commissioner to China spent the evening here. Mamma was at Mrs. Jones, where I joined her afterwards. A little party to Mrs. [Smith] Stansbury who leaves soon with her husband for Bermuda. A refreshing rain last evening promises well for the crops, an absorbing topic just now.

June 8, [1863] Nothing satisfactory yet from Vicksburgh. All we know that it is still holding out without any indications of weakness. At Port Hudson the enemy is said to have suffered a severe repulse—probably a newspaper report only. Nothing of Johnston's movements. If he allows Vicksburg to fall his reputation will be gone past all redemption. Lee has moved his headquarters to Culpepper [Culpeper], and there has been some fighting below Fredericksburgh, where the enemy crossed on a pontoon bridge, in some force, for what purpose is not known. Mrs. Stansbury, & her husband [Maj. Smith Stansbury] & Col Wyatt Aiken are staying with us. Last night we had a room full to tea. Gen. & Mrs. Randolph, Mrs. & Miss Marye, Mrs. [Mary] Jones & Dr. Habersham. I regret much to see Col. Aiken go back to his regiment. His escape at Antietam was so narrow that I fear he may fall in his next engagement. He was struck by six balls—two indented his scabbard—one struck and bent the tip of his drawn sword—one cut the sword knot—one cut his coat on the shoulder—and the last went thro' his body striking inside of the left nipple, & coming out behind near the shoulder blade. His recovery was very extraordinary. The weather is very cool and dry.

Thursday, June 11, [1863]   On the 9th a severe engagement took place on the upper Rappahannock about Kelly's Ford, the enemy crossing in large force. The particulars are not yet received. Col. Sol. Williams of N. Carolina was killed, also Major [Will] Farley of Gen. Stuarts staff. Gen. Rooney Lee (son of the General) was wounded. Two army corps were on this side, according to prisoners taken. Whether this attack was made to cover movements in another direction remains to be seen. Nothing definite from Vicksburgh, which seems in no hurry to be taken. The enemy are said to be ordering troops to the Gulf, & perhaps Mobile may have its turn. Gen. [Samuel] Cooper [Confederate Adjutant and Inspector General] told me troops had been ordered from Charleston in that direction, and if not needed these were to join Gen. Johnston, under Beauregard. Gen. G. W. Smith, wife, & Col. [Eugene E.] McLean [of the Quartermaster's Department] dined with us, on a piece of lamb which cost $13!

June 13, [1863]   The city was disturbed yesterday by rumors of the approach of the enemy, who were said to have crossed the Chickahominy, and to have appeared in gunboats at the mouth of that stream. Our local troops were gotten in readiness, as there are only about 5000 men on the lines. We have organized our workmen into companies and armed them, making 10 companies, altogether about 800 men. No news from Vicksburgh, nor from Johnston. It is said that Kirby Smith has appeared near Port Hudson, but nothing is definitely known of his movements.

June 16, [1863]   A portion of Lee's Army is moving thro' the Valley, & Winchester [Va.] is again in our possession. What the movement means it is difficult to divine. I trust we are not to have the Maryland campaign over again. Vallandingham is now at Wilmington & leaves for Bermuda, by one of our vessels, the Merrimac. He goes probably to Halifax. No satisfactory news from Johnston or from Vicksburg.

[[It is somewhat singular that I should have omitted to notice the fall of N. Orleans in its proper place, in recalling the events of the war. It fell on the 25th of April, with little resistance, Forts Jackson & St Phillip having been reduced after a gallant defence. It is impossible to contemplate this event even at this distance of time with any composure. Major General Mansfield Lovell was the Comdg General, and is here now, attending the close of a court of inquiry into the matter. A dozen courts of inquiry could not re-instate him in popular estimation or my own. He was unfit for his position.]]

June 18, [1863]   Gen. Lee chronicles another victory in his modest way. On Saturday and Sunday, Ewell, comdg 1st Corps attacked the enemy at Winchester, and on the afternoon of Sunday compelled them to surrender, to the number of six or seven thousand—so says the telegram of the press—with wagons, horses, fifty pieces of Ordnance, &c. &c. Two thousand more were captured by Gen. [Edward] Johnson at Berryville, being re-enforcements, so says the press, to Winchester. This clears out the Valley. It is greatly regretted that the miscreant [Gen. Robert H.] Milroy escaped. He has been outlawed by proclamation, & would probably be executed if taken. This good news will be tempered this morning by the news of the capture of the iron-clad, Atlanta, at Savannah. She went out to fight two of the enemy's iron clads and was overpowered it seems. The particulars are not yet known. She came from Europe as the Fingal with a cargo of Genl Stores, and was purchased by the Navy, & covered with iron. Col. & Mrs. Stansbury left this morning for Bermuda, where he will be stationed in charge of a Depot of Ord' Stores.

June 24, [1863]   The captures at Winchester reduced themselves as usual to about one half the reported number viz: to 29 pieces of artillery and 3600 men. Milroy escaped with the remainder. The news from Vicksburg yesterday is that a second general assault was made on Saturday and repulsed with heavy loss on the part of the enemy, & that Kirby Smith had taken Milliken's Bend which would cut off Grant's supplies.

June 28, [1863]   The Capital is again threatened by the enemy, but there is little alarm felt. All the able bodied men are however embodied and armed, & thousands of hardy workmen are parading the streets to-day (Sunday) to confirm their organization. It is reported that the enemy have landed at the White House in force, but it is doubtful whether the force is at all formidable. [Gen. Samuel] Jones' force is ordered here from West Virginia, the enemy having disappeared from there. With the additional force the offensive may perhaps be taken on the Peninsular & [Gen. Erasmus D.] Keyes drawn into Yorktown and kept there. A rumor says that Harrisburgh [Pa.] has been destroyed. If not true now I presume it soon will be. The supplies derived from beyond the Potomac are already valuable, one principal item being a thousand fine beeves.

July 1, [18]63   It is my forty-fifth birth-day, and I have now served 22 years in the Army. We had good news yesterday, part of which is true and a part doubtful. A flag of truce boat arrived yesterday at City Point with 800 of our people, to carry away a part of the 4000 Yankees now on the Island [[Belle Isle]]. Our Signal Officer sent word to the Secy of War that the officers of the truce boat said both Harrisburg and York were in our hand. The latest papers from the North rec'd by the same boat do not confirm the statement, which is therefore doubtful. It is true however that Gen. Dick Taylor has captured the enemy works at Berwick capturing 1000 men and ten guns. This it is asserted gives us command of the Misspi. above N. Orleans, & interrupts Banks' supplies. Vicksburg resists successfully as does Port Hudson where Banks' second assault was repulsed with great loss. Every one is looking anxiously to see what Johnston will do. [[On looking back over these disconnected entries I see that no mention is made of the capture of Messrs [James] Mason & [John] Slidell, our ministers to England & France. They were taken from the British Mail Steamer Trent by Com. [Charles] Wilkes, on her passage from Havanna [Havana] to Liverpool, and carried to Old Point Comfort. Hence they were conveyed to Fort Warren [in Boston]. They were liberated on the demand of England, and sent in a national vessel on board the English Steamer, which conveyed them to England. The Yankee Government disavowed the act, but Wilkes again received a command. The affair caused great commotion in England, and was highly applauded in the United States. The Secretary of the Navy [Gideon] Welles even approved it officially. Ovations were given to Wilkes. After all this, when it was seen that England was preparing for war, Seward deliberately recanted, and declared the seizure unwarranted!]]

July 2d, [1863]   It was said yesterday that Hooker was displaced, & Gen. [George G.] Meade placed in command of the Yankee Army.

The President is ill to-day, and his physician is seriously alarmed about him. The death of the President would indeed be the most serious calamity that could befall us. The Yankees are said to be approaching from the White House, and their pickets are in force at Tunstall's, about 16 miles from here.

July 4, [1863]   I rode out yesterday and the day before to look after the fortifications, the President having expressed some anxiety on the subject of their condition of preparation. The inner line is one of detached works of considerable strength. The works are well constructed and in good order, commanding all the principal avenues of approach to the city. The second line, which is three quarters to one mile farther from the city is a continuous line of rifle pits or covers with places for field batteries. It is placed on high ground generally, but seems to me too much developed. I prefer the inner line, for the number of men we have. Our volunteer companies and militia are all in the field now, occupying the roads, while the regular troops take the field. Our troops skirmished with the enemy day before yesterday between the Chickahominy and the Pamunkey—one man killed and two wounded on our side. The enemy retired and was followed by our skirmishers to within a mile of the White house, so an officer who went out, informed me.

July 5, [1863]   The world of the Conf. States will be somewhat astounded to learn to-day that Mr. [Alexander H.] Stephens has started for Washington. On what errand is not yet divulged, nor whether he will get there. The news yesterday was that Taylor and Magruder were on this side of the Miss. at Kinna [Kenner, La.], 10 miles out of N. O. and that an attempt would be made to surprise Fort Jackson, which it is said is held by a small force of negro troops. Ewell's troops were three miles from Harrisburgh on the 29th. Our news from Lee necessarily comes thro' Yankeeland now. Meade has succeeded Hooker in the command of the army. He was Capt. of Topographical Engr. when the war broke out.

July 9th, [1863]   On Wednesday, Thursday & Friday, the 1st, 2d & 3d, heavy fighting was going on at Gettysburg in Pa. Gen. Lee had apparently concentrated there all his forces; and Meade had done the same. We have telegrams from Martinsburg that Lee has beaten Meade & captured half his army, while the news by the flag of truce boat was to the effect that Lee was retreating on Sunday. Great uneasiness and anxiety is of course felt. It is known that on Wednesday and Thursday, up to Friday morning, our troops had held their positions—that was the last news, & came by way of the Yankee papers. Not a word of any sort from Lee. The people on the flag of truce boat, last arrived refused to give us papers which was suspicious of bad news to them. On the 7th we were told by a telegram from Johnston that an officer had arrived from Vicksburg with the news that the place capitulated on the 4th of July, the garrison being paroled and the officers retaining their side arms. The announcement is so unexpected, after the assurances given heretofore, that it appears incredible. There has been no confirmation of it since. There is news that Taylor and [Gen. Franklin] Gardner [Confederate commander of Port Hudson] have driven the remnant of Banks' force away from Port Hudson and raised the siege of that place. Mr. Stephens has returned having done nothing with his mission, which it is tho't related to the rules which are to govern this war.

Maria with her family is expected this morning. She will probably stay here.

Some very daring things have been done on the water on our side. A party of a dozen to twenty men left Mobile crossed the country to the Miss. below N. O., boarded a steamer lying there, secured the crew, passed out thro the blockading vessels, & ran the blockade into Mobile harbor safely, capturing & burning a prize on the way. This was the Fox. Another vessel was cut out in the same way by a second party. A few days ago the city of Portland was startled by the disappearance of the Rev.[enue] Cutter Caleb Cushing, lying at anchor in its waters. Lt. [Charles W.] Reed [Read], of the privateer Tacony, after burning & destroying forty or fifty fishing vessels, burned his own vessel, which was too well known, and transferred himself & crew to another vessel, the Archer. He then boldly entered Portland harbor & cast anchor. During the night he boarded the Cushing, the officers of which were absent, secured the crew, & put to sea. He was pursued shortly & overtaken by steamers, when he blew up his vessel, having transferred his crew to the boats. He was captured & taken back to Portland. Such things, together with the career of the Alabama and Florida, keep alive the spirit of the Navy, & prevent it falling into utter insignificance.

July 10, [1863]   The news that Vicksburg has fallen is confirmed. It is indeed a terrible blow to our cause. It apparently sets us back indefinitely. It will enable the Yankees to again recruit their armies, and will greatly depress our credit abroad. It is believed that over 20,000 men were surrendered, and of these nearly 17,000 must have been fit for duty. Why an effort was not made to cut thro' is not yet known. Gen. Lee has fallen back to Hagerstown [Md.] where he has a secure position. On the whole our affairs look gloomier now than ever.

July 13, [1863]   Authentic news arrived from Gen Lee himself on Saturday. The fighting on Wednesday the 1st, was destructive to the enemy, that of Thursday indecisive & on Friday we were repulsed from the enemy's position. Our loss is no doubt very heavy, but we appear to have taken as high as 10,000 prisoners. Gen [Richard B.] Garnett and [Gen. Lewis A.] Armistead are killed, and a large number of Gen. Officers wounded. The details are coming in slowly. Gen. D. H. Hill has been promoted to Lt. Gen (?) and sent to the Miss. We are again threatened by Yankee gunboats and transports in the James River.

July 16, [1863]   An officer of Ordnance writing from Gen. Lee's Head Qrs. alludes to the operations of Friday as a "disaster", and as such I fear we must accept it. Gen. Lee will make an attempt to retrieve it, by some signal blow at the enemy. Col. Aiken, 7th S.C. mentions his loss at 133, of whom 18 were left dead on the field. He states our total loss at about 18000. Of this number about 5000 may be prisoners. He thinks we have 11,000 prisoners. If this be correct the loss of the enemy in killed wounded and missing cannot be less than 25,000—about one fourth of his effective strength. Port Hudson has also fallen, and fears are being entertained for Charleston, which was attacked on Saturday and Friday last on its outworks on Morris Island. The enemy effected a landing on the south end of the Island, where there was a small work which our troops soon abandoned. They next advanced to the assault of Fort Wagner, on the north half of the Island, but were decisively repulsed with a loss of 95 killed and about (250) three hundred wounded & prisoners. It is feared the enemy will succeed in taking Fort Wagner, & then reduce Fort Sumter from the North End of Morris Island.

July 17, [1863]   I saw the President yesterday. He is bitter against Johnston, as I judge from a single remark. When I said that Vicksburg fell apparently from want alone of provisions, he remarked "Yes, from want of provisions inside and a general outside who wouldnt fight". We have still no reliable accounts of the killed and wounded at Gettysburgh, or of the prisoners taken and lost there. It is certain that all of Pickett's brigadiers were killed, and his Division wholly scattered. It could not be rallied until withdrawn far behind the field of battle. The weather is disheartening for three or four weeks it has rained constantly. All the crops in this part of the country will be lost—a sad loss to us. Can we believe in the justice of Providence, or must we conclude that we are after all wrong? Such visitations give me to great bitterness of heart, and repinings at His decrees. It is apparent that we are not yet sufficiently tried. The sins of the people of Charleston may cause that city to fall. It is full of rottenness, every one being engaged in speculations. When the fate of Lee's army was as we tho't trembling in the balance at Gettysburgh, the interest was less vivid in it than in a steamer which was expected in; and when a gentleman communicated to a speculator that so-and-so, & a well known officer from Charleston had been killed, he replied, "You don't say so. What's Calypso this morning"—Calypso being a blockade stock! Her fall will be looked on by many as a righteous doom.

July 28, [1863]   Events have succeeded one another with disastrous rapidity. One brief month ago we were apparently at the point of success. Lee was in Pennsylvania, threatening Harrisburgh, and even Philadelphia. Vicksburgh seemed to laugh all Grant's efforts to scorn, & the northern papers had reports of his raising the siege. Port Hudson had beaten off Banks' forces, and "the question" said a northern correspondent was only now, could he save the remnant of his army. Taylor had driven the enemy from the greater part of Louisiana, and had captured immense stores at Brashear. Winchester with 28 pieces of artillery and four thousand prisoners had fallen into our hands. All looked bright. Now the picture is just as sombre as it was bright then. Lee failed at Gettysburg, and has recrossed the Potomac & resumed the position of two months ago, covering Richmond. Alas! he has lost fifteen thousand men and twenty-five thousand stands of arms. Vicksburgh and Port Hudson capitulated, surrendering thirty five thousand men and forty-five thousand arms. It seems incredible that human power could effect such a change in so brief a space. Yesterday we rode on the pinnacle of success—to-day absolute ruin seems to be our portion. The Confederacy totters to its destruction.

V

"Has war ever been carried on like this"

July 29, [1863]   News rec'd to-day of the death of Wm. L. Yancey at Montgomery. He was prominent in the earliest days of the Secession movement, and went abroad as one of the Commissioners of the Confederacy, accredited to foreign governments. After his return he appears not to have agreed with President Davis and has had little influence even in the Senate.

It has rained not less than fifty days almost consecutively, probably 45 days out of the 50. The wheat which had been cut has sprouted in the shock. The loss of the crop will be a most serious embarrassment in feeding the army, especially if as is threatened the corn crop should also be injured. The loss of arms in the Gettysburg fights will not fall short of twenty-five thousand. I fear this with the losses on the Miss. will carry the losses up to 70,000, a serious matter to my department but not I hope irreparable. The singling out of two Yankee officers by lot, to be executed in retaliation for two of our officers executed by Burnside for recruiting in Kentucky is denounced by the enemy & they have placed Gen. Rooney Lee & Capt Winder in confinement, & declare they will execute them. As Buckner is said to have captured three Yankees recruiting in Tenn. I hope the true solution of the difficulty will be found in the execution of these, & the liberation of [Capts. H. W.] Sawyer &——[John Flynn]. Since the fall of Vicksburg which gives a large surplus of prisoners to them the enemy exhibits a malignant spirit on the subject of exchanges.

Aug 1, 1863   No news yesterday of especial importance. It appears to be admitted that Grant has gone up the river with his forces, to what end no one seems willing to predict. The bombardment still goes on at

Charleston with few casualties on our side. We went to see Mrs. Cross last evening. Saw there her mother Mrs. Ritchie, widow of [Thomas] Ritchie the editor of the [Richmond] Enquirer in the days when that paper was a power.

Aug. 2, [1863]   The only good news appears to come from the South West where Gen. Taylor is said to have defeated the enemy in a recent engagement, capturing a large number of prisoners. It is not fully credited. The plans of the enemy will soon be developed and then we shall know where to look for the next attack. Mobile and Chattanooga appear to be the points most likely to attract the enemy. Our freight steamers continue to run to Bermuda, from Wilmington. This is our chief source of supply for arms, and we get our steel, tin, zince, & various other articles wholly in this way. We also import leather, tools, hardware, medicines, saltpetre, lead, &c. &c in large quantities. We own four belonging to my Bureau, & there are others running in which the War Dept is largely interested. Thus far none of our vessels has been captured, tho we have now made some fifty trips out & back. The weather is now extremely warm. Ria is quite ailing, & thin.

Aug 3, [1863]   There was news of a cavalry fight at Brandy Station, in which we lost Cols. [Gen. Lawrence S.] Baker & [Gen. William E.] Jones killed. Our forces got the worst of it, I fear. Longstreet's corps is at Fredericksburgh, & troops were sent yesterday morning from here to replace some taken from Hanover junction to reinforce him. The weather is oppresively warm, and I trust our troops may not have to undergo heavy marches at this season. Went with Mamma to Gen. [Arnold] Elzey's to see Mrs. E. The General is a brave man <without brains for his position.> He is surrounded by four or five <u>youngsters</u> for aids &c. who were better in the ranks.

Aug 6, [1863]   Lee seems to have fallen back behind the Rappahannock, & has his head Qu. probably at Orange C. H. Charleston appears to be doing very well. As long as Battery Wagner is maintained there need be no apprehension. No field officers were killed in the fight, at Brandy Station. Col. Baker (now General) lost a portion of his arm. Johnston has established himself at Enterprize on the Mobile & Ohio R.R. so as to be in position to cover Mobile. For four days past the weather has been excessively warm.

Bayne and myself go out to breakfast with Mr. Freeland "at 7½ to 8 A.M."

Aug 10, [1863]   No event of special importance has occurred. There seems to be a strong disposition to leave the Confederacy to go abroad. [Former U.S.] Senator [from Calif. William M.] Gwynn [Gwin, who had sided with the Confederacy] and his daughter went in the last trip of the

Lee. Mrs. Greenhow went also lately, and now Mrs. Ex-Presdt [John] Tyler applies for a passage on one of our boats. We are burdened with applications, & I suppose the private steamers carry as many as can get on. The state of feeling in Miss. is said to be very discouraging, since the fall of Vicksburg. The soldiers will not fight again under Pemberton in whom they have lost all confidence, whether justly or unjustly. Of the 40,000 men whom we had in service on the lst of May in Port Hudson and Vicksburg we shall never again I fear re-assemble 6000—a large army lost at one blow. Truly Grant's operations were fruitful of results. All now depends for the present on Charleston. If we can maintain it against the determined attack preparing against it, all will go well. If not we shall be driven from the sea-board entirely, to a line of interior defences. Then will our constancy commence to be tested. I have my fears that many who now seem determined will then suddenly show themselves <u>weak-kneed</u>, and will quail before the storm. But I believe the determined men will still retain sway, and keep the timid down, and the spirit of the people is still with the war, and will continue so. A good deal of sensation was created by the appointment of Gen. [Alexander R.] Lawton as Qrm. Genl. Col. A. C. Myers has hitherto been the Qr. mr. Genl. and has fulfilled his duties very well. Lawton is a graduate of the class of '39, but left service almost immediately after graduating. He is a man of but moderate ability. <The President seems determined to respect the opinions of no one; and has I fear little appreciation of services rendered, unless the party enjoys his good opinion. He seems to be an indifferent judge of men, & is guided more by prejudice, than by sound, discriminating judgment. I have been surprised to hear his condemnation of men & measures—in the field and in the Cabinet. Yet apparently without any idea that it was for him to correct them. He sneers continually at Mr. [Stephen A.] Mallory and his navy, and is at no pains to conceal his opinions before that secretary. Yet he never controls him in any respect, nor will he yield to the opinion of the country which has long since pointed to a change in that branch of the service.>

Aug 13, [1863] There is little activity prevailing, the hot weather having no doubt its influence. The enemy are probably continuing their work on Morris Island for the reduction of Fort Sumter. Mamma and I propose going to-morrow to visit Mr. [J. P.] Holcombe [member of the Confederate Congress] at his place beyond Lynchburg. We may stay 8 or 10 days.

Aug 24, [1863] We returned yesterday from our visit to Mr. H. It proved to be a very pleasant quiet one, tho' the going and returning in the present condition of roads and of travel was wearisome. The children (Willie, Minnie and Ria[)] enjoyed the country exceedingly. Here there is little knowledge of the war except thro the newspapers, and the scarcity of articles of luxury and of wearing apparel. Fort Sumter is suffering severely from the fire of the enemy's heavy rifle guns, and will probably be abandoned, tho' the city will not therefore be given up. Beauregard telegraphs that he will defend Wagner and Sumter to the last extremity. Were I in his place, I should endeavor to level off the ruins of Sumter, and immediately place guns on it behind sand bags. It would be a task of difficulty and danger, and to be done in a great measure at night.

All seems quiet with the army of Lee, and his army appears to be nearly in its original good condition. Gen. Bragg is threatened, and an advance into East Tenn. is considered the next most likely move on the part of the enemy. Recent arrivals from abroad have given us a fair supply of arms, and will enable us to equip all the men we can raise.

Aug 26, [1863] Fort Sumter has been nearly destroyed by the 8 inch rifle guns of the enemy, at a distance of 2⅝ miles. This is certainly an extraordinary result, and is startling evidence of the superiority of modern artillery. Mamma, and [her] sister Maria went yesterday on a pleasure trip to Drury's Bluff, returned quite pleased. Mrs. Dain of the party, with whom Maria is much pleased. Not so with her sister Miss Stowell, who it seems made herself disagreeable. Gen. Lee's army increases at the rate of 600 men per day.

Aug 28, [1863] The city is again thrown into commotion by the appearance of the enemy, this side of the Chickahominy, after driving away a small force of ours stationed at Bottom's bridge, of whom some were killed. The local organizations are again called out very much to our detriment, as work people charged with the supply of the army. General Floyd died on Wednesday the 26th, in his 58th year. He has played a very important part in this revolution.

Sept 3, [1863] It appears to be certain that our forces have evacuated Knoxville in order to concentrate with Bragg's army at some point and advance. We shall soon therefore hear stirring news from that quarter. The shelling at Charleston still goes on, with no marked effect. After an examination of the present condition of Fort Sumter, Engineers have decided that the Fort can be held, and it is still held. The probability is that the monitors will make their final attempt to run by during the night. We are throwing projectiles at the rate of about 25 tons per day, 1000 rounds. The large imported gun, 12¾ inches, is probably now in position. Its ball or bolt weighs 670 lbs, the gun 22 Tons, English. General Lee is in town in daily consultation with the President. Willie saw him for the first time on Sunday, & sat in his lap. Willie seemed disappointed— thinks the General does not look heroic! Last evening Maria & Mamma met him at Mrs. Randolph's.

Sept. 6, [1863]   The enemy has not yet succeeded in breaking thro' the defences of Charleston, and the bombardment seems to go on slowly. The 600 pds. is said to be mounted at White Point, on the Battery. Knoxville is evacuated by our forces, and probably occupied by the enemy. This is done for concentration with a view to an advance. I hope all will go well, but hitherto our advances have been lamentable failures. I have no doubt from all the signs that Lee is also meditating an advance against Meade, if not into Maryland. His army is again in excellent condition.

Septr 8, [1863]   After an obstinate defence Battery Wagner and Morris Island have been evacuated. This of course involves Fort Sumter which has but one gun left. This result was expected after the first error of permitting the enemy a footing on the Southern extremity. The next step will probably be the reduction of Fort Moultrie, and then the harbor will be effectually closed. Johnston and Pemberton are both now without commands. They have both lost the public confidence. A corps of Lee's army is ordered to East Tenn. to join Gen. Bragg. Knoxville and most of the road from there to the Va. line is in possession of the enemy. The best news is the falling of gold which has gone down from 1500 to 1000 in a few days.

Sept. 13, [1863]   I observe that I have omitted all mention of the foray of Gen. John H. Morgan into Indiana and Ohio. He started from the Cumberland, traversed Kentucky, crossed the Ohio at or near New Albany, went round Cincinnati, and struck the Ohio at Buffington, fighting his way thro, and doing a vast amount of damage. All this in June & July. He was captured with three fourths of his command, which consisted at first of about 2000 men, on the banks of the Ohio the rains having so swelled that usually fordable river that he could not cross. He was lodged in the Ohio Penitentiary, for safe keeping. It was a most unfortunate enterprize, but would not have been disastrous, save for the unprecedented rains. The great events transpiring about Gettysburgh diverted attention from the daring exploit.

On Tuesday night the enemy attempted to take Fort Sumter by assault in 30 barges, at night. They were beaten off with the loss of over 100 prisoners, & four or five barges. I am pained to hear of the bursting on trial of one of the two 600 Pds. rifle Blakeley guns just rec'd from abroad. In fact the bursting is a sort of national calamity so much was expected of these guns. A triple banded rifle gun of the Brooke pattern has also burst. It is more than difficult to make any of them endure anything like smooth bores. Longstreet's Army Corps has been going thro the city for East Tenn. ever since the middle of the week, Hood first, then [Lafayette] McLaws. Pickett's Division remains here it seems, while Wise, & [Micah] Jenkins' brigades heretofore here, go to Charleston.

Sept 17, [1863]   Bragg has shown his usual readiness for retreating, & has <u>retreated</u> us out of the whole of East Tenn., Rosecrans being in possession of Chattanooga, & Burnside of Knoxville, without the pulling of a trigger. Two thousand men and guns & ammunition have also been given away at Cumberland Gap, where a drunken Brigadier named [John W.] Frazer commanded. A cavalry fight occurred at & beyond Culpepper on Sunday, & our troops have fallen back to Orange. A brilliant thing was done a month ago by Lt [John T.] Wood of the [Confederate] Navy. He captured two [U.S.] Steamers [*Satellite* and *Reliance*] on the Potomac each with 40 men, & two guns, by boarding with a force of some 60 men. Wood is a grandson of Gen. Taylor. No firing has lately been done at Charleston. The enemy is busy establishing guns at Cummings point, no doubt with a view to shelling Charleston, at the distance of four miles.

Sept. 23, [1863]   On Saturday & Sunday the 19th & 20th a bloody battle was fought on the Chickamauga in Ga, near Chattanooga. The enemy was defeated with the loss of it is said over 50 pieces of artillery, and is retreating on Chattanooga. Our joy is damped by the loss of Gen. Hood, who died under the operation of amputating his leg. He left here only two weeks ago scarcely able to manage his wounded arm. His loss is a severe one. Second only to that of Jackson. Besides Hood we have lost [Gen. James] Deshler, [Gen. Benjamin H.] Helm, & a General [Preston] Smith—and heroes of less note—too many, too many. The defeat of Rosecrans will have a telling effect, as they hung their highest hopes on him. One division of Longstreet's Corps only appears to have been engaged. I hope this victory may lead to the recovery of East Tennessee.
   A Prof. McCulloch just from Columbia College, N. Y. spent the evening with us. He told us details of the cruel treatment of our wounded prisoners at Gettysburg. He is a Baltimorean & has just quitted his professorship, rather late, but let our people come, even at the eleventh hour.

Sept. 26, [1863]   Hood is not dead but has had his leg amputated & his condition was critical. Bragg telegraphs that he has taken 7000 prisoners, 36 pieces of artillery 15,000 small arms and a great many standards. The battle of Chickamauga will therefore rank as a great victory in the history of this great war. As however we do not hear that Rosecrans has abandoned Chattanooga the fruits of so great a victory are not yet reaped, and people are still in a state of anxious suspense, fearing that all this bloodshed may have been in vain, and that Tennessee may after all not be recovered. No doubt Rosecrans is being reinforced, & unless dealt with soon may become too strong to dislodge. The enemy is also operating in Western Virginia at & near Bristol, where some buildings were burned. A fight took place at Zollicoffer, where the enemy was repulsed.

These are attempts to destroy the rail-road, & have no design of permanent occupancy.

Gen. S.[amuel] Jones commands there on our side. Exchanges of prisoners will probably now again be effected, after the captures just made. The Yankees have of late had largely the advantage, & have behaved accordingly, refusing exchanges and keeping our men confined in large numbers at Fort Delaware & other places. Dined at Mr. [Burton N.] Harrisons [secretary to President Jefferson Davis] on 6th Street. Mr. Mallory, Sec. Navy, & Mr. [C. G.] Memminger, Sec. Treary. present. A dinner party of 14 & very tedious.

Sept. 28, [1863]　　The weather continues quite cool—a slight frost on Saturday morning. The town was quite excited last evening over news that our cavalry was in rear of Rosecrans, and our troops in position to cut him off. I suppose it too good to be true. It is difficult to "cut off" a superior force, and if we can manoeuvre to force him back on Nashville, by threatening his supplies, I shall be satisfied. The country however expects much more, even the redemption of Tennessee entire. God grant its hopes & wishes may be achieved. Everything is ominously quiet at Charleston. The poor city is I suspect doomed to a fearful ordeal. 10,000 shells may be thrown into it in October, and the destruction these will create may be imagined. But the city will be considered "defended" as long as the site of it is in our hands. The iron clads from England are soon expected.

Oct. 3, [1863]　　On the 8th of Sept. the enemy was defeated in an attempt to force Sabine Pass, Texas, and lost two Steamers, carrying about 12 guns, which were disabled by the fire from land & were captured by our troops. The Situation at Chattanooga is becoming less & less encouraging, as Rosecrans strengthens himself. We have possession of all the Rail-roads, leading to the city, but he appears to supply himself by wagon trains from Stevenson [Ala.]. Should he be heavily re-inforced he may resume the offensive and compel Bragg to retreat.

No movements seem to be contemplated in Virginia. The firing has been resumed at Charleston. Our firing produces little effect as appears from teams moving along the island despite the fire.

Oct 7, [1863]　　No prospect of dislodging Rosecrans at Chattanooga, & the blood of 5000 poor fellows has been shed in vain. The President left for there yesterday morning. It seems to be believed that Mr. Mason has withdrawn from England. Gens. [Leonidas] Polk, Hindman, Forest & one other are said to be in arrest at Atlanta for disobedience of orders at Chickamauga. The weather is clear & cool.

Oct 11, Sunday [1863]　　The situation remains unchanged so far as we know at Chattanooga. The President is now there, probably with a view to assuaging the griefs that have arisen between the General (Bragg) and some of his chief officers. There is no doubt that very heavy re-inforcements have gone to Rosecrans from all directions. It would not be surprising if he had near 100,000 men & would soon have 130,000. With this force he can advance, and I fear will be in Atlanta before the winter sets in. Probably we may be able to defeat him in a pitched battle before he reaches there. Meade has fallen back from the Rapidan, and Lee has followed him, but no results are expected. The probability is that more troops will be transferred to Georgia, and I hope Lee will assume command of affairs there.

Charleston will soon cease to attract attention, as it is practically in the hands of the Yankees, like Savannah. It is an inland town now, & has ceased to be of importance. The only port now left to us is Wilmington. The weather is beautiful fall weather, clear, dry & cool. There seems to be no doubt that Mr. Mason has withdrawn from London. No further news of the iron-clads which seem to be expected to reach here somehow. I have no faith in Mr. Mallory's proceedings I confess, nor has any one else, except his wife.

Oct 16, [1863]   Several important cavalry fights have taken place between Stuart & the enemy's cavalry, and we have made some captures. The enemy has retired beyond the Rappahannock, burning the bridge there, and is probably concentrating about Washington. There are rumors this morning of a heavy fight in the direction of Centreville, but there is no probability of a general engagement. Gen. Johnston appears to have had a brush with the enemy's cavalry in northern Miss. between Grenada & Grand Junction, & retired before a superior force, they burning Wyatt [northwest of Oxford]. His despatch is from Oxford. I suppose he was trying to reach the Memphis and Charleston R.R. with a view to cut off re-inforcements coming to E. Tenn. from that direction. Capt. West, Staff of Gen. Zach[ariah] Deas was here last evening. The failure of the plan of battle before Chattanooga appears to rest with D. H. Hill, on the extreme right. He could not be found to receive the necessary orders in time, & was too late in playing his part, which was to attack the communications with Chattanooga, & draw the enemy down the river. From all I can learn, our forces were not equal in strength to the task undertaken. I have little doubt that Rosecrans outnumbered the combined forces of Bragg, which did not exceed 45,000 men. At Charleston the old story of firing at the enemy's working parties. The big Blakeley was fired there a few days ago with 55 lbs of powder, with entire success. The range was very good.

October 19, [1863]   The enemy advanced thro' Bristol to Abingdon [Va.] threatening the Salt works, but the news to-day is that they are now rapidly retreating—probably because they have learned that we are advancing upon Knoxville from Georgia.

[October] 22d, [1863]   There is no military news of especial interest. The Winter is coming forward & closing around us drearily enough. I look forward to mid-winter with anxiety. There is not food enough to sustain the population here, & altho there is abundance in the country the limited means of transportation and the unsettled state of the markets prevent food from reaching here. I fear we shall see trouble on this Score, especially should we have a cold winter. We have lately lost three ships in which we were interested—"Phantom" (our own), "Douro" of which the cargo was ours, "Venus" belonging to the Collie & Crenshaw line, of which we (the War Dept.) own one half, & the cargo was entirely on govt acct. consisting of Bacon & Qrtmr. Stores. The vessels attached to my Bureau have been very lucky, the Phantom being the first & only loss— her cargo was partly Saved.

[October] 28th, [1863]   The military situation presents no new phase of interest. Gen. Lee has returned to this side of the Rappahannock. The enemy still holds on to Chattanooga but will not I confidently hope be able to continue there without fighting a battle to recover his communications. It was currently believed that Gilmore [Gen. Quincy Gillmore] had gone with the bulk of his forces from Morris Island, whither no one knew. Rosecrans has undoubtedly been relieved from the command at Chattanooga, & is succeeded by [Gen. George H.] Thomas, while Grant is placed in general command of the Armies operating in Tenn. Ken. & Miss. Rosecrans is charged it is said with cowardice on the battle field, & other derelictions—most probably he has quarreled with [Gen. Henry W.] Halleck.

We spent the evening at Mrs. Jones, weather cool but very fine. The seizure of our rams by the English government is the chief topic of interest. Poor Mallory is ever unfortunate in his dept. It is to be hoped he will have better success with those building in France. No one seems to apprehend that the French government will interfere with their delivery. A capture by our cavalry of 700 prisoners with some wagons and artillery was made near Loudon [the] same day last week. Wheeler's operations on the Chat[tanooga] & Nash[ville] R.R. resulted in the capture of some prisoners & the destruction of 800 wagons, 2000 mules & large depots of stores, with "ten miles" of the track. [Gen. Philip D.] Rodd[e]y too is stated to have blown up an important tunnel.

[October] 29th, [1863]   The great fear of every patriot at this moment relates to our currency. The vast over issues of paper money have raised prices to such a pitch as to make the expenses of the Government enormous. The estimate of the Qr. mr. Genl alone requires 54 millions per month after Jany 1st. This exceeds the limit fixed by Congress for issues of paper money by 4 millions. The fear is that a swift national bankruptcy is coming upon us. The poor suffer from this enormous inflation of currency. Beef is 1.25 per lb—Butter $4—Eggs 3—clothing is unobtainable, calico being $8 & 10 per yd—coffee is $8—sugar 3, & so on. Shoes cannot be had under 50 to $60 the pr. for very common ones. God only knows where all this will Stop. When we consider the absolute wealth of the South it is amazing that our finances should have been allowed to run into this ruinous conditon. We are now in a condition to carry on the war for an indefinite period. There is breadstuff enough, & tho the inadequacy of transportation makes prices high in some parts, there is abundance for all if the total be considered. And we have war material sufficient—men, guns, powder—the real pinch is the Treasury, & I fear we must pass thro' a national bankruptcy to get out of that. Perhaps it is better that this paper of 6 or 7 hundred million should come to naught and so relieve posterity of a debt too heavy to be borne. On Monday last we went to the funeral of Mrs. Harrison, daughter of our neighbor Mr. Freeland. She died suddenly—was quite young—had just lost her husband, and the occasion was one to excite deep sympathy. The minister Mr. Hoge prayed & preached over one and a half hours, during all of which time I stood up. Yesterday I heard of the death of Col. [Charles] Dimmock, Chief of Ord. of Va., of paralysis, the night before. His death was very sudden. He was a graduate of West Point, & somewhat advanced—has been useful in this war.

Nov 8, [1863]   During the last three days of October there was some fighting near Chattanooga. The enemy crossed the Tenn. below C. and drove our forces back this side of Lookout Creek, leaving them in possession of Raccoon Mtn. There is little doubt that we shall have to fall back from before Chattanooga, & then for the present abandon all of Tenn. to the enemy. It is a bitter tho't, but there may be even worse in store for us. The President has visited all the principal points this side of the Miss. & has probably just arrived in the city (9th). Flour has sold as high as $125, & people are in fear of absolute want, with plenty in the country. Fear of impressment keeps farmers from sending their produce to market.

Nov 11, [1863]   On Sunday (8th) we heard of a fight which occurred beyond the Rappahannock in which the greater part of two of our brigades were captured ([Harry T.] Hays La. & [Robert F.] Hoke N.C.). They were on duty over the river from the main body of the army. It is very strange how little success has attended the movement of Lee's army since the death of Jackson. On Sunday we heard also of the capture of the Cornubia, and on Monday learned that [Amelia's brother] Dick had been captured with her. This is a heavy blow, in all respects. The weather is quite cold with heavy frosts.

Nov 16, [1863]   The situation Still remains the same at Chattanooga. The enemy, having possession of Raccoon Mtn, have no difficulty in getting supplies by river and R. Road from Bridgeport [Ala.], thus the last fruit of our victory at Chickamauga has slipped from our grasp. The general sentiment is undoubtedly that Bragg should resign his command, none of his subordinates having any confidence in him. I do not think that justice is done to Bragg, & think what he has done is not entirely appreciated, tho' it must be confessed what he has lost is most apparent.

Nov 17, [1863]   Rumors yesterday made Meade cross the Rapidan & that a fight was imminent. It seems to have been nothing but a cavalry dash, tho the ambulance committee was sent for, a certain sign that a fight was expected by Gen. Lee. The conduct of the French at the mouth of the Rio Grande is surprising—they have captured and carried to Vera Cruz, ships laden with arms and Stores for us, under pretence that they were going to Matamoras, a port blockaded by them, & were intended for the Mexicans. The apprehension of Scarcity this winter weighs heavily on the minds of men. Nothing but prompt action on the part of Congress, to rectify the currency will save us from great distress.

Nov 21, [1863]   Gen. W[illiam] E. Jones did a handsome thing in capturing a force of Yankees at Rogersville in East Tenn.—about 800 were taken with 4 pieces of artillery 1000 horses, wagons &c. The telegraph yesterday reports officially that Wheeler is at Knoxville with his cavalry and the infantry close by. The loss of the Cornubia, R. E. Lee and the Ella and Annie, all laden with govt Stores, is a very heavy one. It is a great reflection on our commanders that they allow their vessels to fall unhurt into the hands of the enemy. With the Cornubia fell into the hands of the enemy despatches which excite no little interest, and will attract some ridicule upon us, as exposing all our plans. People abroad will distrust a nation that conducts its affairs abroad with so little skill.

Decr 6, [1863]   On the 25th of November our Army at Chattanooga suffered the worst defeat we have had during the war. Our troops were drawn up along Missionary Ridge, with the right resting near the mouth of Chickamauga Creek, the right under [Gen. William J.] Hardee, the left under Breckinridge. The enemy attacked about 10 A.M. and at 4 broke thro our left centre, routing the left wing, with the loss of 40 odd pieces of artillery, & and about 5000 prisoners, (including the wounded[)]. The right stood firm and covered the retreat. The enemy pursued next day, and after following our troops to Resaca was repulsed with loss by our rear guard under [Gen. Patrick R.] Cleburne, after which the enemy returned to Chattanooga, burning the bridges behind them. Bragg has asked to be relieved & it is believed that Hardee is in command. No permanent commander has yet been assigned. Our loss in killed and wounded is not heavy. Reinforcements are being sent to that Army, & it will soon recover its strength, but its morale is I fear badly shaken, despite the victory it achieved at Chickamauga. Longstreet's Corps was absent at Knoxville, endeavoring to force Burnside to surrender. Had he been on the left as at the battle of C. all would have been well, & the enemy would have suffered a bloody repulse along the whole line as they did on our right.

In Northern Va. Meade crossed the Rapidan at the lower fords, turning Lee's right, & moved his troops behind Mine run, where Lee confronted him with the Stream between them. An artillery duel was begun on the 27th, with no result. Meade again withdrew without loss a few days after, & both armies are again at their old quarters, Lee at Orange C. H.

The best news of late is the escape of Gen. Morgan from the Ohio penitentiary, with six of his officers, & his safe arrival in Canada. It diffuses general joy.

The bombardment of Sumter Still goes on with little result. A few shells are now and then thrown into the city, & a little damage done.

Mamma has been confined to her bed with a painful attack since the 26th, & is still in bed but declares she will get up to-morrow, cost what it will. Provisions are very high, tho' not especially scarce. Flour has sold as high as $125 per bbl.—Potatoes 15 to 20 dollars per bu.—Eggs $3—butter $4½—Sugar 4½ to 6—Coffee any price, & so on. Gold sells at 20 & 22. I have just rec'd a pair of shoes from Baltimore which at the lowest figures of domestic Ex will cost me 87½ dollars. Congress meets to-morrow, & the first thing to be done is to arrange for the reduction of the currency—how is not yet agreed.

Monday, Decr 7, 1863. Mamma is gaining strength, but has not left her bed to-day, as she threatened to do yesterday. Maria is keeping house, and sways her sceptre with the energy of her character. A ham has, with my judicious carving, served as a daily dish for exactly seven days, and there is even a respectable remnant for to-morrow. It was a delicious Westphalia, and worthy the care bestowed on it.

Longstreet is at Rutledge, east of Knoxville, and asks for instructions, whether to wait for reinforcements or fall back to Bristol. The defeat of Bragg was less disastrous than first represented by himself. The chief loss is after all in the self-confidence of the Army, which success alone can restore to it. With the re-inforcements sent to it, it will soon be in condition to act again. It is singular to reflect that had Longstreet remained with Bragg the left of our army where he commanded would have repulsed the enemy, as did the right, and Missionary Ridge, instead of a shameful defeat would have been a bloody repetition of Fredericksburgh; if on the other hand the movement on Knoxville had been carried out as begun a few days after the battle of Chickamauga Burnside would have been captured, & Rosecranz's army forced out of Chattanooga. If again Longstreet had been with Lee, or even two of his divisions, Meade would have been "ground to powder," as one of Gen. Lee's chief Staff Officers expresses it, before he could have recrossed the Rapidan, during the last days of November. For the late advance on Knoxville the President is perhaps responsible, as he was with the Army of Gen. B.[ragg] when the movement began. It was an unfortunate move then, as the result proved. As Longstreets chief of artillery [Gen. Edward P. Alexander] said then, it was undertaken too late, & in inadequate force. It was early in November, six weeks after the battle of Chickamauga, before Longstreet marched!

Mr. [Pierre] Soule [U.S. ambassador to Spain, 1853–1854] called yesterday. He speaks with singular clearness and force, & is a most attractive conversationalist. He has no hopes of an early termination of the war.

Friday Decr 18, [1863]   Bragg having been relieved from the command of the Army of Tenn., Hardee remains in charge. A new commander is to be selected. Bragg has expressed his willingness to serve as chief of Staff to Gen. Johnston, & that combination may be made. The news came night before last that the enemy's cavalry had reached Salem on the East Tenn. R.R. & burned the Depot. No troops to check him there, & he seems to be at liberty to roam anywhere. All is quiet on the Rapidan. The affair of the capture of the Chesapeake, a steamer running from N. Y. to Portland creates great Sensation at the north. Numberless Steamers went in pursuit of the abducted one, but she is not likely to be caught. The escape of Morgan from prison a month ago gives great joy. The weather is very rainy, & the roads will now be impassable for troops. Mamma is Still in her room, a whole month's confinement.

Sunday, Decr 20, [1863]   I have just been looking back over the earlier pages of this journal, and do not regret having begun it however trivial the entries may appear. I feel sure it will interest my children when I am gone, & that is one chief object. Heard a few days ago of the loss of the iron-clad (monitor) Wahawken [*Weehawken*] off Charleston with all on board. It is impossible not to rejoice over the misfortunes of such enemies as we are fighting, cruel and ruthless as they show themselves to be. Has war ever been carried on like this before, among civilized people? Homes, gardens, crops, mills, & all intended for the use & sustenance of the non-combatant population are relentlessly and systematically destroyed. They are going to starve & maltreat the inhabitants into submission. Short sighted people, & policy as misguided as it is wicked. They exasperate but do not subdue.

Johnston doubtless has taken command of Bragg's army unless Bragg remains as his chief of Staff. I do not hope good from the change. That army should with the re-inforcements it has had, be stronger than before its defeat at Missionary Ridge. It ought to be 35, to 40, thousand strong. Longstreet is at Rogersville still, probably. He prefers to stay there to supply his army. No progress made by the enemy at Charleston, save burning a home or so in the city by shells thrown from Cummings point. A fire and 20 odd casualties are reported at Fort Sumter. Congress has not yet achieved action on the currency. Does it reflect that their time may be worth 1½ millions a day to the country? There are rumors that Mr. [James A.] Seddon [Confederate Secretary of War, 1862–1865] intends to resign. Mamma is Still confined to her room, but will I hope soon be strong enough to come down Stairs. She is greatly reduced tho'. I took Willie, Jessie & Mamie to church with me, & heard a good sermon, not from Mr. Minnegerode, bless him!

Decr 28, [1863]   Salem on the E. Tenn. R.R. was visited by Averell with three or four thousand men. Unfortunately a large stock of meat, grain and leather had been collected there and were destroyed. Averell has escaped with the loss of only a few hundred men, but they lost nearly all their trains, & some horses. It is very discreditable to the vigilance of our commanders. Longstreet appears inclined to winter in E. Tenn. near Morristown. The Chesapeake which was so adroitly captured by passengers, between N. York and Portland has been recaptured, at Sambro N.S. [Nova Scotia] by the Ella and Annie, one of our blockade runners just captured.

Johnston has formally assumed command of Bragg's army. Mamma is Still confined to her room, but is gaining strength daily. Christmas was not a merry one to me, & I passed it very quietly, almost sadly at home.

VI

"Such a war, so relentless and so repugnant"

Jan 5th, [18]64   No military event of any sort has happened lately—rain and consequent mud has closed all operations. A few shells are thrown into Charleston occasionally, and on Christmas Eve & morning, the city was heavily bombarded, one killed & one at least (a woman) mortally wounded. The new Year came in very cold, but it is now again raining. Mamma is up & about but has not yet come down.

Jan 10, [1864]   The arrival of Gen. Jno. H. Morgan created quite a stir here on Friday. The city authorities and the Govt received him at the Ballard House, and gave him a handsome reception. No military events have transpired.

Charleston seems to be given up by the enemy who only throw an occasional shell. Having Sealed the harbor against commerce they consider their task no doubt half accomplished. A land attack is probable toward Spring. Wilmington too it is believed will be attacked by land. Lee's army numbers now less than 30,000 infantry. With cavalry and artillery it may be placed at 38,000 men. Longstreet has perhaps 22,000 including a large cavalry force, say 8,000. Gen. S[amuel] Jones in West Va. has I suppose 6 to 8,000, and there are say 10,000 men here and at Petersburgh. This will constitute a force of about 80,000 men in & upon the borders of Va. of whom 60,000 could be concentrated in five or six days on any point. Is not this a force large enough to defeat any force the Yankees can probably bring against us?

Gen. [Jubal A.] Early is operating in the lower valley of the Shenandoah, to get beef, of which the army is in great need. We shall get thro' the winter without manifest suffering, tho' shoes and blankets are still wanting. In the midst of these gigantic wars people will still amuse themselves, and I went with Maria & B[ayne] to see some charades at Mrs. Semmes. They were very good, & Mrs. S. especially successful, & hence I suppose the charades.

Jany 17, Sunday [1864] There is little news of a military character. In consequence of the assignment of [Gen. Benjamin] Beast Butler to the command at Fortress Monroe the exchange of prisoners appears farther off than ever. We have about 35,000 prisoners in their hands against say 16,000 in our possession. Gen. W. E. Jones Seems to be doing a little work in East Tenn. having lately captured 360 prisoners with some wagons, 3 pieces of artillery &c. It is stated that with his brigade he has captured over 1200 men in the last two months. Gen. [Dabney H.] Maury at Mobile and Gen. [William H. C.] Whiting at Wilmington both apprehend early attacks on their places respectively. Our armies are filling up and will I hope, be strong enough for their work by the 1st of May. A law abolishing all substitution has just been passed. While I don't think this will materially Strengthen the army, it will give general satisfaction.

A scheme of restoring the currency passed the house yesterday, its features are not known.

The Yankee Congress appears disposed to prosecute the war with vigor, tho the opposition amounts to nearly 70 votes, on a test question. Gen. Morgan came to my office during the week. He is a very handsome man, about six feet high with light brown hair and blue eyes, about 37 to 40 years old. His hair had not quite recovered from the cropping it rec'd in the Ohio penitentiary. Capt [Thomas H.] Hines one of his escaped comrades was with him, a modest young looking man of active build. These men will be heroes of our history. On Wednesday evg at Mrs. Randolph's charades there were present Hood, Stewart [Stuart], Buckner, Elzey—all Maj. Gens. and several Brigadiers. Stewart is fond of society, but entirely abstemious as to drinks. Last night I met an officer, Major [S. Bassett] French in the Comy. Dept, who had never tasted liquor. Would these were the rules in the army, unfortunately they are rare exceptions, the vice of drinking being nearly everywhere prevalent. Mamma is again ill, having fatigued herself too much going to Mrs. R's charades.

Jan 21, [1864] Movements reported seem to indicate designs against Mobile. Its present armament would have been considered powerful three years ago, and with the land force at Meridian under Gen. (Bishop) Polk, it may be considered pretty well prepared for defence. A couple of good cargos have lately arrived there for us from Havanna. Charleston has daily some 150 large shells thrown into it from the distance of four miles, without very great effect as reported. Troops are to-day moving thro' the city Southward, probably to be prepared to assist Wilmington. Longstreet seems to be active and some successes are reported in that quarter. The bill for improving the currency has passed the house, & is before the Senate. Its features are not known, but it is doubtless sufficiently Stringent. The danger now seems to be a too eager disposition to sacrifice everything to putting men in the field at the expense of the industrial interests.

A letter from Dick rec'd by last flag of truce assures us he is well & well treated, but tired of his confinement & longing to be exchanged. The commandant of Fort Warren is Col. [Justin] Dimick a good officer of the old Service, and humane.

Jan 31, [1864]   Slight events of varied character have occurred in East Tenn. Gen [Robert] Vance [brother of N.C. Governor Zebulon Vance], comng in Western N. C. with about 50 men has been captured, by the Yankee Gen. [S. D.] Sturgis. He was returning from a partially successful foray into the Yankee lines. Under Longstreet Gen. [William T.] Martin met with a reverse, losing 2 pieces of arty and several hundred men, killed wounded & missing. The troops are getting supplies of food and clothing, and their spirit is represented as generally good. The ranks are decidedly filling up as is evident from the number of arms called for. There is a disposition in the Senate probably instigated by the Secy of War, to drive the enginery of war under too great pressure. A bill has passed it to place in the Military Service, for details all men between 45 and 55. This is unnecessary. In such a war as this—a war for national existence the whole mass of the nation must be engaged. It must be divided into those who go to the field and fight, & those who stay at home to support the fighting portion, supplying all the food, and material of war. Between the age of 18 & 45 has been fixed on for the fighting population—the rest must be devoted to Agriculture, Arts, mines, and manufactures. It is simply absurd to call on all to fight. Some must labor or all will starve. There is much crude legislation going on, but we shall work thro' this revolution with some blunders. Gen. Pillow came to my office yesterday. He & I served in Mexico together—at least we were there together. He is charged he says with organizing two brigades of cavalry to cover northern Alabama. He is a man of energy and ability and were he content to <u>serve</u> would I think be very useful; but his great ambition leads him to seek commands to which his military status is hardly equal. To a General by whom he would be controlled he would be very useful.

Feby 4, [1864]   A party of 150 Yankees landing from a Steamer at Smithfield [Va.] on the Nansemond [River] were nearly all captured and the Steamer destroyed last week. The news came this morning that Gen. Pickett had encountered the enemy eight miles from Newbern [New

Bern, N.C.] & had killed & wounded nearly 100 & captured 280 & two pieces of artillery. One gunboat was also destroyed. The object of the expedition—the capture of Newbern—was not attained it seems. The movements of the enemy down the Miss. coupled with the evacuation of northern Miss. have lead [led] to the surmise that Mobile is to be attacked. I saw an officer from Charleston to-day. The injury done to the city by the shelling is by no means great. The country is still awaiting with eagerness the action of congress on the currency. I fear it is too late to redeem it now. Since Congress met an additional 100 million have no doubt been added. Their action to do good should have been prompt.

Feb 14, [1864]   During the week 109 of the Yankee officers escaped from the Libby prison, by making a tunnel under the street some 60 feet long. Thirty only appear to have been recaptured. It is a serious misfortune just as the exchange question is pending—diminishing our prisoners so sensibly. [Gen. William T.] Sherman is moving eastward from Vicksburgh, and when last heard of was reported at Morton, half way from Jackson to Meridian. A demonstration has also been made from Jacksonville toward the interior of Florida, and at Charleston on the lines on John's Island. Both advances were repulsed. Some think Sherman's movement threatens Mobile, others that its only object is to devastate upper Miss & Alabama. The enemys movements are now no doubt partly political. They try to get possession of the capitals of the States & institute State governments, for effect on the next elections. All such governments would be subservient to Lincoln.

[February] 18th, [1864]   Nothing definite concerning Shermans movements. An attack appears to have been made at Grant's pass, without success. Gen. Polk has withdrawn his forces behind the Tombigbee [River]. It is Still doubtful whether Sherman's object is Mobile, or to devastate the grain growing region about & above Demopolis [Ala.]— perhaps a march on Selma. Fifty-four of the Yankee officers have been recaptured. The prisoners on Belle Isle are being sent to Americus, Ga, at the rate of 400 a day. The currency and tax bills, are at last out, & are sufficiently stringent to satisfy the most craving. These with the <u>military bill</u> will form a series of measures calculated to restore courage to the timid, and it is needed. The weather is the coldest known here for many years it is said.

Sunday [February] 21st, [1864]   Gen. Bragg spent Tuesday Evey with us. Willie now boasts the personal acquaintance of two Generals (Lee & Bragg) and three Lieut Gens (Hood, Ewell & Hill A.P.). Bragg was talkative. We had a good game of whist—Mr. [Francis S.] Lyon [Confederate congressman from Alabama and friend of Amelia's father], Capt. Brown & myself—some good supper and egg-nogg; altogether a pleasant evening. Sherman as far as heard from has not advanced East of Meridian, but is no doubt doing great damage to the [Mobile & Ohio] R.R. & destroying the corn, of which there is great store in that region— & doubtless some cotton. Mr. Holcombe was here this evening with Mrs. Jones. He goes to Halifax on a mission in relation to the Chesapeake. He is not very hopeful about the currency.

Thursday, March 3d, [1864]   The city has been in commotion since Monday from a threatened attack of cavalry, coming from the Army of Meade, & commanded by [Gen. H. Judson] Kilpatrick. On Tuesday they appeared on the north side of the city & shelled the batteries, or outer defences. They were driven off with the loss on our side of one killed & 5 or 6 wounded. This on the Brooke turnpike. About the same time they appeared about 5 miles from the city on the plank road, and were met about sundown by the battalion from the Armory here, which lost three killed or mortally wounded, and four or five wounded more or less severely. The enemy were finally driven off them losing 8 or 10 killed and a good number wounded. Some fifty of our men were taken prisoner and paroled by the Yankees. Yesterday it was reported that the enemy were approaching Bottom's bridge, but it is again said that they have retired. The local forces are however again sent out on the lines to-night.

Last week we had news of a considerable success over the Yankee forces invading Florida from Jacksonville. They marched westward 10,000 strong it is said to within ten miles of Lake City (Alligator) [the battle of Olustee] where they were met by our troops under Gen. [Joseph] Finnegan [Finegan] rated at 4 or 5 thousand & defeated with the loss of several thousand killed wounded & captured & five pieces of artillery. The tide of invasion seems therefore to have been thus far turned back in Miss. & in Florida. Gen. Bragg is in command here, having been assigned to duty with the President, to direct under him "the military operations of the armies of the Confederacy."

[March] 4th, [1864]   To-day were captured Col. [Ulric] Dahlgren & his command of raiders—outlaws—bandits. He was dead, but on his body were found the orders to his command, which were to enter the city, set it on fire in as many places as possible, liberate the prisoners, capture & kill the Presdt & his cabinet, & to commit every possible horror on the capital. What beasts and murderers. Hereafter those that are taken will not be heard of! We have passed a social pleasant evening. Mrs. Robinson & Mrs. Jones—Col [Julius A.] DeLagnel [one of Gorgas's assistants] & Judge Robinson. Heard of the arrival at Charleston of the Don (blockade runner) and of two vessels at Wilmington, perhaps three—Steamer City of Petersburgh, & Alice— some from Nassau, & some from Bermuda—with provisions, lead and general supplies.

[March] 6th, [1864]   A flag of truce boat with 900 prisoners arrived yesterday. It is hoped this may lead to the resumption of the cartel. We shall not however return a like number, but probably a number in proportion to the whole numbers held by each. The sinking of the Sloop of war [U.S.S.] Housatonic, of 13 guns, by the torpedo [boat] David—a submarine affair—is chronicled. Unfortunately the David was it is feared lost with all her crew.

[March] 11th, [1864]   The affair at Okolona [Miss.] in which Forrest with very inferior force repulsed [Gen. William Sooy] Smith & [Col. B. H.] Grierson seems to have been a very handsome one. Its result too was the retreat of Sherman, whose plans were thus entirely deranged. Over three hundred of the late raiders have been captured, pity that more of them were not killed. The shelling at Charleston still goes on slowly, without it is said much additional effect. Three torpedo boats are ready there to make an attack on the gunboats or iron clads. It is said the wonder boats now go to sea at night to avoid being blown up.

[March] 13, [1864]   The failure of their military operations seems to have had a decided effect on gold among the Yankees—it has gone to 169. I trust a few more failures will send it to 200. Partial exchange of prisoners is going on—600 were delivered to us yesterday, I learn. We return about two-thirds. Willie & I took a walk of 7 miles to-day, the weather being very pleasant.

[March] 16, [1864]   Numerous torpedo boats are building, to the number of say 30, with the view of destroying the blockading vessels at Charleston. These are cigar shaped, have a Steam engine—are 60 ft long by a little under 6 ft dia, & bear a torpedo on a spar at the bow. One of these struck a vessel last week, but for some reason the torpedo failed to explode, & the vessel struck never knew how near destruction she was. A torpedo boat with two engines it is supposed will make 12 to 14 miles, & may it seems to me make attack in open day-light. I prefer a system which I have sketched, of boats armed with a 16 inch shell gun—the gun placed in the bow weighs 8 or 9 thousand lbs. One shell, holding say 28 lb of powder would destroy any wooden ship. The exchange of prisoners if kept up will soon give us large additions to our veteran troops—say 25,000. The exchanged prisoners were received with music and other demonstrations yesterday. The President went among them, & was received with great enthusiasm. Weather clear but cool—gardening just beginning.

[March] 22d, [1864]   On Sunday afternoon we all went to the Capitol square to see the returned prisoners, another lot of whom had just arrived—over one thousand. We took along two small baskets of provisions and 1 demijon of cold tea. Jessie & Mamie each carried a basket &

Willie the tea, Minnie a little basket of cakes. There was a great crowd, and we barely saw a few of the prisoners by penetrating thro the mass. The President and Gov [William "Extra Billy"] Smith said a few words, & about dark the mass moved off to Camp Lee. Grant has been made Lieut Gen. at the North, and has assumed command of all their armies.

[March] 23d, Wednesday, [1864]   The heaviest fall of snow this winter began yesterday. It lies 8 to 10 inches deep. Maria is in utter despair at this renewal of winter which she so much dislikes. We four sat down quietly as tho' there were no war and played a game of euchre. Anticipation of reduced prices under the new currency are Still entertained. The State of it is now deplorable Flour $300 the barrel. A shad costs $35. Turkey 5 to $9 per lb. Beef $5 to 6. Eggs, $7, and so on. How the poor live is incomprehensible. Even meal sells at $30. per bu.

March 25, Good Friday [1864]   It is raining fast, & with the snow we shall have plenty of water in the River, & plenty of mud in the roads. A bad prospect for the Yankees. Maj. [R. Milton] Cary dined with us to-day. He commands the Bellona Arsenal & foundry, and is one of my best officers. He has been good enough to send us four or five wild turkeys lately—a great addition to our bill of fare. Minnie is his especial pet, & he is her "sweetheart." Her airs with him are comical.

Gen Elzey has been relieved of command here and placed in charge of the 'Maryland line', to be more fully organized with head quarters at Staunton. The message of Gov. [Joseph E.] Brown of Ga. and the speech of Vice Presdt Stephens excite much remark, & are looked upon with general disfavor. The former denounces the suspension of the habeas corpus, and the latter speaks cold[ly] of the three great measures of the government—the h[abeas] c[orpus], the currency & the military bills.

March 27, Easter Sunday [1864]   The morning is bright but a cool raw wind is blowing. It is just three years ago to-day since I sent in my resignation in the U. S. Service. Another year of hard struggling will I hope serve to consolidate this Confederacy, & establish its right to enter the family of nations. Then it will I believe rapidly recover from the wounds it has received. I go to breakfast with Mr. & Mrs. Jones.

April 1st, [18]64   The weather Still continues raw, damp rainy, chilly. It is raining to-night. We are alone again in our quarters Bayne and his family having taken rooms on Main St. <Two families can rarely get along without some discontents in the house, & it is well that we have quietly broken in two. We have however passed nine months together pleasantly. Bayne is the most amiable & best man to get along with I have ever known. Maria is a little more difficult to please, and is too fond of havng her own way, to get along perfectly well with others.>

There is no war news. The bad weather prevents all military operations; and there is no information as to the plans of the enemy. They openly threaten Richmond, but it is Still believed their main attack will be in Georgia. I saw to-day in the hands of Gen. F. H. Lee the pocket memo. book of Dahlgren, in which is a rough draft in pencil of his published address to his troops, differing a little here & there; and among other memo on another page "Jeff Davis & his cabinet must be killed on the spot."

Bragg's quick decided spirit is I believe felt here. His presence I have no doubt does good. Every one feels that he will <u>assist</u> the President in the conduct of military matters.

April 4, [1864]   The news from Forrest to-day is very good. He attacked Union City on the 25th & took 450 prisoners. Paduca[h] afterwards & captured it, but did not hold it, the Small pox being prevalent. He returns about 600 prisoners who are on the way to Demopolis. He states his loss at only 25 killed and wounded, while the Yankee accounts had made it as high as 1300! It appears that the Yankees have succeeded in making their way some distance up the Red River & were above Alexandria at last accounts. They captured about 250 of our men at Fort DeRussy near Alexandria, with a few pieces of artillery. Grant appears to be with Meade's Army, and it really looks as tho' serious work were intended on this line. The weather is Still very bad—it snowed hard on the 2nd. Bayne has moved to a house on the upper end of Main St. & we feel quite lonesome here. Mamma has gone to bed with a face-ache, and it is time for me to follow.

Apl 7, [1864]   The weather has cleared up, and 8 or 10 days of such will make the roads passable. Grant really seems to intend operations against Richmond. It will I trust prove the final test & discomfiture of the enemy. I saw the President yesterday—he asked me whether the proportion of artillery with the army was not too large,—a subject I had lately brot to his attention in a paper—and then desired me to have some portable mills for making meal constructed to carry with the army. Prices of food are Still exorbitant—flour 1½ dollars per lb—potatos 40 dollars per bu.—tea 30 dollars—and so on. There is I fear real suffering in many families. I feel chagrin at times that <u>we</u> should be so well off. The funding & taxation have evidently had no effect. About 240 millions have been funded, & that with the tax on the remainder (33⅓ pr ct) reduces the volume of currency full one half. The five dollar bills are now taken reluctantly & at a discount as they have only till July to run. It is a real financial bewilderment. By the 1st of July matters will be somewhat arranged I hope.

April 8, [1864]   It is three years ago to-day since I took charge of the Ord. department of the Conf. States at Montgomery—three years of constant work and application. I have succeeded beyond my utmost expectations. From being the worst supplied of the Bureaus of the War Dept. it is now the best. Large Arsenals have been organized at Richmond, Fayetteville, Augusta, Charleston, Columbus, Macon, Atlanta, & Selma and Smaller ones at Danville, Lynchburgh and Montgomery, besides other establishments. A superb powder mill has been built at Augusta, the credit of which is due to Col. G. W. Rains. Lead smelting works were established by me at Petersburgh, and turned over to the Nitre & Mining Bureau, when that Bureau was at my request separated from mine. A cannon foundry established at Macon for heavy guns, & bronze foundries at Macon Columbus Ga. and at Augusta. A foundry for shot & shell at Salisbury N. C. A large shop for leather work at Clarksville Va. Besides the Armories here & at Fayetteville, a manufactory of carbines has been built up here—a rifle factory at Asheville (transferred to Columbia S. C)—a new and very large armory at Macon, including a pistol factory, built up under contract here & sent to Atlanta, & thence transferred under purchase to Macon. A second pistol factory at Columbus Ga. All of these have required incessant toil & attention, but have borne such fruit as relieves the country from fear of want in these respects. Where three years ago we were not making a gun, a pistol nor a sabre—a pound of powder—no shot nor shell (except at the Tredegar Works) we now make all these in quantities to meet the demands of our large armies. In looking over all this I feel that my three years of labor have not been passed in vain. Mamma is again suffering—she is not at all well. There is no news. The daily papers are carping at the renewal of exchanges thro' as they say Beast Butler, the outlaw.

April 10, [1864]   It is reported that the enemy is landing troops at Newport News, or somewhere below on the James' River—said to be Burnside's troops. It is very doubtful. If it be so we must get the ironclads of which there are three nearly ready, to hold the course of the River. The heavy rains will prevent active military operations for some time to come. It is said that Gen. Lee is anxious to attack Grant before he can be reinforced. This seems probable. As I have had to-day a telegram from him asking that the arms from Wilmington be hastened to him I judge he is getting his troops ready to do work. It is raining incessantly. An arrangement to resume the exchange of prisoners tho' not announced has doubtless been made.

Apl 11, [1864]   There is nothing further as to the reported movements of the enemy on the lower James. The floods have caused some destruction of bridges, &c, & apprehensions of injury to the canal are entertained. The river is higher than it has been since '47. There is much anxiety on the subject of food for the capital. It is said—on the authority of the assessors—that the popn of Richmond is now 130,000 against

50,000 three years ago. The increase seems hardly credible. With proper energy in the use of the Rail Roads, there is no doubt food can be bro't forward from the South & troops & Capital fed, but the passenger trains must be interrupted for a time.

Bayne is little pleased with his new chief, the Secy of the Treasury. Mr. Memminger treats others with rudeness, & is besides dogmatical, narrowminded & slow. He places every fresh paper at the bottom of his pile, & makes it await its turn patiently without much regard to its importance. His time, & his method are more important than any subject can possibly be! Whenever I leave Mr. M after an interview I feel somehow as tho' I had been trying to do something very much out of the way—so injured and put upon does he represent himself. He always assumes a bristling defensive & makes you appear to be on the aggressive, toward him. Mr. Seddon compares him to a dog who when a new dog enters his domain runs along side of him erecting his bristles & curving his back! Gold has gone to 171 in Yankee land—within one per cent of what it was at its highest a little over a year ago.

Apl 24, [1864] A brilliant feat of arms was done at Plymouth [N.C.] on Sunday Monday & Tuesday. Gen. Hoke (of N. C.) marched against it with about 5000 men and with the aid of an iron clad just finished took it partly by storm. —2500 men were taken—2 gunboats destroyed and one captured—100,000 lbs of Bacon and 1000 Bbls of flour—25 guns (among them one 200 pds Parrott) and other spoils. The town was surrounded with fortifications of which both ends rested on the river (Roanoke). The water front was left to be covered by their gunboats. As soon therefore as our iron-clad appeared and destroyed the boats, our troops landed & occupied the town taking the works in reverse. Some of them were however very strong. The garrison was summoned to surrender, and after some fighting in which one fort was carried with heavy loss on our side, it was again summoned. Gen. [Henry W.] Wessels now asked an interview in the course of which he told Gen. H[oke] that the defences were comparatively intact, and that his government held its officers to a strict accountability. He could not therefore surrender. Gen. H. replied in substance—"My force is as you must see adequate to the storming of your works. I shall storm them at any cost of life, and I warn you that if you expect to save your men by hoisting the white flag at the last moment you deceive yourself. After my troops surmount the defences no quarter will be given. The laws of war will be exacted." The fighting recommenced and our men were thrown forward to assault, but now the Yankees were discovered coming out of their works, first singly then in squads & platoons, & finally four hundred threw down their arms and gave themselves up, and then the main fort surrendered, & all the works fell.

No negro soldiers were taken prisoner, but about 300 were taken as laborers and put at work; and an hour after the surrender were busy placing the captured bacon, flour and other stores, on our boats to be bro't up the [Roanoke] river to Halifax [N.C.]. Our iron-clad was fairly hit three times by the shot of the 200 pds Parrott, which broke the outer layer of 2 in. iron & indented the inner without breaking thro'. Further news are expected from the same expedition, which it is hoped may capture Newbern.

Apl 25, [1864]   Went to service in the morning yesterday but instead of sitting thro the sermon, I took the children out during the singing of the hymn, and walked with them in the Capitol Square which they enjoyed more than they could the sermon. No further news from Gen. Hoke and the Newbern expedition. Gen. Beauregard is at Weldon. He has been assigned to the immediate command it seems in that quarter, the limits of his command having been extended. News of an advance by Lee is every day expected. Our troops are in excellent condition but the cavalry is not yet all to the front. News of Yankee disaster up the Red River [at battle of Mansfield, La.] is gradually being confirmed; but without sufficient distinctness. They confess to a loss of 2000 killed wounded and missing. We claim now 7000 prisoners and 19 pieces of artillery. The Yankee Gen. [Thomas E. G.] Ransom comng their cavalry is reported by them wounded. A good deal of excitement is created by the moving away of the lady note-signers to Columbia. It was proposed to move the chief portion of each department leaving only the chiefs, & such as were necessary to the business of the army. This would have been very embarrassing to us. It has since been reconsidered. The object is of course to diminish the number of mouths here—the question of feeding Gen. Lee's army & the Capitol being a very critical one.

April 26, [1864]   The weather is now beautiful, and very favorable to military operations. The news is that a large force is landing at Yorktown, & that an early advance may be expected against this place from that direction. It is still doubtful where the enemy will endeavor to strike the heaviest blow here or in Georgia. Our armies are maintained in full force at both places. Johnston has about 40,000 men, and Lee with Longstreet full 55,000. It is supposed that Lee will take the initiative immediately.

That he has not done so is I suppose because all his cavalry and artillery is not yet to the front.

The problem of the currency is a curious one. We have stricken out of existence 500,000,000 of dollars of currency yet prices have not receded. It is evident that parties holding food & supplies mean for the present to hold on to them. There will thus be a scarcity of money, yet high prices. Until the farmers are forced by taxation to sell their produce it is possible these prices may continue. It is now better to buy with gold when gold can be commanded. Eggs can be had for 12½ cts in gold while they cost $6 in currency. I have ceased to draw my pay & am determined to live on the sale of such things as I can spare. Gen. Sam. Jones has been assigned to command at Charleston, & Gen. Robt Ransom to Richmond. Gen. Hoke is a Major Gen. for his capture of Plymouth.

Friday, Apl 29, [1864]   There seems to be no longer reason to doubt that Gen. E. K. Smith met the 13th Army Corps on the 8th at some point on the west side of the upper Red River [the battle of Mansfield, La.], and defeated it with heavy loss say 4000 men in killed wounded and missing; & twenty pieces of artillery. The Yankees claim that Gen. A. J Smith came up next day, & drove back our forces with loss re-capturing some of the artillery. It is probable therefore the Enemy have been beaten before they could unite their forces, & that the second column simply saved the remains of the first from destruction. At all events the Red River expedition is frustrated and Louisiana safe. I had a short conference with Gen. Bragg yesterday. His views are so startling & decided that I am tempted to think him a little cracked. The subject was the removal of machinery & operatives from here on account of scarcity of food. He said movements would begin in a few weeks which would compel people to leave to escape starvation as all the food would be taken by the troops—"it is probable that the town will be pillaged by our own men for want of ability to supply them"—meaning when the R. Roads should be cut about Richmond.

April 30th, [1864]   The indications are now that Burnsides Corps may reinforce Grant it having gone to Washington from Annapolis there can be little doubt I suppose that a powerful army is collecting in front of Lee. His army is as large, perhaps larger than it was a year ago when it defeated Hooker; but then he had Jackson. I saw the President yesterday, having succeeded in making a corn-mill for him, which is to be used with the troops. He was much pleased at the specimen of meal made by it; and added that every body to whom he had imparted his views as to getting up a corn mill of this Sort "had told him how & why it could not be done, but that I had shown how it could be done." Possibly I ought to be master miller in place of Chief of Ordnance.

Congress meets day after to-morrow (Monday).

Sunday May 1, [1864]   We attended this afternoon the funeral of one of the Presidents little boys (Joe), who was killed yesterday evening by a fall from the back piazza. No one saw the poor little fellow fall, & he probably had been lying some little time when he was found. His legs were both broken & his head fractured. It is a very sad thing to see a fine healthy child, gamboling about yesterday, & to-day carried along in his little coffin. The President is very much attached to his children, & very caressing toward them, and this is a heavy sorrow to him. Last winter I once saw him take this little fellow off to hear him say his prayers as he went to bed.

May 2d, [1864]   News to-day that Washington N. C. is in our hands having been evacuated by the enemy. Should we now be able to reduce Newbern the waters of N. C. would again be in our possession, & the series of reverses beginning with the fall of Fort Hatteras would be redeemed. The recent battles on the Red river seem to have taken place on the 8th & 9th of April. The Yankees report Gen. [Alfred] Mouton as certainly killed. As yet we have no authentic advice from confederate sources. Two yankee gunboats and three transports are reported at West Point. The great scene of the drama of this year—perhaps the last one of this war (joyful tho't[)] must soon open. The omens are all good for us. Thus far military events have been every where in our favor.

May 4, [1864]   The enemy are reported to have crossed the Rappahannock at Ely's Ford, & to have advanced to the old ground near Chancellorsville. The crossing may be only a reconnaissance in force.

Rode out yesterday to attend the trial of the siege 8 inch gun, & the 9 pds light gun. The first was found spiked by the accidental breaking of a gimlet in the vent. A charge fired from the muzzle failed to drive the vent clear. The trial with this gun had therefore to be postponed. The 9 pds did very well, & gave very fair ranges. I had a brisk ride out & back & feel quite shaken. The day was clear & cool—wind sharp. The fortifications on the Manchester side are very strong & well built.

May 5th, [1864]   The enemy it is ascertained has landed in some force on the north side of the James River below Westover. 34 transports are reported. No further news of movements on the Rapidan. Troops are coming in from the South as far as Charleston. From Savannah & points further South they are ordered to Dalton [Ga.], so that Johnston ought now to have an army of nearly 60,000 including his cavalry. The great points of collision are evidently here and with Johnston's army. There are advices here from Shreveport to the 12th of Apl. There can be no doubt of the serious defeat of Banks & his withdrawal to Alexandria [La.] & perhaps to the Mississippi.

May 6, [1864]   The enemy crossed at Elys and Germanna Fords on the 4th & were met on the 5th by Ewells and [A. P.] Hills Corps the former on the old turnpike the latter on the plank road. They were repulsed at both points with a loss of 4 guns and "many prisoners". Gen. J[ohn] M. Jones (my classmate) was killed, & Gen. [Leroy A.] Stafford mortally wounded. Our loss is apparently heavy.

To-day the fight was renewed, but there is no news of definite character, except that all is going on well. Gen. Jenkins of S. C. is reported mortally wounded, and Gen. Longstreet severely wounded in the shoulder, both by their own men ([Gen. William] Mahone's brigade). 1200 prisoners are reported as having arrived at Orange C. H. The effort appears to have been to turn Lee's right.

A large force has landed at City Point & marched toward the R.R. but at latest accounts had not yet cut it. This effort, commanded by W. F. Smith, is doubtless aimed at Drurys Bluff. An enemy's gunboat was blown up on the river by a torpedo, & entirely destroyed. The forces here are adequate to holding the defences of Richmond, and if Gen. Lee is successful against Grants attack no fears need be entertained. Gen. Beauregard is at Petersburg by this time with 3 brigades besides some troops of Picket[t]'s.

The enemy is reported advancing in Western Va. to destroy the Salt Works. At Chattanooga the enemy is also reported moving, tho slowly. One of the officers on duty here came to me at midnight to say that his brother Col. J. Thompson Brown was killed in the fight to-day (6th) and desired leave which was of course given him. Col. B. is well known & a great favorite in Richmond. When will these terrible things come to an end. Capt. [E. S.] Hutter (stationed at Danville) stays with us to-night. The weather is beautiful, & the day has been quite warm. The stars are looking down upon many a poor wounded man lying in pain, & on the mangled corpses of many thousand brave men.

May 8, [1864]   No further official news of the fight of the 5th. On the 6th Gen Lee reports our troops thrown into momentary confusion by the attack of the enemy on the Divisions of [A. P.] Hill, which were being relieved by fresh troops. As soon as the troops got in position they recovered the ground which had been lost, and then attacking the enemy's left drove it off the field, leaving its killed and wounded, and forcing it back to its position behind the Brock road where it is entrenched. Rumors are rife of further successes. Our killed are not many, but a good many wounded—the fight having been in a wooded country with musketry. Fighting has been going on during the day (7th) below on the Petersburgh road—where the further progress of the enemy is disputed by our forces, by this time I hope twelve or fifteen thousand. It is stated they are entrenching. Another gunboat has been sunk or destroyed, having been captured by the men of [Gen. Eppa] Hunton's brigade. Beauregard is probably at Petersburg, tho' he was ill at Weldon on the 6th. Reports believed to be authentic state that Price has captured the greater part of [Gen. Frederick] Steele's command. The ironclad Albemarle returned to Plymouth after having had a fight of 48 hours (?)

with gunboats. She broke the muzzle off her after gun. We are preparing to move our Carbine Factory with all the operatives & their families to Tallassee, Ala.

May 10th, [1864]   On yesterday morning a despatch from Gen. Lee reported that Gen. R. H Anderson had met the enemy at Spotsylvania C. H. and repulsed one army Corps ([Gen. Gouveneur K.] Warrens), and a Division of Cavalry, "with heavy slaughter." Receiving re-inforcements the enemy renewed the attack and was again "handsomely repulsed."

On the 6th, [Gen. John B.] Gordons brigade attacked the extreme right of the enemy & drove it forcing him to abandon his communications by Germanna ford. In this fight Maj. Gen. [Truman] Seymour & Brig Gen. [Alexander] Shaler were captured. The enemy afterwards took up his bridges and withdrew toward Fredericksburgh our columns keeping parallel to his march. In this movement the collision at Spotsylvania C. H. took place. The body of Gen. [Micah] Jenkins of S. C. was taken to the Capitol yesterday evening, & Gen. Stafford was buried in Hollywood [Cemetery in Richmond] in the forenoon.

The day was one of excitement; in the morning it was reported the enemy had reached Chester on the R.R. between here and Petersburg, and that they were fighting at Drury's Bluff. Later news showed that this was incorrect, and that the attack was directed toward Petersburg. All the local forces were called out—alarm bells rung—&c. At night news of a raid at Beaver Dam, on the central R.R. again caused excitement. It is reported this morning that the enemy was driven from there by the local cavalry.

Evening. The news is bad from western Va. Brig Gen. [Albert G.] Jenkins cavalry command was attacked by a Yankee force and defeated. Dublin Depot [in Pulaski County] is now in possession of the enemy. Col. [John] McCausland, said to be a very good officer is in temporary command at New River. It is hoped that Morgan & W. E. Jones may restore our fortunes in that quarter. There is no definite news from Lee, fighting has doubtless been going on, but the result is unknown. Yesterday a party of Yankee cavalry, estimated at a thousand, took possession of the central R.R. at Beaver dam, capturing three trains laden with commissary stores, including over 200,000 lbs of Bacon. This is a very Serious loss, at this moment.

This morning there was fighting in the vicinity of Drurys Bluff. Gen. Ransom having advanced with two Brigades—[Gen. Archibald] Gracies & [Gen. Seth M.] Bartons—& attacked the enemy. The affair was done to attract the enemy from Petersburg, and resulted in a loss of about 150 of Barton's brigade. Gracie was not engaged. The affair was I judge unfavorable to us. Troops are concentrating at P[etersburg]. Every body complains of the tardiness of Beauregards movements.

The woods are on fire where the fight took place to-day and the horizon is lined with fires to-night in that direction. Hoke has it is said relieved Picket[t] at P[etersburg]. Picket[t] is very dissipated it is asserted.

I hope all will go well. People look very anxious as well they may with 30,000 Yankees close upon the city, & not 12,000 troops here to defend it.

Wednesday, May 11, [1864]   The day has been one of the greatest excitement. I slept but a few hours last night having been called up by messages, and kept awake by the ringing of alarm bells & the blowing of alarm whistles the most of the night. At 5 this morning I went to Mr. Seddon's office and found him laboring under the impression that the last hours of Richmond were at length numbered. The entire cavalry force of Meade's army were reported to be rapidly approaching the devoted city from the direction of Ashland, with Stuart at their heels it is true, but having a good deal the start of him.

All the city militia were transferred to that side of the city, & a brigade of old troops (Hunton's) from Chaffin's farm. We breathe more freely now (11. P.M) as Stuart is on their flank & the city defences in their front. It is hoped therefore that they may be worsted if not caught.

As all my officers and clerks are in the field I am obliged to attend to details myself and have trudged about the Streets until I am thoroughly tired. The news from Gen. Lee shows that there has been sharp fighting on the 9th and 10th the enemy being continually and as it appears easily repulsed. Still the enemy shows a bold front, & makes desperate assaults on Lee's position which appears to extend from Spotsylvania C. H. on the right to Shady Grove church on the left. Gens. Hays and [James A.] Walker are reported wounded yesterday. How this continued fighting will end cannot yet be predicted. If supplies do not fail I have no doubt of Lee's ability to maintain himself. Meantime the attack on Richmond from the large force landed at Bermuda Hundred, is repelled by the forces now under Beauregard; and he is to take the offensive to-morrow, and drive them to their gunboats. He has now all told a force of fully sixteen thousand men. The three iron clads will be ready to partake in the conflict as soon as they can get thro' the obstructions (the "Richmond" the "Virginia" and the "Fredericksburgh"). I fear they are too vulnerable to the heavy guns of the monitors, of which there are four. In the fighting with the cavalry force to-day Col. H. Clay Pate was killed, & our cavalry had to give back before the superior forces of the enemy—who number about 5000 it is said. Stuart has about 2500.

May 13, [1864]   Richmond is again breathing freely for the moment. After severe fighting at the Yellow church [Yellow Tavern], in which Stuart was mortally wounded at about 2½ P.M. on Wednesday, and after some skirmishing yesterday the enemy at last retired by Mechanicsville, without any serious loss. There is much dissatisfaction at this result. The enemy were however very strong—say 8000; still with three veteran brigades & a large force of "locals" something might perhaps have been done more than was done.

On the South side the enemy yesterday crossed the Petersburgh R.R.[d] and went to the Coal pits on the Danville road, cutting that & doing some other damage. Troops have been sent after him. It is tho't that Gen. Hoke is to attack the enemy to-morrow in some force. A courier brings despatches from Lee, which are I fear very unfavorable. He has been forced out of his lines on the left, and Major Gen. [Edward] Johnson & Brig Gen. [George H.] Steuart captured, losing besides a good deal of artillery. The courier poor fellow knew nothing of our misfortunes, & was retailing gay stories of recent successes, which will be detailed in the morning papers no doubt.

May 14, [1864]   The enemy has effected little damage to the Danville Road, and it is again in running order. Trains also left to-day for Gen. Lee on the Central R.R. So the city is again free for the time being, but I have little confidence in its remaining so long. Our enemy is here in very great force & will harrass us in every possible way. The newspaper despatches from Gen. Lee's army, are rather favorable to us, but I expect to hear that he is falling back. In truth I see no solution of our defence of Richmond except in this: to concentrate all our forces here, & keep open communications with the city. Heavy firing has been going on to the right of Drury's bluff all day, with some casualties to us. Beauregard is there, and I hope the troops are sufficient for an attack on the enemy.

May 15, [1864]   The despatches from Gen. Lee & his principal officers are quite hopeful. Still he has lost 2000 prisoners and 20 guns.

The loss of the enemy in the struggle of Thursday must have been enormous. An officer who was in the fight describes the attacking force to have come up in line after line, ten in number; & to have been mown down by our artillery in heaps. The "Herald" of the 12th states the minimum loss of Grant in the fights of the first week, to be 27000 killed wounded & missing. At that rate their losses must now sum up nearly 50,000. Ours cannot exceed 15,000. They have lost seven general officers killed & wounded Sedgwicke [Gen. John Sedgwick] is certainly killed. I knew him very well at Old Point Comfort. A fight occurred yesterday in which we took 300 prisoners & 4 colors. Gen. Lee does not ask for reinforcements, but for supplies of provisions, tho' he is in no danger of starvation as the country behind him still affords supplies. Lt. Col [Briscoe G.] Baldwin his chief Ord officer reports his ammunition holding out very well—100 rds yet per man, of small arm ammunition. Supplies are again going forward.

On the South side of James River, we have beaten the enemy off at the Appomattox bridge, & restored the Danville R.R. Gen. Beauregard is preparing an attack in force, and ought to have full 20,000 men. Gen. Whiting has joined him from Wilmington. Firing has been going on all day chiefly artillery with some skirmishing. We could see smoke of the guns & the bursting of shells from the cupola of the War Dept. Willie saw & watched it with interest.

A flag of truce was sent up to Curl's neck by the enemy—for what purpose is not known. [Gen. Philip H.] Sheridan's Cavalry is said to rest from its fights about Richmond about Malvern, & may again resume its raid after a brief repose. In Western Virginia Averill [Averell] has certainly been defeated by Morgan, Jones & Jackson, & is said to be lying wounded at Christiansburg a prisoner. I <u>hope</u> this may be true. For the past week it has been raining every day. If we could receive 15,000 men from Johnston's army, as we ought to, all would soon be well. If Johnston had the happy inspiration that Desaix had at Marengo, he would send here one of his corps without waiting for orders; [When the Austrians had attacked Napoleon unexpectedly, Desaix had heard the guns, hastened to the battlefield, and allowed Napoleon to take the offensive successfully.] as the enemy is evidently not to attack him & he must have 65,000 men idly waiting there, while the roar of battle thunders over a dozen battle fields in Virginia & the fate of the nation is being decided here.

May 16, [1864] A severe engagement took place on the South side to day, beginning at early light between the forces of Gen. Beauregard & that of Butler. We began the attack and drove the enemy capturing a Brigr Genl ([Charles A.] Heckman) with his staff & over a thousand prisoners. Seven pieces of artillery, & many of the horses are reported captured. Our losses are not reported, but are said to be heavy in Gracie's brigade, & in the Washington (N. C) Artillery. At 5 o'clock Beauregard despatched that he was preparing to renew the attack & hoped to effect a junction with Whiting who was at Port Walthall junction. The enemy is to the East of the R.R. about the half-way house. I have had great trouble to get ammunition for the Enfield arms, the troops having come up from N. C. with only 40 rounds.

Breckinridge has met and driven back [Gen. Franz] Sigel in the valley with considerable loss, & in some confusion [at New Market]. He is retiring behind the Shenandoah burning the bridges.

The news from Johns[t]on is that the enemy is in line in front of him, & on the 14th two attacks of his were repelled.

Gen. Lee says the enemy still moves toward our right apparently with the view of flanking, but has not renewed his attack since Thursday.

People look quite hopeful to-day. I hope their hearts are grateful to the brave fellows who are standing between us & our enemies, & pouring out their blood for our safety. I think of it every hour in the day with gratitude & sorrow for the noble fellows, who never flinch nor falter before the enemy.

May 17, [1864]   Our losses yesterday were quite heavy, amounting I fear to quite two thousand in killed wounded and missing. It was Barton's Brigade (commanded by Gen. [Birkett D.] Fry) which it seems suffered chiefly. [Gen. Johnson] Hagood's, (S. C) also lost heavily—18 men being killed in one company. We captured quite 1500 prisoners, and 5 pieces of artillery. One regiment from Springfield Mass, commanded by a Col. [William R.] Lee, was captured almost entire. The enemy have fallen back to their lines extending from the James River to the Appomattox, about 3 miles long, strongly defended, & of course supported by the gunboats. It is rumored to-night that they are crossing some troops to the north side below Chaffin's farm, communicating no doubt with Sheridan whose cavalry is still about Malvern hills.

No fighting above, the enemy still extending to the left and taking position behind the Ni River. Gen. Lee will I suppose occupy the range of heights south of the same River, his right just in front of Guinea's station. The road to Petersburgh is again cleared of the enemy, & may soon again be placed in running order. It is also repaired south of Petersburgh. Spent the evening at Mrs. Jones, meeting Mr. Lyon, Mrs. Marye, Col. Marye, Mrs. Miles, Mr. [William P.] Miles [Confederate congressman from] (S. C), & Col. [John E.] Baldwin (M.C [from Va.])

May 20, [1864]   One of the victims of the fight of Monday lies in our house—Lt. Robt. M. Taft, of Charleston. The poor fellow, whose family we know very well sent for me on Tuesday at noon, but owing to some stupidity I did not receive the message until late at night, after his death. It will be a sad blow to his poor mother who is a very fond mother.

There are reports of another fight below, & that Beauregard attacked & drove the enemy out of their rifle pits. I know the ambulance committee of Richmond was sent for to-day to Chester station. My heart sickens at the thought of another day of Slaughter like that of Monday. There is little doubt it seems that if Gen. Whiting had performed the part allotted to him by Beauregard on Monday, the yankee army would have suffered a severe defeat—he has been relieved from command at Petersburgh in consequence. I saw the President to-day. He was in better spirits than I have seen him in for a long time, and told several anecdotes, en passant [in passing]. One of Gen. [Zachary] Taylor in Mexico, who in passing by a soldier lying by the wayside during a fight, accosted him: "My poor fellow where were you wounded". "I'm not exactly wounded, General, but—["] "Yes, and taking good care that you won't be, you d——d rascal" said the indignant General, when he found it was one who was skulking.

The President called for an aid, & Col. Wood came in. "But" said the

President smiling "I want a writing aid." "Then I'll call Col. [J. C.] Ives" said Col. W. blushing a little but good natured. "Never mind" said the President "you'll do, I was jesting. And to relieve you from any embarrassment, I will tell you a little anecdote of Gen. Jackson.

There was an officer by the name of Capt. Bean apptd from the Rangers to the 1st Dragoons. He could not write his name, but had learned to sign his name Capt. B. "Capt Rangers" & when he was transferred to the Dragoons he continued the signature as before. Col. [Philip] Kearney went to Gen Jackson & told him, "Capt. B. is too illiterate for an officer—he cannot even write". The old Gen. threw up his specks & said "Can't write eh?—Well, he fought with me at —— Springs, and I know he made his mark"!

The story is somewhat old but did very well under the circumstances, & Col. Wood went on to write a letter to Gen. Beauregard from the Presidential dictation.

May 21, [1864] The fight yesterday drove the enemy nearer to their gunboats but cost us four or five hundred in killed and wounded. Gen. W.[illiam] S. Walker Comng [Gen. Clement A.] Evans brigade is missing, supposed captured. The enemy to-day evince no design of moving away down the river. The number of transports is reported at 70. The enemy again cut the Central R.R. at Hanover C. H. but have been forced off. It is said they are all about the other side of the Chickahominy about Mechanicsville, plundering and destroying. It is reported that the negro troops on the Peninsula are committing the most revolting excesses.

Our cavalry force is not adequate to driving them away & keeping them off. It is heart-rending to hear of the mal-treatment of the inhabitants. No news of fighting in Gen. Lee's army.

Gen. Johnston is falling back as hard as he can & has placed himself behind the Etowah River with his head Quarters at Altoona [Allatoona, Ga.]. It is surmised that he will reach Macon in a few days at the rate he is retreating. I trust the country will sooner or later find out what sort of a General he is. I don't think he will suit the emergency.

Sunday May 22d, [1864] Listened to a very long & very tiresome Sermon this morning in St. Paul's [Episcopal Church], from an old clergyman. He must have preached over an hour.

Gen. Lee has his head Qrs. at Hanover C. H. with [A. P.] Hill's Corps, the others following him. The movement of Grant down the Mattaponi [River east of Richmond] renders this necessary. It is probable that Grant is seeking to unite with Butler. No further news from Johnston, & nothing from Beauregard. Hugh [Aiken] arrived to-day with a part of his regiment. There are nearly 5000 cavalry here & on their way here from the South.

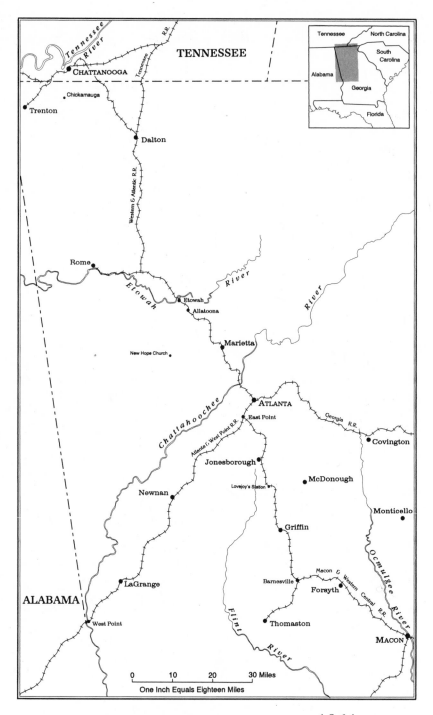

THE CAMPAIGN FOR ATLANTA, 1864

May 23d, [1864]   No items of news of any interest. With the cavalry now arriving here there will I think be no difficulty in keeping open our communications. It is said that the body of Grant's army is at Bowling Green and Milford Depot. A few heavy guns have been heard to-day in the direction of Drurys Bluff but it has not transpired what they meant.

May 25, [1864]   Yesterday we heard that the enemy had crossed the North Anna at three different points, and fighting had begun at Hanover Junction, the operator having left as he wrote the despatch.

A great battle must be fought to day then on the ground directly South of the N. Anna extending from Jericho Ford to beyond the Junction. I cannot but think that Lee is as well prepared to fight now as he ever will be. He is nearly as strong as when he breasted the first shock of battle at Wilderness, having been reinforced by six brigades from here, & by Breckinridges division from the valley, they having joined him after defeating Sigel at New Market. I suppose Lee's strength to be 60,000. Grant may still be able to muster 85,000 to 90,000 men if the reports of his original strength are not exaggerated. We have therefore reduced the disparity of numbers very greatly, and ought to hope for Grants defeat, without presumption. The rapidity of his movements indicates strength and confidence. To-day or to-morrow will tell the tale of defeat to us, or of disaster and ruin to him. We can still fall back upon our intrenchments; but Grant is irretrievably ruined if defeated. He has never before ventured so far from his gunboats. It is said our iron-clads are getting out thro' the obstructions. I fear they will never get back again.

Johnston verifies all our predictions of him. He is falling back just as fast as his legs can carry him. As I did him wrong in underestimating the strength of the force in front of him, I hope he will so vindicate himself still further by beating them in spite of our predictions. He is falling back behind the Chattahoochie [Chattahoochee], and will I fear give up Atlanta. The Chattahoochie can be "flanked" as well as any position he has held, and it is this process which is driving him back. Where he will stop heaven only knows.

May 26, [1864]   No fighting seems to have occurred yesterday. Grant pauses before he trusts himself beyond the North Anna. He does well to collect his strength before the perilous advance, from which I hope he is never to return without a thorough defeat, for defeated he is already, if a General who makes an unsuccessful attack & recoils from his adversary can be said to be defeated. Our position appears to be behind the North Anna immediately in front of Hanover Junction. Gen Lee is understood to have left bridges & boats on the N. A. after crossing it. This may have given Grant pause, tho' a part of his army is understood to have crossed. No definite news of Johnston's position. The Atlanta papers continue to assert that he is "master of the situation," a meaningless phrase copied from Yankee papers. A week ago the new iron clad <u>Raleigh</u> crossed the bar at Wilmington & drove off the blockaders without however doing any mischief. In returning she got aground inside and is lost. Such is the fate of the Navy under its present administration. Our three iron clads here are now below the obstructions. I fear they will next be lost tho' care will I think be taken not to venture down too far.

May 27, [1864]   Skirmishing yesterday only at Hanover Junction, and some artillery firing. Reinforcements are still going forward to Gen. Lee. No doubt both sides are preparing for the final struggle. God grant us success. Defeat will indeed be woe to us! According to accounts from Atlanta Gen. Johnston's position is not a bad one, & all there feel confident of success yet in that campaign, unpromising as its beginning is.

A heavy battery is to be placed in position at Howletts farm, below Drurys Bluff with a view of annoying the enemys shipping. Two 8 inch rifles (one captured) are to be placed in position, & 5 ten inch columbiads. The body of Lt Taft has been with us since last Wednesday, & leaves to-day for Charleston in charge of his brother Walter. His grief last night at closing the box containing the metal coffin, which has been lying in my little <u>study</u>, was very touching, my wife says. Yesterday I heard of the somewhat unexpected death of my old friend and [West Point] classmate Major Smith Stansbury. He died at Halifax, N. S. on the 26th. He & I were always side by side in our classes, & I had hoped much from his assistance in this war. His mind was of the highest order.

May 27, Evening, [1864]   Grant is known to have recrossed such of his troops as were South of the North Anna, and to be crossing the Pamunky at Hanover town. Lee is making corresponding changes and was at Ashland this morning. Whether he will strike Grant between the Chickahomina [Chickahominy] and the Pamunky remains to be seen. Such was doubtless his intention, but he may have reconsidered it & conclude to occupy the lines this Side of the C. No official information from Johnston. Bragg is bitterly assaulted in two Journals this morning, without much harm done. I walked up to Capitol Square this evening where the "Cadets" of the Lexington School were being reviewed by Gen. Bragg. They moved very well. A flag was presented by Govr Smith, & a speech made to them by Mr. [Thomas S.] Bocock [of Va.] in presenting the resolution of thanks passed by Congress.

May 29, [1864]   Gen Lee was yesterday at Atlee's Station on the Central R.R. Grants position was not exactly known. He was supposed to be bearing toward West Point, perhaps facilitating a junction with Butler, who it was said yesterday was striking his tents. If so our battery at Howletts will be too late. No official news from Johnston. From the

Red River we hear that Banks has escaped with most of his army and fleet. The latter was Saved by building a dam across the river below the falls & then raising the water so that the vessels could float out over the rapids where they had been caught by the low water. If our boats had been so caught, we should simply have blown them up.

Gold has risen at New York to 186. When Grant began his movements it was 171. The weather is quite cool enough for a little fire. Provisions are coming in somewhat more freely. Trains laden with corn are constantly arriving. The fear of Starvation has therefore nearly subsided. Four vessels have arrived thro' the blockade at W[ilmington].

June 1, [1864]   I have been quite indisposed for the past three days.

The army is now in position from about Atlee's Station on the left to Cold Harbor on the right. The enemy's line extends from the Central Road to Dispatch Station on the York River. Heavy firing was going on this morning, and a general engagement may be bro't on any day, or any hour. Gen. Lee has been quite indisposed with bilious dysentery, but is able to be out again. Gen. Breckinridge appears to be rising in favor as a dashing commander. A. P. Hill does not sustain himself. Early is looked upon as one of the best leaders.

Yesterday there appears to have been an assault on the enemy's lines at Bethesda Church in which we lost heavily—four field officers killed & wounded—three mortally. It was Pegram's brigade led by Col. [Edward] Willis which suffered so seriously. Some prisoners were taken by us. Beauregard's forces have been moved chiefly to the north-Side[,] Butler having drawn off most if not all of his forces, probably to West Point. No news of interest from Johnston who Still appears to maintain his position west of Marietta [Ga.].

11 P.M. No general engagement to-day beyond the Chickahominy, despite appearances to the contrary. Hugh went out toward Atlee's Station with a portion of his regiment. So many cavalry officers have been killed in the last few fights that we parted from him with a feeling of gloom. I hope all will turn out well with him. Beauregard is still on the Southside confronting Butler tho' rumor had assigned him to Gen. Lee.

June 2d, [1864]   There was some fighting yesterday between McLaws and Anderson's Divisions and the enemy on the right; and Breckinridge on the left, the latter capturing 150 prisoners. The general engagement Still appears to be delayed however; tho' from the circumstances that the local forces are called out & sent to Bottom's Bridge, I judge the final dispositions are made. Should the day be favorable we may hear the roar of artillery in the morning. Our iron-clads have as yet made nothing out of their passage thro' the obstructions. They appear to treat the enemy with distant respect. It has been raining freely since 5 P.M.

June 4, [1864]   Rode out to the battle fields yesterday afternoon, returning about 9 P.M. A heavy fight had taken place in the forenoon and a field to the front was covered with dead Yankees. Our casualties were very small amounting to but two in one of the brigades engaged. We (Major Merlin & myself) had scant time for observation as the enemy's sharpshooters, about 700 yds distant were evidently taking aim at us, & several balls struck close by. Met A. P. Hill as we were coming away. Said he was arranging for a little expedition to drive the enemy from a position. We heard sharp firing after we got 6 or 7 miles away doubtless this expedition. Our troops were lying behind triple lines of breastworks.

They have acquired quite a respect for this sort of intrenchment, & work like beavers when they take up a new position. They began the war with a contempt for the Spade, but now thoroughly believe in it. They use bayonets tin pans, & even I am told split their tin canteens to get a utensil that will throw up earth. Met Gen. Lee near the field, with the President. The General kindly stopped & beckoned me to him, cautioning me not to go near the lines as I might be shot, with my blue cape, by either side—would rather he added in half jocular way, that I would return & send him ammunition. I agreed to send him a Whitworth gun which I did as soon as I got back. All were in excellent Spirits, and agreed that the Yankee loss that morning must have been enormous. The weather is beautiful, clear & not too warm—nights cool.

It is Minnie's birth day—5 years old. I have just given her a little book like this & wrote her name "Christine Amelia" on it, which seems to make her quite as happy as an elaborate present.

June 5, [1864]   There has been a good deal of rain, tho' not very violent, and military operations have been somewhat Slack. There is a report that a portion of Breckinridges line was broken thro' last night & that we lost a good many men. I have not been able to get anything authentic.

The "Herald" of the 1st has a ridiculous report from Butler saying that a meeting had been held in this city, at which the giving up or burning of the city was discussed—that the Mayor (Mr. [Joseph] Mayo) was in favor of surrendering & had in consequence been arrested & thrown into Castle Thunder! The enemy appears to be established on the Chickahominy opposite Bottom's bridge within sharpshooting distance of our troops on this side.

June 6, [1864]   The morning is beautiful, would it were as peaceful as it is lovely. What have we done that the Almighty should scourge us with such a war, so relentless and so repugnant. There was apparently no fighting yesterday. Grant seems inclined to try a passage of the Chickahominy at Bottom's bridge. What good that would do him is the question. It brings him further from instead of nearer to Richmond. He is now as near as he ever will be, I trust. Getting over to Butler & taking Petersburgh from below City Point might annoy us, but would hardly advance his object. I think he is at his wit's end.

June 7, [1864] The report is that Grant has withdrawn his forces from our left front. It is not known what his movements are but suspected to be to the South Side at Some of the lower bridges over the Chickahominy.

The painful news of the defeat & death of Gen. W. E. Jones [near Piedmont, Va.] was rec'd yesterday. He met Hunter's forces at Mount Hope about 7 miles from Staunton & fell early in the fight. Staunton appears to be in possession of the enemy, & it is rumored they are also at Lexington. Jones was a graduate of the Class of '48 & a very good cavalry officer. He was known as Grumble Jones from his grumbling disposition & manner. Breckinridge probably goes to the valley in command to-day. He was bruised by a cannon ball which passed thro' his home. I saw the President yesterday in reference to a bill for increasing the number of Ord Officers. He objected to a proviso in the bill which gave preference in the appointments to persons already acting as officers in the field. He construed this into an interference with Executive prerogative, and showed more sensitiveness than seemed becoming to appt of officers of such inferior grades. The capture of the U.S Steamer Water Witch near Savannah by boarding seems a bold & brilliant affair. We lost the Lieut ([Thomas] Pelot) in command & three men killed.

June 9, [1864] I have been suffering greatly from neuralgia in the face for some days, and yesterday suffered intensely, until relieved by a dose of opium & quinine. This gave me pleasant dreams or hallucinations all night long. No news from any direction. Grant apparently does nothing. Breckinridge is opposing the further advances of the enemy at Meacham's River. Affairs look to me more and more critical. I cannot see where further re-inforcements are to come from. Lee is waiting and Grant is gathering strength here. The same appears to be the condition of things at Atlanta. Johnston is waiting while Sherman is receiving re-inforcements. What the issue will be is in God's hands—nothing but an unforeseen event can it seems to me save us from the gradually rising strength of our opponents; or rather from the defeats our waning strength must entail. Our losses here all told are about 25,000 men killed wounded & captured, in Lee's army alone & perhaps 5000 on the South side. Where can we supply such a waste of men? We can hold out in all else. Lee's strength altogether is about 5000 less than when he first met Grant at the Wilderness, say 50,000 infantry his cavalry is now larger.

Monday, June 13, [1864] I have suffered severely with face-ache since Thursday. It left me suddenly last night but the medicine I have taken makes me feel badly. There is no change in Gen. Lee's Situation. The enemy attacked Petersburgh on Friday in some force, & were finally repulsed. The militia lost about 10 killed or mortally wounded, & about 27 wounded. They fought very staunchly, but were overpowered before the re-inforcements arrived. It is said their stubborn resistance saved the town.

The battle at New Hope [Church in Ga.] was a severe disaster to us, resulting in the loss of some 1500 in killed wounded & captured, & in the capture of a great many of our sick and wounded at Staunton, which was entered by Hunter on Monday last. He was joined here by Crook & Averell, making an aggregate force of about 14000. The loss of the battle at New Hope is attributed to the giving way of the 60th Va. Regt. Gen. Jones is said to have lost his life in the attempt to rally them. The troops then fell back to Waynesboro, saving all their artillery & trains. The enemys advance is said to be within 25 miles of Lynchburgh, & to be in possession of Lexington.

The news from the north is that Lincoln & Andrew Johnson were nominated at Baltimore by the [Republican] convention which met on the 7th, and that gold was 194½ on the 8th, a very satisfactory commentary.

VII

"Can we hold out much longer?"

Wednesday June 15, [1864]   We heard yesterday of the wounding of Hugh [Aiken] (comdg 6th S. C. Cavalry) at the fight at Louisa C. H. on Saturday. He was shot thro' the left breast, the ball coming out at the edge of the Shoulder blade. After being placed in an ambulance the train was captured by a dash of a yankee brigade in the rear of Gen. [Wade] Hampton. After being four or five hours in possession of the enemy, he was again recaptured by the cavalry of Fitz Lee, and is now at the house of Mr. Hunter at Louisa doing quite well. Saw to-day Capt. Gregg of his regt who was shot thro' the right arm at the same time & also captured & re-captured.

Hampton has whipped Sheridan pretty thoroughly and sent him over to Fredericksburgh. Early with Ewell's Division is on his way to Washington via the valley. What effect this will have on Grant remains to be seen. Grant has left his lines at Cold Harbor, crossed the Chickahominy with part of his forces at Long Bridge, & gone to Westover, perhaps. Some part of his force appears to have gone to embark at the White House. Lynchburgh is threatened by a portion of Hunter's forces; & a small body of cavalry has crossed the James, & burned the bridge at Concord on the South side R.R. Gen. Lawton, Qr. M. Genl & his wife, Mrs. Jones, Dr. Richardson, & Gen Elzey spent the evening here & took tea.

Congress adjourned yesterday. The news of Gen Polks being killed by a cannon ball yesterday was in the papers this morning. He was a brave Christian Soldier, beloved by his troops. Gen Ewell is placed in command of Richmond vice Ransom sent to command the cavalry in the valley. It is a practical <u>retirement</u> of the maimed old soldier, to which he must submit on account of his infirmities. He does so sorrowfully & with an ill grace.

Forrest's victory [Brice's Crossroads] over [Col. B. H.] Grierson at Tishomingo creek near Baldwin [Baldwyn, on the Mobile & Ohio Railroad between Tupelo and Corinth] is a complete one. He seems to have utterly destroyed the enemy's column [commanded by Gen. Samuel D. Sturgis], & was Still pursuing it relentlessly.

June 16, [1864]   Hugh telegraphs that he is better. His brother Gus [Augustus Milton Aiken] & his servant Perry left last evening & have reached him I hope by this time (10 P.M.[)]

The news from Petersburg is unfavorable, the enemy having captured a portion of the entrenchments, & some pieces of Sturdivant's battery. I hope Gen. Lee will be able to correct this very soon. It will not do to lose Petersburgh.

A Mr. Austin, an English merchant spent the evening. Mrs. Commodore [French] Forrest called. They have lost all their wealth & can hardly get their daily bread it seems. It is sad to see people plunged into utter destitution, from a state of entire affluence. Three years ago this lady did not know what it was to want money, or any thing that money could buy. Now she is dependent on a portion of her son's pay. He is in the navy, & gets 100 dollars a month, & being abroad draws his pay in gold. Of this he gives his mother one half, worth eight or nine hundred per month.

June 19, [1864]   Mary [Gayle Aiken] arrived Friday evey. Hugh is improving. She proposes joining him to-morrow. Mrs. Capt Adams is here with us—her husband is also wounded. She is a niece of [Amelia's late brother-in-law] Dr. [William B.] Crawford(?)

No fighting at Petersburgh yesterday nor to-day, a thousand wild rumors to the contrary, one of which was that a great battle had been fought there with the loss of 5000 on ours & 25000 on the Yankee side! Such rumors prevail mostly on Sundays.

Thursday June 23d, [1864]   Yesterday our right wing attacked the left of the enemy, captured 1600 prisoners, some colors & 4 guns. The enemy have thrown a few shells into the suburbs of Petersburgh. Hunter is retreating toward Western Virginia with Early in pursuit. Not much damage has been or is likely to be done to him. Our forces are inadequate to punish him. Gen. & Dr. [William Edward] Aiken [another of Hugh's brothers] came to-day from Hugh. Mary went up with the Dr. on Monday. He is doing well. The wound is close by the jugular vein, & the ball came out 8 inches down by the back bone, Hugh having been in a stooping posture when shot. Col [John W.] Mallet [Superintendent of Confederate Ordnance Laboratories], who has been staying with us a few days, left us this evening. I am taking daily rides hoping to restore my strength which is somewhat shaken.

June 24, [1864]   The news from Petersburg is still good. The party which occupied the Weldon R.R. below P. was driven off and 500 prisoners captured. The enemy took possession of Burkeville last night, but have been dislodged after doing some damage. They took it is said the direction of the high Bridge on the S. Side road. Willie & I saw the prisoners marched thro' town this morning, a dirty Set.

June 26, [1864]   The enemy have cut the Danville Road in various places, & tho' they have been driven from the Weldon Road below Petersburgh, their proximity to that Road renders it practically valueless to us. We are thus for the present without communication with the South. Fortunately we are provided with meat for 40 days, and with the wheat which we shall soon get from Central Va. many will laugh at Grants efforts at a "Siege" as he terms it.

Hampton attacked the enemy's cavalry (Sheridan) near Charles city C. H. yesterday & drove it from its position with loss. Gen. Lee speaks of it as a very handsome affair. Our loss in the attack by Hagood on Friday (probably a reconnaissance) on the City Point Road is stated by Gen. Lee at 93 killed & wounded & 207 (?) missing. Hunter appears to have disappeared into Western Virginia, with some loss of artillery & wagons. The Yankees now systematically shoot their worn down horses. Can anything be more diabolical than thus to treat these noble animals?

This is the hottest day we have yet had.

June 30, [1864]   No striking military events have occurred if we except that Johnston telegraphs he repulsed a general attack of the enemy with "supposed" heavy loss. There are no particulars & I have little confidence in the State of affairs in that quarter. I fully expect to hear of his retreat behind Atlanta probably in the direction of West Point. Early is at Staunton & down the valley his artillery having been heard of at Port Republic. I hope another invasion of Maryland is not contemplated, yet there is no other explanation of this movement. The raiders have left the line of the [Richmond and] Danville R.R. & made their way back to Grant's main body. They were decidedly repulsed at the Staunton River bridge by the "Reserve" forces stationed there. Our friends the two Aikens & Col Mallet left yesterday by way of Petersburgh for the South. Gold has certainly risen to 244 & some say is selling at 5 premium in Washington (5 dollars in "greenbacks" for 1 in gold).

July 1, [18]64 15 minutes A.M   It is after midnight and Minnie & I are sitting up waiting for Hugh & Mary who started from Louisa C. H. on the Central Road. Something has doubtless delayed the train which was due at 6 P.M. There is good news from below Petersburgh where the returning raiders were attacked & defeated with heavy loss of prisoners, horses, & wagons. It is surmised that Grant is preparing a grand bombardment of Petersburg for the 4th of July.

Mr. Memminger Secy of Treasy resigned his post a few days ago, but continues on duty until his successor is appointed. No name is yet mentioned. The President sent for me day before yesterday to show me a big sword made at Columbia S. C & sent to him. He seemed to think highly of it, tho' I objected to its length. He opened the conversation by saying as he took the sword to hand it to me "Col. I find my conversations with you have more reason & less politics than any others". He likes to talk of matters purely military, especially about guns &c which he used to pay much attention to as Secy of War under Mr. Pierce. A little girl was born to him day before yesterday.

I am 46 years old to-day. I may still live to see the country recover from the effects of this terrible war, if it should cease soon.

July 3d [1864]   The number of prisoners taken below Petersburg is ascertained thus far at about 1000, and 700 darkeys recaptured. The yankee cavalry seems dispersed over the country in bad plight, giving itself up in squads. Little mercy is shown to them by our cavalry—they are shot down wherever found. A Confederate naval officer coming from Wilmington to Richmond was surrounded by them, & seeing his Shoulder Straps, drew their revolvers shouting "Kill him. Kill him—no prisoners" & but for the negro boys with him they would have fired upon him. Our people are exasperated to the last degree by the burning, plundering, & mal-treatment inflicted by these marauding Scoundrels. Tomorrow (4th) will be Grants great day and if he does nothing he will inflict great disappointment on his admirers. Only one or two houses have thus far been burned in Petersburg. The [Richmond and] Danville R.R. has been destroyed for about 28 miles beyond Burkeville, & it will take three weeks to repair it say until the 20th of July. In the meantime we have very little corn to live on. Wagon trains will no doubt be established at the break. Hugh arrived last evening, in pretty good condition.

July 7, [1864]   No fighting at Petersburg. It is reported that Early met Pope & Sigel at Martinsburg, & captured 1200 prisoners. Would that we could hear of no more captures. The war has now assumed that phase in which no mercy can be shown to the enemy. He burns, robs, murders, & ravishes & this is to be met only by killing all. Johnston has I fear fallen behind the Chattahoochee [River] just as I surmised long ago. Will he fight at last? I do not expect it, & yet I do not see how he can give up Atlanta without a fight—a general action. An expedition is it seems in preparation at Wilmington looking to the liberation of the prisoners at Point Lookout. I know nothing of it, except what I hear, but was directed to send 2000 Stand of arms there at once. It seems however impossible to keep State Secrets & the expedition is talked of on the Streets. We had just a sprinkling of rain to-day after five weeks of total drought. There was scarce enough to lay the dust. Hugh is evidently getting stronger daily. The resignation of [Salmon P.] Chase, the Yankee Secy of Treasy, & the rise of gold to over 250 are the chief subjects of interest in the northern papers.

July 10, Sunday [1864]   The drought still continues & the weather is very warm. To-night there is a strong breeze from the South which may eventually blow up a rain.

Bad news from beyond the Sea. The Alabama was sunk by the Kearsage after a combat of 1 h. 40 m., on the 19th of June. Capt. [Raphael] Semmes & most of the officers and crew were picked up by an English yacht, the Grayhound [*Deerhound*], which carried them to Southampton. The fight took place off Cherbourg. News from the North of the 6th and 7th places gold at 259. The new Yankee Secy of Treasy, [William P.] Fessenden [of Me.] had been installed. The progress of Early created some alarm, & troops for 100 days were called out in Penn, New York & Mass. He was in possession of the Balt. & Ohio R.R. from a few miles East of Cumberland to below Harpers Ferry, & had captured a good deal of property & stores.

At Charleston the Yankees made an attack on James Island (Fort Johnson) on the 3d of July & were repulsed with the loss of 5 to 6 hundred killed wounded & captured. From Mobile Gen. [Dabney H.] Maury telegraphs that he is threatened with an attack. The enemy appears to have advanced upon Jackson from Vicksburgh & to have occupied it, but at last accounts were retiring upon their lines. At Petersburgh the enemy is using mortars with effect upon the city, and burning a good many houses. A few days ago a party landed at the fine plantation of Curls Neck and destroyed by fire the entire crop of wheat in the fields.

July 13, [1864]   It is reported that Gen. Lee has gone to Georgia. Gen. Bragg has certainly gone. Everybody has at last come to the conclusion that Johnston has retreated far enough. Mr. [D. H.] Hill is I understand here on the mission of getting additional troops (cavalry) to operate on the communications of Gen. Sherman, as the only means of saving Atlanta, & what is to be done must be done quickly, they say. He wants the forces of Gen. S. D. Lee (Lt. Genl) brot over from Miss. for this purpose. The news from the North to the 9th shows great excitement over the appearance of Early's columns on the Potomac. They are unable to decide whether there are 5000 or 35,000 men there. Our forces seem to have advanced into the skirts of Pa.

Nothing further heard of the column reported by Maury as marching upon Mobile from N. O. The enemy do not appear to make any impression on Charleston or its defences. An expedition to liberate the prisoners at Point Lookout has been on foot at Wilmington for some ten days past. The removal of the prisoners to Elmira, N. Y. renders that prospect abortive. Early movements alarmed the enemy on this point. It rained briskly several hours day before yesterday but the earth was so baked that it appears to have done little good.

The death of poor Capt. Walter Wynne, at Petersburg of a wound in the knee reached us last Evening. Amelia knew him as a boy, & his Sisters. It is a sad thing. His wife is on the way here but had not arrived at the date of his death.

July 14, [1864]   News to the 11th from the north announces the defeat of their own forces at [the] Monocacy [River near Frederick, Md.] on the 9th, with the capture of Gen [Erastus B.] Tyler & Col. [William] Seward. Our troops seem to be moving toward Baltimore. It is Still unknown here whether or no Gen. Lee has gone to Atlanta. I presume he has not, as such a thing could hardly be kept secret, he being too well known personally along the line of Rail Roads. In Miss. our forces on the 11th were at Pontotoc [west of Tupelo], while the enemy was [to the north] at New Albany & moving forward Slowly. A battle has probably occurred of which we shall hear soon. At Charleston various attacks of the enemy on John's & James Island have been repulsed.

The weather continues warm & the drought destroys our gardens, the rains of Monday having been of no great extent. Partial rains are however occurring about us which will keep the corn from burning up.

Major [Norman S.] Walker, Gen. Randolph Mr. J. Alfred Jones, and Bayne dined with us yesterday.

July 17, [1864]   Early defeated the enemy at [the] Monocacy [River] and tho appears to have advanced upon Washington, whether with a view to make a dash upon it or simply to frighten it is not known. He has however again withdrawn, & on Tuesday last was on the retreat. Doubtless he is by this time behind the Potomac. The only good he has done is to arouse the waning enthusiasm at the North & draw a few additional recruits to their Standard. He will lose a good many stragglers on his way back to the valley.

S. D. Lee seems to have attacked the enemy in position at Tupelo [Miss.], & been repulsed. He says it was a drawn fight.

Took a long ride last evening out by the Brooke road to the intermediate lines, along those to Grove Road, & back by that about 12 or 13 miles. Major Pierson, from Europe, & Col. McLean Qrms. Dept spent the evening. Major P. is a Frenchman in our Service who has served bravely for some time in the Artillery. He has been at home. The drought still continues, the little rain a week ago having done no perceptible good.

July 19, [1864]   Johnston has been relieved of his command and Hood placed in charge of the Army [in the West]. This of course means fighting, and a battle must soon be the result. Gen. J will doubtless have a strong party who will condemn his removal. Rumors have been rife for several days that Grant is dead, believed by many but hardly true. A slow rain to-day has done a great deal of good, & the clouds look as if it might continue.

July 22, [1864]   A fight took place day before yesterday on the Chattahoochee in which we were the assailants, & as the despatch says drove the enemy to their breastworks. An attack was made on Wheeler's Cavalry & repulsed. A despatch I rec'd from Columbus [Ga.] says that place is threatened by a heavy force and the Ordn Stores and machinery were being sent away from there. So after having run to Columbus from Baton Rouge, we have run from Columbus to some other place. Too much running, & too little fighting, Gen. Joe Johnston.

P.M. A despatch from Gen Hood announces an attack on Gen. Cleburnes division of Hardee's corps, and on Wheeler's Cavalry on the right, & that the attack was handsomely repulsed. Col [Samuel] Adams 33d Ala. killed. In the previous attack Gen. [Clement H.] Stevens (of Charleston) was mortally wounded. People are I think generally satisfied with the removal of Gen. Johnston. They have praised him, & waited for him to fight until he has lost all of Georgia, and they have gotten tired of him. Nevertheless if Hood fights & is victorious there will be plenty who will exclaim "behold the fruits of Johnston's strategy", while if he is defeated these people will cry "see the fruits of the removal of Johnston!" The Administration will gain nothing in the estimation of such in either case. It is a pity President Davis did not act earlier on his own judgment which has always been adverse to Johnston. His tardy action was at last induced by the action of distinguished Georgians represented by Senator [Benjamin H.] Hill, who came on here after a full interview with Gen J. & urged a change of commanders, having ascertained to his entire satisfaction that Johnston would not fight even for Atlanta but would continue to retrograde under the flanking movements of Sherman.

July 23, [1864]   A despatch from Gen Hood states that the enemy attacked yesterday and were repulsed after which our troops assumed the offensive. Gen Hardee on the right moved around the enemy's left to his rear, capturing 1500 prisoners and 16 guns. Gen [Benjamin F.] Cheatham in the centre captured 500 prisoners and six guns. 5 stands of colors also captured. Gen Wheeler drove the enemys cavalry back at Decatur [Ala.]. We have lost Maj. Gen. W. H. T. Walker killed and Brig. Genl* Smith (?) [Gen. S. R.] Gist and [Gen. Hugh W.] Mercer* wounded. Our

---

*errors of the despatches

loss is I fear heavy. The success appears to have been decided. Hardee is represented in a press despatch as being still upon the enemy's flanks and rear. [Gen. James B.] McPherson is reported killed, by yankee prisoners.

At Petersburgh the enemy is reported moving across the Appomattox; and our "local" forces are ordered to hold themselves in readiness.

News from the north places gold at 263, & the tone of the papers is desponding.

In the valley our forces are said to have defeated the enemy at Snicker's Gap, [Va.] & to have driven him across the Shenandoah [River], we holding Winchester. On the whole the atmosphere brightens, but we cannot predict what a day may bring forth.

July 26, [1864]   The "Situation" here appears to be unchanged except that the enemy has thrown some troops to the North bank of the River at Deep Bottom. A Yankee regiment was run over by our troops yesterday and entirely broken up, but we only succeeded in securing 48 prisoners. Heavy firing of artillery continues at Petersburg with great waste of ammunition, no doubt unavoidable. From Atlanta Hood corrects his first despatch & now reports 13 in place of 22 guns and 18 stands of Colors in place of 5. Gen Mercer not wounded. The enemy is now throwing occasional shells into Atlanta, and appears to have gotten to the R.R. at Stone Mtn. He has also broken up say twenty miles of the West Pt & Monty [Montgomery] R.R. and is at Opelika [Ala.]. This party it is said is directing its course toward Andersonville [prison in Georgia] to release the prisoners there (now 30,000). There is a despatch to-night from Gen. Lee saying that Early had attacked Crook at Kernstown & routed him driving him beyond Winchester. The community is a good deal stirred at the publication from Yankee Sources of the correspondence between Messrs Holcombe Clay & Geo. Saunders on the one side & [Horace] Greel[e]y [editor of the New York *Tribune*] & Lincoln on the other, relative to peace. It is not flattering to us.

July 28, [1864]   A disgraceful affair occurred yesterday morning at 7 o'clock below Chaffin's Farm. The Yankees attacked a battery of 20 pds Parrott guns and captured it, our supports flying without firing a gun, and yet these supports were [Gen. Joseph B.] Kershaw's brigade, some of the best in Service. They were flanked it Seems on their left and at once ran, leaving the battery (Rockbridge Artillery) to its fate. The Captain fired he told me double canister, & at last saved his caissons and limbers with all the horses. The President sent for me yesterday to ask me something about the number of men that could be spared to go out to the trenches without suspending work. He read me an extract from a letter written by a high French military authority calling attention to the use of rockets, against shipping & cavalry. He is looking quite well, but is growing not only gray but white with his cares.

July 28, [1864] The enemy appears to have crossed to the north side of the James in force & to threaten us from there. The local forces were called out to-day, it being reported that cavalry had moved toward our left, & might threaten the city from the north east. It appears probable that we shall soon hear of forces from the Trans-Miss. having crossed over into Tenn. to operate on Sherman's communications there. Little Rock is undoubtedly now in our possession and Arkansas is redeemed. Spent the evening at Major [John] Ellicotts, who has a charming wife, & who gave a pleasant supper (tea or coffee). Dr. [James B.] McCaw [head of the Chimborazo Military Hospital in Richmond] & wife there. This morning Mr. [William] Aubrey [military storekeeper], Dr. Spotswood, Col. Aiken, & Bayne breakfasted with us. A very nice breakfast of one chicken and tomato omelette! The weather is quite warm but the breeze good. We need rain again.

July 31, Sunday [1864] Grant it appears sprung a mine under one of our batteries at Petersburgh yesterday, & did some damage, but failed to break our lines. The enemy were it seems re-crossing to the South Side & we were yesterday following the movement. A fight of some Severity appears to have been going on at Atlanta on the 27th, as it is reported from Macon on the 28th, yet we have no definite or official news concerning it. [Gen. Alexander P.] Stewart & Wheeler were both said to be wounded. Went to Drury's Bluff yesterday to see the examination of the midshipmen on the Patrick Henry [[Yorktown]]. There were about 30. The exm was very cursory in navigation, firing making sail & broadsword exercise. The little "Squib" torpedo boat passed us. She is only about 45 feet long, & makes about 9 miles. This is the little boat used against the Minnesota. Others of the Same Sort are building. Lt. [William H.] Parker commands the Patrick Henry. Mr. [Lt. William B.] Hall is her first officer.

P.M. Good news from Petersburg. In repelling the attack of the enemy after firing their mine, an assault appears to have ensued which resulted in the capture of 850 privates & 75 commissioned officers including Gen. [William F.] Bartlett & his Staff—12 Stands of Colors & the recapture of the guns which had been taken with the position. 500 dead Yankees were left on the Spot. Gen Mahone's division appears to have done the work. The enemy seem to have returned chiefly to the South Side. Grant is certainly at his wits' end, & is simply moving his men about idly & without plan. No good news yet from Georgia.

Aug 3d, [1864] The news from Georgia yesterday was cheering. [Gen. George] Stoneman [U.S.A.] with 500 of his raiding cavalry were captured by Gen. [Alfred] Iverson not far from Macon & bro't into that city. They were first repulsed from Macon by the "Reserves" & in retreating were attacked & routed by Gen. I. The remainder of the command (originally 2800) were dispersed thro' the country. So that party has, as the saying is "come to grief". In an attack on the 27th on our left [Gen. Alexander P.] Stewart & [Gen. William W.] Loring were wounded, & the day before Gen. Rector. Our losses have been quite heavy, as I see the enemy reports the arrival of over a thousand prisoners at Louisville— in the operations of the 19th to the 22d of July. A bad accident occurred in the Armory close by yesterday. An armorer (Smoot) drawing one of the guns to be repaired toward him it exploded & the ball passed thro' the ankle joint. In two hours afterward his leg was cut off some distance above the joint. He is lying in the office at the other end of this building & Mamma looks after him occasionally & sends him his meals. It is a sad affair to this poor working man. His wife is some distance in the country.

Aug 6, [1864]   Nothing new of Special interest. The burning of Chambersburgh [Pa.] by Early gives intense satisfaction. Gen. Mc-Causland seems to have been in command of the troops who did the deed—a very good one. It is stated in the papers this morning that the officers recently placed under fire in Charleston, & at Morris Island have been exchanged, a good solution of an awkward move. Gen. Johnston is said to be in town—for what purpose is not known.

Aug 7, [1864]   The news of the destruction of our fleet at Mobile creates no surprise, nothing but disaster comes from that unfortunate branch of the service. The news which is meagre represents that we have lost three iron clads—one captured by the enemy (the Tennessee) one sunk & one blown up. What effect this will have toward the capture of Mobile remains to be seen—not much, I think—tho I fear it will lead to the reduction of Forts Morgan and Gaines [near Mobile]. Beauregard it seems sprung a mine yesterday (or evening before) under some works of the enemy, blowing up their mines, & doing some damage. I hope it may be so, but I haven't much faith in the reports. Troops were moving from Petersburgh thro town yesterday, destination unknown.

Aug 8, [1864]   Admiral Buchanan has it seems lost a leg and been captured. The Tennessee and Selma are captured—the Gaines is ashore & the Morgan alone escaped. The first is alone Iron clad. The whole of Longstreets com and Fitz Lee's cavalry are said to have moved north-ward. I doubt whether more than a Division and the Cavalry have yet gone. It is probable that Grant too is sending off troops. The northern papers it is Said announce the removal of Meade and the appointment of Hooker, on account of the disaster of Saturday (the mine). The drought still continues to the total destruction I fear of all crops especially of our vegetables. I omitted to note heretofore the accession to our domestic establishment of a good milch cow. She was taken out of her Stable at Petersburgh under fire. She adds greatly to the good living of the children, & of us all.

Aug 10, [1864] The news from Mobile continues decidedly bad. Fort Gaines appears to have been shamefully surrendered by its commander Lt. Col. Chas Anderson with its garrison of 600 men. It could have held out for three months, & was provisioned for six. This is indeed shameful. There are rumors of the capture of a considerable portion of [Gen.] Bradley Johnson & McCauslands comds.

A portion of the fifty exchanged officers from Charleston arrived a few days ago. These officers were the ones sent by the enemy to be placed on Morris Island as retaliation for placing 50 of theirs in Charleston. For a weak measure it has turned out very well. Mary is quite ailing & we begin to feel anxious about her condition. [Mary was pregnant.] Hugh's wound is nearly well, but he is far from Strong. No rain yet. Willie & I took a bath in the river last evening.

Aug 12, [1864] The yankees claim that they surprised and captured a portion of McCausland & Bradley Johnson's command at Romney, [Va.] with wagons & artillery. Some such thing happened I fear but not to the extent named. The explosion which was lately heard in the Yankee lines at Petersburg seems to have been an explosion of powder & Shells at City Point—a great many employees killed & wounded. An Artillery officer just from Atlanta gives me a gloomy view of the situation. The probability is that the city must be evacuated, as the enemy is closing his lines about it. They extend from the river to near the Macon R.R. That once seriously endangered the city must of course be evacuated. There are no intelligible explanations of the surrender of Fort Gaines. Col. Anderson was it appears 2 years at West Pt. Saw yesterday one of the exchgd officers Gen. [James J.] Archer, but had no opportunity to talk with him.

Aug 14, [1864] The President sent for me yesterday to tell me about a report that the powder at Battery Danzler (Howletts Farm) had given very inferior ranges. He was reading to Mr. Mallory & Mr. Seddon a report from Gen. Lee that the yankees were at work digging a canal across Dutch Gap, and told Mr. M. with his usual clearness what would be the effect of the "cut-off" thus made viz: that the depth of water above will be diminished while below it will be increased. This he illustrated by citing instances of similar effects on the Miss. & referred to Gen. Bragg in proof of one where lands were reclaimed above the "cut-off". Having stated the general effect, he called Mr. Mallorys attention to the position of his iron-clads, asked him at what point above the Dutch Gap was the first bar, & whether his iron-clads might not be caught below it, unable to return, adding after discussing the matter "very well Mr. Mallory, forewarned is forearmed."

He then went on to discuss what could be done to interfere with the cutting of the canal. Talking to me of an officer (Col. L. M. Clarke of Mo.) who was at West Point with him he said—"He is a good conscientious man with abilities of various sort. He can draw, & has a fondness for machinery. He is out of position—has lost two sons—one at school, having been killed by a Dutch boy on account of his politics, the other in command of a battery in one of the battles in Mo. He has been sick & has had something like paralysis. He has now nothing to do tho' willing to do anything. I dislike to see such a man walking about trying to get into position, looking like a horse outside the lot at fodder time!" He then asked me whether I could do anything with him, & seemed relieved when I told him that I had appropriate duty. He spoke again of a long Sabre that Gen. Hampton wanted made for his cavalry, and remembered that on a previous occasion, he spoke of the armament of cavalry and said that if they had sabres they should not have guns, but be made to depend on the sabre. He referred to the "pistol carbine", the barrel of which was 12 inches long & had a movable stock, which he had adopted in the U.S. Service when Secy of War. He referred to it as "the old government," which somewhat attracted my attention. He tho't that if our cavalry were to depend on the sabre alone that they would then come to close quarters, & run off their antagonists who depend on their long range guns.

No news & no rain.

Aug 17, [1864] A sharp engagement took place yesterday on the Charles City road below White's tavern, in which the enemy were driven back. We lost Gen. [Victor J. B.] Girardey killed, & Gen. [John R.] Chambliss wounded and it is believed a prisoner. No details of our other losses seem to be known. It seems to have been a tolerably determined attempt of the enemy to break thro' our lines on the north side of James River. The day before we lost 4 8 inch howitzers which were in position to shell the enemy's pontoon bridge at Deep Bottom. The infantry supports appear to have been again at fault. These guns were in charge of Lt. Col Pemberton [formerly the general commanding Vicksburg]. Gen. G[irardey] was advanced from the grade of Capt. A.A.G. to that of Brigr. and commanded [Gen. Ambrose R.] Wrights Ga. Brigade. Our local forces were again called out yesterday in consequence of the proximity of the enemy. They go with reluctance, & only one-fourth were present last evening for the march. From Ga. there is nothing cheering. It is probable that Atlanta will be given up, & East Point held. A heavy force of the enemy under [Gen.] A. J. Smith appears to be advancing thro north Mississippi. Forrest has but 7000 men to hold them in check. He was last at Oxford. A division of the Trans-Miss. Army was to cross the River tomorrow. Its strength not over 500. We ought to have 12 or 15,000 men to operate on Sherman's communications in middle Tenn. Wheeler left Atlanta on the 10th to cut Sherman's communications—not yet heard from. The enemy appear to have come up pretty close to Mobile, but the city will be held at all hazards.

A good rain on Monday and cloudy & showery since.

Sunday Aug 21, [1864] Gen [A. P.] Hill attacked Warren's (5th) Corps on the R.R. South of Petersburgh and captured 24 to 2700 prisoners among them Gen. [Joseph] Hayes and some 60 com'd officers— this on Friday. On Saturday the attack was attempted to be renewed, but it was found that the enemy had massed their two Army Corps, and the attack was deferred. It is reported that a heavy fight has been going on to-day.

A despatch rec'd from Gen. Lee to-day states that Early attacked the enemy at Front Royal and captured two hundred prisoners the enemy retreating toward Harpers Ferry, burning the wheat in stacks and in the fields. A heavy force of the enemy appears to be advancing in Mississippi, and Gov. [Charles] Clarke [Clark] is assembling the Reserves. Urgent calls for arms there, which the break in the W.Pt. & Montgomery R.R. renders it difficult to get forward. The "Tallahassee", Capt. J Wood is doing excellent service capturing & burning the shipping of the enemy on the coast, as far up as New England. News from Northern papers show that Wheeler is operating on Sherman's communications at Dalton, breaking the R.R. & destroying supply trains.

Aug 24, [1864] The attack on the enemys position upon the Weldon [Rail] Road, on Sunday was a decided failure. Our troops were not up, the crossing back from this side not having been effected until Monday morning. The enemy is now firmly established on & across the Weldon Road his left extending to over a mile to the west of it. This is a serious advantage gained by him. Our loss was not very heavy, & chiefly in Hagood's brigade. This from being one of the largest brigades when it came from S. C. here about the 1st of May is now reduced to not many hundreds. No news of interest from Mobile since the surrender of Fort Gaines. The Yankee papers report that Farragut had ordered an attack on Fort Morgan on a certain morning, but it does not appear to have been made. They say that Gen. [Gordon] Granger has invaded Fort M. on the land side. This is not reported from Mobile. In the valley nothing has been heard of Sheridan since his retreat down the valley before Early. The cavalry there is very inferior & should be thoroughly re-organized. From the Mississippi we hear that Dick Taylor has suspended the movement to this side of the River in consequence of the desertions from his ranks. His troops will not serve on this side if they can help it. If we get no troops from Trans-Miss the plan of operations for the relief of Hood will be seriously interfered with.

A flag of truce on Monday bore I hope to the north the papers necessary for the exchange of Dick, so that he <u>may</u> be among us in a short time. The yellow fever is making havoc at Bermuda. Several of our clerks have died there & others are down with the fever.

Aug 26, [1864]   No news of special importance. Rumors of fighting at Petersburgh yesterday. Gayle [son of Maria and T. L. Bayne] is still very ill, & parents much distressed.

Aug 29, [1864]   Midnight. I have just returned from the sick-bed of poor little Gayle. He is struggling hard to hold on to the little remnant of life Still left to him. If a mother's love and devotion can get him thro' he will live. She still has hope, despite the Doctor's sad conviction that he will die. His disease seems to be in the chest, and is manifested by hot fever, great debility & attenuation, & chiefly by violent paroxysms of pain which at first made him writhe, but appear to be diminishing in violence. Whether this is a symptom of amendment or decline remains to be seen.

The fight on Thursday was severe and resulted in the capture of over two thousand prisoners & 9 cannon, with several stands of colors by [A. P.] Hill's Corps & Hampton's Cavalry. The enemy were dislodged from their works towards Reams' Station tho Still holding on to their position along side of & East of the R.R. It has cost them ten thousand men thus far captured & perhaps half that number in killed and wounded. Can we hold out much longer? The captured killed and wounded tho' half that of the enemy are still seriously depleting us. I doubt whether Lee now has 30,000 men of all arms under his & Beauregard's joint command.

Hood says the enemy is contracting his lines, & is now nowhere nearer than four miles from Atlanta. It is supposed that he has had to send off a portion of his force to recover his communications, interrupted by Wheeler.

The surrender of Fort Morgan seems certain. The circumstances are not yet known. All that Mobile business indicates a poor head, Maury. The Tallahassee is safe back in Wilmington after her destructive cruize. Another vessel, the Edith, is nearly ready to go out on a like errand of vengeance against the enemy's commerce.

Peace begins to be very openly talked about.

I saw the President last week on the subject of the promotion or appt of some officers. He talked about various subjects. Showed me a telegram from Hood, saying that a brigade of infantry and cavalry had driven off a party of raiders and captured colors and a gun. "He says nothing of prisoners," remarked the President significantly, and repeated the remark so that I could not misunderstand what he meant—that Hood did not choose to take prisoners when the enemy went on such errands—and such is the sentiment of the country. He was inclined to be dissatisfied at the loss of the Tennessee, without being injured. A letter from one of her officers explains that her wheel & afterward her rudder tackle were shot away, & she lay unmanageable. The 15in shot penetrated the iron but did no great damage, not coming quite thro'. In the attack on Friday, week, Gen. [J. C. C.] Saunders [Sanders] was killed. He was from Alabama & the youngest Brigadier yet made being only 24 years old.

Aug 31, [1864]   Hood telegraphs that the enemy has wholly changed his position his left being thrown back to the Chattahoochee, & his right resting at some point near the West Pt R.R beyond East Point [Ga.]. This takes him beyond shelling distance from Atlanta. I saw Gen. Hoke to-day who tells me that they have ceased to fear Grant, & believe themselves to be his equal in numbers. Our lines are so strong that no assault can be made on them with success. Our ranks are again filling by men returning to duty. Hoke was made a Maj. Gen. for the capture of Plymouth, but has not maintained his reputation. He is a very pleasant looking, young man of rather sanguine disposition, I judge.

Gayle is I fear declining, & there is little hope of his getting better.

Sept 2d, [1864]   No news of importance from the points of chief interest. I judge from the length of a telegram from Gen. S[amuel] Jones that he apprehends an attack on Charleston by the fleet as he calls for large supplies of rifle projectiles.

Gayle is still alive but hopes of his recovery are very feeble. The weather for the last three days has been quite cool.

Sept 4, [1864]   Gen. Hood telegraphs that he has evacuated Atlanta, and is now some 20 or 25 miles South on the Macon Road at Lovejoy's Station. The series of events which led to this seem to have been that Hardee's Corps & Lee's were sent to Jonesboro to counteract a movement of the enemy by his right flank. That these two corps made a feeble attack on the enemy who had effected a lodgment on the east of the Flint River, & were unsuccessful that Lee was withdrawn & in his absence the whole weight of the enemy was thrown at his single corps & he was driven back with the loss of 8 pieces of artillery. To prevent the isolation & destruction of this corps Hood had to leave Atlanta & effect a junction with it which he has done, with what loss of Stores does not yet appear. This is disastrous, tho' the mere acquisition of Atlanta by the enemy cannot be of much value to him now. Hardee is said to have inflicted heavy loss on the enemy in the engagement. Efforts must now be made to cover Augusta, & for this perhaps all the local & reserve forces there have been sent to the front.

Gayle appears to be better & strong hopes are entertained of his improvement. He appears again to be conscious.

No movements about Petersburgh. Gen Lee was in town to-day.

Wednesday Sept 7, [1864]   Gayle died this morning at 4 o'clock. He began to sink rapidly yesterday morning. The funeral Service takes place at 5½ P.M. to-day, & the body is taken to Mobile by Mr. Bayne & a friend (Mr. [Stephen] Chalaron).

Hood telegraphs that the enemy is retiring from his front in the direction of Jonesboro. It is quite apparent that Hood besides being outnumbered is out-generaled, yet the enemy have gained no great advantage. The northern papers announce that McClellan & [George H.] Pendleton (of Ohio) are the nominees of the Chicago (democratic[)] convention. Pendleton is a decided peace man, but with such successes as Mobile and Atlanta there will be little left for the peace party to stand on as the republicans think.

Sept 9, [1864]   The enemy are retiring from their advanced position at Jones[boro] upon Atlanta, preparatory to another campaign. It is confidentially whispered that Hood has applied to have Hardee relieved, and that Gen. Dick Taylor be assigned in his place. It is also rumored that Beauregard is to be assigned to the command of the army at Atlanta—not at all probable. It would however be popular. The general judgment is that Hood has not capacity for such a command. The President is strongly prejudiced against Beauregard. No news from Early. Grant is said to be building a Rail Road from City Point to the left of his line on the Weldon R.R.

Sept 12, [1864]   We lost at Atlanta one hundred cars & six Engines—an Ordnance train of ammn & large supplies of Comy Stores. These latter were distributed to the people. Sherman has directed all the white inhabitants to be removed from Atlanta—those taking the Oath North, the rest South. Hood has consented to an armistice for ten days for this purpose.

Gen. Jno. H. Morgan was surprised and killed on Sunday morning (4th Sept.) at the house of Mrs. [Catherine] Williams in Green[e]ville, East Tenn. He with his Staff slept there & were betrayed to the enemy at Bull's Gap by her daughter who rode thither, informed of his whereabouts & returned with the enemy. [Mrs. Williams's daughter-in-law was incorrectly credited with these events.] He was killed fighting, endeavoring to escape. The rest were captured. He was determined not to be taken. He was buried with military honors at Abingdon on Monday evening at Sunset. It is singular that with his habits & vigilance he should have slept at a house so far advanced without the simplest precautions against surprise.

Sept 15, [1864]   No especial news. I saw Gen. Lee to-day looking very well. He returned to Petersburgh to-day. Met to-day Gov [Francis A.] Lubbock of Texas, who has been made A.D.C. to the President. He is a small, middle-aged man with pleasant open face.

What a farce it is to have here "Senators" from Kentucky—especially such Senators as [William E.] Sims—a long lank, unprepossessing man, who they say is making money here in speculations. I go to Danville in the morning.

Sept 24, [1864]   I returned from Danville Tuesday [the] 20th, having passed three days there very pleasantly. It is a not unattractive town of about 4000 inhabitants.

On the 17th Gen Wade Hampton penetrated to the rear of Grants army at Sycamore Church and captured 2450 beef cattle and near 300 prisoners with some wagons, arms etc. About the same day Early was attacked by Sheridan in front of Winchester and defeated with heavy loss on both sides. Gens. [Robert E.] Rodes and [Archibald C.] Godwin killed & Fitz Lee & [Zebulon] York (La) wounded. Our troops fought well but were overpowered. I fear our so-called cavalry, in the Valley, behaved badly. Early fell back to a position in front of Strasburg, said to be very strong, but it was reported yesterday that he had been again worsted and driven back. The reports from Georgia represent the people as very despondent & ready to make terms with the enemy. It is even currently reported that Stephens, Toombs, & Brown have had a conference with Sherman. This is of course an exaggeration, but it is believed & shows the state of the country. The President went south on Tuesday. I learned yesterday that our Navy prisoners would be exchanged, & we may expect Dick in the course of a month.

Sept. 25, [1864]   Early was again attacked in his position at Fisher's Hill and defeated, retiring with the loss of 12 pieces of artillery & a few men to New Market. These recurring defeats are due it is said to the inferior quality of our cavalry, which is routed by the enemy's cavalry who then gets into our rear. Hood is at Lagrange [Ga.] edging off toward Sherman's communications which will force him to fight probably out of Atlanta. If he should beat him in such an encounter Sherman & all his stores would be ours. God grant it. We need a victory to close this bloody year. It is believed & hoped that Beauregard will take command of Hood's army. There is little doubt that Grant who has again returned to his forces will now soon move. With the disasters in the Valley Lee must meet him with greatly diminished forces. I doubt whether he can now bring thirty thousand infantry into line. The time is coming now when it will be necessary to put our Slaves into the field & let them fight for their freedom, in other words give up a part of the institution to save the country, or the whole if necessary to win independence.

Sept. 27, [1864]   Early is still retreating tho' it is rumored that he has checked the enemy near Port Republick [Republic]. These reverses in the valley will greatly augment our difficulties in holding Richmond this fall campaign, now about to begin. Longstreet has doubtless assumed command by this time. In the South Hardee has been relieved of the command of his Corps at his own request. President Davis was in Macon on Friday last.

Rode along the fortifications of the "intermediate line", from the James River above the city to the Mechanicsville turnpike about ten miles, making a ride of about twenty miles. The line is continuous with places for artillery at the various roads leading to the city, and at other commanding positions.

The news from Forrest is that he has captured Athens, Ala. with 1300 prisoners, 500 horses, fifty wagons, arms &c. It is to be hoped that the tide of reverses has ebbed & that we may hope for victories again. All will however depend on what we can do against Grant who must soon move now.

Sept. 29, [1864]   The enemy's cavalry is reported to be on a raid thro' the upper portions of the valley. The depot, iron bridge &c at Waynesboro' are reported destroyed. Early appears to hold the infantry and artillery of Sheridan in check near Port Republick. Gold at the north has fallen to 199—indication of very exuberant confidence on their part. It is a curious nation. Why should they exult over a little victory like that at Winchester & at Fisher's Hill? They have lost almost all they held in the Trans-Miss, & have gained nothing in Va. during this campaign. What they have gained in Georgia they have lost in Miss, North Alabama & in N. Carolina. They think these little reverses are evidences of exhausted resources, but really we are better off now than we were two years ago when no one doubted our ability to wage the War. The only point against us is the Scarcity of men to fill up our armies. This must be met by placing negros in ranks giving them their freedom. We must meet the use the north makes of our negros by using them ourselves, & giving them the Same reward.

Sept 30, [1864]   Yesterday & to-day have again been days of excitement. The whole population of the city has been turned out & armed & sent to the defences. In the morning yesterday the enemy attacked & carried Fort Harrison, one of the outworks of Chaffin's Farm. But few were in the Fort, & it was easily taken by the enemy. Lt. Col [John M.] Maury comdg Chaffin's Bluff, & Major —— an artillery officer have not been heard of since & were doubtless captured. Soon after an assault was made on Fort Gilmer, another dependency which was repelled decisively. The assault was made in part by negro troops & their loss was heavy tho some of them actually clambered out of the deep ditch of the work, up the Slope & got into the work. About two hundred of the enemy were killed, & four or five hundred captured. To-day there has been an effort to re-capture Fort H. The first attempt, feebly made failed—the result of the Second has not yet been learned. Our loss has not yet been heavy.

Oct 2d, Sunday [1864]   The weather was very bad yesterday, & there is little improvement to-day. We did not retake Fort Harrison, & the attempt is given up. Retrenchments are to be made which will exclude Fort H. & give us a good line. During the operations on this flank the enemy advanced on his extreme left & broke thro' our line but was met at one point by [A. P.] Hill's division with a loss to him of 450 prisoners; & on the extreme right by Hampton's Cavalry with a loss of 500 prisoners. The enemy were driven back and our lines recovered. The total loss of the enemy has therefore been about 1400 prisoners, and perhaps 1100 killed & wounded. Our loss will probably reach one half that say 10 or 12 hundred, but even this disparity will ultimately ruin us, unless we can open up new resources of men. There is no help I fear except to use negros, giving them their freedom. The common Sentiment of the country is rapidly verging to this point. Judge [John A.] Campbell [Assistant Secretary of War] thinks it would be the knell of Slavery as it exists, but I do not see that that necessarily follows. Nevertheless the country is prepared to throw Slavery into the purchase of our independence if that be necessary to achieve it. The opening wedge to this use of Slaves is found in law of last Congress conscribing 20,000 for cooks, teamsters &c. The next thing will be to put them in as Soldiers giving them their freedom. The news from West Va is favorable, the enemy having been driven back to Jonesboro' & repulsed at another point. Early sends word to the comdg office at Lynchburg that if the citizens will defend themselves against raiders he will look after Sheridan. Thus affairs are brightening in those directions. The loss of Fort H. is serious but not irreparable. The President is on his way back from Hood's army.

Oct. 4, [1864]   The news from Western Va is that our troops whipped the enemy coming from Ky. at Saltville & are pursuing them. Our forces were composed entirely of reserves and detailed men, armed for the occasion. The enemy had 6000 men. Early holds the enemy in check in the Valley, & is even forcing him back. Kershaw's Division is on its way back, and is much wanted here. I attribute the partial Successes of the enemy to its absence. The accounts from Mo. are encouraging. [Gen. Sterling] Price at the head of a large force is advancing upon St. Louis & was at last accounts at Pilot Knob some thirty or 40 miles from the city.

Oct 6, [1864]   Our poor harrowed and overworked soldiers are getting worn out with the campaign. They see nothing before them but certain death and have I fear fallen into a sort of hopelessness, and are dispirited. Certain it is that they do not fight as they fought at the Wilderness and Spotsylvania. The cure for this is I think to limit the term of Service. They are now in for the war, and as there appears no end to it, at present, they begin to look upon themselves as doomed men. A term of Service for 5 years would perhaps correct this without imperiling the existence of the Army. Under such a term the men would begin to go home in the middle of 1866 but most of them in 67, and there would be constantly veterans enough to keep up the quality of the Army. This with a proper employment of Slaves as cooks, teamsters, and even as guards, & soldiers would greatly relieve the burdens of the war on the white population. Willie is still at Mr. Seddon's, so pleased that he dont want to come home I fear.

Oct 8, [1864]   Yesterday morning our troops attacked the enemy between the Darby town and Charles City road, & drove them out of their works capturing 10 pieces of artillery with all the caissons & a hundred horses. The attack was however less decisive than was expected. The object was to pierce the enemy's line and isolate the 10th ([Gen. David B.] Birney's) Corps, & destroy it. It is partly composed of negro troops. The brave Gen [John] Gregg of Texas fell at the Head of his troops. Gen. [John] Bratton of S. C. severely wounded. Col. [John C.] Haskell artillery mortally wounded. He is one of four brothers, of whom two have now fallen, & one lost an arm.

Willie came back yesterday highly delighted with his visit to Mr. Seddon's place, where he had plenty of playmates. The weather has turned suddenly cool this morning, with a bright sun however. Hood is now in position across the Ga. R.R. & Sherman must fight, or evacuate all his conquests. Forrest was said to be marching on Altoona tho he was last expected by the enemy at Huntsville [Ala.].

Oct 11, [1864]   No news from Hood. What is Sherman waiting for? His provisions must be nearly out, & his horses pretty well starved. Will he march out & fall upon Hood, or will he perhaps form a moveable column and strike across the country for Charleston. Our situation here is getting very critical. We have no men. Gen Lee's Army is reduced to about 30,000 Infantry and say 10,000 Cavalry & Artillery. Grant is being re-inforced daily to the extent of 1000 per day, so Col. [R. H.] Chilton says. He told me that Gen. L said "if we can't get the men, all that is left for us is to make peace on the best terms we can." I cannot think he was serious, but I regret to hear such language from his mouth. I heard almost the same expression now attributed to him uttered by him in June 1861. He must be subject to fits of despondence. Our brave President never wavers thus, in act or thought.

Oct 16, [1864]   On Thursday the enemy attacked our lines between the Darby town & Charles City Roads, and were repulsed with heavy loss. It is ascertained that in retaliation for our placing negro prisoners at work on fortifications the enemy have put our Officers & men at work on Butler's Canal. The news from the valley is that Early attacked Crooks command and drove it back with loss—Sheridan having detached two of his corps to rejoin Grant.

From Georgia it appears that Hood has withdrawn from his position on the Rail Road, and intends moving either up the road towards Dalton, or if Sherman follows to strike over to Huntsville & up toward Nashville, thus compelling Sherman to return into Tenn. to cover Nashville.

The President made a very awkward speech at Macon on his way to the Army, which creates a great deal of comment. It was a very unfortunate speech to say the least of it. It seems probable that the naval prisoners, after having been brought to Varina for exchange were, at the instance of Butler, sent back to Old Point—so that poor Dick has not reached here as we hoped he would.

Willie had a little fever yesterday and to-day—nothing serious I hope. The death of poor little Gayle makes us anxious about him.

Oct 22d, [1864]   Early was again whipped on the 19th with the loss of 23 pieces of artillery. This makes about 80 pieces that he has lost since May 6th. It is time to let him retire! It seems he attacked the enemy's camp early, and surprised two corps, routing them & capturing 1300 prisoners with 19 pieces of artillery. He pursued them until they rallied & turned upon him & attacked him in line. Then comes the old Story—our left gave way—a total rout ensued, the men behaving disgracefully & scattering into the woods. The prisoners were recovered however. It is really ludicrous this business in the Valley.

Oct 23d, [1864]   Dick reached here on Tuesday evening looking a good deal the worse for his years imprisonment at Fort Warren. About 120 Naval officers returned with him. Hood appears to be striking out for Tennessee & when last heard from was at Gadsden [Ala.] on the Coosa [River]. I fear his campaign will not effect its object, & that his army will be disorganized in the attempt to draw Sherman back into Tenn.

Oct 28, [1864]   There was fighting yesterday on both ends of the lines. On our left the enemy attacked at two points—between the Power House and the Charles City Road & on the Williamsburgh Road, & was repulsed losing 7 Colors & four hundred prisoners. On our right the enemy drove back our Cavalry, but was afterwards assaulted by Mahone & Hampton, & driven to their original lines, with some loss. Our losses Slight on this side—heavier probably on the South side. One of Gen. Hampton's sons [Frank P.], is reported killed, the other wounded [Wade]. No news from Hood who has not been heard from since the 22d. Mary [Gayle Aiken] had a little daughter on Tuesday—both well—the birth somewhat premature. Hugh commanded his brigade in yesterday's fight, & earned the commendation of Gen. H[ampton].

Oct 30, [1864]   Gen. Lee telegraphs that Gen. Hampton drove the enemy across Rowanty Creek & re-established our lines—so that in the several attacks of Thursday he has gained no ground, and has lost in killed wounded & missing not less than 2500 men. Our loss from all causes will scarcely reach 500. No news yet from Hood. Forrest advises from the interior of West Tenn. that [Gen. Lovell H.] Rousseau has left his Qr.ms & comy trains—taken all his infantry & hastened toward Huntsville. [Earlier Rousseau's raid (July 10–22) had cut the Montgomery and West Point Railroad, the most important rail line into Atlanta, and contributed to the city's fall on September 2.] As soon as he [Forrest] can cross the Tenn. he will advance rapidly on Nashville. Will he & Hood unite to attack that point?

Nov. 3, 1864   A little boy was born to us at 15 minutes before 6 this evening (Thursday). Mother and son [Richard Haynsworth] doing very well—but these are events involving terrible suffering. I hope it may be the last. Two boys & four girls in a family will do very well. May Heaven bless & protect them all & bring them safely to years of maturity. It is a wet miserable evening, & as I sit writing by the blaze of a cheerful wood fire, I sorrow over our soldiers exposed to the slow, cold, penetrating rain. Heaven watch over them too. No further news from Hood. I fear Price has met with bad luck in Missouri, but as our accounts come wholly thro federal sources little reliance is to be placed on them.

Novr 6, [1864]   Mamma and the youngster are both doing well. I heartily wish he were a year old. Mrs. Jones stays constantly with Mamma.

Nothing of an exciting nature going on at the front. No news from Hood. A paper of the 2d in the War Dept. States that gold is 260 & that Gov. [Horatio] Seymour [of N.Y.] has called out the militia in New-York to protect the ballot box. Deserters & prisoners coming in say that there is good news for us in Missouri.

Nov. 8, [1864]   Active operations were expected on our right yesterday & to-day, but the bad weather or other causes prevented no doubt. It is said that many of the enemys troops have gone home to vote. To-day is their presidential election & by this time it is settled who is to be their President for the next four years. Lincoln will no doubt be re-elected over McClellan. In East Tenn. our troops under Gen. [John C.] Vaughn have been defeated losing 5 guns. Early is re-organizing his demoralized troops at New Market. From Hood there is nothing definite tho he appears to have crossed the Tennessee at Gunter's landing & perhaps near Tuscumbia [Ala.]. Price does not seem to have been seriously defeated tho he has withdrawn to S. W. Missouri about Carthage. Whether the enemy is to attack at Wilmington does not yet seem to be determined. The loss of the

Albemarle at Plymouth loses to us the Eastern part of North Carolina, & the blood shed at Plymouth in the spring was in vain.

Nov 17, [1864]   No mil. operations of especial interest have occurred. Breckinridge defeated the enemy at Bull's Gap on the 14th with the loss of 6 pieces of Artillery, 10 stands of Colors, 200 prisoners, 50 wagons &c. Sherman is Said to have returned to Atlanta with 4 corps. With the 5 he has now in hand he is capable of marching on Savannah & Charleston, & capturing both places holding them & Augusta thus cutting us in two again. Lincoln has been re-elected President of the United States by overwhelming majorities. There is no use in disguising the fact that our subjugation is popular at the north, & that the war must go on until this hope is crushed out & replaced by desire for peace at any cost.

Sunday Nov. 20, [1864]   Definite news was received yesterday that Sherman had left Atlanta & was marching on Macon with 35000 men including Kilpatrick's cavalry. To-day we learn that the enemy's cavalry were yesterday at Clinton [Ga.] 12 miles or so from Macon, & that a corps had advanced toward Augusta as far as Madison some 60 miles from Atlanta. It is said to be [Gen. Henry W.] Slocum's Corps. Rains is moving stores to Columbia [S.C.] from A[ugusta, Ga.].

Hardee has been sent to Macon. There are about 5 or 6 thousand Reserves & Ga. militia & Wheeler's cavalry, say 3500 men between the enemy & Macon. On the other route there is no force to oppose the progress of the enemy to Augusta, where I hope however some force will have been assembled by the time the enemy appears before it. The Secretary looks very much disturbed. I cannot learn that any provision had been made against such a movement tho' the probability has been evident for some time past. I fear the President is no military genius, tho' genius avails not much without resources. I hope the roads & the distances will destroy Sherman if the military dont. The steamers (war) Tallahassee & Chickamauga are both returned to Wilmington after very brief cruises (10 to 15 days). The navy is decidedly out of luck. Mr. Mallory lacks earnestness & devotion to his duty. He is too good company & too generally informed to be worth much at any one thing tho' a man of undoubted ability. He beats the Secretary of War in every discussion that arises—is in fact too smart for Mr. Seddon.

Nov 21, [1864]   The enemy were yesterday evening at the Oconee River; & fighting was reported near Macon with cavalry of the main columns no doubt. The impression appears to be that the troops of the enemy will combine on Augusta. Gen. Beauregard is still at Florence [Ala.] or rather the army is. What a decrepit movement that has been! If Sherman's columns are properly met the movement must end as disaster to him. I cannot see why a Division is not sent down to Augusta from here. Perhaps it has been tho I fear not. Hardee directed Wheeler to attack the enemy's cavalry at Clinton yesterday to develop their intentions. Vice President Stephens published a letter to Senator [Thomas J.] Semmes [of La.] defining his views, & declaring that the Union as it was is so dead that no hand save that which raised Lazarus from the tomb could resuscitate it! This is very well, & will reassure those who thought eminent Georgians were going astray. Mamma & baby are getting on well. Sister Mary has lost her poor little baby, two weeks old. The weather is very bad, with continued rain which if it extend[s] to Georgia will be one of our best allies.

Nov 24, [1864]   The column of Shermans Army (left wing) marching on the Georgia R.R. turned south at Madison & appears to have gone to Milledgeville. The cavalry of the other column was attacked by Wheeler at Clinton but without gaining any advantage. Hardee has gone with the troops from Macon toward Savannah. He does not know exactly where the enemy is. Dick came here on Tuesday. He will probably leave in a day or two for Wilmington. I was confirmed a Brigadier General by the Senate on Saturday. I owe my promotion to the President himself. Mr. Frank Lyon wrote him a note on the subject, which he endorsed over to the Secy of War directing the promotion.

Nov 26, [1864]   Gen. Bragg telegraphs that the enemy was met in force yesterday at Buffalo Creek near Sandersonville [Sandersville, Ga.]. He has thus made very fair progress—nearly half the way to Savannah in 12 days from Atlanta. Wheeler with his cavalry is ordered to obstruct him in every way—hang upon his flanks—& destroy everything eatable in front of him. I trust he will yet have a difficult path to traverse in getting to the Sea-coast. The prisoners (Yankees) confined at Salisbury [N.C.] ran yesterday & killed two of the guard. They were immediately fired upon with musketry & artillery and forty to fifty killed.

Nov. 28, [1864]   The news last evening was that the enemy had struck the [Augusta and Savannah] R.R. between Millen & Augusta at Briar [Brier] Creek, severing communication with the front from Augusta where Bragg is. Gen. Wheeler confronts the infantry of the enemy at Sandersonville. Lt. Gen. Taylor was ordered to bring all his forces from Macon to Savannah via Albany & Thomasville, the interval between these two places being a land march. Little confidence is felt in the ability of Gen. Bragg to cope with this movement. There are say 5000 troops at Macon 6000 at Augusta, 7500 under Wheeler and the garrisons of Charleston & Savannah. Of course many of them are Reserves.

Nov 30, [1864]   Gen. Bragg telegraphs that Wheeler, leaving a force to confront the enemy near Sandersville followed the party which cut the road at Briar Creek & attacked him at Wadesboro [Waynesboro], gain-

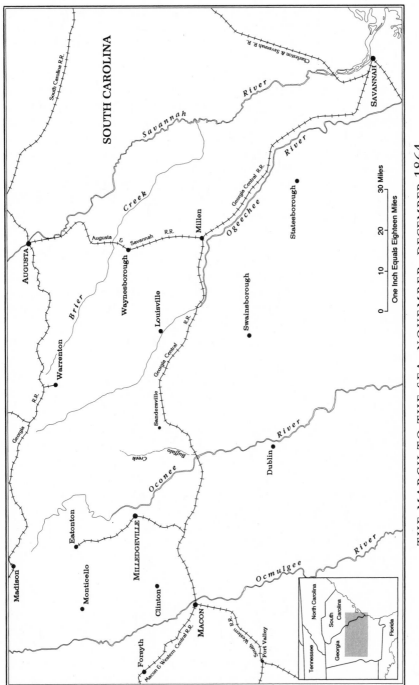

THE MARCH TO THE SEA, NOVEMBER–DECEMBER 1864

ing some advantages. Fighting was going on. It is hardly possible to divine Sherman's intentions. Bragg fears he may cross the Savannah [River] & go to Beaufort [S.C.], & adds that it is "entirely practicable". No doubt. I wish he were there & all our cities safe. We can rebuild the Rail Roads destroyed on this extraordinary career thro' Georgia; & if he thinks the possession of the Sea Coast at Beaufort a compensation for the giving up of Atlanta—a place he fought so hard to gain—he is the best judge of his bargain. I fear he will turn upon Macon & Columbus, & resume his position on the Chattahoochie say at Marietta. Still if he had an object worthy the risks he runs it must be the possession of the two lines of communication between the northern & Southern states, say at Branchville [S.C.] & Pocotaligo [S.C.]. This would involve the fall of Charleston & probably Savannah & Augusta. We shall soon see. I doubt whether Sherman sees his way quite clearly, & hope disaster is before him.

Decr 2, [1864]   The enemy appears to be not far from Millen, & has apparently met with little obstruction thus far. He is inflicting much individual misery, burning & destroying homes, crops, cotton, gins, & implements, but the military results are comparatively small. At Augusta they are Still doubtful of the direction of Shermans march. It is to be hoped he will meet with more determined opposition after he leaves the Savannah.

Hood is approaching Nashville or rather appears to be bearing toward East Tenn., perhaps to effect a junction with Breckinridge & march into Kentucky.

Decr 7, [1864]   Nothing of much interest has occurred on the lines here. The monitors come up to the obstructions occasionally & open fire on Battery Dantzler, & are replied to. The distance 2400 yds is too great to do much execution on them. Gen. Archibald Gracie was killed on Friday last by a Schrapnel. His neck was cut & dislocated by a fragment & three balls struck in his shoulder. A fight took place at Grahamville [S.C.] between forces from the fleet & our Georgia militia, on Wednesday in which the enemy were repulsed with considerable loss. On Monday Sherman is reported as marching down both sides of the Ogechee [Ogeechee River] with four corps.

Decr 11, [1864]   Hood appears to have attacked the enemy at Franklin (17 miles from N.[ashville]) on the lst, with success perhaps, but with heavy loss. The enemy report Genls [John] Adams & [S. R.] Gist killed. He is now before Nashville. We hear no later news direct from Hood than the 27th at which time he was at Columbia, the enemy retiring before him. We have probably not sufficient force to effect much against the troops of Thomas entrenched in Nashville. Besides [Gen. Frederick]

Steele from Arkansas & [Gen. A. J.] Smith from Mo. are hastening to join him.

On the 9th Beauregard telegraphs from Savannah that the enemy is approaching on the River road, the middle ground road, & the [Georgia] Central R.R., skirmishing going on. Wheeler despatches to Bragg on the 8th that he is pressing the rear of the enemy who is obstructing the roads. He says the 14th Corps is marching on the River road—the 15th on the Middle Road & the 17th & 30th on the R.R. Very few west of the Ogechee.

Yesterday Longstreet made an attack on the enemy on the Darbytown road, results not yet known. Hampton telegraphs that he drove the cavalry of the enemy back upon the infantry of the Corps marching South by the Jerusalem Road, & saved the Mechanics River Bridge. Our force in front of this city is now about as follows—Longstreet's, [A. P.] Hills, & [Richard H.] Anderson's Corps with two Divisions of Early's 44,500 Infy—Ewell's command of Infantry, Cavalry and Artillery 6700—Artillery of Gen Lee's Army 3000—Cavalry of Gen. Lee, under Hampton 7,500—Total 61,700. The Infantry count is taken from the return of arms in the hands of troops & is therefore reliable. I am surprised to learn that there are only 7000 men at Savannah. I fear the place will fall & the garrison be captured, tho' Hardee talks bravely & believes he can defend it. Wheeler is behind with 7 or 8 thousand cavalry—tho' how he got behind I am at a loss to tell as he was in front at Louisville [east of Milledgeville] with his main force. Should Sherman receive a check at S. it will go hard with his army. His northern friends are as anxious about him as we are about Hood.

Lincoln's message to Congress spawns nothing but subjugation. He says the door of reconciliation is not yet closed, & we may lay down our arms & return to the fold. I hope six months hence a different story will be popular at the north—especially should we catch Sherman tripping.

Decr 15, [1864]   A despatch from Hood says that he drove the enemy from their breastworks at Franklin on the 30th, capturing several colors, and a thousand prisoners. His losses in Generals are enormous [two major generals and ten brigadiers]. Cleburne, Williams [wounded], Adams, [Otho] Strahl & Gist killed 6 wounded & 1 captured. It is fearful & our loss in killed & wounded, tho' he says out of proportion to the Generals must be depressingly great. He gives no estimate—a bad sign. Fort McAllister, on the Ogechee [River], one of the outworks of Savannah was "carried by storm"—not much of a storm I suspect however. The garrison was only 150 men. Troops are still moving down from the valley. I think still that my notions were correct at the outset of Sherman's movement when I advocated the detachment of 10,000 men to Georgia, even at the risk of losing Petersburgh & the Southern R.R. It would have ruined Sherman, & with his ruin, gone far to make the north tired of the war. What can be the object of moving down troops now I cannot see. It is too late—the golden moment for action in Georgia has passed by. A raid toward Abingdon & the Salt works [in southwest Va.] creates some alarm. Chattanooga & all of the enemy's posts in East Tenn. & north Ga. are reported evacuated. If we can recover E. Tenn & n. Ga. we shall have done well.

Decr 18, [1864]   Sherman is probably in possession of Savannah. One of our iron-clads has been captured & the other cut off, so that we have lost command of the River. The Navy is always foremost in misfortune. Gen. Joe Johnston came to see me last evening. He is looking very well & complimented the condition of my department. He spoke feelingly of the loss of Generals lately at Franklin.

There is a speck of war between the U.S. & England in the present aspect of their relations. Seward's insulting letter to [James A. Stuart-Worthy] Lord Wharncliff[e], in reply to the proffer of aid to our prisoners in Yankee land—the notice to terminate the reciprocity treaty—the order of General [John A.] Dix to pursue & kill raiders in future upon British territory—the resolution to build six gunboats, combined all with Will's Brazil letter look very ominous. Yet it may all come to nothing. Let us continue to rely on our good right arms.

Baby [Richard] was christened Sunday before last—two weeks ago. The fight at Grahamsville turns out to have been a bloody one to the enemy as they confess near a thousand killed & wounded. At Griswoldville [Ga.] near Macon we met with bloody loss, over 600 killed & wounded nearly all Reserves.

Decr 19, [1864]   This is a gloomy day here—one of the gloomiest in our struggle. The news from Hood, thro northern papers asserts that he was defeated before Nashville on the 15th & 16th with heavy loss and is in full retreat. If so his army will be nearly destroyed before he can reach a place of security. This army defeated & demoralized there is no force to cover Alabama & Georgia, & the enemy may penetrate these states at his leisure. The plan of campaign which has terminated so disastrously is due probably to Beauregard whose favorite plan has it is understood, been always to enter Kentucky & carry the war to the Ohio. Savannah cannot probably be held against Sherman.

Decr 20, [1864]   Savannah appears to be yet uncaptured, notwithstanding the loss of our gunboats. The news from Hood thro' Yankee sources continues to be unfavorable, & they say he is retreating after great losses of men & material. Troops are moving toward Wilmington from here, and a heavy armament has departed from Hampton Roads supposed to be destined to the attack of that place. The great trouble to be met now is to feed the army here while the Rail Roads southward are being repaired, which will take from six weeks to two months no doubt, tho partial communication is already re-established.

Decr 26, [1864]   A despondent Christmas has just passed, yet people contrived to eat hearty and good Christmas dinners. The Soldiers unfortunately have not even meat, & have had none for Several days. The Commissary General has signally failed in his duties. While there is plenty of food in Georgia there is none here. There is no sufficient excuse for this. The food must be brought here & the means to do so provided & organized.

Savannah was evacuated on Wednesday or Thursday. All the armament & much material lost. My officer telegraphs that he saved nothing but his arms & ammunition. I presume our prisoners were lost. It is denouement to such laborious preparations. For nearly four years has it been prepared for a defence which lasted about four days. The key to the situation Fort McAllister seems to have been taken by surprise thus establishing communication with the fleet of the enemy. The Yankees claim the capture of sixty pieces of artillery from Hood & I fear it is but too true. I hope to hear however that he has escaped with 20,000 men, as the nucleus for a new army.

Decr 27, [18]64   Savannah appears to have been evacuated on the night of the 20th (Tuesday) the last troops crossing the river about 5 A. M. of the 21st. Hood is reported by the Yankees to have lost 17,000 men and 60 pieces of artillery since he entered Tenn. The probability is that he has lost about ten thousand killed wounded & captured, & that he will recross the Tenn. with 20,000 men besides his cavalry, army enough to cover Alabama & northern Ga. if properly disciplined & led. There is deep feeling in Congress at the conduct of our military affairs. They demand [that] the Gen. Lee shall be made Generalissimo to command all our armies—not constructively & "under the President"—but shall have full control of all military operations & be held responsible for them. This Tenn. campaign altho' the President can hardly be called responsible for it, except that he suffered it, has completely upset the little confidence left in the Presidents ability to conduct campaigns—<a criticism I fear I have made long ago.>

Fort Fisher [at Wilmington, N.C.] was attacked by the [Capt. David D.] Porter Fleet on the 24th & again on the 25th without much effect. Troops were also landed above & assaulted but were repulsed. The federal fleet is about sixty vessels.

Decr 28, [1864]   Gen. Bragg advises that the enemy re-embarked, & desists from the attack on Fort Fisher which has suffered very little damage from the heavy bombardment. [Lt. Col. John S.] Mosby was badly wounded last week. He is a great favorite and everyone asks about him with interest. It is hoped he will soon recover. S. D. Lee advises Beauregard that he will be at Okolona in a few days & wants his (B's) views on recent events in Tenn. I saw the President to-day & conversed with him for half an hour, chiefly on business. He remarked "I will say to you in confidence that since Bragg has gone I can get very little information of things about Richmond. (We were talking of bringing back our workmen from the trenches, & replacing them with the militia). I am almost deprived of the assistance of two valuable officers by the prejudices existing against them. I mean Bragg & Pemberton. The murmurers & fault finders will not let them alone." He said he did not think that Hoods losses would be found to be near as great as was now supposed, & that he had still strength enough to turn upon the enemy & achieve a victory. To-morrow is the eleventh anniversay of our marriage. We will have a few friends in the evening.

VIII

"The prospect is growing darker & darker about us"

Jan 4/ [18]65   Our "anniversary" evening passed off very pleasantly with a little supper and cards. Everybody is depressed and somber. Military events have as in '62 & 63 closed against us. Still gaiety continues among the young people, & there is much marriage & giving in marriage. We were last night at a ball at Judge Campbells, where dancing was kept up until 4½ in the morning.

There is deep feeling in Congress relative to the Situation of mil. affairs. Committees are investigating to determine what is to be done—& how it is that Lee's Army is almost without bread & quite without meat. The Com. Gen. [Lucius B. Northrop] is trying to fasten the blame on the Secy of War [Seddon], because he would not allow provisions to be bro't in & paid for on this side in cotton. I trust it will end in the ousting of the Com Gen. He is not the man for the place which requires plain practical Sense—just the sort of sense that Northrop has not.

From Charleston we hear that Sherman is crossing the Savannah in force. Troops are moving Southward from here, but will I fear be too late to save Charleston. It is sad to think that after so brave a defence it is after all to be triumphed over by the foe. Hood was heard of "in the field" on the 27th, sending troops from Corinth to drive the raiders from the Mobile & Ohio R.R. I am glad to hear he is anywhere. It seems to be true that Price died of apoplexy—a great loss at this time. [Price actually died on September 29, 1867.]

Jan 6, [1865]   No positive news of Sherman's intentions. Indications are that Charleston, too, will be given up. Where is this to end? No money in the Treasury, no food to feed Gen. Lee's Army, no troops to oppose Gen. Sherman, what does it all mean. As Judge Campbell says of the declaration of the Comy General that he cannot feed the Army, what is the "significance" of it? Is the cause really hopeless? Is it to be abandoned and lost in this way? <I fear as I have feared for two years past. There is no master hand at our helm? When I see the President trifle away precious hours & idle discussion & discursive comment, I feel as tho' he were not equal to his great task. And yet where could we get a better or a wiser man? Where, indeed!> I saw the President yesterday. The question was about the removal of Pemberton from the command he now holds of the Artillery defences of Richmond. He said he was about to do him an injustice in obedience to popular clamor, and wished to make it as little disagreeable to himself (the President) as possible; he desired therefore to put him on as honorable & high a duty as possible, and it was agreed to assign him to the Inspection of Artillery & Ord. in the field. He agreed that Pemberton's manners were very ungracious and that he contrived to quarrel with nearly every one he came in contact with, but thinks him a good soldier and excellent man—which I believe he is.

Jan. 10, [1865]   The repulse of the enemy at Fort Fisher assumes larger proportions as the enemy's force becomes known, & it is seen how little damage they effected. Over 600 guns were brought against the work, & pounded it for two days with little effect. Hood telegraphs that his trans-Miss. troops must have furlough for 100 days. This is looked on as a bad sign of their condition. I have just returned from an examination before a committee of both houses on the "public defence".

Jan. 12, [1865]   The topic of remark today is the presence here of Mr. Frank Blair Senior [Francis P. Blair, Sr., in Richmond on a peace effort]. What his business is no one can guess, & yet every one is wondering what it can be & why he was permitted to come here. On Saturday last a fire at Charlotte burned up 22,000 Sacks of corn, 500 bales of cotton, & a variety of stores. It was accidental, but is a terrible blow in our straightened circumstances. To add to our troubles a heavy rain on Tuesday washed away a portion of the Piedmont R.R. & stops the trains for 6 or 7 days.

Gen. Lee's army has but two days food left, & an order is issued to-day to call on the citizens of Richmond for a part of their supplies. Willie still absent at M.A's [in S.C.].

Jan 15, [1865]   In this dark hour of our struggle there is of course strong feeling against the administration for having mismanaged our affairs. This must be expected in adversity. I have cherished and long ago expressed my conviction that the President is not endowed with military genius, but who would have done better? It is impossible to get any one to Say who—and it is probable that as much has been done with our armies as ought to be expected. The odds against us have been very great. But our finances have been badly conducted. For this the President can Scarcely be held responsible. It is not a province he is expected to control. The hostility to the administration will however force some change in the cabinet no doubt. [Judah P.] Benjamin, Mallory & Seddon are obnoxious, especially the latter. The Commissary Genl [Northrop] too, who has failed wretchedly will be replaced I have no doubt. He has hitherto been supposed to be very partial to the President & the President to him—on acct of old friendship at West Point—but this appears to have ceased, & those about Northrop abuse the Presdt grossly, from which I infer that their principal has changed his tone. The bombardment of Fort Fisher began again on Friday, yesterday the Fort was still in good order. Blair left the city on Friday—no one appears to have learned the nature of his mission. I learn that a portion of Hoods army is ordered up—to Augusta I hope, which I told the Secy three weeks ago was the place for two corps, leaving one corps & Forrest to cover north Alabama. The force of Gen. Lee's Army including the troops under Ewell immediately about the city is about 61,000 men (aggregate), of which 50,000 infantry 3500 artillery, & 7500 cavalry. Hoke's Division 7000 is at Wilmington, & [Gen. James] Connors brigade at Charleston in addition to above. With this number of troops before us I see no cause for despondency, if we can infuse energy enough into the Comy Dept. to feed them.

Jan. 18, [1865]   We have just come from dinner at Mrs. Jones—a party of twelve—a good dinner without wine which is getting rare. The prospect is growing darker & darker about us. On Sunday night Fort Fisher fell by assault. After having repulsed the enemy until half past six, it fell at 10 o'clock by a night attack most of the garrison being captured. A distinguished Virginian, Mr. [J. P.] Holcombe [of Bedford County], tells me there is a strong disposition among members of congress to make terms with the enemy, on the basis of the old Union, feeling that we cannot carry on the war any longer with hope of success. Wife & I sit talking of going to Mexico to live out there the remnant of our days.

Jan 25, [1865]   I have outlived my momentary depression, & feel my courage revive when I think of the brave army in front of us, sixty thousand strong. As long as Lee's army remains intact there is no cause for despondency. As long as it holds true we need not fear. The attacks of the enemy will now all be directed against that Army. Sherman from the South, Thomas from the West and Grant in front. We must sustain & strengthen this army—that is the business before us.

Old Blair has returned to this city from Washington & is again gone. What does it all mean? Are we really to make terms with the enemy, before we are half beaten? Mr. [James W.] Singleton [a peace advocate] has I believe gone off. His mission was more I think to see what could be made out of cotton, than one of peace. Would that these birds of evil omen could be kept outside our limits. They do us no good. The Virginia legislature has requested the President to appoint Gen. Lee to the command of all our armies. He replies that he would be only too happy if Gen. Lee would undertake it, but he declines. There is a great outcry against the President but I predict a re-action in his favor. The three iron clads went down the River yesterday. One got through the obstructions, the other stuck, & all returned. The object was to strike at the enemy's depots at City Point. Sherman is still lingering near Savannah, & making feints against the line of the Combahee [River]. I fear he will be heard of on the right bank of the Savannah & will Strike at Augusta.

Jan 30, [1865]   Old Frank Blair left last week, and on Sunday morning (yesterday) three so-called peace commissioners started off for Washington. They are Judge Campbell, Mr. Hunter and Mr. Stephens. Will anything come of it? I doubt it. They have no credentials nor authority but go simply to see whether anything can be agreed on, or hit on, as a basis for negotiations. Last week our flag of truce boat returning in the evening ran down one of the torpedo boats, crushing her & drowning her commander Lt. [Aeneas] Armstrong. The movements of Sherman are not yet determined, tho the Augusta authorities seem satisfied they are to be the next victims of his success. Floods have destroyed they say more property & done more damage in Ga. than Sherman did on his march. Verily, we need patience and courage to fight man and Providence. Is this double affliction Sent merely to assure us of our Strength? I think so. I have been confined for two days with a Severe cold, & to-day Mamma is in bed with a severe neuralgia in the face, the effect of a bad cold. The weather has been very severe for four or five days past, it was milder to-day. A good stock of ice has been laid in.

Feb. 3, [1865]   The "peace commissioners" probably reached Washington yesterday & are now pow-wowing. No one expects any result. Sherman appears to be moving up the Savannah probably to the [South Carolina] R.R. between Branchville [S.C.] and Augusta [Ga.]. In that case I do not see what our tactics will be—to separate by leaving a heavy force in Augusta, & then get beaten in detail; or give up Augusta & unite our forces at Some point near Branchville with the forces in and about Charleston. I fear Sherman has too many men for us & will do pretty much as he pleases. Gen. Lee has been appointed Gen-in-chief, & Gen Breckinridge Secy of War. The country continues to cry out for the re-appt of Gen. Joe Johnston to the command of the Army of Tenn. but there is nothing yet that looks that way—on the contrary it is asserted he is to be assigned to the command of this Army. I trust not, for I desire to see it commanded by one of Lee's generals, who will get inspiration from him.

Beauregard & Hardee are both at Augusta, & the two corps ordered from [Gen. Richard] Taylor's Army are beginning to arrive there. The desertions from these troops en route were said to be very numerous. I hope the story is exaggerated. Our unfortunate brother in law Dick has again been captured with his vessel (the Stag) at Wilmington.

Feb 8, [1865]   An attack in some force was made on our right on Monday, our troops driven back & Gen. Pegram killed [near Petersburg]. No great loss of men was sustained on either side, but the enemy maintained the new position they acquired.

The road between Branchville & Augusta Seems to have been cut by the enemy somewhere about Sunday or Monday.

The troops seem to be everywhere short of ammunition again & are clamoring for cartridges.

The "peace commissioners" returned on Sunday, & with the answer I expected—no terms save Submission will be listened to. It has had a good effect on the country.

Feb 10, [1865]   Yesterday there was an enthusiastic meeting on the war, at the African Church. Mr. Hunter, Mr. Benjamin & others spoke. The war feeling has blazed out afresh in Richmond, & the spirit will I hope spread thro' the land. Gen. Pegram was buried yesterday, & Gen. [G. Moxley] Sorrel is reported desperately wounded. The fight of Monday cost us some five or six hundred killed & wounded & the enemy, it is said some fifteen hundred. They gained a fresh position however & held it. It is said four corps were massed against our right. There is no doubt, that a portion of Thomas' army has been sent here. The enemy have spread along the [South Carolina] R.Road from the Edisto bridge, 5 miles from Branchville [S.C.] to Blackville, a space of some 20 odd miles. We have a heavy force concentrated about Branchville. Col Wood told us this evening that the President had intimated the strongest desire to Gen. Beauregard to have Charleston held, at any rate, for the present. I hope it will be done. It is of great importance to us to hold it for further supplies.

The feeling against the President because he will not restore Johnston, & because he will not make the changes in the Cabinet demanded by public sentiment is growing very strong.

Feb. 16, [1865]   The enemy appears to be approaching Columbia, [S.C.] & there is evidence, from telegrams, of great uneasiness there. We must expect more disasters I fear. The cup of bitterness is not yet full. Exchanges of prisoners, man for man, appear to have been fully resumed. Two thousand of our men came up yesterday. This method of exchange will leave us without prisoners, if carried out to the full extent, will leave 20,000 of our men in their hands, as they are at least that number ahead of us. We have just had a little dinner party of nine—very dull. It is impossible to shake off the despondency that hangs over us. I saw Gen. Lee yesterday. He looked very much troubled & received me somewhat sternly, as I thought. The President looked pretty well, and was as kind and courteous as ever. One cannot help being pleased with him. Gen. Breckinridge carries his duties cheerfully, & will I hope make a good Secretary because he evidently intends to push work off upon others, & not involve himself in details, which is right.

I hear that Judge Campbell, Asst Secy, may retain his position—a thing greatly to be desired. He is the main stay of the War Dept.

Richmond Feb. 19, [1865]   On looking over my notes, I find that Gen. Price is reported dead—this has since proved not to be so. I also predicted the change in the War Dept. and the Commissary. These have both come to pass. Gen. Breckinridge assumed charge of the War Dept about the lst of the month & Col. St John, (Chf. of N[itre] & M[ining] Bureau) has been made Com[missary] Gen[eral] with the rank of Brig. Gen. It is a difficult post, but the change will save the army & perhaps the cause. We held a meeting (or rather he did) at his office last night. He invited a dozen of the principal citizens to advise him & assist with suggestions. It was a good inauguration. With Gen. Lee in command & a good Commissary Gen. we need now only vigorous measures in the dept. of finance. Congress must act by passing a good tax bill.

Charleston has been evacuated (17th) and Columbia occupied by the enemy. My losses in valuable machinery and I fear Stores, have been very great, greater than ever before, perhaps than the sum of all my former losses. Why it was necessary to evacuate so hastily is not yet known. Poor Charleston! I believe however the courage of the country is really rising instead of falling; at least such is my hope from what I see & hear.

Feb 21, [1865]   The greatest consternation prevails on account of the continued advance of Sherman, who was yesterday at or near Winsboro. Beauregard fears that the enemy will reach Charlotte [N.C.] before his troops can get there, and people join in his fears. Unless troops are detached from this army to enable Beauregard to check the advance of the enemy I doubt whether Sherman's career can be stopped, & he will be in Virginia before many days—possibly the condition of the roads may arrest or check him if Confederate arms cannot. Hardee's command from the lower S. Carolina, was at Florence yesterday, & ought to be at Cheraw to-day, thence it has three days march to Charlotte.

Feb 23, [1865]   There is no definite news of Sherman's whereabouts to-day. The morning papers announced that Gen. Johnston is assigned to the command of the troops in North Carolina now under Beauregard's command, he being it is said unfit for duty from ill health. This will at least inspire confidence if it does not lead to improvement in our military status. Every body is getting dumbstruck at the rumor of the proximate evacuation of Richmond, & Mamma & myself are anxiously canvassing what is best to be done, to go away or to stay. She is most inclined to stay, with her Six little children, within the enemy's lines, & perhaps it is better than to fly one does not know whither. Did we dream six months ago that Hood's movement to Tenn. would bring us to this pass?

It is now said that the enemy refuses to receive our prisoners at Wilmington after we had ordered them there for exchange, & will try to capture & release them. This after a Solemn engagement with Grant for an exchange!

Feb 27, [1865]   I learned with pleasure yesterday from Col. [Robert] Ould [C.S.A. Chief of Exchange of Prisoners] that our exchanges would go on at the rate of say 2000 per day. Instead of Wilmington, Goldsboro [N.C.] will be the point of delivery. Sherman's movements seem to be illy understood. It is supposed he is moving toward Fayetteville and Goldsboro. He will I hope find Hardee's, Hoke's & [D. H.] Hills forces in his way. I have strong hopes that some harm may yet come to Sherman before he reaches a place of safety. Here there is a good deal of consternation lest Richmond be evacuated. An order has been given to remove all cotton and tobacco preparatory to burning it. All the departments have been notified to prepare to move. The President sent for me on Saturday & expressed his uneasiness at the effect of this order on our people at home & our prospects abroad. He thought the policy of Gen. Lee ill-judged, & likely to have an effect contrary to that intended, viz: to hasten legislation on the negro bill. He afterwards caused the Virginia Legislature to be assured that in no event would Richmond be evacuated. Gen Johnston has again been assigned to command, & has assumed charge of the troops in N. C. These when collected ought to aggregate 30,000 men, besides artillery and say 4,000 cavalry (Wheeler's, not included in the 4,000). Besides [D. H.] Hill is marching with the greater part of his corps southward. He can reach Fayetteville before Sherman can possibly get there.

Saw Mr. Benjamin yesterday, he denounces these representatives and Senators who are still hankering after peace, as "cowards & traitors."

Mamma is halting as to whether she with our children Shall in case of evacuation Stay in the enemys lines.

March 2d, [1865]   People are almost in a state of desperation, and but too ready to give up the cause, not that there is not patriotism enough to sustain it, but that there is sentiment of hopelessness abroad, a feeling that all our sacrifices tend to nothing, that our resources are wasted, in short that there is no leadership, and so they are ready to despair. It must be confessed that we are badly off for leaders both on the council & on the field. Lee is about all we have & what public confidence is left rallies around him, and he it seems to me fights without much heart in the cause. I do him wrong perhaps, but I dont think he believes we will or can succeed in this struggle. The President has alas! lost almost every vestige of the public confidence. Had we been successful his errors and faults would have been overlooked, but adversity magnifies them. He has undoubtedly done much, perhaps irreparable wrong by adhering to the wrong men. Mr. Memminger ruined our finances (with the able assistance of a weak Congress) & yet the President refused to the last moment to acknowledge that Mr. M. was the wrong man. The Commissary General has brought this army to the verge of starvation, & the country to the utmost verge of ruin thereby, yet the President has for three years kept Col. Northrop in place, tho' the whole country exclaimed against his unfitness for his duties, and the country was undoubtedly right. The President has great qualities & shining virtues, & may yet win back the good opinion of the country in the trying times before us. We cannot lose this cause, & the President will perhaps show his strength of character in sustaining it when others have lost all hope.

We went to the wedding of Gen. St. John, our new Commissary Gen. on Tuesday evening (28th). He married Miss [Ella] Carrington, living about 3 miles out of town. The roads were very bad, & with a bad driver we had poor work in getting there. There was a large company chiefly connexions & old friends of the family. The bride is a most feminine looking woman, but of decided character, & will make a most excellent companion for him. He has won the regard of every one, & has the good wishes of all. Sherman is reported moving toward Darlington & Florence [S.C.] & crossed Lynch's Creek in some force at Tylerville on Tuesday. He seems to be tending toward Wilmington, or perhaps some point above it on the Cape Fear River. Johnston's order assuming command of the army is a very appropriate one. It is a pity he was not returned to Tupelo [Miss.] two months ago. That army, which started last May 60,000 is to-day reduced to about 12,000, disheartened & dispirited men!

March 4, [18]65   To-day is the great Yankee jubilee [Lincoln's second inauguration] and jubilant are that people. I trust their crests will be br'ot lower by next 4th of March. Sherman seems to be making some progress towards Cheraw on the way to Fayetteville. I suppose he will be able to open his way to the Cape Fear & thus get supplies. In that region of sweet potatoes he is in no danger of starving. Were Gen. Lee to detach 20,000 men from the army it appears to me Sherman's defeat & perhaps destruction could be accomplished before Grant could overwhelm Richmond. Mr. Singleton has again arrived here, this time not to make peace probably, but to make money. Met last night at Baynes, Gen. Zach Deas, just from the Army of Tenn, Mr. Harrison, the Presidents Secy—his financee, Miss Conny Carey [Cary], Mr. Lyon, Mr. & Mrs. Jones & Mr. Aubrey four of us played whist while the rest talked until 12. It is raining fast this morning. We are still, as every body is, in the greatest perplexity as to our future movements, to go away or to stay is the question. The enemy threatens to advance from N. Orleans & Vicksburgh on Mobile, & from Tenn on middle Ala, capturing Selma & Montgomery. So there is no assurance of safety in that direction.

March 5 [1865] (Sunday)   Sheridan's cavalry moved on Staunton and our forces fell back to Waynesboro' where they were attacked and routed by the enemy on Thursday. They made little resistance altho over 1500, while the attacking force is represented as about 5000. Our cavalry were sent to the rear early in the winter to get forage and there was nothing but one division of infantry ([Gen. Gabriel C.] Wharton's) which has become so demoralized by defeats as to be worthless. This lays the whole [Shenandoah] valley open & the enemy is effectually destroying the Central & the Orange & Alex[andria] R.R. by tearing up rails & destroying bridges. It is very strange that Gen. Lee persists in keeping Early in command after his uniformly unsuccessful career. Rumors in the streets give us vast victories in the Carolinas. Would it were so. There has probably been a cavalry fight with Kilpatrick's cavalry. If we could overcome that we might threaten Sherman's movements & destroy his foraging parties. We had a few gentlemen to dinner yesterday—Gen. Deas, Mr. Aubrey, Col. Williams & Mr. Goldthwaite (Lt.). The weather has turned sunshiny again.

March 6, [1865]   The crisis of our fate is rapidly approaching, and men's minds are harrassed with doubts, fears & perplexity. The weak are for submission and those who have more fortitude are affected by the fears of the timid. A few men remain Strong & if they have them conceal their fears. Wherever three or four are gathered together there are ominous whispers & dubious shakings of the head. Even those whose faith remains unshaken find it difficult to give a reason for their faith. The Senate it is now Said are ready for any terms—the cowards. Pity a few could not be taken out & hung or shot. If a soldier yields to his fears in the hour of trial & is shot for it, why may not the craven Senator be made to yield his dastard life in the Same way? Is it less a crime, & is not his example just as pernicious as that of the coward soldier? A few brief months, weeks perhaps, will decide whether this cause is to fail, & all the blood shed in it be for naught—can it be possible? Are the names of the illustrious dead to go down to history as traitors, instead of patriots?

No definite news of Sherman. Our forces seem to be drawing toward Raleigh. Fayetteville where we have an armory and an arsenal will probably be left to its fate. Sheridan seems to go along unmolested. He did not go to Gordonsville, but seems to have taken a road back toward Lynchburg.

March 9, [1865]   A little good news comes to-day from Bragg. The forces under him attacked the enemy near Kinston [N.C.], drove them back and captured 1500 prisoners and 3 pieces of artillery, without sustaining very heavy loss. Yesterday the enemy were reported across the James River, & on the Southside R.R. 25 miles this side of Lynchburgh. This is ascertained to be untrue—none having crossed the River—but he is approaching Lynchburgh & will no doubt try to take it. I hope we shall repulse him, but our troops have fought so badly of late, that we cannot predict anything with much confidence. Gen Johnston is at Fayetteville which was however being evacuated yesterday, so that we have lost the Armory and Arsenal there. There are also 8 cotton factories. We heard to-day the reported death of Hugh [Aiken, husband of Amelia's sister, Mary]. There is Still a hope it may not be true—a faint hope. It was said he was killed in a skirmish near Cheraw. I went to the market this morning. There was but one Turkey visible, & that held at $140. Veal was selling at $10 per lb, & none at that.

March 11, [1865]   The fast yesterday was generally observed, and many good Sermons were preached, no doubt with effect. They are needed to strengthen the failing faith of the people. There is a little additional good news to-day. Gen. Hampton attacked Kilpatrick's camp yesterday morning, took his wagons and artillery and captured Some prisoners, & re-captured many that he held. Is this the last gleam of an expiring cause; or is it the dawn of its rise from the night which has shrouded it?

We had definite news of the death of Hugh. I saw Major [John G.] Stokes, Adjt. Gen. of [Gen. Evander M.] Law[']s cavalry brigade who saw him buried, & was not far off when he was killed. It occurred on the road to Cheraw from Chesterfield, about 14 miles from the former place. The enemy was reported in front, skirmishers thrown out, and Hugh with a group of others rode out in front of the line of skirmishers. A volley was fired into this group from an ambush & four fell, among them Hugh, hit the Major says, (on hearsay) by nine balls. The body was taken along, placed in a rude coffin, as were the others & decently buried at Mount Hebron Church, 11 miles from Cheraw. The church stands in a pine wood about 300 yds back from the road—poor Mary! What a life long sorrow is there. But he died like a gallant soldier, on the soil of his native state & defending it against her foes.

March 14, [1865]   After defeating Early at Waynesboro, and dispers-ing his force, Sheridan has been careening over the country without opposition, and has destroyed the system of Rail-Roads north of the James River so that they cannot again be repaired for this war probably. Yesterday it is reported he was crossing the James River to the South side, whence he would doubtless proceed to join Grants left severing the Rail-Roads in his way. The enemy behaved pretty well at Charlottesville, not destroying the university nor committing unnecessary outrage. It is reported they shot Commodore [George N.] Hollins, who took to the mountains. Several well known gentlemen are missing, but will doubtless turn up in due time.

March 15, [1865]   Sheridan is to-day reported to be about 15 miles from the city with his whole force, consisting as Gen. Early declares of 8000 men, each armed with a 16 Shooter & four revolvers—a moving Armory truly! Some fighting has been going on to-day, with what success is not yet ascertained. The whole of Pickett's Division, & Fitz Lee's cavalry is after him, and he ought to be bro't to bay, but he will probably escape after having caused us damages it will take four months to repair. From Sherman there is nothing more authentic than that we are concentrating about Raleigh, & that Johnston apparently proposes to give battle. He will however I think fall back, even perhaps behind the Roanoke. The President sent in a message to Congress on Monday which appears to have waked them up. He demands a suspension of the habeas corpus, some gold to feed the army with, a militia law, & then they may go home. They appear inclined to respond. A month more & the war will be full upon us again.

Mch 19, [1865]   Hardee resisted the advance of the enemy a few miles South of Winnsboro, & foiled his advance upon Raleigh. It may have been a heavy feint to cover his advance upon Goldsboro where he will effect a junction with Scofield [Gen. John M. Schofield] who has 10 or 12 thousand men. Our loss in this action (16th) is rated at 500, that of the enemy much larger. Sheridan has joined Grant, & will doubtless soon emerge from the left of that army & operate on our communications. The Spirit of the people appears to be again rising—that of the army remains good. Desertions are decreasing. Bayne and I are still discussing where we shall move our families. Mama desires to remain. To-day & yesterday large bodies of returned prisoners arrived. The weather is beautiful & is rapidly drying up the roads, & rendering the resumption of hostilities imminent.

March 21, [1865]   On the 19th Gen. Johnston attacked the enemy at Bentonville [N.C.] and drove him. He was reinforced but still driven. Reinforced still further he attempted to take the offensive but was readily repulsed whereupon he intrenched. The country was wooded & difficult. This looks as tho' he were covering his march toward Goldsboro where he expects to effect a junction with the forces of Schofield. It is scarcely probable that Johnston has Strength enough to prevent this. What will be his movements after this junction remains to be seen.

Rumors to-day of a victory over Sherman are rife, but not much credit is given to them. Lee seems entirely indisposed to send any portion of his force to the assistance of Johnston, yet 10,000 men so detached would enable Johnston to stop & perhaps overwhelm Sherman. No one can divine the reason of this inaction of Lee. The apprehension now is for our communications with Danville on which our supplies depend. If these are interrupted for ten days Lee's army cannot be fed, & it must fall back. It is a most critical situation.

The confidence of the country is again rising. Stragglers from Johnston's army are said to be returning.

Everything depends on his ability to meet Sherman.

Mch 26, [1865]   Yesterday morning at 4 o'clock Johnston's [Gen. Bushrod Johnson's] Divn with a part of [A. P.] Hill's Corps attacked the enemy's lines on the Appomattox. They carried the curtains easily, but these men swept by redoubts which overwhelmed us with their fire & compelled a return to our lines. We captured about 700 prisoners including a Brig. Gen. ([Napoleon B.] McLoughlin), & lost 1000 in killed wounded & missing. Col Baldwin calls the affair a bad failure. We lost many valuable officers. Sherman has effected his junction with Schofield & the combined force will now doubtless march on Raleigh or on Weldon. As Gen. Breckinridge Said yesterday "Something must be done Soon". Either Lee must uncover his position & with [Gen. Joseph E.] Johnston fall on Sherman, or Johnston combine with Lee & together fall on Grant. We are preparing to move our goods and chattels to Danville for the present. It is in vain to predict where safety resides & we must wait to see.

Mch 29, [1865]   We are still discussing as to what place we shall retire to. Danville appears the most feasible, & we are packing up to go there. It grieves Mamma to leave our comfortable quarters here, & go to a new home.

Mch 30, [1865]   Last night at about 9 o'clock, the enemy made a furious attack on our lines at Petersburg. It seems to have been an attack of artillery, chiefly. The enemy yesterday moved a heavy force out upon our right, & have apparently gained a position not far from the Southside R. Road. When he gains this road I fear the lines about Petersburg will no longer be tenable. The accounts of our attack on the enemys lines on the Appomattox show a very unfavorable result for us. Our losses cannot have been less than 2000 in killed wounded & missing chiefly the last.

Winsboro, April 30, [1865]   On the 2d of April news came in, in the morning from Gen. Lee that his lines had been assaulted and broken by the enemy; and in a few hours afterwards a second despatch that his line could not be re-established and that Richmond must be evacuated by 8 o'clock at night. This I learned about 1 P.M. We had been making arrangements to move to Danville on the 3d (Monday). It was now impracticable to get the family & our effects ready by the time indicated, & Amelia concluded at once to remain & we began moving all our effects up to Marias house. At about midnight I left her, still standing like a brave woman, over the remnants of her household goods which would be moved up before day by a wagon & horse I had left for that purpose. She had with her two faithful women of the neighborhood to whom she had been kind during the winter, & Willie, who dropped off to sleep about this time. At a little after midnight Bayne & I wended our way down Cary St. to the Danville Depot. All was Still & orderly on the Streets. In passing out of the Arsenal gate, I left the Sentinel on duty at the gate as usual, & everything promised an orderly evacuation. I had given directions that nothing in my control should be burned lest fires might be general, & the innocent inhabitants suffer. At a little after 1 A.M. Monday morning the train to which the car on which I was belonged moved off but it was 3 o'clock before we left the neighborhood of Manchester. Toward 6 o'clock in the morning as we have since learned the tobacco warehouse on Shockoe Slip was fired, & set that part of the town on fire. About 7 A.M. the three bridges—[Richmond &] Danville & [Richmond &] Petersburgh R.R.[s] were fired & the result was the burning up of a large part of the city, extending from 14th up to 8 or 9 St, & from the Water to Franklin. It was due to our own ill-advised orders. I heard Gen. Breckinridge give orders to fire the bridges, & regret I did not interpose, as I had heard Gen. [Jeremy F.] Gilmer, Chf Engineer express [the] most decided opinion as to the wanton destruction of R.R. bridges. I had on Saturday addressed a letter to Gen. Ewell, deprecating the destruction of tobacco in the warehouses by fire & suggesting that it might be effected as well by breaking barrels of turpentine over the top of it as it lay Stored. The Arsenal was fired from the [Richmond &] Petersburgh [Railroad] bridge, & the explosion of powder & shells must have terrified the inhabitants of that part of the city, & must have spread the fire.

We reached Danville Monday evening & were received by Major Hutter. Here we stayed until the news of the surrender of Gen. Lee made it necessary for the Government to remove still further Southward. The surrender took place on Sunday the 9th. The news of it reached Danville on Monday evening. I saw the President the same evening, as he was preparing to leave Danville. He was evidently overwhelmed by this astounding misfortune. He had sent for Gen. Cooper, myself & Col. [Richard] Morton [Superintendent of the Nitre and Mining Bureau], the only Chiefs of Bureau present. But he had no instructions to give me, & I told him I would probably receive some from the Secy of War, who would be in the following day. He left Danville the same evening with such of the cabinet as were with him, by rail for Greensboro. We left in two ambulances about 1 P.M. on Tuesday. Our party consisted of Bayne, Capt Aubrey, myself, & three others. We stopped that night at or near Yanc[e]yville [N.C.] at Mr. Bow's, who treated us very kindly. Next day we crossed the Haw River, at a very bad ford near Haw River Horne, where the bridge had been swept away. Our dumb Chief Eng. for Johnston was then preparing to build bridges for that army. We continued on to Graham, & about a mile & a half beyond & slept in our wagons. Next morning we moved on to Judge Ruffins & breakfasted. It had rained most of the night & the roads were very bad. Judge R's family including mostly ladies, were much alarmed at the prospective approach of Sherman's Army. Running a short distance on the road to Graham we took to the left, on the old Salisbury road, & traveled to Mr. Winslows near Carraway mountain, a somewhat picturesque country. Mr. W was evidently no "rebel." On Friday night we stopped at the home of a widow with three grown daughters who all "dipped"—i.e. chewed snuff. On Saturday night at [space] where a horse thief had been shot the week before & one hurt in a stream of [?].

On Sunday night we stopped, after crossing the Yadkin [River] at Stokes Ferry, at a Mr. Moose. The people all live very plainly but still have enough to eat & we could procure all we needed for coffee, yams, or spices, of all of which we had some. On Monday we broke one of our wagons, & stopped at a blacksmith Shop, 9 miles from Concord, & stayed 24 hours to repair damages. His name was also Moose. On Tuesday night we went to Pioneer Mills & the next day to Charlotte.

At Charlotte we found that the President and most of the Bureau Officers had arrived, and the town was crowded with cavalry, & straggling infantry. We found quarters at a hospitable Inn named Mayer Baer, who gave up his best room with two sofas, & a Brussels carpet to sleep on. The good woman served our meals in the parlor and took good care of us. I have a grateful recollection of Mrs. Baer. (She said the children called her boys "cubs", & laughed heartily). The total dispersion of Gen. Lee's army affected that of Gen. Johnston, & it soon became evident that no further effectual mil. resistance could be offered. The consequence was a mil. convention & Armistice, between Sherman, on the one side & Johnston & the Secy of War on the other. This took place at or near Hillsboro about the middle of April & caused a suspension of hostilities—to be resumed after 48 hours' notice by either party. The armistice was based on 7 articles the principal of which provided for the disbanding of the Conf. troops which were to be marched back to the State Capitals where the arms & munitions were to be deposited with the State governments; for the recognition of existing State governments—the Supreme Court to decide in case of conflicting governments; the protection of persons & property & <u>general amnesty</u>. This latter

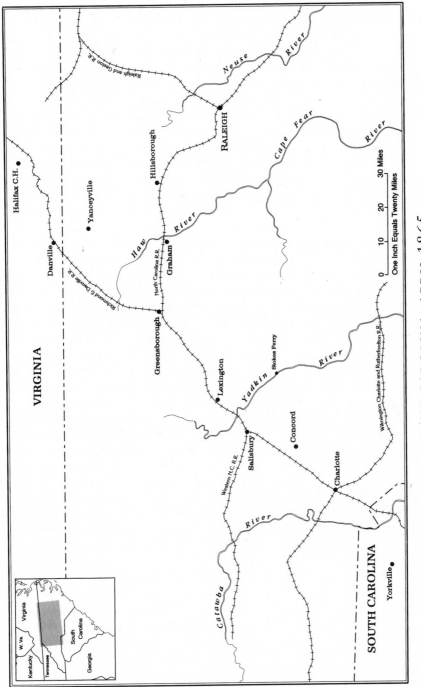

NORTH CAROLINA, APRIL 1865

article was dictated by Gen. Sherman. Nothing was Said about Slavery.

The convention was sent to Washington & there instantly rejected, tho' it is understood approved by Gen. Grant. The notice of termination of armistice took effect on Tuesday or Wednesday (25th or 26th).

Meantime Lincoln had been assassinated (on Friday eveg the 14th) while at the Theatre, and [Secretary of State] Seward badly if not mortally wounded.

On Wednesday at 11 o'clock we left Charlotte for this place, Winnsboro. As I rode out of the town I met the President, booted and spurred with one of his aids, Gov Lubbock, ready to take Saddle. He was going with a large escort of cavalry by the way of Yorkville, Union[ville,] Abbeville [S.C.] (where Mrs. Davis was) and thro' upper Georgia to the Trans-Miss. All the cabinet except Mr. [George A.] Trenholm [Confederate Secretary of the Treasury] who is sick were with him. Before he reaches the Miss. events will have shaped themselves. Whether I shall follow remains to be determined.

Wednesday night we stopped 16 miles from Charlotte. Thursday we forded the Catawba which was deep, & floated away part of our "furniture"—such as tin basin, water pail—bag of useful things—corn &c. We drove on, after drying & reloading to "Col. Sturgis", about 8 miles from Hay Ford, where we had crossed. This was the most forlorn looking place we had yet Stopped at. Tho owning 600 acres of land, & Several Slaves, & tho' the "Col." was a "public" man, not unknown to local fame, there were none of the comforts of civilized life—nothing to eat & nothing to eat it with. But one spoon with half a handle to Stir all our cups. There were three daughters, one of whom did a great deal of courting with a Soldier whom she had seen for the first time that day.

On Friday night we stayed with Mr. Robt Caldwell, 17 miles from Winsboro, & fared sumptously. Here there were beautiful flowers & a piano—in short civilization which we had left behind us at Danville. Mr. C. had been stripped of everything eatable & much of his Stock, first by friend & next by the foe. He would receive no pay, but we left with him a small supply of Coffee. We drove here by 1 o'clock on Saturday & are comfortably distributed—Bayne & myself at Mary's, & Aubrey & [Joseph] Denegre & Jas. Aiken [older brother of Hugh and Wyatt Aiken] Mr. Wiltz at the hotel.

We had heard of the surrender of Johnston's army before we left Charlotte.

Wednesday, May 3d, [1865]   The orders of Johnston & Sherman on the Surrender are being published. It capitulates the whole country east of the Chattahoochie, and paroles all officers on duty within the limits of Johnston's command.

There is a Strong disposition to possess themselves of all property of the Conf. Govt on the part of the people. Augusta is ruled by a mob who have broken open all public Stores, & it is said private ones. All public property has been carried off at Chester & Blackstock [Black Stocks, S.C.] (the terminus of the [Charlotte and South Carolina] R. Road) [north of Columbia]. The citizens here take whatever they can lay their hands on, and have even shown a great desire to lay violent hands on a large quantity of powder here.

Reconstruction
May 1865–July 1878

Josiah Gorgas as a civilian (Courtesy of Hoole Special Collections, University of Alabama, Tuscaloosa, Alabama)

IX

"I am as one walking in a dream"

Thursday May 4, [1865]   The citizens here are destroying powder in Store here lest worse befal[l] & the whole town be blown up. I have suggested that some of the common powder be reserved for blasting.

We are discussing the propriety of setting out again on our progress Southward, & will probably leave on Saturday. I desire to set forward to Alabama, as my adopted State, before again coming under the control of the authority of the U.S. Govt. We took tea at Mr. Jos. Aikens last night, & are to dine with Mr. Taft to-day.

The calamity which has fallen upon us in the total destruction of our government is of a character so overwhelming that I am as yet unable to comprehend it. I am as one walking in a dream, & expecting to awake. I cannot see its consequences, nor shape my own course, but am just moving along until I can see my way at some future day. It is marvelous that a people that a month ago had money, armies, and the attributes of a nation should to-day be no more, & that we live, breathe, move, talk as before. Will it be so when the Soul leaves the body behind it?

Thursday May 11, [1865]   Left Winsboro on Saturday at 1½ P.M. & slept at Mrs. Lyles, 18 miles out. Mrs. Lyles' mother is first cousin to my wife. She was there—a talkative old lady of 64. Her husband was Wm. Hainesworth [Haynsworth], & her own name was Moss. She is from Conn. They reside at Sumter [S.C.]. Mrs. Lyles' place is called <u>Rat Hall</u>. It is 3 miles from Broad River.

Sunday morning we left at 8½, crossed Broad River on a good flat worked with a rope. A poor woman sat under a big tree on the West side of the Ferry, with her household goods under two old tent cloths. She was waiting here for the body of her daughter who was drowned here some 10 days before in crossing with a skiff & the body had floated down some 14 miles before it was recovered. I gave her $50 Conf. money—worthless to me—but which she said would assist her. We passed thro Newberry [S.C.], inquiring the way beyond at Mr. Jones (Lambert—having picked up on the way & deposited at his home a limping Lieut. named Owen, formerly residing at Charleston (son of G. W. Owen). Newberry is a pleasant looking town with plenty of space & shade trees about the homes. We passed on 3 miles to Judge O'Neil's mill where we crossed the [Greenville and Columbia] R.R. track & continuing on to Mr. Longshores took the left hand road & stopped at Mr. Benton's 1½ miles from the fork & 9½ from Newberry. Mr. B. is a wealthy planter owning 6000 acres, all of which he has accumulated by his own labor tho only 48 years old. He Still had Sugar, coffee, & tea— treated us most hospitably & took no pay. On Monday (8th) we crossed the Little River and at 15 ml from Mr. B's the Saluda at Island Ford, in a good ferry boat, where they still charged in Confed. money. It rained a part of the day. Reached Wyatt Aikens at 3½ P.M. having driven 24 miles since 7½. On Tuesday evey at nearly 8 o'clock Bayne, Denegre, Fred Gayle [one of Amelia's half brothers] & Mr. Jas Aiken arrived. Stony Point [S.C.], formerly a place of note in the old Piedmont Stage route to N. Orleans, is a mile from here. Three sets of stages formerly left there twice a day, & there was a Dry goods & a grocery store kept there by old Mr. Smith grandfather of Mrs. Aiken. Col. Aiken has a good plantation here with excellent outhouses, & good stock. His Gin, & Press are driven by Steam & he has good boilers for Syrup. Little cotton is now being raised in any of this region.

To-day Judge [William W.] Crump, Asst Secy of Treasy, Capt. Irwin (brother of Mrs. Elzey) & Mr. [Edward M.] Tidball Chief Clerk of Navy Dept. arrived on their way back to Richmond. From them we learn that the last vestige of the Conf. Govt was dissipated at Washington Ga. The escort of the President proving wholly worthless, it was dismissed & the President left with Col. Wood, Col Lubbock, Col. [William P.] Johnston & Mr. [Charles E.] Thorburn (formerly in the Navy) for Florida, it is supposed. The rest of the cabinet went off separately—Gen. Breckinridge leaving with his two sons. The government being then utterly destroyed, there seems to be nothing left but to give our paroles, & remain quiet— moving in meantime toward Ala. We shall leave in the morning probably for Washington [Ga.], & there give our paroles.

Friday, May 12, [1865]   Left Stony Pt [S.C.] in the morning. Stopped at Blacksmith Shop at the homestead to repair something. (Bayne is always stopping at Blacksmith shops to repair damages, due I expect to his ambitious style of going down hill). Drove to Abbeville. Aubrey & I

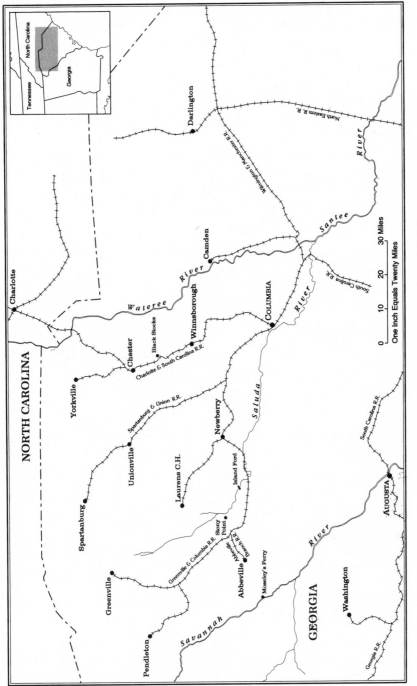

SOUTH CAROLINA, MAY 1865

went to Mr. Gus. Smiths, to whom Wyatt [Aiken] gave me a letter—
Bayne & Denegre to Major Bow's. Had a most comfortable room & A.
& I slept well.

Saturday, [May 13, 1865]   Left in good time (say 7½) drove a mile on
the wrong road. Crossed the Savannah river [into Ga.] at Moseley's Ferry
and stopped at the Widow Gary's about 5 miles from the Ferry. Were
well entertained without charge. It would be a nice place to spend a
summer month or two.

Sunday, [May] 14th [1865]   Heard that the enemy were at Elberton
[Ga.] in force; & crossed Broad River at Bakers Ferry, taking the road to
Washington & Centreville [Centerville, Ga.]. Met a squad of 6 Yankees
whom we mistook for our own people. Bayne asked them whether there
were any "Yankees" at Washington! They seemed to be quite as willing
to pass us as we were to pass them. B. & I rode on to Washington while
the wagons went on to Centreville. We got paroles for ourselves & the
two others, met Gen. Alexander and talked an hour, rode on and reached
C a little after dark, 41 miles from Mrs. Gary's by W. Mr. Maddox's
house constitutes C. & he was our host.

Monday, [May] 15th [1865]   Mr. M. wanted to charge us $10 for our
night's lodging food &c. B[ayne] pd him $5 & $300 Conf. money (which
is now worthless) & drove to Poullain's Mills & bivouacked on the
hither bank of the Stream. No Sleep on account of fleas, & kept watch
from 1¼ to day light.

Tuesday, [May 16, 1865]   Drove to Mr. Hardee's who charged us
$7½ for a bushel & a half of corn & supper with a lunch, paid him
sovereign & $100 in Conf. money.

Wednesday, [May 17, 1865]   Crossed Snapping Shoal, & went to Mr.
Hartsfield whose daughter mistook us for Yankees. Passed a most comfortable night, all sleeping indoors for the first time.

Thursday, [May 18, 1865]   Drove thro McDonough, stopping on the
way to drink buttermilk at Mr. Cloud's, drank a gallon I think among us.
McDonough a decayed town, went on until dark & bivouacked at Mrs.
Jackson's, a poor widow who baked some corn bread for us. (Passed
Gen. Hardee at our noon rest, or rather he passed us & we afterward
drove by him).

Friday, [May 19, 1865]   Passed thro' Griffin, & passing Cedar Shoals,
drove to Mr. Atkinson's where we were hospitably entertained, &
charged only $2½. Mr. A. had lost a son at Manassas to whom he
referred with much feeling.

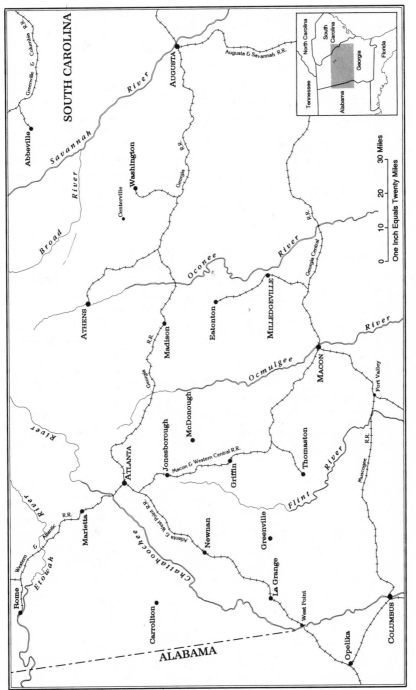

GEORGIA, MAY 1865

Saturday, [May 20, 1865]   Passing by Mr. Howe's blacksmith shop & stopping 1¼ hours, we reached Greenville about 12. Parted from Mr. Aubrey ½ mile this side, & reached La Grange [Ga.] a little after sundown.

Sunday [May] 21, [1865]   Breakfasted at Mr. Banksmith's & dined at Col. Phillip's. Mr. Mallory & Mr. [Benjamin H.] Hill arrested at midnight of Saturday night & taken off by a special train. Saw Mrs. M. in the afternoon. She is greatly afflicted, & very helpless.

Monday, [May 22, 1865]   Am going to dine with Mr. Solomon Levy, where Gen. Hardee who comes in this morning also dines. Spent two hours with Mrs. Mulford this morning, who sings charmingly & is a cultivated musician.

Leave in the morning for Montgomery [Ala.] via [space]

Tuesday, May 23d, [1865]   Left Lagrange (stayed at Mr. Howards whose family including his mother-in-law, had refugeed as they called it three times having been driven first from Northern Ga & afterwards from near Jonesboro; & again from Atlanta) crossed the Chattahoochie 9 miles from Lag[range], & passing thro the little dilapidated town of Fredonia [Ala.], where 3 abandoned shops had signs of "bar-room." Stopped all night at Lafayette [in eastern Ala.]. Gen. H[ardee] stayed in the same town, & went hence by Wetumpka to his home near Demopolis.

Wednesday, [May 24, 1865]   Cooked our own breakfast, & started early, travelled 27 miles & stopped at a Mr. Brown's 2 miles beyond Loatchipoka [Loachapoka, near Auburn, Ala.]. I slept in the house the rest (reduced now to Bayne & Denegre) in the wagon. It is very difficult to get corn & the country is very destitute—(crossed the Alabama line yesterday about 1½ to 2 miles this side of the Chattahoochie).

Thursday, [May 25, 1865]   got a cup of coffee (Parker restaurateur) & drove thro' Notasulga [in northern Macon County] on the [Montgomery and West Point] R. R. & thro' Franklin which had just one abandoned house, to Mr. Webb's 27½ miles, & 23 from Montgomery. Mr. W. is a very wealthy man, or was, has a fine home, & a pretty married daughter. Yet he charged us $5. for our corn and entertainment. We all slept in the house. People are so desirous of getting a little specie that they charge people for entertaining them, a thing hitherto almost unknown, among the planters.

Friday, [May 26, 1865]   reached Montgomery passing by many large fields of corn in which the grain was growing at 1 o'clock. Stopped to see Gov [Thomas Hill] Wat[t]s who is of course deposed. Went to the Exchange [Hotel]—too late for dinner—took tea with Yankee officers at the same table. The sensation is novel, but we must get used to the

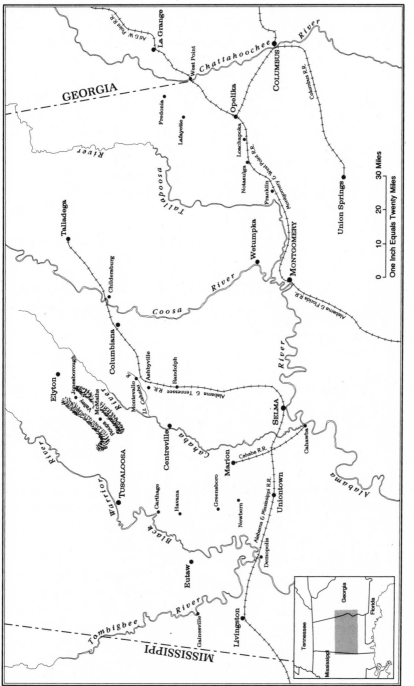

ALABAMA, 1865

presence of our late enemies, now our masters. The town is full of Yankees, & the negros abound everywhere, idle tho not insolent. Three thousand are in camp on the opposite side of the [Alabama] River, & the smallpox is making sad havoc among them. Poor victims of their northern friends.

Saturday, [May 27, 1865]   Saw Gen. A. J. Smith & asked him as to the policy of his Govt toward the members of Conf. Congress & Govt. & also toward army officers. [He] Tho't army officers would not be molested, & has no orders to make arrests. He has grown very old & gray since I saw him 20 years ago. He is a man of moderate calibre a good soldier no doubt and seems to give satisfaction. Talked with freedom as to my coming South at the beginning of the war. He is himself from Tenn. Found Dr. Potts at his room, who is also from the old Army, & had served with Smith. Left M. at 4 P. M. by Steamer Coquette (U.S. Qr.M Dept.) with horses and ambulance on board. Ex Gov. A. B. Moore [at the time of Alabama's secession convention], & Col [George W.] Gayle came on board, the first accompanied by a Yankee officer, & in arrest; the second under guard, two sentinels constantly sitting over him with muskets. He foolishly it seems published an offer to be one of a number that should make up a purse of a million dollars, as a reward to assassinate Lincoln [Seward, and A. Johnson. Gayle was jailed for several months until officials decided he had nothing to do with Lincoln's death]. Gov M[oore] kindly said to me as I left him that if he came back safely he could be of service to me.

Sunday [May] 28th, [1865]   Left Selma at 7 P. M. & drove to Marion [in Perry County], taking with us Mr. [William M.] Brooks, who was the President of the convention which voted this State out of the union. We stopped all night at his house. Mrs. B[rooks] is a very charming woman & refined. Mr. B[rooks] thinks he will be arrested, & talks of leaving the home which he had hoped to embellish for his children. Denegre left us at Selma & continued on to Mobile. Met Lt. Col. White at the landing at S[elma].

Monday [May] 29th, [1865]   Drove to Greensboro [in Hale County], 18 miles, and found all well—[Amelia's stepmother] Mrs. Gayle, [Amelia's older brother] Matt, [Amelia's half brothers and half sister] Fred, Helen, Johnny & Eddy—Capt. James Wemyss her nephew absent temporarily. Matt looks perfectly helpless, vacant almost imbecile. [A C.S.A. surgeon, Matt suffered a nervous breakdown at the end of the war and never recovered.]

Wednesday [May] 31st, [1865]   Drove to Eutaw [in Greene County], 21 miles & found [Amelia's sister] Sarah [Crawford and her children], Clara, Milly, Billy & Sally all well. Eutaw & Greensboro are both rural, shady pleasant towns, the latter has most wealth. Both afford good society.

Friday June 2d, [1865]   Drove to Demopolis. The roads thro the swamp developed some of the worst mud holes I ever rode thro'. Found Mr. Lyon ill with a severe chill. He was well enough however to see us & left his bed on Sunday. The slaves are of course in great commotion. Their freedom has been announced to them, & they are in a state of excitement & jubilee not yet knowing what responsibilities their new condition brings with it. They are idle but not insubordinate nor disrespectful. It is a curious problem which is being solved by the sword— this freedom of the African race. It will cause many a cruel pang on both sides. The master sees his property suddenly swept away, & the negro does not find in his freedom compensation for the ills it brings upon him. But the world will wag on & his freedom will cling to him and the master will continue to cultivate his land, with black labor or that failing with white. The energies of the white race will halt but temporarily before this catastrophe. At Mr. L's was Mrs. Lyon, an admirable wife & mother, [and their children and in-laws] Mrs. [Sarah Lyon] Prince & daughter and 2 boys, Mrs. and Gen. Deas, Amelia[,] Eugenia, & Ida Lyon & the only son Frank. Mrs. [Mary Lyon] Ross, another married daughter, lives close by.

Mr. Bayne left on Sunday for N. O. leaving me, the last of the company, alone with "John," the last of my Staff.

As we were going with B[ayne] to the boat we met Mr. [William H.] Ross just from Mobile with the "Amnesty Proclamation" which allows all except a couple hundred thousand people to take the oath of allegiance. The most curious & significant "exception" is that of all worth over $20,000. I expected the rest. Another amnesty will follow later which may perhaps include me. At present I am a hopeless traitor—with no right to life, liberty or property! I have debated gravely with myself whether I should leave the country or not. My decision is for the present to remain, & take the consequences, unless I find that my life is really in danger, which I cannot think.

Tuesday June 6th, [1865]   Drove back to Eutaw alone. Crossed the Warrior river 2 miles from town, after driving thro thick swamp. There is a Yankee picket, to prevent desertion no doubt, for they ask for no passes. Dined at Col. [James I.] Thornton's—half way—who is the owner of a very large estate [the palatial Thornhill]. It struck me very uncomfortably that his convictions should be so largely interladed with retrospection of his opposition to the doctrine of secession, & the necessary deduction that we fought so valiantly & bled so freely in a cause radically wrong. He has I learn however done his share to sustain the war, & perhaps that consciousness makes him talk the more freely of his former views. Missed my way before getting to Col. T's & consequently drove 33 miles under a hot sun.

Friday June 9th, [1865]   Drove with Milly to Greensboro, leaving ¼ 7 & arriving at 12¼. Day very sultry.

Saturday June 10th, [1865]   Drove with Col. Jones to Gen. Hardee's plantation, & dined & passed the day with him. His wife (nee Lewis) is a pleasant woman, cultivated, & much in love with her husband, who tho' still young looking is quite double her age. Had a good plain dinner, served on all sorts of odd china. Crockery, being fragile; has suffered its full share of the ruin brought by this war, & cannot yet be replaced.

Monday, [June] 12th, [1865]   Have just rec'd a note from Mr. [Frank] Gilmer addressed to Mr. Lyon asking me to meet him at the mountain where his coal & iron interests lie. Must wait to see Col White who promises to be here to-morrow, & then I shall try to get to this rendezvous with Mr. Gilmer tho I don't as yet know my way there.

Thursday [June] 15th, [1865]   It has been raining every day since Sunday, much to the advantage of the crops. Called to-day to see Mr. [Richard H.] Cobb[s], rector of the [St. Paul's] Episcopal Church, a young minister of excellent physiognomy. Also on Dr. [John H.] Parrish, who reminds me a little of Kingsbury, and to see Miss Sallie Walton. Saw Mr. W. her father. He is a wealthy planter owning some 7 or 8 plantations, & is much troubled at the present condition of things—his slaves all freed & his past life as he seems to think wasted. This state of mind is most natural, & leads to despondency in his case, but not so in the case of most planters, and nothing surprises me more than the equanimity with which they meet existing <u>facts</u>. Their slaves are suddenly made their (almost) equals & they, with them; they are withdrawn from their control & they talk to them & advise them. A Yankee Captain ([Henry T.] Crydenwise of the Freedman's Bureau) makes an appointment to meet <u>them & their slaves</u>, & expound the views of the Yankee govt. & they <u>attend and listen</u> to declarations made to their slaves that they & their children are <u>free</u> for all time, & will be protected and maintained in that freedom! And they stand and ask questions of this yankee Captain as to their new relations toward their Slaves! It seems a gigantic dream. Four months ago that Yankee capt. attempting to make such an address to their Slaves, would have been hung on the nearest tree, & left there. It is a good omen for the future of this country. Where sense & discretion guide & direct the masters they will be sure to regain in time the sway, in some shape which they have at present lost, thro' the total failure of military operations. We may still hope for a future I think.

Friday June 16, [1865]   Left with a buggy and a pair of horses for Tuscaloosa on my way to see the mineral region of the Red Mountain, but especially to look at the iron works of Mr. Gilmer. Passed thro' Havanna [Havana] (15 m.) [a town north of Greensboro in Hale County] and Carthage (8 ms.) [then in Tuscaloosa County, now the village of Moundville] the former a dozen houses tavern &c, the latter one house open the other two or three unoccupied. Stopping to rest at 12 M at a stream I found a planter with three wagon loads of negros & their plunder, returning to his place in Miss. He had been planting in Georgia for two Seasons. Said there would probably be food enough raised in his section of Miss. to sustain the pop'n. Carried the inevitable big whip of an overseer or small planter, which always strikes me uncomfortably. Reached Tuscaloosa at 6½ P.M. (40 miles) and stopped with Col. [Robert] Jemison (late Conf. Senator) who was just recovering from a fight in which two of his ribs had been broken! He lives in a fine large new house, not quite completed. The wood work is all of selected native wood— walnut, oak, china tree, long leaved-pine, &c. The doors, which are large panel, are highly varnished & have a very rich appearance. His family consists of his wife and daughter Cherry (Cherokee). He began life as a stage driver & made a fortune as a contractor. Col. Mallet came round to see me in the evening.

Saturday, [June 17, 1865]   left with Col. Mallet at ¼ 10, crossed Hurricane Creek (8 m) & drove to Mr. [William] Vance's (24 miles). The country is broken, & the roads hilly but at this season good as any road can be expected to be which has not been worked on for four years. We got some oats for our horses, & stayed all night for a dollar which Col. M[allet] paid for with a plug of tobacco.

Sunday, [June 18, 1865]   Started at a little before six, passed McMath's, where there is a Cold Spring (7 m) & Jonesboro (15 m) [in southwest Jefferson County] & rested 2 miles beyond a Mr. Smith's. Jonesboro is a village of several hundred inhabitants. It is a pleasant valley from Vance's up, well watered & healthful. Mr. S.'s house has a pretty site, & his farm is a good one. He gave us a pitcher of buttermilk oats plenty for our three horses & charged us a dime! He had lost 14 head of stock (mules & horses) & much of his meat & corn in [U.S. Gen. John T.] Croxton's raid. He appears to have been the devastator of this valley [on March 27, 1865, during Gen. James H. Wilson's raid through Alabama]. Mr. S. had made a bargain to give his negros one half of his corn crop, leaving them to find their own food after his present stock is exhausted. Left at 3¼ P. M., passed along strata of lime stone tipped vertically along which the road runs the strata being thin & worn by wheels make grooves for the wheels out of which it is somewhat difficult to turn. It is called the "Devil's race track" tho quite different from the stony road to which the same name is applied in Randolph Co. N.C. Reached Mr. Grace's house, with but 3 wheels to our buggy at 6½ P. M.

Monday, [June 19, 1865]   Rode to Elyton (2½ m. north west) to get our wheel repaired. It is a deserted looking town, the county seat [until 1871] of Jefferson Co. A female school on the edge of town was burned lately (<u>not</u> by Croxton I think). Returning S. E. by Mr. G's house we went 5 miles on the Montevallo Road to the works of the Red Mtn Iron Co. There are two substantial stacks with good engines for the blast the boilers for which are heated from the gases escaping from the stacks. Everything combustible was burned by the terrible Croxton, the engines & one set of boilers seriously damaged &c. The ore used is the red haematite, which with the flux [limestone], & good building stone are found within the circle of a mile & a half. A Saw mill, grist mill, foundry & machine shop about a mile off, were also burned, & the machinery pretty well ruined by the fire. Rode to the top of Shades Mountain (Shades Creek runs at the base of it) which is some 800 feet high. Examined the bed of iron ore near Mr. Grace's in the rail-road cut. It is very extensive & comes boldly to the surface for a long distance. [[Mem. Slept on a piano last night to get out of the way of the chintzes]].

Mr. and Mrs. Grace gave us some music which was pleasant if not artistic. Mr. G. helped his wife's voice out with his flute, a pleasant voice without sufficient cultivation [[Another bout with the chintzes after the music, notwithstanding Mrs. G's vigorous efforts during the day, in scalding & washing & scrubbing]].

Tuesday, [June 20, 1865]   Left Mr. G's early. Stopped at Dr. Davis (an old scamp) 9 miles S. of Jonesboro & reached Mr. Vance's (32 m) before sundown. Crossed an apparently fine out crop of Brown haematite on the road not far this side of McMaths. It is the vein on which are Mr. Sanders furnaces. Col. M[allet] took the cradle & cut enough of oats to feed not only our horses but Mr. V's, had a good sleep, paid one dollar again (of course we have supplied our own provender all along the way) & started early for Tuscaloosa, reaching there at 5½ P. M. on Wednesday.

Thursday, [June 22, 1865]   Saw Dr. & Mrs. [LaFayette] Guild who have just arrived from the north. Dr. G[uild] was Gen. Lee's Medical Director. They saw our wives on the 10th of May, & left them all well & still hopeful, [despite] the news of Mr. Davis' capture. The Monday (April 3d) of the occupation of the city must have been a day of terror to them. My wife they say saved the house by keeping wet blankets over the combustible parts; & a shell or fragment of one entered the parlor! Dr. G[uild] found Gen. Lee in a little 8 by 10 room on the third story of his home on Franklin St. with a pile of letters, chiefly from Yankee women, asking after things which belong to dead relatives, which he was himself laboriously answering, all of his Staff having left him. Yankee soldiers covered the sidewalk opposite scanning the windows to get sight of the redoubted General whom they had at last conquered. He was about to go down to Shirley [the Lee family plantation] to escape annoyances.

Friday, [June 23, 1865]   Saw Mr. Joe Davis elder brother of the President at Mr. Jemison's. [Joe Davis had refugeed to Tuscaloosa from Mississippi late in the war.] He resembles the President somewhat, & was anxious to hear anything he could about him. Met Mr. and Mrs. Nicholson (sister of Mrs. Mallet) & Dr. and Mrs. Guild & Dr. and Mrs. [John Edward] Hall (sister of Dr. G.) in the evening at Mrs. Mallet's and drove back here on Saturday. Stopped to <u>noon</u> at Mr. Avery's (12 Ms). The negro foreman an intelligent fellow, <u>said</u> he tho't the slaves were better off to remain on their master's plantations, & got nothing by going off. Discussed a most excellent lunch provided by Mrs. [Mary O.] Mallet.

Monday, [June 26, 1865]   Mounted my horse at 1/6 3 P. M. & rode to Demopolis reaching there (25 m.) in time to see the Yankee dress parade. I wonder how I could even interest myself in the military displays of that nation. Shall I ever do so again? Stopped all night at Mr. Lyon's. Left at 5 P. M. and reached here at 10 minutes before ten. The road is uninteresting tho the country is a very rich one. Artesian wells supply the needed water. Such running water as exists lies deep in beds & is almost inaccessible. [See diagram on p. 180.]

Thursday, [June 29, 1865]   Went to hear [the] Bishop [of Alabama, Richard Hooker] Wilmer preach but he was not at church. He is going to reside at Mobile.

(Greensboro) Saturday July 1, 1865.   I enter upon my 48th year. Amelia was born June 1, 1826, & is therefore 7 years and 11 months my junior, a good difference. I am now at the age of 47, beginning life anew so far as my provision for my family is concerned. If the country were in a prosperous, or even a settled condition, it would be easy enough to earn one's bread & something more but prospects are gloomy enough, & it may be some time before I can get at settled work.

Sunday, [July 2, 1865]   Heard Bishop Wilmer preach. His voice, manner & delivery are excellent, but I cannot recall anything striking in his Sermon. Good appearance goes very far in all professions, tho' the Bishop is said to be able; & has certainly shown character in his dealing with the federal authorities in his church matters. He instructs his clergy to omit the prayer for the President [of the United States] until civil government is restored in the Diocese.

Monday, [July 3, 1865].   Started early for Eutaw with Milly & Matt, driving myself & "John" riding a spare horse, reached there at 12 M (6 hours) the weather being very warm. [See diagram on p. 181.]

do so again? — Slept all night at
Mr. Lyon's — Left at 5 A.M. and
reached here at 10 minutes before ten —
The road is uninteresting tho' the
country is a very rich one —
Artesian wells supply the need of
water — Such running water as exists
lies deep in beds & is almost inaccessible

Thursday — Went to hear Bishop Wilmer
preach but he was not at church
He is going to reside at Mobile —

Diagram from journal entry for Monday, [June 26, 1865]

to be able, + has certainly shown character in his dealing with the federal
authorities in his church in allow - the
instructs his clergy to omit the
prayer for the President until civil
government is restored in the Diocese,

— Monday — Started early for Eutaw
with Molly + Matt, driving myself
+ "John" riding a spare horse —

reached there at 12 m (6 hours) the weather
being very warm —

Tuesday — took tea at Mr. Weaver, whose
son was an officer of Ordnance — Had
some good Piano music from Bofura or
Braune — Mrs. W. a short pleasant lady
her little daughter of 8 years old plays
quite well — ~~xxxxxxxxxxxxxxxxxxxxx~~
~~xxxxxxxxxxxxxxxxxxxxxxxxx~~
~~xxxxxxx~~ — Weather very warm.

Diagram from journal entry for Monday, [July 3, 1865]

Tuesday, [July 4, 1865]   Took tea at Mr. Weavers, whose son was an officer of Ordnance. Had some good piano music from Professor Browne. Mrs. W. a stout pleasant lady her little daughter of 8 years old plays quite well. <Mr. W. does not stand well among the gentlemen I find for uprightness.> Weather very warm.

Friday, [July 7, 1865]   Took tea (or coffee) at Mrs. Crawford's. Met Col. Robt. Smith, a man of fine capacity, Col. [Lewis T.] Woodruff, a well known citizen of Mobile, who was badly wounded in Johnston's last campaign, "Col." Blocker of Tuscaloosa, a planter & whom everybody appears to know, "Col." [Joseph W. Taylor,] editor of the newspaper at Eutaw and a man of education & reading. Stayed till 10½ and drove home by a beautiful moon. Col. S[mith] has no confidence in the future of this country and is going to Maryland or Virginia.

Saturday, [July 8, 1865]   Rode to Gainesville (18 miles) [a cotton port on the Tombigbee River in Sumter County] was joined by Col. W[oodruff] at Mr. C. Passed Col. [James] C[rawford]'s plantation, 12 miles out. He has 10,000 acres together here. Crossed the 'Bigbee on pontoon bridge at G. It is not over 100 feet wide now, tho it is sometimes 6 miles wide, flooding the whole country about. Dined at table of Mr. [Robert] Bradshaw, with Mrs. (was Miss [Elizabeth] Pickens) & [Confederate Adjutant] Gen. [of Ala.] Duff C. Green. He is collecting the cotton of the late C. S. Govt. for the U. S. officials. The place is a small one & full of soldiers and negros. Rode home thro' Col. C's place & stopped a few moments. One of his plantations is managed almost wholly by a mulatto "John," who is very intelligent. He manifested no desire to take advantage of his newly acquired freedom. Arrived home at 8½, having ridden about 37 miles since 5½ P. M.

Sunday (July 9), [1865]   Went to Presbyterian Church, & heard a good sermon from the story of Jacob's dream. The heat continues unabated.

Monday, [July 10, 1865]   Drove to this place thro a furious rain of an hours duration which wet me thoroughly the top of the carriage proving leaky. Arrived 20 minutes before ten, the moon shining, and having passed out of the storm.

Wednesday, [July 12, 1865]   Drove to go to Demopolis stopped at Gen. Hardee's to dinner & until next morning. Gen. H. [is] much interested in his plantation which belonged to his wife (Miss Lewis). His daughter Anna, his wife & himself the only persons at the house. He lives in two somewhat dilapidated log cabins.

Thursday, July 13, [1865]   Reached D. at sundown, stopping at Major Lewis' and at Mrs. Wynne's. Got a letter from Mamma here, which I read in part to those present nearly all of whom were old friends of hers; Gen. Bocock Jas Lyon & his wife, Mrs. Wynne & one or two others.

Friday, [July 14, 1865]   Dined at Mrs. Ross (daughter of Mr. Lyon) & had some music in the evening from Miss Rosa Foote (niece of Mrs. Alfred Jones) and Miss Lightfoot.

Saturday, [July 15, 1865]   When the boat reached D. got the papers from which we learned the agrarian reply of the President to the committee from Richmond. Mr. Lyon is a good deal disturbed at this evidence of intention to rob the planters who are worth more than $20,000. Walked over with Mr. L. to look at the ten acre lot which Mr. L. insists he gave to my wife long ago. He invited me quite earnestly to put a little house thereon.

Sunday, [July] 16th, [1865]   Heard [the Rev.] Mr. [William A.] Stickney [of Faunsdale] preach. He married Mrs. [Louisa] Harrison, a rich widow. He is a most positive, restless, & energetic man who seems to manage the negros & Yankees equally well. Rained in the evening. Rev. Mr. Harrison [Stickney] stayed all night.

Monday, [July 17, 1865]   Returned here stopping to dinner & as it rained stayed all night at Gen. Bocock who lives in a very nice home not far from Prairieville [a village southwest of Greensboro]. Left Tuesday morning & stopped at Gen. H's to dinner, reached here at 8 P. M. Mrs. Bocock knew Amelia very well she having made a visit to the plantation before we were married. The servants still remembered her.

Thursday [July] 20th, [1865]   Rode with Dr. Parrish to Newbern [a town southeast of Greensboro] & dined at Dr. Higgins, having gone there to see Dr. Nichols, who married Miss Jenny Pollard niece of Gen. [George W.] Randolph. My chief object in going to Newbern was to see Mr. [Caswell C.] Huckabee who used to be engaged in the iron business in this state, a business I desire to connect myself with now that my profession is gone.

Friday, [July 21, 1865]   Reading "Clarissa Harlowe," which is a superior book and writing to Mamma & Bayne. Weather excessively warm. I leave early in the morning for Montgomery—(10½ P. M.)

Saturday, [July 22, 1865]   Left for Montgomery via Uniontown [in Perry County] at 5¼. The way to U. is bad & not sandy. Reached there at 10. 18 miles waited till 2½ for cars. Selma at 5½, 30 miles. Stopped at the "Gee house." Weather very hot indeed. Slept very little at night from the great heat. The aspect of S[elma] is desolate in the extreme—many of the best regions, comprising nearly all the business part of the town are mere rows of crumbling walls. I walked up after sunset toward the square where the [Confederate] "Arsenal" was. All vestige of its arrangements had disappeared, except a tall stack; & fragments of rows of gun carriages lay about to show where gun carriages were stored in iron making. It was not thus I had hoped to visit it—one of my principal establishments.

Sunday, [July 23, 1865]   Left at 12½ P. M. for Montgomery on the "Virginia" a Stern wheel boat, & reached M. before dawn Monday. Spent the evening & slept at Mr. Frank Gilmer's whom I came chiefly to see to talk with him over the iron prospects.

Tuesday, [July 25, 1865]   Saw Gov [Lewis E.] Parsons [of Talladega] the Provisional Governor, a stout dark skinned & rather pleasant looking man. He declined acting on any "pardon" (humiliating word) until he had gotten civil Govt in operation when he would take them up. The capitol was filled with people seeking to see the Governor, chiefly on matters of "pardon." Saw Gen. A. J. Smith, Comdg. His Corps is about to go to Texas. Dined at Col. Powell's with Mr. Lyon & Mr. [Augustus] Benners [Sr.] (of Greensboro) and went on board the "Flirt" to return at 4 P. M. The boat was crowded with federal soldiers who were quiet & well behaved. They were western men & generally good looking fellows, young & healthy.

Wednesday, [July 26, 1865]   reached Selma at 9 A. M. too late for the train, & took hack to depot to go by a train which was to carry the Soldiers. Got into a box car loaded with commissary stores, which went no further than Uniontown. Stayed all night with Col. [James L.] Price, Presdt of the Selma & Meridian R. R. His wife, a brisk black eyed woman was Miss Shearn, and knew Amelia's mother. She has four daughters, fine looking girls.

Thursday, [July 27, 1865]   reached Demopolis at noon & found "John" there with the buggy. Stopped at Mr. Lyon's.

Friday, [July 28, 1865]   Left at 12, after seeing the Comding Gen. [Lucius F.] Hubbard, & finding that they would not administer the "oath" for want of forms. Arrived at Eutaw (28 miles) at 9 P. M. stopping 2 hours on the way, the heat being very great.

Tuesday Aug 1, [1865]   Went to a Storm party at Mrs. Picton's—a very nice supper & dancing in which latter I did not join of course.

The time passes very heavily with me having no occupation & our future being so uncertain not to say gloomy. I seldom hear from wife & children & this adds to my disquiet.

Miss Charlotte Hamilton, of Mobile is staying with Sarah [Amelia's oldest sister]—a very nice girl, who sings ballads prettily, & is a girl of good sense. Miss Kate [space] a very attractive (not pretty) young lady is staying at Col. Crawfords.

Saturday, Aug 5, [1865]   Left Eutaw at 4 P. M. & reached here (Greensboro) at 9 (21 miles) the road somewhat sandy.

Sunday, [August 6, 1865]   Went to [St. Paul's] Episcopal church and heard Mr. Cobb[s] preach from the text "For the children of this world are wiser in their day than the children of light & I say unto you make to yourselves friends &c"—a text which he confirmed presented singular difficulties but which he endeavored to explain.

Wednesday Aug 9, [1865]   Rode to Newbern to see Mr. Huckabee about machines for making nails. The morning was excessively hot. Went on to Gen. Hardee's & dined there. Got home about 8½ P. M. Met Miss Amelia Lightfoot & Miss Sue Tarleton there. The first is named for the same person as Mamma (i.e. for Mrs. Ross), is very agreeable & well instructed, the other was engaged to Gen. Cleburne, & wears mourning for him.

Thursday, [August 10, 1865]   Reading "Clarissa Harlowe" by [Samuel] Richardson, which Rousseau pronounced the best novel ever written in any language. It is certainly the work of a man of genius. I am also getting some knowledge of the geology of the mineral regions of Alabama & looking into the structure of furnaces rolling mills &c.

Friday, [August 11, 1865]   Sent John with a basket of fruit to Gen. H's. The fruit is from Dr. Parrish's orchard, & quite fine. Called to see Gen. Longstreet at Mr. Gid Nelson's.

Saturday, [August 12, 1865]   went with Gen. H to see Longstreet & dined there. Drove with him to Mrs. Withers, 7 miles out, & stayed all night. She has three fine daughters grown, & one about 14. Met Rev. Mr. & Mrs. Menius (a Greek). Mrs. M. is a Withers also. Got home before sundown on Sunday. Gen. H. is not pleased with L[ongstreet], thinks him somewhat self sufficient & engrossed with himself. I was suprised to hear how little credit L. was inclined to give Gen. Lee. The credit of suggesting the movement against McClellan he gave to Gen. Johnston, That against Pope to Jackson.

Wednesday 16th Aug, [1865]   Weather continues hot. The chapter in "Clarissa" which describes her conduct in prison seems to me incomparable. No one can read it unmoved. No rain nor prospect of any. I shall go to-morrow to pass two days at Gen. H's, pursuant to promise to him & Mrs. H.

Tuesday Aug 22, [1865]   Returned from Gen. H.'s Saturday Evey— found the vicinity full of federal cavalry. I learned that the town came near being sacked, some imprudent men having fired into a Yankee camp. The men were so incensed that they asked leave to plunder the town as revenge. The Col. commanding said that he had rec'd so much ill treatment from the inhabitants by which his men had been greatly irritated, that he hesitated whether he should or should not grant them the license they asked!

I have to-day taken the oath of amnesty before a federal officer (Capt. [John D.] Kelly, 9th Ill. cavalry) and forwarded my petition for pardon!— pardon for having done my duty in a cause I deemed the best on earth! But the conquerors have a right to dictate terms and ours have not been magnanimous.

I am about to ride over to Eutaw. No letter yet from Mamma. Her last is dated June 26!

Saturday Aug 26, [1865]   On my return from Eutaw found that Dick had reached here on Thursday. He looks very well but graver than of yore. Bro't me a letter from Mamma of July 28. She and my little darlings are all well and comfortably settled at Cambridge on the "Eastern Shore" of Maryland. They are staying at a hotel a sort of life that suits Amelia exactly. I hope to be able to join them before long. The separation is extremely irksome, and I am getting depressed for want of occupation.

Wednesday Aug 30th, [1865]   Dick started from here by carriage with John for Eutaw while I rode on horseback via Demopolis. I wished to see Mr. L[yon] about appt to a position on the Selma & Meridian R. R. found Mr. L[yon] feeble from chills, and not hopeful on the situation of affairs. All look forward with doubt and some with apprehension to the lst of January, when the present contracts made by planters and negros expire, & new ones are to be made. These have been for a portion of the crop in every case. Whether new contracts are to be made or the negro simply hired remains to be seen, probably the latter. The negros seem still to expect a division of lands and hope for some undefined good on the 1st of January, what they don't exactly know. Mr. L[yon] has received his pardon, & is reinstated in all his rights as a citizen!

Aug 31, [1865]   It is the day of election for members of convention to reconstruct the State back into the Union. This is the bitter end of four years of toil & sacrifices. What an end to our great hopes! Is it possible that we were wrong? Is it right after all that one sett of men can force their opinion on another sett? It seems so, & that self government is a mockery before the Almighty. He permits it or refuses it as seems good to him. Let us bow in submission & learn to curb our bitter thoughts.

Wednesday Sept. 6, [1865]   Reached Greensboro from Eutaw where Dick & I have been spending a week. I felt a good deal depressed, & Sarah appeared so also. Our affairs are all unsettled and no one can see his way before him. All is unquiet. We find on reaching here the details of an affair which came near ruining this town on election day. Yankees and

Confederates got to drinking, & thence to quarreling & shooting. One soldier was killed and another wounded. This so incensed the Yankees that they spread over the town and attempted to fire it several times. The houses were entered and searched for arms, & in some cases money [was] carried off. I lost a little fancy pistol which had been presented to me. In other cases threats were made to burn private cotton, and money exacted to guard it! There was however no further personal violence.

Saturday [September] 9th, [1865]   Rode down to see Gen. H[ardee] & dined & passed the night there. Col. [Thomas Benton] Roy one of his late Staff was there—quite a young man who is going to study law in Mobile. Dick and I are still talking over our project of setting up a Saw mill on Fish River, but cannot see our way very clearly, and nothing is likely to come of it.

Wednesday Sept. 13, [1865]   Drove with Dick to Demopolis. Stopped for the night at Dr. Reese home, 2 miles this side, where we were hospitably entertained to dinner, tea and breakfast. Mrs. R.'s maiden name was Wynne. The Dr. is grateful to me for having taken pains to send from Richmond last summer the body of Capt. Wynne who died of wounds rec'd at Petersburgh. I talked to him about position of Supdt of Meridian & Selma [Selma & Meridian] R.R. He would gladly give it to me (he is a Director) were there a vacancy, or should it occur.

Thursday, [September 14, 1865]   Drove Dick to town, to take the cars for Mobile, but found there would be no cars from Meridian until Friday. Stayed all night at Mr. Lyon's.

Saturday, [September 16, 1865]   stopped last night at Gen. Bocock's, took tea & breakfast & drove here by 1½ o'clock. Gen. B[ocock] would also I see be glad to have me on this R. Road, of which he too is a director, Mrs. B. sent kind messages to Mamma. He has little hope of being able to make a crop next year, the negros, he thinks, cannot be prevailed on to work. An attempt was made some weeks ago to steal his private cotton from near his home. With the assistance of his negros he frightened the teamsters & captured two teams at dead of night. The life of a planter is just now no sinecure.

Monday Sept. 18, [1865]   Writing letters to send by John to Demopolis. Took tea with Mr. Benners & sat till 8 o'clock. It has been showering most of the day.

Wednesday [September 20, 1865]   Mr. Ross writes that he has spoken to several of the Directors of the Mobile & O[hio] R.Rd. and that they appear inclined to give me charge of their Road as Supdt. I am therefore going down to-morrow to see after it.

Greensboro, Ala. Octr 7, [1865]   Left here on Thursday Sept 21 for Demopolis to go to Mobile, left D. Friday noon & reached Meridian at 6¼ P. M. It is a collection of small frame houses with no shelter or conveniences for the passengers. While waiting I spoke with a Yankee soldier, a western man, who deprecated the freeing of the slaves & tho't it was a "bad thing all round," meaning for blacks as well as whites. Took cars at 8 o'clock for Mobile & got there at about 9 A. M. (135 miles, fare $8)—raining very hard. Went to Battle House [Hotel], waded about the streets delivering letters and seeing people, dined at table with Gen. Hardee who went up the river at 4. Found Col. Mallet at Hotel, engaged on preparations of Salt Works at New Iberia, La. On Sunday went to church at 1st Presbyterian (the Episcopal churches being all closed by order of Gen Thomas, Comdg. this Division [Third Military District in response to Bishop Wilmer's instructions to his clergy in June. In December President Andrew Johnson directed Thomas to revoke the suspension of the clergy]). Dined with Mr. Chas. Foote, his daughters Mary & Rosa, & Mr. Jno. Lyon (brother of Mrs. Jones) present. Mr. F[oote] is one of the directors of M[obile] & O[hio] R.Rd. Took tea with Dr. [Josiah] Nott [eminent Mobile physician]. On Monday took Steamer with Col. M[allet] for N. Orleans, arrived at daybreak, & went to St. Charles Hotel. Bayne came in & took me to his rooms on Bourbon St. Spent the time until Friday making inquiries about machinery &c for saw mill which Dick & I propose to put up near Mobile. On Thursday Dick, Bayne, a Mr. Farley, & myself dined very handsomely with Major Noble (late on duty (in cotton) at Montgomery) at Victor's restaurant on Canal St. The rest of the party played cards until very late at Bayne's room, & Dick with whom I slept, passed a very restless night. I saw on Tchoupitoulas St two ice-making machines, imported from Paris, patented by a Monsr Carre. The material used is Sulp. of Ammon. They make good ice in blocks 2¾in. × 14in. by 30in. The ice is produced at a cost of ¼ct per lb. as the proprietors assert.

Left N. O. for Mobile at 5 P. M. on Friday & arrived at M. at 12 M Saturday. Continued my inquiries as to the feasibility of a Saw mill on Fish River. My inquiries led me to the conclusion that the best plan is to place the mill at Mobile & get the logs down the Alabama & Tombigbee Rivers. A good site may be had on 3 Mile Creek, & a good engine with power for two saws. It now remains to determine whether we will risk our capital in the enterprize. Sunday Octr 1st went to Presbyterian Church, dined at Mr. Peter Hamiltons Vice Presdt of M & O. R.Rd, took tea at Mrs. Tom Hamiltons (Miss Kate Bayard) and went with them to 3d Pres. Church. Monday afternoon drove out to Spring Hill with Col White & passed the night at his father in laws' Mr. Tuthill. Tuesday evening kept [to] my room with a most violent cold. Maj. Myers came to see me & talked an hour. He & other gentlemen (Mr. Hamilton Brown especially) gave me every assistance in my inquiries. Dick & I left M[obile] at 4 P.M. Wednesday, reached Meridian at 4 A. M. Thursday whence he went on to Eutaw, & I to this place via Demopolis. Got there at 12 M. Mrs. Lyon made me take a good hot foot bath, & a strong whiskey punch, for my cold, and I got up on Friday very much improved & refreshed, having had no sleep the night before on the cars. Rode over here with Willie Glover who was coming to G in an ambulance & got here at 1½ P. M. Took tea last evening with Prof. [Nathaniel T.] Lupton [chemistry professor at the Southern University in Greensboro and former chemist at the Confederate Nitre and Mining Bureau], who has just returned from Washington. Thinks there is little chance for a general amnesty at present, & that we West Pointers must wait yet awhile. Shall go up to Tuscaloosa and the Roup's Valley iron works on Monday on horseback taking "John" with me (This is Saturday the 7th). Expect to be back about the 20th. Read "Enoch Arden" Tennyson's last poem to-day. It is profoundly touching, & very beautiful.

Monday, Oct 9, [1865]   Left G[reensboro] at 7 A.M. & rode to Tuscaloosa, weather very fine, reached there at 5½ P. M. Stopped at Judge [John J.] Ormond's. Went round to Dr. Guild's to see him & his wife. He has just returned from the North, and gave me a good many items of information.

Tuesday left at 10 A. M. after seeing Col. Blocker, stayed at Mr. Vance's 25 miles from T[uscaloosa].

Wednesday, rose at 5, got some breakfast, paid $5 for my very poor night's entertainment & rode on to the iron works, stopping to see the somewhat famous Spring at McMath's. It is not worth looking at now, having been filled with stones & all its beauty destroyed. Reached the works at noon, and in the afternoon visited the ore bed which is a very fine one—brown haematite in exhaustless quantity.

Thursday, rode to the deposits of coal & to the proposed site of a rolling mill, on Shades Creek. There is not enough water. Stayed with Mr. B. J. Jordan, a well known iron master from Va. who is staying here with his wife, just eking out a livelihood out of the cupola furnace, until something better turns up. This property consists of 3 wretched looking furnaces, 6000 acres of land, excellent ore beds, some good coal lands, & a small water power, capable of driving one small furnace. A tram gently graded runs from the furnaces to the ore bed. It will be valuable when Rail Roads are opened.

Friday rode to Mr. Jno. Alexander's 3 miles from Montevallo, & stayed all night. It rained heavily & we got very wet.

Saturday reached Shelby Iron Works about noon, & stopped at Mr.

Hall's. This property is five miles from Columbiana [in Shelby County] & has a track laid to it. It has very good ore beds very convenient. There is one fire stack—11 feet bosh [lower sloping part of a blast furnace where diameter increases to its maximum]—& another smaller partly finished. There is also a rolling mill. The improvements are very good. The country is pleasant, & altogether the establishment is very attractive. They will have to bring coal & coke a distance of about 30 to 35 miles by rail. The destruction by the enemy did a good deal of damage to the works. The company is preparing, however, to go on.

Sunday, left after breakfast & rode back by Montevallo to the Bibb Works, 6 miles S. of M[ontevallo]. Here are rolling mills, on the Mahan Creek, & two stacks 2½ miles west of the Mills. The R.Rd from Montevallo to Selma passes thro the rolling mills (Briarfield—so named by Lt. Col. Hunt, C.S.A.). A good train connects the mills to the furnaces. There are two good stacks[,] 10ft 4in & 11ft. boshes, the latter arranged for hot blast. There are 4000 acres of land. The ore is scattered, & not very abundant but sufficient. I am greatly pleased with this property and will try to organize a company to buy it. I stayed with Mr. Wilson, the furnace man, a big sensible Pennsylvanian who evidently understands his business. He however talks a little too much of his past successes in running furnaces, which are always feminine in his vocabulary.

Monday left at 10½ & rode to Mr. Henry Adams to see Mr. Huckabee's nailery on the little Cahawba [Cahaba River], a good water power, machines not set up. Dined with Mr. A and rode to Pratt's Ferry thro' very blind piney woods paths. Passed the point where 6 mile Creek sinks beneath a precipice (bluff) of limestone, & disappears for ¾ of a mile. Rode 10 miles beyond Pratt's ferry to Mr. Hills which we reached an hour after dark.

Tuesday, paid $3½ for a good nights entertainment & rode to Tuscaloosa by 1 o'clock—found Judge O[rmond] & [his daughter] Mrs. Mallet at dinner, all the rest of the family absent. Col. Mallet arrived about an hour after. Walked up to see Col. Blocker, & in returning saw Mrs. Stafford.

Wednesday rested at Judge O[rmond]'s saw Mrs. Guild, & got some information relative to N.E & S.W. [Northeast and Southwest] R.Rd. Col. M[allet] took me to the Asylum [Alabama Insane Hospital] in charge of Dr. [Peter] Brice [Bryce]. It is about to be discontinued for want of funds. It is a large well built structure.

Thursday, rode by Foster's Ferry to Eutaw, road very hilly after crossing Ferry.

Saturday left Eutaw at 9.40 & rode over here in 3½ hours. Shall leave to-morrow (Sunday) for Demopolis & Mobile to carry out my present designs. If I meet with no adequate encouragement I shall go on at once to the North.

Distances—to Tuscaloosa 40, to Roups Valley Works 34, to Mr. Alexanders 18, to Shelby Iron Works 15, to Bibb Works 24, to Mr. A's 4, to Pratts Ferry 7, to Tuscaloosa 35, to Eutaw 35, to Greensboro 21 = 233 miles.

X

"Our works progress slowly"

Cambridge [Md.] Nov 4, 1865   I left Mobile on Wednesday the 26th
on the 4 P. M. train for Columbus Ky, having ascertained that the iron
property I had come down to purchase could not be arranged for without
a good deal of delay. Reached Meridian at 4½ A. M. 27th, & Corinth at
9 P. M. (or later) same day. Left C[orinth] at about 6 A. M. 28th & reached
Columbus at 11 P. M., took steamer for Cairo, & thence took cars at
2 A. M. 29th for Cincinnati, breakfasted at [space] and changed cars at
Odin [Ill.] where we got on the route from St. Louis to C[incinnati],
reached C. at 11½ P. M. Rested over Sunday 30th there being no trains
out. I left at 10 P. M. for Baltimore via Belaire, where we crossed the
Ohio. Reached Baltimore at 10½ A. M. 1st Nov. and dined with Aubrey.
Took boat at 8 P. M. & arrived here 10 A M. 2d Nov.

Distances—Mobile to Columbus 490, to Cairo 25, to Cincinnati 379, to
Baltimore ——. Fare to Cairo $30.50/100—to B. $31. The cars to Columbus were filthy & uncomfortable the road in bad condition, & the
rate of travel very slow—on this side of the Ohio the cars are clean—
conductors & guards Surly & rate of travel 20 to 25 miles the hour. I had
in charge Mrs. Bonsall of Norfolk, & her five children from Columbus
Ky to Baltimore. She could not walk except with great difficulty, & had
often to be carried.

I find Mamma established at an old country-house converted into an
inn. Good living but very cramped quarters, the children look well & for
refugees the life is not bad. The shores of this bay (Chesapeake) are very
low & fertile, & are studded with pretty looking places. Oysters & fish
are pretty plenty, and living sufficiently cheap. My family of wife, six

children (11 to 1) & nurse board for $104. per mo. having one good sized room & two very small ones.

Sunday Novr 19th, [18]65   We leave this to-morrow morning for Baltimore where I have taken rooms at the Grant (!) house, corner of Franklin and Calvert. On the 10th I went to Phila[delphia] to look after our furniture, and found it safely stored at Messrs. Heaton & Denkel, 507 Commerce (?) St. No charges for storage on it which made me feel two hundred dollars richer than I tho't I was. I did not meet a single person going to P. or returning from or at P. that I had ever seen before. On Saturday (11th) I went to Washington, saw [William] Maynadier (now Bvt Brig. Genl) and [Thomas J.] Treadwell (now Bvt Lt. Col), and made some inquiries at the Treasury Dept relative to the sale of the Bibb Iron Works.

Saw Mr. Knop (Charles) whom I desired to get interested in the purchase of an iron property in Ala. Returned same day & took boat from Baltimore down here, arriving Sunday morning.

Took a long walk yesterday to see several farms which I may think of buying if I can do no better. The life of a farmer would suit me very well but would not be so pleasant to Mamma, who has no liking for the country.

Sunday Decr 17 [1865], Baltimore   We are established at the Grant House(!) corner of Franklin and Calvert in two rooms, which are sufficiently pleasant & convenient. We have been here nearly four weeks. I have been confined to the house for nearly two weeks with most severe catarrh accompanied with cough.

We have met with every attention from the Baltimoreans we could expect and [if I] had been well would have gone out a good deal, in a quiet way.

I went to Washington at the close of last month & got a letter from Gen. [O. O.] Howard [head of the Bureau of Refugees, Freedmen, and Abandoned Lands] to Gen. [Wager] Swayne [Bureau commissioner for Alabama] at Montgomery to sell to us, if not needed for the Freedman's Bureau, the Iron Works in Bibb Co. I got a copy and sent it to Mr. Lyon by first mail.

I have received private intimation that I have been apptd Supdt M & O R.R. but without some authoritative notice I cannot go on, as I must dispose of my family. We are much perplexed as to our course, whether in case I go to Alabama, we shall all go together or whether we shall get a home and establish ourselves with our Philadelphia furniture at this place. I am annoyed and embarassed at receiving no news—no letters—from my friends at the South—the last date from Bayne is of the 13th ult. I do not understand it. Gen. [R. H.] Chilton was here night before last &

yesterday. He is very despondent as to his personal affairs. He undertook to farm a little in Glocester Co. Va. but could do nothing for want of labor. Said he had not seen a single negro for hire yet in his neighborhood. Gen. Lee's salary he says is $1500 per annum. Compare this with Gen. Johnston's salary of $10,000 as Presdt of the New National Express Co. Johnston's course by the way in this latter position excites criticism—he seems to be little ardent except for his own sett, & pays little attention they say to attachees of Lee's army in his appts to office. Gen Elzey has also been here several times, talking very despondingly of the prospect before him tho' as his wife has $1200 a year, and a farm my sympathies are not especially enlisted in his case as in that of Chilton.

The distinction between Union and Confederate is very strongly marked here & generally over Maryland. I had to drop my blue U. S. cape, a part of my old uniform, because it was always noted in the Confederate circles in which of course I am seen. In Alabama it was not noticed.

Wednesday, Decr 27, [1865]   I leave to-day for Ala. I have been confined to my room for the most part since early in this month, & have felt ill & desperate. I shall feel better no doubt as I get on the road, unless indeed my cough & catarrh return. I think tho I have really had a slight attack of chills added to my cough & catarrh. The country is surprised at the arrest of Admiral Semmes which happened 10 or 12 days ago at Mobile. The charge is taking up arms after having surrendered to the "Kearsarge". I leave my wife and babies behind with great reluctance. I had hoped we would never again separate; but we are both agreed that it is best for me to go & prepare a place if we are to stay there. The future is still uncertain to us, & we must wait patiently, & take our lot as it comes trying to do the best all the time.

Briarfield, [Ala.] January 20, 1866   I reached here yesterday to take up my permanent residence here. The company of which I am a member bought this property on the 9th of Jany. for $45,000, and I am to manage it for them. The members of the Co. are Messrs. Lyon, [John] Collins, Frank Griffin, Mrs. Wynne, Dr. [Bryan W.] Whitfield & Dr. [James D.] Browder of Demopolis, shares of $10,000 each and Mrs. Bruce half a share, and Col. [James] Crawford, Wm. H. Ross of Mobile & myself, one share each making $95,000 in all. $5000 are held in reserve. I expect to spend $30,000 in machinery & repairs, & shall then have $25,000 to start with. The company can readily be increased if necessary.

After making the purchase, Mr. Lyon being the active party, of the U.S. Govt, I was obliged to go to Demopolis quite sick with diarrhea & cough. I was rubbed with croton oil, by Mrs. L's direction, & Dr. [Cincinnatus] Ashe forced a probing down my throat which nearly suffocated me. The result was that after a sojourn of a week I was well enough to come over here to go to work. And a work of great magnitude it is that is before me. The expenses of such an establishment are so great that it requires some boldness to undertake it.

Jan 21, [1866]   The weather was very cold last night and the ice made nearly ¾ inch. thick. It is Sunday & very solitary here. I am staying in the home of Capt. Arms, whom I have taken as asst. The inmates are besides Mrs. Arms & her four children, a Mr. Norris from the North, who has bought pig iron here, and Capt Seaman who commands the guard of soldiers here.

Feb 6, [1866]   Returned from Montgomery yesterday. Mr. Lyon & myself were up there to perfect our title to this property & pay over the $45,000. The deed is to Mr. L[yon] & his heirs but recites (or rather the certificate of Mr. Knott who sold the property does) that he is the purchaser for himself and others. These others are myself, Dr. Browder, Dr. Whitfield, Mr. Collins, Mrs. Wynne, Mr. Frank Griffin of Demopolis, and Col. [James] Crawford & Mr. Ross of Mobile—9 shares of $10,000 each—one share not disposed of. Mr. [Giles] Edwards [who had recently rebuilt the Shelby furnace near Columbiana] master machinist goes to N. York to-day to buy machinery. I find that the charge of these works is likely to be a heavy one, & gives me great anxiety of mind. I hope as the work progresses the way will seem clearer.

Feb. 11, [1866]   Have rec'd several letters from Mamma. She is [I] am rejoiced to observe, impatient to rejoin me, isolated as our life here will be. I am almost afraid to bring her here, so desolate does this place look, with its ruined shops, bare chimneys, and its silence where once there was so much noise and bustle. This is Sunday, and I took a walk along the Stream, Mahan's Creek. It is quite precipitous in places, with cold spring coming from beneath the rocks which underlie the hills. Col [Moses H.] Wright, whom I desire to associate with me in the enterprize I have attempted, visited me on Friday, & stayed all night. I took him over to the furnace and ore pits, & talked with him a good deal. I dont think he will come, as he has a good place in Cincinnati. He was one of my best ordnance officers, & commanded ably the arsenal at Atlanta, Ga. It is raining very heavily & [I] fear we are likely to have a good deal of bad weather which will retard the work of rebuilding.

Saturday Feb 24, [1866]   Last Saturday & Sunday I passed very pleasantly at Mrs. Lyons house, tho' it rained incessantly. Miss Amelia Lightfoot, Miss Eugenia & Miss Amelia Lyon were there—the latter two myself & Capt [William M.] Polk played euchre all evening. Miss L. went home indisposed. She has I see told of my criticism on the application of croton oil to the throat. I suggested that the ladies were unfortunately deprived of this remedy, or eschew low-necked dresses. I suggested that in their case the application must be made to the back of the neck! Gen H. a great friend of hers alluded to it the other evening as a good joke. Wrote to Willie & Jessie and to Mamma to-day. It is cold & has just been raining heavily. Our work is much interrupted by the bad weather, & we cannot make much headway for some time to come, as good weather cannot yet be expected. The veto of the Freedmans Bureau bill is published in the Selma papers to-day. It is supposed to be a declaration of hostility by Mr. Johnson toward the radicals. I feel little interest, and shall be satisfied if I am allowed to work quietly for my family. I wish they were with me, but the prevalence of the Small-pox about Selma & over this part of the country generally inclines me to let them stay at Baltimore yet awhile.

Feb 25, [1866]   The weather has turned clear & cold again. I took a short ride to the furnace & coal pits, & meditated on where we shall place our church—good Sunday thoughts. Wrote a short article headed "Selma & her railroads" to urge the running of accommodation trains, & sent it to the "Messenger" office. I spoke to the same effect last Monday Evy to Gen. Hardee & some Selma gentlemen. They approved my views.

March 13, [1866]   My occupation is now so incessant and my duties so absorbing that I am forgetting my entries in this journal. I will try to be more attentive hereafter. Since my last entry I have gotten rid of all my federal friends; and the armies have departed never more to return I hope. It is a great relief to get rid of all federal associations. Dick arrived here on Friday and will stay here of which I am glad. His society is a great pleasure to me, & I have confidence in him. He will run a Saw-mill connected with this property. To-day he has gone to Selma. Wrote this morning probably my last letter to Mamma, for this separation. I hope she will leave Baltimore about the 25th. The house will hardly be ready, but we must make the best of it. The work gets on slowly and gives me much anxiety, but I try not to allow myself to be depressed. I have just (10 P. M.) gotten clear of two of our country visitors—Mr. Mahan, a respectable neighbor, & Professor(!) Humphreys, who is teaching a school close by.

Mch 14, [1866]   Quite warm to-day. Engaged in planting fruit trees, extending garden &c. Rode over to furnaces at 2 P. M. my now daily ride. Dick returned from Selma, and has improved our fare by the addition of a fine cheese, & some good Bourbon. I do not feel very strong for some reason.

March 20, [1866]   Rec'd a letter from Mamma to-day enclosing one from Willie, which is very well written. I am glad to see he improves. The letter makes me very sad for it speaks of our beloved chief in his imprisonment. His hair & beard have grown snowy white they say. Mr. [Andrew] Johnson confesses to Mrs. [Virginia] Clay [wife of Clement Claiborne Clay, imprisoned with Jefferson Davis] that the incarceration is unjust, & yet he does not seem to have the hardihood to act the manly part which his better nature prompts, & release him and others.

We are getting on with our work here, and are raising the machine shop. Our Saw Mill engine started for the first time to-day, & gives promise of doing good work. It is showery to-day.

May 3d, [1866]   I have been so much occupied as to have neglected my journal. Wife and babies arrived here on the 12th of April, having lost a trunk and 8 big gold pieces ($20) on the way. We hope to be settled here for a long time, but look longingly toward N. Orleans as a place where we are to see a little of the world during our winter months.

The political aspect of the country is still very lowering. President Johnson seems to give way to the radicals, who have overwhelming majorities in congress; and the Southern people will be sacrificed. The revolution is not yet ended & one cannot predict the result. If some soldier of nerve were to step in, Sherman for example, nothing would be easier than to inaugurate a military despotism now.

We are progressing less satisfactorily with our works here than I had hoped, and I am much troubled about the result. I fear I cannot accomplish what I desire & what I undertook with the means at my command. I am expecting Col. White every day, & think he will engage in this business with me. Col. Mallet came to see me about the middle of April, & thinks seriously of joining me here. My desire is to surround myself with men capable of assisting in the extension of these works.

July 1st, [1866]   It is my 48th anniversary. How changed from two years ago. Then I hoped for an honored future in my profession. No doubt of an ultimate success haunted me. I knew we had trials and disappointments before us, but believed in the goodness of our cause & that come what would it must in the end triumph. Alas! It has failed & leaves my life as to its future bitter & barren. I cannot believe that there is no future for this country but abject submission to the puritan. I have been reading with absorbing interest the "Prison Life" [of Jefferson Davis] of our fallen chief, by Dr. [John Joseph] Craven. It shows him to be what the world will one day confess him—one of its greatest men. The conversations are well reported, & remind me in the tones of expression of Mr. Davis. He is an admirable talker—never vain and frivolious—but full of matter.

About the middle of May Col. Mallet joined me here, permanently, having taken an interest in our works. I sent him at once to Baltimore to get data for the construction of brick coal ovens in which to burn our charcoal. Our furnace is getting on very well now & I hope to have it in blast about the 1st of August. Then if successful I shall feel relieved from the great sense of responsibility under which I have been working. Our income will then I hope be sufficient to carry on the rest of the works to completion.

After we get the furnace in blast our forces will be concentrated on getting the Small rolling mill going. We are just putting in the wood foundation for the rolls. These can then be placed, & the fly wheel made & put up, the Steam Engine put in place, boilers repaired & connexion made, which is all that is needed. One heating furnace is to be built up we having all the plate & parts. After that is done the putting up of the "muck train," the repairing & putting up of the large Engine, & fly wheel will be next in order; & then the nail plate rolls, & finally the building for the nailery & the nail machines. This will complete our work to be done, as now laid out. I cannot hope to finish it under three months & fear it will be the 1st of Nov before we make nails. I had hoped much earlier results but have not the means to accomplish them. We must get the furnace in blast & with the proceeds of that complete building up the rest. We cannot drive the whole forward together, I have found without greater means than I have at my command.

We have just completed our Rolling Mill building the main room 160ft long, the transept 140ft, width 58ft. It looks well & is a good substantial building except that the posts should have been 12in sq instead of 10″. The foundry is in successful operation cutting pipes &c for the furnace. Our expenses are very heavy amounting to over $200 per day for labor alone, & the purchases continue very heavy. It takes full $10,000 per month to cover our outlays. I shudder at the rapidity with which our resources are absorbed, & cannot meet my expenses longer than about the middle or end of August. By then, if the furnace is not productive, I shall be penniless. It is a fearful gulf, this of bankruptcy, which I am approaching.

The weather is beautiful—days warm & nights cool. I am wearing thick woolen clothing to-day. The thermometer went down to 50° at Shelby Iron Works on the night of the 28th.

Aug 6, [1866]   My entries despite good resolve are at long intervals. We are progressing slowly with our work & shall not get our furnace in blast for six weeks, say the 15th of September. Meantime I am harrassed by want of means. The outlay is far beyond what I anticipated & there are no returns, nor can I hope for any for two months to come.

The political aspect is extremely critical. A collision between radicals and conservatives seems extremely probable, & war, civil war is predicted by many, should the radicals succeed this fall. The completion of the Atlantic cable at the close of last month is the great event of this year on this continent. In Europe the battle of Sadova [Sadowa, Austria], & the defeat of the Austrians is the absorbing event.

The hot weather for two weeks past brings sickness, & Jessie & Ria are both in bed. Uncle Tom Bayne was with us last Sunday & went away on Thursday. Uncle Dick has engaged himself to be married to Miss Flora Levy [of New Orleans], & appears to be very happy.

The death of my friend Gen. M[artin] L. Smith, greatly grieves me. He was with us just three weeks ago, in excellent health & is dead at Rome Ga a week ago yesterday. He graduated a year after me at West Point, was Second in command at Vicksburg; and was at difft times chief engineer to Gen. Lee, & then to Gen. Hood, with the army of the Tenn.

Aug 21, [1866]   The great national [Union Convention in] Philadelphia met on the 14th & has adjourned. The resolutions or platform for the great national party thus to be inaugurated, have not yet been published, but are no doubt humiliating enough from what we hear of them, as for example, provision for federal soldiers & their widows & orphans, repudiation of the Conf. debt, maintenance of the federal debt, &c.

The war in Europe, between Italy & Prussia against Austria seems to have been definitely settled against Austria by the great battle of Sadova. She loses Venetia, & a good deal of the little military prestige she had.

The Emperor Napoleon does not it would seem insist on extending his frontiers to the Rhine as was at first stated. Prussia declined yielding her Rhinish provinces.

Our work here is progressing, but very slowly. The furnace is all ready, except the lining up of the machinery and the connexions of the blast, & the water connexions. The bridge house is nearly framed & ready to be put up. Six barrows are to be made for charging [loading the furnace with] ore, flux & charcoal.

Yesterday our third Steam Engine arrived. This is for the small rolls for making merchant iron. It is the last I hope we shall need.

Capt. Polk (the Bishop-General's son) will leave us on the 1st of November, to go to planting [actually to enter medical school]. I shall regret his departure. The brick for 8 coaling ovens are being made, & we hope to begin laying in a month. This job will require about 350,000 brick. Meantime we have to burn the lime we need. Indeed the work seems endless; & continually unfolds some new feature.

We have not all been as well here this summer as I had hoped we should be. The children have all had slight attacks of chills & fever, and Ria was dangerously ill.

Sept. 16, [1866]   I regret that I cannot keep up my entries in this journal.

No great events have occurred. The Mexican Empire seems about to be dissipated, by the abdication or departure of Maximilian. Such is the tone of the Northern press. I doubt whether Napoleon will so utterly lose the fruits of his labors. [In April 1866 the French ambassador to the

United States pledged that French troops would be withdrawn from Mexico by November 1867.]

The President (Johnson) has lately made a <u>progress</u> to Chicago, which has developed the bitterness of feeling between radicals and conservatives. [In the 1866 congressional campaign Johnson made a series of speeches, August 28–September 5, known as the "swing around the circle."]

Mr. Davis' health is said to be declining & he is very feeble. God help him. He has the earnest prayers of millions ascending for him every night and morning. Dr. Craven's book called "The Prison Life of Jefferson Davis" aroused general interest. It is not wholly truthful it now appears. It must have been a breach of confidence to have published it at all, <u>but it</u> has probably enriched the author.

Our works progress slowly. The furnace is now perhaps within 3 weeks of being ready, yet I fear even greater delays. I say fear, for I am in constant terror lest our funds may fail before I can get any returns from them. The load of responsibility is even greater than was that of Chief of Ordnance in the Confederacy.

Mr. Hambleton, the blind preacher, as he is called, Mr. [W. H.] McMain, Capt Polk, & Mr. Watson dined with us to-day.

Yesterday we shipped off our first product in the shape of a screw-press for cotton. We are to make a good many of them & I hope to make the foundry & machine shop sustain itself thro this & other cuttings. It is weary work to me, from some cause. I am not well.

Richard [the youngest of the Gorgas children] has inflamed eyes, an epidemic & is very fretful. Mamma [is] a good deal harrassed. We are talking of sending Willie away to school, poor little fellow. However he wants to go, to leave the nest.

Sept 17, [1866]   I will try to note each day hereafter the progress we make at the furnace, & at the Rolling mill. The situation of the furnace is as follows. Lining of [the] furnace completed nearly three months ago, stack boiler completed six weeks since, hot blast finished two weeks ago, & waiting now for binders which are being cast, boiler set complete, bridge house covered in, floor being laid, Engine house covered two months ago, now being weather boarded, water tank to supply tuyeres [the opening in the furnace wall where hot air blast is delivered to the furnace] & sometimes the boilers, framed and will be put up to-day. Blast receiver put up six weeks ago, & connexion about completed. Ductor for pumping water into tank, & Worthington pump in position & connexion partly made. Hot blast pipes in position & connexion with tuyeres to be made to-morrow. Casting house to be raised up & covered. Sand to be filled in for pig bed. There are charging barrows [carts on which fuel, ore, and flux are carried to load the furnace] to be made, &

casts to be gotten ready, a cinder wagon & some minor things. We have say 7000 tons of ore about 500 Tons of flux, and nearly 100,000 bu. of charcoal on hand.

Sept 21, [1866]   The weather has suddenly turned quite cold after a heavy rain. The thermometer 60°. Did not go to the furnace yesterday to note progress. Capt. McMain joined up for duty on Monday (this is Friday). He will take the position Capt. Polk vacates.

Sept 30, [1866]   <I am very much depressed to-day. I fear the failure of all my plans here. I doubt whether we have funds to carry us along. Yet we are so near having the means to sustain ourselves from the products of our furnace, that I cannot think without anguish—keen anguish—of the possible result. Perhaps I am too gloomy. God grant that we may not fail.>

All the steam & water connexions at the furnace are now made, & there seems to be no reason why everything should not be ready by the close of this week. The casting house is making progress & will doubtless be partially covered by Saturday.

Here at the rolling mill we have laid the foundation of the heating furnaces with attached boilers, & some work has been done in lining up the steam engine of the small mill.

At the foundry the cupola blast has been re-arranged & is now in excellent condition, bringing down the metal in 40 minutes.

We went to Methodist meeting this morning to hear Mr. Woodard. Mamma declares she won't go again to hear such nonsense. The children (Ria & Richard) are getting over their epidemic sore eyes.

The thermometer goes from 60 to 72, and the weather is cool, with a great deal of rain. In case of failure what shall I do next? I prefer taking a professorship of mathematics somewhere, as involving no responsibilities, no care, of which I am heartily tired.

Oct 15, [1866]   <Never have I suffered so much mental anxiety, nor have I ever experienced so much depression. I rise in the morning with a feeling of depression & a reluctance to encounter the duties of the day. Last evening Col. M[allet] & Capt. McMain were at my house. I could scarcely hold up my head, I was so wearied & dejected. Is this dyspepsia? I verily believe it comes much more from the condition of my stomach than from the pecuniary embarassments which surround me in the conduct of this work.>

Willie slept with me last night and was wandering a great part of the night. He has slight fever. His head is easily affected.

Mr. Lyon and Mr. Edwin Glover came up last Tuesday & spent two nights & a day with us. They went away apparently well pleased.

Novr 16 [1866]   Our Furnace went into blast on Friday Nov 2d at 10½ A. M. The first cast was made Saturday morning at 5 A. M. I staid over at the Furnace Friday night & was present at the cast Saturday morning 5 A. M. The cast was about 4½ Tons. Since then the furnace has been working along slowly, making about 9 tons a day. The ore is very dirty & we cannot hope to do much until we get the ore in better condition.

XI

"Harrassed with debt & surrounded with troubles"

Sunday January 6, [18]67   <My life has been one of hope and fears for the past 4 months. For the most part I have lived in a state of profound depression, which has made life a burden to me. Whether this is wholly due to the evident condition of our finances here, I can not tell, but I am certain that for no imaginable recompense would I live this life over again. I can now understand how these poor, doomed, destroyed wretches whose self-destruction we daily see chronicled, are forced to their doom. To many annihilation must be the only thing left. Nothing is so terrible as despair.>

Since my last entry the furnace has been kept in blast with indifferent results. It is however now doing better. We are burning charcoal & mineral coal, 20 bu. & 400 lbs. to the charge, with a burden now increased to 1050 lbs of ore, and yesterday were running 6 & 7 beds to the cast. If this improvement continues we may hope to run 8 & 9 beds, the utmost of our expectations.

About the last days of November (or lst days of Decr) Dick bro't his bride (Flora Levy, a Jewess, of N.O) and spent two weeks with us. They appeared to pass away their time very pleasantly. A few days after their arrival Gen. Jos Johnston came & spent a couple of days with us. I took him over to the furnace and ore beds, and the next day rode with him to Mr. Brown's mine, 5 miles from here. He talked freely & rather forgivingly of the people in the war who are regarded as his enemies—Mr. Davis, Mr. Benjamin, Gen Hood, &c.

Of course I have my own views as to the matter of controversy between him & the President. He was greatly pleased with Willie, & has sent him a Christmas present of a powder flask & shot pouch. Willie shot his first bird while the Gen. was here and the glow of joy with which he burst in upon us as he & I were talking, to relate his exploit delighted the General.

We should have had a Merry Christmas were not I so much harrassed & dejected & did not Mamma have her own troubles. However, the children were very happy with their little gifts, & that made us contented.

On looking back to the entries under the lst of July, I see that I even as late as that continued to anticipate making nails by the lst of Novr. I did not even have the first part of our enterprize—the furnace—in operation on that day; & the second part—the rolling mill—will not be running yet for a month, while the last or nail making, may take until the lst of July. I certainly knew little of the difficulties that lie in the way of getting up machinery. It is the slowest of all work that one can undertake.

Since Christmas day, which was bright, we have scarcely seen the sun until to-day. It has rained, snowed, & made sleet, incessantly. The fuel for our furnace threatened to run short, our tram cars broke down, our roads were cut up, & altogether the past 10 days have been about the most uncomfortable of my whole life. Daylight begins to appear however. I am to meet the stockholders about the middle of the month & I hope we shall put things on a more satisfactory train, by that time.

<Meantime I must contain myself as best I can, harrassed with debt & surrounded with troubles.>

Sunday Jan. 13 [1867]   The weather for the past week has been quite pleasant, and our work has progressed more satisfactorily, tho' strange to say the furnace did better in the bad weather, and is doing quite poorly now. I went to Selma on Thursday to get the means to pay our men, yesterday having been pay day. I passed Thursday Evey very pleasantly with Gens. Johnston & Hardee. We played a game of whist, Mrs. H., Miss H, Gen. J. & myself. On Friday I succeeded in getting $5000. to pay up the men for Decr, & to liquidate some pressing debts due in Selma. A letter from Mr. Lyon informs me that the act of incorporation for our company had not passed, & we must await the re-assembling of the Legislature which will be in a few days. We expect to get our little rolls at work this week, possibly. Mr. L[yon] & three of the stockholders are to be here this week, to look into matters. We are a good deal in debt & I think the stockholders are somewhat alarmed at the prospect before us. Gen. Johnston expressed a strong desire to take the coal mine nearest to us & to work it, with a view to supplying us with coal. The thermometer is up to 71° at this moment 7 P.M. The political aspect is not encouraging, the radicals will evidently have their own way in all things, because they cannot be arrested except by force, and Mr. Johnston [President Andrew Johnson] is not the man to apply that. An effort at impeachment is being made but that will evidently not be pressed. The [Fourteenth] Constitutional Amendment will not be accepted by any of the Southern States, of their own volition, & some means will doubtless be found to impress upon them the resolves of the victor, which are "universal suffrage & general amnesty." The sooner it is effected the better. It is unwise, to give votes to uneducated people, black or white, & still more unwise, to the negro, who is but an infant in intelligence & especially in moral training, but the unwisdom is not ours; & the harm has already been done. Voting won't make the matter much worse, if any. The negro will disappear in any event before the moral & intellectual superiority of the white. Cotton is quoted in Mobile at 31½. Mamma is not very well, but the children are all enjoying the beautiful weather. Willie expects to be away at school by next Sunday.

Jan 27 [1867]   It is quite cold to-day. I rode out to the furnace on a lame mule & found things going on pretty well. But our charcoal oven is still unmanageable. As soon as we open and begin to draw the charcoal some part of the kiln takes fire and we are obliged to shut it up again. We got out three or four hundred bushels, & have the second kiln burning. With patience we shall succeed at last. I returned from Selma yesterday having made sale of 1000 tons of iron, to be delivered here at $30 for the short ton (of 2000 lbs). We cannot afford to work at this permanently, but our necessities for ready money are so great that we must sell our iron at what we can get for it. It will take until the 1st of May to pay this up. About July I hope we will be in condition to work up all our iron, as I had planned & thus reap all the benefit ourselves. I doubt whether the stockholders of the works will applaud my action but I believe it to be for the best and it gives me infinite relief to have a definite, immediate, tangible income. With this and the product of the small rolls, I hope we shall be able to get along. Our little rolls began to work on Wednesday, & are now in working order. We shall I think find sale for all our iron as we make it at about 6½ cts. per lb and with a production of 8000 lbs. this will give us an income of about $500 per day. We can I hope rely on $10,000 from this source up to the end of February, allowing for all draw backs. I came up on the cars with Gen. Jno. W. [H.] Forney. He graduated in 1852. He is now engaged in managing a plantation on shares, near Demopolis. He told me of the very narrow escapes he had of being utterly penniless immediately after the surrender, having started from Jacksonville with $100 in his pocket to seek his fortune.

Willie has not gone to his school yet, but Wednesday next is fixed for his departure. I think he begins to feel a little sober over it, tho' he looks forward to the change with boyish pleasure. As he lies asleep before me now, how earnestly I pray for his future welfare. How my heart yearns toward him; & how glad I would be to shield him from the troubles of life. It makes me understand, & in some measure respect the desire people have to accumulate, in order that they may leave their children in affluence. It is the natural desire of the parent to protect & watch over the offspring—to work hard, & bear the brunt of the struggle of life, that the child may be saved the same struggle in some degree. No new developments in Congress affecting our political situation. The Mexican Empire seems to have been put to death by the determined opposition of the United States. If our struggle had been successful it would have been otherwise. France would have gained a foothold on this continent. Napoleon was not farsighted when he deferred acknowledging the existence of the Confederate States.

Feb. 3 Sunday [1867]   Weather mild and pleasant. It rained yesterday & day before. I rode to the furnace this P. M. and found the stock of charcoal exhausted, & the furnace will have to stop for 15 hours. This is owing to our being unable to "draw" our new oven, which has resisted all our efforts to cool it off entirely. We hope for better success with the next oven. Our furnaces were doing very well last night & this morning, running on charcoal & coke, making 7 & 8 beds & good iron. Pity our stock failed. Mamma was taken very sick on Monday last toward dark, & is very feeble still, but I hope slowly recovering her strength. The children are always greatly distressed when their mother has to stay a-bed. A thrill of indignation has run thro' the hearts of Southern people on learning that honors to the dead hero Albert Sidney Johnston were forbidden at Galveston by Gen. [Charles] Griffin. On appeal to Gen. Sheridan by the Mayor he confirmed Griffin's action in language far more wounding than was the order of Gen. G. [In 1862 Johnston had been buried in New Orleans. In 1867 when his body was enroute from New Orleans to Austin, Tex., for reburial, his former comrades attempted a funeral procession in Galveston. After military authorities refused, thousands filed past the coffin on the Galveston wharf.] No matter, we are conquered & must bear with our fate, val victus [woe to the vanquished]. The passage of Mr. [George] Boutwell's bill, nullifying the decision of the Supreme Court in the case of the test oath, has given it seems more uneasiness at Washington than any act of the radicals heretofore. It looks like revolution sure enough.

[February] 24 [1867]   The stockholders of the company met here on the 14th. Mr. Lyon, Dr. Browder, Mr. Collins, Mr. [Edwin] Glover, Mr. [Daniel J.] Prout, and myself the absentees being represented by proxies. There being some objections made to Mr. Prout I consented to serve as President for the present, tho' I am anxious to be relieved of the financial responsibility. Mr. Prout was made Vice President, and will take charge of sales & purchases for the works. He will also attend to the sale of the surplus capital, $50,000. The capital stock was fixed at $300,000 & $250,000 divided among the original shareholders. The party left here on

Saturday the 16th, & I went with them taking Willie with me as far as Selma where I put him on the train for his first school with the [Rev.] Mr. [Anastasius] Menaeos near Greensboro. The little fellow went off courageously. It is sad to see him so early separating from us. On Thursday last Col. [John S.] Williams (Conf.) and Col. [Daniel] Flagler (U.S.Ord) came up with me from Selma to stay a day. Col. F. is a young but very intelligent officer, who seems to have been actively engaged in the late war as Ord officer. Col. Williams is chief Engr on this road. The weather is quite warm to-day, Ther. 74°, and the peach trees are beginning to blossom, prematurely I fear. Mamma is recovering strength but slowly. We walked over to Col. Mallets new house, which is not finished, & she was greatly fatigued with the short walk.

March 1, [18]67   The weather continues quite warm & pleasant. Mr. W. P. Brown [a pioneer coal operator] our neighbor of three miles distant passed the day with us. He has had a stroke of paralysis, & is very much changed. Mamma talked to him (or listened rather) the whole day. Rode to the Furnace, my usual ride, at 4 P. M., furnace running Pretty well, tho the cinder looks green. Am going to town in the morning, & hope to bring up Col. Wright, one of my Ordn Subs, with me. The telegraph chronicles the death of Mr. DeBow the author of the [DeBow's] Review, which he had transferred to Washington, at the age of 47. We knew him very well both before and during the war.

[John] Sherman's reconstruction bill, which establishes military governments at the South, is likely to become law, as the President was going to return it on Wednesday (27th) which will give time to pass it over his veto. He evidently lacks the force to contend with Congress, and will go under. It would have been better never to have opposed them, than thus to give in to them, & be <u>driven</u> from power, where with proper will he might command.

Mch 9, [1867]   The Sherman military bill has become a law over the veto of the President and the negros can now vote. I yesterday saw the first a political gathering of negros in Selma, for the first time in my life. Mr. Prout, the Vice Presdt of our company came up on Tuesday, & spent Wednesday here. We had a good deal of business to talk over. It has rained incessantly nearly all this week. Our poor furnace has had a hard time of it, & we were forced to lay her up for several days, for want of charcoal, which the bad weather prevented us from receiving. To-day a fine athletic capable blacksmith was instantly killed, in the rolling mill, by the tilting up of a piece of iron which he was putting into the shears. It struck him on the side of the neck below the ear, & produced instant death, probably by dislocation. Letters from Mary [Aiken] & Bayne to-night. She is established in a comfortable house at Winsboro. We are much dependent on the mails for relief from the solitude of our isolated life here. Mamma has not been away from here since she came in April a year ago. I have been persuading her to go to Selma with me, without effect. It is a dreary life to us, a fit sequel no doubt to the deplorable loss of country. But the children amuse themselves playing, the livelong day.

Apl 3d 1867   We have had continued rain during the month of March, & a frost which destroyed all prospect of a peach crop. The wrath of Heaven seems directed against this poor unfortunate country. Our furnace was obliged to suspend for eleven days in the latter part of March, for want of charcoal. Our rolling mill followed suit, the boilers behaving badly & forcing us to inactivity for 5 or 6 days. All is going on now pretty well again. But these delays and interruptions are greatly against us, & drive us to the verge of distraction. It is impossible to say whether we will not be obliged to succumb at last to the overwhelming adverse circumstances which surround us. Our iron will not sell at re-numerative rates, and it seems impossible to get through. I will persevere to the last, but fear the worst. I go to Selma to-morrow to see whether some of our capital stock cannot be sold to relieve our necessities. Mamma & I took ride to the furnace yesterday & to-day. I hope the out-door exercise will do her good. The weather is again pleasant, and spring like and we may hope for progress in our gardens.

Apl 9, [1867]   It is the anniversary of Lee's surrender, sad, sad day, with what force & suddenness it broke upon us as we heard it at Dan-ville. I never saw the President moved but by that shock. It unnerved him completely. He sent for me & several chiefs of Bureaus, the Secretaries not having yet arrived, & when I entered said, "We have just received, Gorgas, the worst news that we could have. Gen. Lee has surrendered his army." He never before addressed me without the prefix of my rank. He was standing when he spoke & then sat down & bowed his head upon his hands for a moment. After further conversation as to the direction we were to take from Danville, he referring me to our respective Secretaries who were to arrive, he got up buckled on his sword & pistol, & dis-missed us. He looked as he stood, thin, spare, erect, every inch a chief, sorrowful but self possessed, hopeless but self-reliant to the last.

How little we are disposed to criticize Gen. Lee, yet to me the fact of our unpreparedness for the news of the catastrophe, even on the part of those who knew the military strength & dispositions, is the best com-mentary; & is good evidence that Gen. Lee fell short of his reputation. He had not made the preparations necessary to save the army from capture. The truth is, I think, he thought it a useless sacrifice to continue a hopeless struggle. If he thought it hopeless, he should have spoken out when the commissioners went to Fort Monroe. A decided word from him would have made peace.

Apl 21 [1867]   The weather is to-day balmy and beautiful. It is the
blessed Sabbath, a day the value of which I have of late learned to
appreciate in that it affords cessation from the hard toil of the week. We
very much need some place of devotion & a minister to remind us of our
duties to God & to man, duties we are so apt to think of lightly.

I went to Selma on Thursday to meet Mr. Prout. The city was para-
lyzed by the heavy defalcation at the 1st Nat Bk. The deficiency which its
President, Mr. [John G.] Parkman, had advertized as a robbery, turned
out to have been created by losses in [cotton] speculation. He was arrested by military authority, eluded his guard & fled. It is sad to see a
man one day honored & trusted & the next day see him advertized as a
felon, his stature, hair & clothes described, & a reward set on his head.
He is a young man with wife & children, who drop down from luxury to
penury, probably. [Parkman subsequently was imprisoned at Cahawba
and drowned in the river in an escape attempt.]

Our works are kept <u>afloat</u> with the greatest difficulty. They absorb a
great deal of money and the hard times, making it difficult to sell the
product of the works at any price. If we can sustain ourselves for the next
four months, we shall I hope do well, but it is a serious question as to
whether we can do so. Of course the thought of failure distresses me
beyond measure & makes me cheerless & gloomy. I have no relief from
the thoughts which constantly crowd upon me. I trust there will be a
happy end yet to our difficulties.

May 19, Sunday [1867]   Since my last entry I have been to N.
Orleans. I stayed there a week with the hope of effecting some arrangement for the sale of our iron & with the faint hope of disposing of some
of our surplus stock. I could do neither. And now our difficulties will I
fear compel us to stop work; or rather the want of a market will compel
us to stop. If we could sell our pig iron & our bar iron at even lower rates
than I ever dreamed of we could sustain ourselves. But such is the prostration of the entire South that nothing can be sold to the interior, & we
cannot compete with imported iron in the Seaport towns. Of course I am
greatly distressed at this state of things, but I do not see that we could
have anticipated it when we began this enterprize.

Mamma began her Sunday school last Sunday in our little schoolhouse
church, & is prosecuting it to-day. She is now sitting on the piazza with
her young friends singing hymns! I hope she will persevere, because she
can thus do a great deal of good.

During my absence Bishop Wilmer came here (about the 28th) &
preached at night in our little church. In the morning early he had communion in our hall, & after breakfast took the cars to Randolph [a
settlement in southeastern Bibb County], & thence by private con-

veyance to Tuscaloosa. He is very democratic in his notions, & disappointed my wife in not occupying the pulpit of her little church which, she had taken great pains to decorate prettily.

It has rained a good deal to-day. The weather is not yet warm. Yesterday even a fire looked pleasant.

Mr. Prout, our V. P. stayed here all last week talking over our prospects, & looking at the coal lands in our vicinity. He goes to Mobile to-morrow, & will telegraph to me by Tuesday or Wednesday what is to be done.

The political condition of the country is not improving. The negros in the city are growing troublesome, & I fear we shall have bloodshed. They show a turbulent spirit in Mobile & N. Orleans. A collision, with bloodshed, happened at Mobile last week. [On May 14 a riot had disrupted a speech in Moble by Pa. Congressman William D. Kelley. A more serious riot had occurred in New Orleans in July 1866, when forty people died.] I fear there are times ahead still more disastrous than those we have passed thro.

The children, Ria & Jessie, are still predisposed to chills.

June 25 (Tuesday) [1867]   Therm. 72 at 8 A. M. We have beautiful weather.

June 30 (Sunday) [1867]   To-day I complete my 49th year. To-morrow I must fairly confess that I am middle-aged. I have no dread of growing old. Gen. Johnston came up on Thursday evey from Selma & stayed a day, on his way to Washington whither he goes to look after the business of the A. & S. [Selma, Rome & Dalton] R.R. of which he is Presdt. I went to town on Tuesday & stopped all night at Gen. Hardee's. Gen. H is absent in N. Y., also on the business of his R.R. the Selma & Meridian. His daughter Miss Sallie did the honors of the house, a very lady like attractive girl. Gen. Johnston stayed there also & talked until 12½ at night. He is implacable as to Mr. Davis, & Gens. Hood & Bragg. He seemed to enjoy his stay here very much. He is still very active in his walk, & seems perfectly preserved, tho' I suppose he must now be on the shady side of Sixty. The aspect of the country does not improve. The registry of negros & of whites under the military bill shows the former largely in the ascendant, of course, for most of the whites are excluded. This will throw the local government into the control of negros. It is impossible to predict the consequences a year may bring forth. The land South may again be deluged in blood. I fear we have not yet seen the worst of our condition.

At 9 A. M. to-day we all went to our Sunday School, which Mamma began about two months ago. It has become a point of interest, & to-day there were quite sixty children present, besides about 20 grown people. The fathers begin to come with the children. After the school I went over to the furnace on the tram, & walked back—2¾ miles. It was very warm. I walked slowly & beguiled the way by stopping to pick blackberries. Dined at ¼ 2, quite plainly, on chicken & plenty of vegetables. Col. Mallet came over after dinner to tell me of the furnace, but as I had been there he stayed but a few minutes. He is greatly depressed, as I am, at the unfortunate condition of our works here. We are heavily in debt, and in the present condition of our country, the South, it is impossible to sell stock or to borrow money. This leads us to fear that we may have to sacrifice our property, and perhaps lose all we have invested here. It is a sad termination to all our high hopes, in great measure attributable to the total prostration of the country. We could make money now & work ourselves out of debt could we but find a market for our products at any rate which we had a right to calculate on. We cannot sell our wrought iron at all, & pig iron will not afford profit when we have to send it to N. York.

On turning back to the entry made a year ago I see that the shadow of failure which is now upon us even then pressed fearfully upon me. What a life I have lived for this twelvemonth, constantly pressed with debt, & not knowing where the means to continue the works were to come from. When the furnace went into blast I fondly hoped my troubles would be over, & I should have revenue enough from that to sustain us. Alas, the furnace was a comparative failure, and has run us in debt instead of assisting us with the other work. After that I thought if I could only get the rolling mill going we should make a good deal of money out of that, but the rolling mill was if possible worse than the furnace. All burned to ashes in my mouth. Hope after hope disappeared, & at last I awake to the certainty of entire failure in our enterprize, & the stoppage of works, before they are wholly done. It is a bitter close of my 49th year.

In the afternoon I went with Mamma & the children to her colored sunday school, pretty well attended, in spite of the rain. Millie Crawford & Mamie Bayne [two of Amelia's nieces] are with us. Mamie has a very good ear for music, & can sing a second to some airs of the Sunday School music. Willie comes back from his school day after to-morrow. Fred Watson went over in a buggy to Greensboro to bring him & Eddy [Edmund D. Gayle, one of Amelia's half brothers] over. It is raining so hard I fear they will be delayed.

July 4, [18]67 Thursday   I cannot remember when this glorious 4th has given me much pleasure. It has certainly given me none to-day. There was a Barbecue at the little Methodist Church, half-a-mile from here, to which the country people & negros flocked. It was a congregation of the "Union League," a society which seems to be organized in this hopelessly benighted country out of those who skulked during the war, and are now rampant for the Union. Willie had a slight chill to-day. He returned from

Mr. Menaeos school on Sunday, with Eddy. Eddy has his face bunged with poison ivy, and Willie swam too much yesterday, probably for his good. Dined at Mrs. McMain's on roast pig, so big.

July 7 [1867]   Therm. 74°. The day opens gloomily and threatens rain. A heavy rain would just now be disastrous to us, as it would prevent our getting in charcoal for the furnace, on which our ability to pay off our men depends. If we can run until Wednesday, five more days, we shall do very well. Willie was quite sick yesterday, & Mamma complains of feeling seriously unwell. Milly has just recovered from a sharp attack of biliousness. On the whole we are a very dilapidated set. We took tea & spent the evening at Col. (Dr.) Mallet's.

July 9, [1867]   Went to Selma on business, nothing but gloom & dejection among the businessmen. One declared there was nothing left for us but to leave the country & I fear he is right. The affairs of our own company look gloomy enough, & I fear we may lose all we have put into this work, which is nearly all I have in the world. At fifty (nearly) I shall have to begin where I was twenty years ago, except that then I was alone & now I have a wife & six children dependent on me. Alas! that I should have ventured at such an unlucky moment, but I acted from the best dictates of my judgment, & thought we had every chance of success here. Congress met on the lst of July & is continuing its radical programme by over-riding the opinion of the Atty Genl on the re-construction bill. The political horizon is darkening. The registration of voters shows that the political power will be in the hands of our late slaves. What shame! What humiliation for us. Would it not be better to take up arms & defend ourselves to the last against such infamy.

July 10, [1867]   Therm. 72 at 7, 84 at 3 P.M. Weather pleasant cloudy towards evey. Rode with Mamma to the furnace, joined by Col. Mallet on returning. A beautiful sunset. The Col. & I are in better spirits as it seems probable the proceeds of the furnace will enable us to close up our work here without discredit to the company, so far as the workmen are concerned. Found Col. Williams here when we got back. Willie & Eddy returned from a day's shooting proud of a crow, a lark & a dove! The evening is genial & delightful. The climate is indeed all we could ask. Would that our works were prosperous.

July 14 Sunday [1867]   The thermometer has been as high as 87° (on the 12th) and the weather somewhat sultry but not oppressive. The item of news which creates most sensation is the death of Maximilian, who was shot by the Mexicans on the 19th of last month. He died with great dignity & firmness, breathing his wife's name "Poor Carlotta." It is an act that will cause the name of Mexico to be execrated. The radical congress have passed a bill in the house, taking away all lands granted to Rail Roads in five of the Southern States. There seems to be no end to the oppression we are to undergo. We now are wholly under military government, and that imposes blacks as officials over us. We have negros who swear in white people & decide on their right to vote. In Selma we have negro policemen, & in Mobile Gen. Sweeny [Wager Swayne] has appointed a negro alderman, on city council. [After the riot in Mobile in May all offices in Mobile were declared vacant. Gen. Swayne offered positions to blacks, who refused. Black policemen were appointed in both Selma and Mobile.]

Misfortunes follow us in these works. It seems probable that we shall lose all the proceeds of the sale of 400 Tons of iron made to the First National Bank amounting to $12,000. This would indeed be a serious misfortune. I had a letter a few days ago from my sister Christiana [Gorgas Zerbe] whom I have not heard from for 8 or 9 years. I do not know that it gives me much pleasure to revive communication with kindred who live among & sympathize with those who have so much oppressed us, but I used to be strongly attached to this sister who is the youngest of my sisters, & is only 5 years my senior. Our furnace is still in blast & turning out 8 or 10 tons of good iron per day. This will help us to close up our works creditably, by giving us funds to pay our workmen. Our prospects are however very gloomy, & I fear we shall lose nearly everything we have put into these works. Would that I had settled down somewhere quietly for a few years, after the war, & done nothing. I should have been better off, but I thought differently two years ago, & was anxious to employ myself on something which would be permanent, & important. The state of the country has baffled all my hopes.

July 21, [1867]   The week has passed away without startling incident. We heard of the birth of another little girl in Bayne's household [Amelia Elizabeth (Minna) Bayne]. Willie is quite unwell again, bilious no doubt & inclined to chills. Mrs. Mallet, too, our neighbor over the creek has been sick, & a physician came up yesterday evening from Selma. I hope this don't indicate that our place is to be unhealthy again. The creek which flows thro here is dammed below us, makes the water sluggish. Our works are very quiet now. The furnace was blown out on Thursday morning (18th) and all the men have been paid off. The rolling mill did its last work last week, and there are only a few men at work on the nail plate rolls or muck train. The foundry & machine shop are closed. It makes us all very sad to see this destruction of our high hopes. Instead of making money, we shall have great difficulty in extracting our money from the concern. It changes my plans of life entirely for I expected to make this my future business. The weather continues quite rainy, too wet for cotton & perhaps not good in future for corn, tho this looks now very well. The thermometer ranges from 74° at 8 A. M. to 80° & 84° at the warmest part of the day, a pleasant temperature for this latitude.

July 28 [1867]   Ther. 76° 7¼ A. M. I went to Demopolis on Tuesday to meet the stockholders. No one came but Mr. Prout & Mr. Lyon, but there were proxies enough to make up a majority of the stock, and it was agreed that we should sell the property as early as possible. I shall accordingly go on to the north as soon as I can leave here to see what can be done. I fear there is little prospect of an immediate sale. The crop especially the corn is looking very promising, and we may hope for a little relief from our present distress as soon as the crops are sent to market. The weather was very warm at D., mercury at 83° at 7½ A. M. & 90° at sundown. The scarcity of money is almost ludicrous if it were not distressing. Three rich planters, who have heretofore hardly known what it was to want money, could not raise $300 each, & we are obliged to postpone the payment of debts which ought to be paid at once, & which could be paid if each one of these could but raise $300. But they are positively without money until relieved by the sending of cotton to market. Mr. Lyon speaks very despondingly of the future, & says he would leave the country at once if he could.

Aug 4, [1867]   7 A. M. Ther. 71. The weather continues beautiful and pleasantly warm. Our place looks of course very quiet and the men sit idly about in groups, but behaving very well. There are four men at work here, & two guards at the Furnace. Our expenses are now reduced to about $300. per month, instead of about $18,000 that we were spending two months ago, but without income it is difficult to pay even the $300. I am hesitating as to whether I shall enter on the making of cotton ties on my own account. The prospect to make 4 or 5 thousand dollars before January is very tempting but we are so very timid here now that we dare not venture even where the risk is so very small. The political condition remains about the same. Senator [B. H.] Hill of Ga. continues writing letters on our situation which are spirited & attract a good deal of attention. It seems Ex Gov Brown of Ga is writing in reply on the side of the "Military Bills." Gen. Sheridan is spoken of for President, & if things progress on as they are going now I should not be surprised to see him taken up, & of course elected, as I see no signs of reaction which would lead to defeat of the radicals. What will become of us is hard to tell.

We heard of the shooting of Mr. Shepard in Mt. Vernon, by a federal officer there. He had posted this officer as a coward & liar. Mamma and I are discussing plans of reform in our household. I have no salary now, & therefore not a cent of income & we must economize. Mr. Prout came last evening, more to benefit himself probably than on business of the company.

Aug 11 [1867]   The weather continues very hot, the thermometer going up to 87° to-day. Sunday, we had our usual Sunday school, present 60 pupils, besides teachers, about 70 in all. The afternoon school of darkeys is omitted to-day on account of meeting in the afternoon at the church half a mile from here.

Mr. Johnson seems to be trying to get himself up to the sticking point to sustain his authority, & even to remove some of the military commanders who almost defy his prerogatives as commander in chief. But there is nothing announced as certain. I fear he is but an indifferent successor to Andrew Jackson. The manly "notes on the situation" of Mr. Hill of Ga. attract attention at the South, where people are so timid that a little manliness is refreshing. Mr. Bayne is expected toward the close of the week, & I hope will go on North with me.

[August] 14 [1867]   Ther 86° to-day. It ranges from 76 in the morning to about 88° at 4 P. M.

I have recd. advices from Mr. Lyon which will prevent me from going North for some time to come. Mamma and I are just going out to ride, 6 P. M.

Aug 25 [1867]   The weather is very pleasant, nights cool, the thermometer sinking to 70 & 72 & rising in the day time to 85°. Bayne arrived on Wednesday Evey & is enjoying himself doing nothing, which he requires very much.

On Monday I went over to Demopolis to see Mr. Lyon about a contract made with Mr. [Horace] Ware [of the Shelby Iron Works], in which we are likely to get into trouble, found Mr. Lyon quite indisposed & nervous. The season is there a very sickly one, & I congratulate myself that I have my family in so comparatively healthy a location.

The political event of the week has been the removal of [Secretary of War Edwin M.] Stanton (which took place about ten days ago) & the subsequent removal of Sheridan from command [of the Fifth Military District] at N. Orleans. Sheridan had been guilty of decided disrespect to the President in an official communication to Grant. Besides he did all he could to oppose the President's views as to reconstruction. The President desires to reconstruct on a white basis, while Sheridan & Pope [commander of the Third Military District] seem determined to give the black element political control. It is strange to see the northern fanatics endeavoring to convert the Southern States into a Jamaica.

Sept 8 Sunday [1867]   The morning is beautiful & temperature charming. Therm. 72°. I wish the condition of the country were as cheering as this climate is delightful, but things seem to be going from bad to worse. The President directs the removal of Sheridan from N. Orleans, & other changes to correspond, and Grant protests! What a spectacle of military subordination. Grant orders Sickles from Charleston, & he suspends the execution of the order until he can be heard! Sheridan is however at last relieved & [Gen. Winfield Scott] Hancock takes his place. There are scarcely any courts & the whole machinery of civil government in the States seems fallen to pieces. Still we get along without much civil government as we did in Confederate times, but then we had a great central idea, that of the war & its success, which kept us in subordination. (No allusion I see is made in the pages of this journal to the liberation from prison of President Davis, which occurred in the spring after a confinement of two years. He now lives near St. Catharine's in Canada—this did much to alay the bitterness between the two sections.)

We are going on to make cotton ties but are too late to do much, I fear. We ought to have been in the market a month ago with the ties. It is the misfortune of joint stock companies that the direction is too often controlled by considerations which weaken the energetic conduct of the work. If I could have followed the dictates of my judgment we would have been early enough.

Bayne went down on Wednesday after Maria who telegraphed she was at Mobile & the baby sick. I think they will be up on Tuesday perhaps when we shall have, let me see how many whites in the house, 9 of us, Matt, Milly & Helen, 12, Bayne's family 7, making 19 & we hope to have Ma with T. L. & nurse & Eddy, making 23, besides servants.

Helen took a ride with me to the furnace. I took Ria en croupe [behind]. She is perfectly devoted to horses. Willie had holiday yesterday & rode after butter in the afternoon. He has stayed in my office until 12 M and at 4 P. M. goes to the store to assist there. Matt has a very singular affliction. On alternate days he is active, excited & talkative—on other days he can scarcely stir or say a word. It is perfectly intermittent—tertian—and is a singular case. I suppose it will result in mental aberration. I fear so.

Sept 15 [1867]   The proclamation of amnesty just issued by the President includes all except the President & his Cabinet, Governors of States, & officers above the grade of Brig. Genl. So that I am now amnestied, by taking the oath of allegiance. This measure excites little remark.

It is taken however as an indication that the President feels himself strengthened, & able to take the offensive against the radicals. The result of elections in California, where there is a democratic majority of 7000, in Montana, in Connecticut & in Maine, in which latter state the Republican majority is reduced from 28000 to 10,000 indicate a change which bodes no good to the present system of misrule. Yet I hope in my heart the misrule will triumph until utter chaos is produced, when we may emerge with our Confederacy as we struggled for it. Negros are now being appointed to city offices in N. Orleans. It appears incredible that such a revolution could be affected by force in the space of 5 years, since the city fell into the hands of the Yankees. Maria arrived on Monday Evey, & is looking as beautiful as ever.

Bayne goes North to-morrow. We are going on here with cotton ties, & hope to have some ready for the market by the end of the week, too late to dispose of many, & I shall have great trouble in getting supplies for our hands. Thermometer ranges here from 72 to 82. We saw a beautiful natural eclipse of the moon which was full on Friday evey, & the children looked at it thro' the opera glass from the back porch.

Oct 10, [1867]   12 midnight. I am sitting up to overlook the work at the Rolling Mill. The night is a beautiful moonlight with the thermometer at about 62°. Bayne left for N. York nearly four weeks ago & may possibly arrive to-morrow. He will bring us all the news from the North—what is said and thought in New York as to the state of the country. The elections for a convention [in Alabama] to adopt a State constitution have been held, & are wholly radical. Among the members returned are 16 negros! Scarcely any white people voted. Elections have just been held in Ohio & Pennsylvania & indicate large Democratic gains, which would seem to point to a re-action at the North. The trial of Mr. Davis, it is said, will certainly take place in November. It will be a mere argument of counsel, as the facts will be admitted.

Gen. Johnston who has been Presdt of this R.Rd [Selma, Rome & Dalton] went north two weeks ago not to return again. Under the lease of the Road a son-in-law [brother-in-law, Franklin A. Delano] of Wm. B. Astor [of N.Y.] becomes President, and the road is now to be completed thro' to Rome Ga. in a twelvemonth. We shall see. We are all living very comfortably here in our cottage—8 grown white people, and 10 children—with 4 colored Servants. Ma is expected here next week with Bayne's little boy (T. L.) which increases the white folks by three, a pretty fair family. Besides we expect some visitors soon! Mamma seems to think the more the merrier. I have been trying to teach Willie & Jessie a little Latin, but it is impossible to command the time to hear them. Ma when she comes will undertake the education of the children & Willie will probably go to N. O. with Bayne to go to school there. It is now nearly one & I must go & look at the puddlers [ironworkers converting pig iron into wrought iron], & then go to bed.

Nov 14, [1867]   The elections at the north seem to have inspired some hope of ultimate good results. Even the radicals seem to be awakening at the north to the insanity of placing these states under negro rule. At present the State [Constitutional] convention is sitting at Montgomery, mixed black & white, the delegates sitting mixed indiscriminately as to color. We shall have apparently the singular spectacle of democratic reaction at the North, and radical-negro rule at the South. The trial of Mr. Davis it is positively said now is to take place at Richmond & he is expected there on the 22d. Mr. Chase Chief Justice is to preside with the infamous [Judge John C.] Underwood [of the U.S. Circuit Court in the District of Virginia, where Davis was indicted,] & the jury is to be mixed black & white! Bayne left here last Thursday, & Maria expects to follow next week. The yellow fever has been very severe in N. O. but has ceased to be epidemic. I have a letter from B[ayne] relative to taking a position on the Mobile & Ohio R.R. of which I was elected V. Presdt two years ago. It would be a little singular if I should after all go on the road where I might have gone two years ago, thus losing two years of my life, a serious loss at my time of life. We have tried the making of cotton ties here, & have again lost money, tho' not much.

Nov 28, [1867]   The Rolling Mill is again at work making a few more cotton ties, Capt. [Thomas S.] Alvis undertaking to get the coal & do the work. I fear he will have up-hill work, but I am glad to see it going on even if but a few tons more of ties are made.

To-morrow Maria leaves for N. Orleans. Willie & Helen go with her, & we shall be bereft of half our family. I go with them as far as N. Orleans & then to Montgomery, where I am a witness in a suit brought against us by the National Bank of Selma. Ritchie is quite feverish and a little "wild" this evening.

A few days ago the news from Washington was that the President would be impeached. The impression now appears to be that there will be no further attempt to prosecute it, that it will be passed over. Mr. Davis' trial is put off until March, & it is probable will then again be postponed. He came down from St. Catharine's in Canada where he has been living to attend the court at Richmond. It is said he will not go back this winter.

The mixed black & white convention to frame a constitution in this State, under the military bills, is still in session. Their proceedings are very radical, & their constitution will be bad enough, so bad that it will perhaps not be adopted.

Decr 8, [1867]   The weather is clear bracing sunshiny & beautiful. I took Maria to Selma on Friday week (29th), but returned without going to Montgomery the court having adjourned its meeting to the 14th of January. It rained furiously on the morning Maria left, & she had a very uncomfortable time of it. Congress is in session & the President's message published. It is much more determined in its tone than I expected it would be. He is doubtless encouraged by the results of the recent elections in the northern & western states. The constitutional (black & white) convention at Montgomery has produced a constitution and adjourned.

Children all well except Minnie who has a bad cold. Walked 9 miles yesterday to coal mines & do not feel very good to-day, tho' I felt distressed yesterday.

Decr 14, [1867]   Therm 30 at 8 A. M. Yesterday clear & beautiful tho cool, to-day promises the same. No news of special interest in the papers of yesterday. Gen. Hancock [commander of the Fifth Military District] appears to give great satisfaction at N. Orleans. Gold fell to 133 but rallied to 138 (so say the figures, which are often incorrect, perhaps the rally was to 135).

We are still making a few cotton ties & have some bar iron.

The chief occupation of my thoughts is now to sell our works, of which there is little hope in these disastrous times, and what we are to do with the many debts pressing on us, surpasses my comprehension. Our situation is sadly depressing. Mamma remarked some time ago, that our misfortunes seem to come toward Christmas, & that it was never a season of rejoicing with us. This year it certainly is not. My own future is very uncertain. As the prospect here at these works closes I look around for some occupation, but find it difficult to decide what to do for a livelihood. We must remain here until this property is disposed of, as my interest in it is so large that I cannot afford to trust to another, else I would resign the Presidency & look for a position elsewhere.

Sunday, Decr 22, [1867]   The Therm stands at 68 (2 P. M.) and the weather is very pleasant, altho it has been quite rainy early in the day. We went to our usual Sunday School at 9½ A. M. Mamma has 50 to 60 Scholars, & takes great interest in her School. Last night she rec'd a letter from Helen telling her that a Christmas box for her scholars was on its way. She has despaired of being able to give them any present, everybody is so poor, never was the country in such a state of destitution. There is literally no money in circulation. Christmas comes on Wednesday, & the children are all anticipating such little pleasures as we can give them.

Christmas, Decr 25, [1867]   Therm 62°, day cloudy & threatening rain. Children all in glee at their little presents. I feel much depressed & will take a long walk by myself.

Decr 26, [1867]   The thermometer stands at 72° to-day. Dr. Broughton dined with us. Every body is gloomy & depressed. I have been visiting most of the day.

[December] 27th, [1867]   Therm 78° at 2 P. M. & 74 at this moment, sun-down. Weather very beautiful. Mamma had her box from N. O. last evening & her Sunday School celebration this morning. The little church-school-house looked very pretty with its holiday trimmings.

XII

"Our company affairs are very much embarrassed"

Jan 3d, [1868]   (Ther 64 at 8 A. M.) The New-Year came in warm & cloudy. The chief news is the removal of Gens Pope & Swayne from this Mil. District, & the shooting of Judge [Richard] Busteed by the U.S. District Atty [Lucien Van Buren Martin] in the streets of Mobile. Busteed began to be better liked, and there is some sympathy for him. He began I think to feel with the South. But they are both Union men alike, & let them fight it out. Our holidays have been anything but merry, somewhat my own fault. I cannot look the future into the face with equanimity. I have a dread of being poor & old together.

Jan 25, [1868]   Ther 26 at 8½ A. M. Sun shining brightly and Capt. McMain & I propose to take our usual Saturday walk. Stanton's return to the War Office was the latest Sensation at Washington. It happened about 10 days ago.

Jany 26, [1868]   Therm 42 at 8½ A. M. Sunday, cloudy, Sunday School at 9½. Mr. Nix, foreman of the Foundry & chief class teacher announces his going to Meridian, knocking away Mamma's last prop. A long letter from [Amelia's] Sister Sarah last evening which as exposing the trials in store for us makes me feel very sober to-day. I am constantly trying to shake off thoughts of the future, harrassing as they are. There are no developments from Washington in last evening's news. Gold 141 which again indicates uneasiness in New York.

Jan. 31, [1868]   Yesterday morning the mercury stood at 7° at 8 o'clock & had been down to 5° no doubt. This morning it is 11° & has been down to 8°, no doubt. This is the coldest weather that has been known here for many years. The days are clear & beautiful. Snow fell on Tuesday night to the depth of 4 inches & is still lying on the ground tho' it thaws in the day time. The trees are covered & breaking down with their white loads. Yesterday (Thursday) was a fast day, recommended by the conference of distinguished citizens who met at Montgomery last week & who recommended to the white people not to vote on the mongrel constitution on the 5th of Feby.

Feby 2, [1868]   The Snow is still lying on the roofs & in spots about tho we have had beautiful sunny days. The nights have been quite cold. Our walk to Sunday school or rather from it was quite muddy from the thawing of the frost. Ria was quite overcome with toothache last night, but did not fail to have appetite enough to enjoy her share of turkey to-day. One of our winter troubles here is to get fresh meat, and we have almost grown tired of chickens. Affairs at Washington show no special development. The President has done nothing decided as to Stanton. On the 5th the people of this State are to vote on the mongrel constitution. The white people have all been requested to stay away, by the conference at Montgomery, so that a majority of the registered voters may not vote, in which case the constitution fails. We get good accounts of Willie's success at N. Orleans, his Uncle Tom [Bayne] praises his assiduity. His mother is of course very proud to hear every one speak in praise of him.

Feby 22, [1868]   There is nothing new in the papers of yesterday. Cotton retains its advance & is quoted at 24 in N.O. Mobile & N.Y. Gold 140½ . The impeachment of Presdt Johnson is finally relinquished, the chief impeacher [Thaddeus] Stevens [of Pa.] abandons it confusedly.

The mongrel constitution [written by Republicans] was defeated, not half of the registered voters voting for it, only about 1500 white votes were cast in all the State. [70,812 voted for the constitution (including 500 whites) and 1,005 opposed it.] About the 8th of this month I was in Selma & rec'd there a letter from Presdt Davis. He is now at Vicksburgh with his brother Joe who is still living.

Feb 23, [1868]   The therm stood yesterday at over 60. This morning 48°. The weather is very fine. The President has nominated Gen G. H. Thomas as Lieut. Gen. & brevet General, promotion which Sherman declined. The President is going on as if he intended to oppose Congress & use his own power. He has nominated McClellan to the court of St. James. I hope he will prevail against his drunken opponent Grant, whose downfall is I think not distant. But it is possible that Congress will prevail in this contest & that the revolution the radicals are attempting will yet be consummated & end in despotism.

Feby 27, [1868]   Therm 46° at 7¾ A.M. Rained for three days Past. The House has passed impeachment resolutions. The President seems to have miscalculated in getting the support of the Army thro' Sherman or Thomas who have both declined to sustain him. I think he will be deposed & [Benjamin F.] Wade [of Ohio] as President of the Senate become Acting President. It is perhaps fortunate for the north that Johnson is not a man of high self respect & resolution. He will give away before Congress where a firmer man would use his power to protect himself in his position under the Constitution. I am to go to Demopolis to-morrow to meet some of the company no doubt.

Mch 8 [1868]   Ther 61 at 8 A. M. The peach trees show in the swollen buds the approach of Spring. The Apl 27r has been very fine for the past week and I have been planting potatos, corn, peas &c. I hope we shall have a good garden, the season is thus far promising. My fruit trees, 223 of which I planted two years ago, will I think bear peaches & pears this year. The trial of Mr. Johnson on articles of impeachment, actually began on last week, tho' he is cited to appear on the 13th. He objected to Wade being sworn as Senator [[impeaching court]], on acct of interest as Wade becomes acting President in case of conviction. Wade is a low vulgar man. The President has Dudley Field of N.Y. and Judge [Jeremiah S.] Black (said by Mr. Lyon to be a very able lawyer) as counsel in his defence. It is believed that the radicals have determined to depose Mr. Johnson & merely go thro' the form of trial with him. As the Senate has already by formal vote declared his action towards Stanton a violation of law, this looks probable. The articles of impeachment relate with one exception entirely to his suspension of Stanton as Secy of War. The charges all hang on this thro' 9 articles. The 10th relates to a conversation with [William H.] Emory (Gen) as to his powers as commander-in-chief of the Army. I cannot help hoping that all this turmoil may end in a chaos at the North from which our Confederacy may again emerge. Would it not be wonderful! I spent last Saturday & Sunday at Demopolis & returned with a lease of the Furnace which I hope to carry on with the assistance of some northern men who can command money. We do not like this close association with even good northerners, but cannot now help it. The necessities of our business take precedence over likes & dislikes.

Your poor Uncle Matt continues to have his alternate days of exultation & depression. He does not seem to grow better nor worse. We had a pleasant Sunday School to-day. Have had no <u>Service</u> since last October.

[March] 9, [1868]   Ther. 48° at 7½ A. M. now 1 P. M. it is 72°. Am gardening to-day, spading & planting, the former is as hard work as one need wish.

Mch 15, Sunday [1868]   Ther 12½ P. M. 77°. Peach trees in full blossom. Corn in the garden well up. Potatos planted on the 14th of Feby just up.

Went to Selma on Friday & returned yesterday evening. Stayed all night at Hardee's. His family consists just now only of his wife (Miss Lewis, she was) and his daughter Sallie who is not looking well. Col. Roy (formerly on his staff) joined us & we played whist. I talked for 15 minutes on the side walk with Judge Tom Brooks. He thinks Mr. Johnson will be deposed without doubt. He & others of the Democratic club were to have a meeting in the evening to recommend some course of action to the white people of this State in view of the forced adoption of the negro constitution for this State, by Congress, & the admission of the State to representation. [The Alabama constitution failed to be ratified in February 1868 when a majority of registered voters did not participate in the election. However, Congress subsequently passed an act that validated that election and returned Alabama to representation in Congress.] He proposes a convention at Montgomery, & that that convention should recommend separate elections for the white people in the fall for President, Congress &c.

Mch 17 1868   Ther at 7 A M 69°. At 8½ A M it had fallen to 62°. It is Jessie's birthday. She has no presents this time, but will have an egg-nogg after dinner. I rode out by the Saw-mill thro the standing timber to Day's Saw-mill, my steed an obstinate white mule. It is showery to-day, but not enough to keep one in door. Mamma has not been well for Several days past.

[March] 20 [1868]   Ther. 2 P. M. 73°. At 8 A. M. 47, clear sunshiny & warm. Potatos & corn well up. Potatos planted on the 13th Feby did not appear above ground until the 15th Mch. Corn planted on the 9th was up on the 17th. Peach trees were in full blossom by the 15th & a few days earlier. Strawberries began to blossom on the 13th & are now full of blooms. There was little if any frost last night, tho the ther was probably down to 43 or 44°.

Capt Alvis is still running the Mill. Fan broke this morning & mill stopped. Rode to Montevallo yesterday, & got the mail.

[March] 21 [1868]   Thermometer 32 at 6½ A. M. Smart frost, tho not enough to kill in the garden. The peach trees are I trust safe.

Mch 22 Sunday [1868]   Ther 34 at 7 A. M. Slight frost. Col. Mallet returned from N. Orleans last evening. The woods are on fire about us. This annual burning of the woods is no doubt a chief cause of the poverty of the soil & the "piney woods." If the leaves & pine straw & old wood were allowed to lie & decay, a rich soil would be formed in the course of years.

Am discussing the propriety of running the furnace at my own risk. As I have nothing to lose, the risk cannot be great. No further developments in the Impeachment of the President. It is strongly rumored that there will be defections among the radical Senators.

Mch 23, [1868]   Ther at 2 P. M. 74°. Night cool but no frost, fires simply comfortable. Jessie seems to have something like a chill to-day. We do not feel quite sure of the healthfulness of this place, on account of the creek near us.

[March] 26 [1868]   Ther 62° at 8 A. M. Pleasant, warm, refreshing rain which promises well for our garden and crops. A Mr. Marshal of N. Orleans stayed here on Tuesday to look at our Works. He desires to get a purchaser for them. In the impeachment business time has been given until Monday for the President to prepare himself for trial.

Mch 30, [1868]   The thermometer for three mornings past has been at from 39° to 41° but no frost. A Mr. Thomason from Troy stayed here two days to look at our works, left here this evening. Col Mallet has also gone off to Virginia, to assume his [chemistry] Professorship at Charlottesville. Went out at 9 P. M. last evening to "fight fire" in the woods north of the Stable, & stayed until 10½. Have ridden over the furnace grounds to-day. Mamma has been a good deal indisposed since Saturday with neuralgia.

Apl 4 [1868]   Ther 38° this 7 A. M, no frost. We had a long steady rain in the afternoon and night of the 2d. I have been a little indisposed for the past two days. On Tuesday Col. Moore & Mr. Pearce of the Ca. Coal. Co. were here. They desire to lease the whole sett of works.

The impeachment trial is going on. It is probably settled that Mr. Johnson must be put out, & Wade installed so that there may be no further obstruction to the career of the party.

Apl 13 [1868]   On the 8th of April there was a heavy frost but no great damage was done by it. Even beans showed little effect from it. It is to-day very warm with signs of heavy weather. Easter Sunday was duly celebrated with flowers at our little Sunday school, which now numbers some eighty. The impeachment trial still goes on with what result cannot yet be predicted.

Rec'd a letter to night from Buffalo saying that Mr. [Philip] Dorsheimer [husband of Josiah's sister, Sarah] was on his death-bed, & sent kind messages to me, but there is no doubt bitter feeling against all "rebels," and I do not look for good feeling from northern friends or relatives. Took tea this evening with Mrs. Mallet, by special invitation to eat waffles.

Went to Selma last week to see what if any arrangement could be made to sell pig iron with a view to putting a furnace in blast. Could effect nothing, as the merchants are too weak financially to assist me in any way. I shall persevere & may still succeed.

Apl 27, [1868]   We have had constant & heavy rains all the month. Last Sunday night & Monday (19th & 20th) the rain was heavier than I have yet known. The creek in [the] rear of our house [is] now about 12 feet & threatens to destroy the little bridge between us & Col. Mallet's. It is now raining steadily & we shall have another freshet.

The streams have done a good deal of damage to the bottoms, & the rain was so heavy as to erode the uplands a good deal. I fear the wet weather will injure the wheat crop.

The impeachment trial has concluded the testimony & the counsel are going through the arguments. Boutwell [of Mass.] began, the other managers are [John A.] Bingham [of Ohio], [Thomas] Williams [of Pa.], [John A.] Logan [of Ill.], Stevens & the notorious Butler who conducts. The Presidents counsel are [Benjamin R.] Curtis, [William M.] Evarts, [Henry] Stanbery, & [William S.] Groesbeck.

Apl 29 [1868]   Ther. 65° at 7½ & 80 at 3 P. M. Rained heavily for half an hour yesterday afternoon. To day is bright.

May 3, [1868]   Ther 70° at 7 A. M. May-day was warm and beautiful. I rode out to Centreville on business starting at 5½ A. M. & returning at 7 P. M. The distance out & back is 33 miles. Mamma goes to Demopolis to-morrow to see her old friend Mrs. Deas (Helen Lyon). Have just read [U.S. Senator] Mr. [Henry] Wilson's speech [of Mass.] (a part of it) before the court of impeachment. It is able, abler than its opening promised.

May 14, [1868]   Ther 51 this A. M. It has rained a great deal in the last 4 days, & the weather is quite cool. We have had fine mornings & evey for a week past. Went to Selma yesterday to perfect arrangement for sale of iron with Maj. Ferguson & to provide provisions, have effected both & will now go on to put the furnace in blast. Went down with Mr. Delano, Presdt of this R.R.—son in law of Wm. B. Astor & of course very rich. Mr. Adger & Mr. Dato, rich N. Yorkers, & Col. Printess Presdt of the Rome & [Selma, Rome & Dalton] R.R. I hope these people will leave some of their money here. We are helpless almost without the assistance of these people, who hold the money of the country.

June 7 [1868]   Sunday Ther 68° at 7½ A. M. The last six days have been very warm with no rain, the mercury going up to 85 to 93 at 3 P. M. On the 23d I went to Montgomery to attend court as a Witness. Our suits were not called & I got home on the 30th.

The chief sight at M was the Judge of the U.S. District Court named Richard Busteed [of N.Y.], a man appointed in '62 or '63 [1864] by Lincoln in a sort of bravado, & as a good joke. He was what they call in N. Y. a Toombs lawyer. His outrageous conduct on the bench, his lawless decisions, & his probable corruption make him notorious in Ala. He was shot on the streets of Mobile a few months ago by one of his own set of dirty people whom the times have collected & put into office in the South. He behaved very well during this court & Mr. Lyon who went to see him was rather agreeably surprised to find him a pleasant man. The chief political events have been the acquittal of the President on the articles of impeachment. 7 of the radical Senators voted with the Democrats, making a vote of 19 to 35. These seven just men called down on themselves the bitter denunciations of the chiefs of their party. At once Butler & his crew accused the Presidents friends of having used money to obtain his acquittal, & private telegrams & letters were ransacked to obtain proof. All this resulted only in the discovery that Senator [S. C.] Pomeroy (radical) [of Kan.] had offered to sell his vote. They have now dropped the matter having found out more than they wanted. A Mr. [W. W.] Woolley [of Cincinnati], who with [N.Y. newspaper editor and politician] Thurlow Weed & others have doubtless been employed in underhand transactions with members of Congress, is now confined in the Capitol for refusing to answer certain questions put to him by Butler. [Woolley subsequently sued Butler for false imprisonment.]

Schofield is Secy of War, nominated by the Presdt & confirmed by the Senate. Stanton has relinquished the War office, which ends all this impeachment business.

Grant & [Schuyler] Colfax were nominated by the radical [Republican] convention at Chicago early in May. The nomination it is agreed excites no enthusiasm.

Minnie's birth-day (June 4) was celebrated by a little party, & a nice little supper. Her mother fatigued herself too much in getting it up.

We went the same evening to Mrs. Mallets & ate a good supper of chicken salad, claret, & berries.

The furnace will progress very slowly I see, as it will be difficult to get hands together until the corn crop is laid by & the wheat crop gathered, but I will not be impatient.

Our company affairs are very much embarrassed, & it gives me great trouble to answer the many calls made for payment of debts.

Willie writes to his mother (& spells it very badly) that he goes to Pascagoula [Miss.] on the 13th of June with his Aunt Ria, this is 10 days before his school ends in N.O.

There is some talk of my taking the position of President of the Sewanee University (Episcopal) in Tenn. It has not been offered to me. Gen. Kirby Smith & Com. [Matthew Fontaine] Maury have declined it.

Mamma went over to Demopolis on the cars with seven young men of Eutaw on their way to the Dry Tortugas having been sentenced by a Mil. Commission sitting at Selma to 5 years imprisonment at hard labor, reduced to two years by Gen. Meade [commander of the Third Military District]. The offence with which they were charged was compelling an obnoxious citizen to leave Eutaw, under threats of punishment (tarring & feathering). What they were guilty of was thrashing this man who was caught stealing wood, and being a companion & teacher of bad negros they ordered him to leave the place, under threats &c. His name was [Joseph Benjamin Fitzpatrick] Hill, a notoriously bad fellow. Such is the government under which we are now living.

Gen Meade has released these young men upon coming here to Selma & learning from Mr. Lyon & Gen Hardee the real state of facts, tho' he warns them & others against a repetition of such offences.

June 14 [1868]   Ther 85° from 11 A. M. to 5 P. M. We have had not a drop of rain since the 29th of May, & then only a brief fall. Our garden is parched & there is danger of total loss of the corn crop.

We had 85 in Sunday School to-day. Mr. Bird held service here on Wednesday Evening to a good congregation.

Went to Selma & returned yesterday. Mr. [Henry] Tutwiler [principal of the Greene Springs School near Greensboro] has been apptd President of the University at Tuscaloosa.

The bill for the admission of all the States has passed both houses, & will pass over the veto of the President. So we are to have a government of negros, at the South, but rejected at the North.

June 18, [1868]   Ther at 7½ A. M. 72°. No rain & the mercury stands at from 82° to 85° in the heat of the day. All is parched up. Rode yesterday to where a gang of men are getting out Sand Rock for the furnace. In the afternoon I worked with "Dick" getting up a bath place in the creek for the children. The heat & work exhausted me very much. After six o'clock I took a pleasant bath in the creek for the first time this year. On Tuesday Father O'Leary was here, & held mass in our sitting room, 8 Catholic men women & children present. I see nothing in the worship calculated to "proselyte," yet the church is said to be growing rapidly in this country.

June 20 [1868]   Yesterday was by much the warmest day we have had. The Ther ran to 88° & stood at 85° at 6 P. M. It rained all around us but not a drop fell here. The ground is literally parched. I rode over to the Stone quarry yesterday, a very warm ride.

[June] 28 Sunday [1868]   Ther 65° at 7 A. M. The weather continues hot & dry, not a drop of rain since four weeks ago last Thursday, & then only a smart shower. Everything is burned & the garden a bed of dust. Dick came here a week ago & left on Wednesday last. I rec'd a letter from Bishop [William M.] Green [of Miss.] inviting me to come to Sewanee to see them in reference to a position at the University. I shall leave to-morrow and be absent about a week. In putting up a temporary bath house on the creek, & cutting out the weeds & undergrowth I have had my skin badly poisoned & am much annoyed by it. I am pondering the stoppage of work at the furnace—not having the means to meet the heavy expenses.

Friday July 10 [1868]   Weather cloudy. It has rained at last, & for three days we have had showers. On Monday I returned from my visit to "University Place" Tenn. pleased with my visit. I shall accept the position offered, but not to take effect until next March. I went and came by Blue Mtn. [now Anniston in Calhoun County, Ala.] & Rome [Ga.], stopping a day on my return at the latter place. The stage ride from Cross Plains to Rome 39 miles was excessively hot dusty & disagreeable—8 miles.

I have quietly passed into my 51st year, having completed 50 July 1st, while at Sewanee.

I have 20 years more to live. I hope they will be less disturbed ones than my last 30, & more profitable to me.

July 26 Sunday [1868]   It is a wretched rainy day. No one can stir abroad, & the house is dull & gloomy. Capt [Charles C.] Sims [Simms] formerly of the U. S. and C. S. Navy passed from Monday until Friday with [us]. He is an incessant talker & therefore "very good company" as they call it.

On Saturday the 18th the Thermometer touched 90° the highest I have seen it in three Summers here. That week was a very hot one the mercury ranging up to 78° at night.

There have been continued rains & some heavy ones for the past 10 days.

The nomination of Horatio Seymour of N. Y. & Frank Blair of Mo. [Democratic nominees for president and vice president] seem to give general satisfaction to the country. It seems to me however that the unscrupulous politicians now in power will find a way to attain their ends & defeat the will of the people.

The Ala. Legislature now in Session contains 26 to 30 [27] negros, & a negro chaplain prays every morning!

Aug 4, [1868]   Ther 5 P.M. 73°. Incessant rains for two weeks past have deluged the country & seriously endangered the cotton & the corn crops. I was out to-day on the train with Willie & "Dick" and I have seldom seen such a torrent of rain.

On Thursday last there was a great barbecue ratification meeting for Seymour & Blair. The speakers were Judge [Samuel F.] Rice of Monty, [former] Gov. [A. B.] Moore & Gen. J. T. Morgan [future U.S. senator from Selma]. All passed off well.

Aug 9, [1868] Sunday.   Thermometer at 5 P.M. 81°. Read the Sunday School service in place of Mamma, who is still not strong enough to go there. There were about 60 at School. It is the one point of interest on Sundays to the whole neighborhood. I am still at work trying to get the furnace in blast, & hope to succeed in time. The difficulty lies chiefly in getting charcoal.

I am going again to University Place to-morrow. The day is very fine & warm, no rain for three days now save a little sprinkling.

Aug 21, Saturday [1868]   I returned from University Place on Monday. Stayed there from Wednesday to Saturday, commenced on Thursday morning. Met there Col [L. N.] Whittle of Macon, Dr. [M. A.] Curtis of N. C., Dr. [H. M.] Anderson of Rome Ga., Rev. Mr. [John M.] Bannister [of Ala.], Rev. Mr. [George H.] Hunt [of Tenn.], Maj. [A. M.] Rutledge [of Sewanee], & Col [T. E. B.] Pegues of Miss., all these trustees, & Bishops [C. T.] Quintard [of Tenn.], [Alexander] Gregg [of S.C.], & [William M.] Green [of Miss.]. On my way back traveled with Mr. Breed the lessee of this road from Cape Cod, a rather pleasant man.

Went to the Furnace yesterday with Willie on the tram, our horse behaved badly, & I had a fall on the cinders. Willie shot 7 doves, 3 at one shot & came back greatly delighted.

Thermom. this morning at 7 A. M. 68. Mamma is gradually recovering her strength but still complains a good deal.

Aug 31, [1868]   Thermometer at 7½ A.M. 71. The weather is somewhat warm but very pleasant. Rev. Mr. Cotton of the Meth. Church preached last evening in our School house on the 4th commandment, and spent the night with us.

We had a little dinner for the Mallets on Friday, & Saturday Evey ate a turkey at their home. On Friday Mr. Thomas, Mr. Mikels & Mr. Hunt, nephew of Mr. T., came to look at our Works. We have had some hopes that Mr. T. would buy a part at least of our works. Unless we can sell by Jany 1, I see no end to our troubles. The earlier mortgagee will sell them I fear. Mamma is so well recovered that she resumed her Sunday School yesterday to the great delight of the children & the grown people as well. Col. Mallet leaves for Virginia to-day. It makes me very sad to see him go away. Two years ago we hoped to pass many of our years together here.

Sept 23, [1868]   I returned from my third visit to University Place on Tuesday (21st). On Friday the 18th the University was inaugurated in its Junior Department by appropriate religious Services, Bishop Green of Miss. & Bishop Quintard with 3 clergymen assisting. On Monday last recitations began, the number of the boys present being <u>nine</u>, more arriving.

There is little news in the papers. The great earthquake on the West Coast of So. America destroyed it is said 32,000 souls, & ruined many cities. There are few particulars as yet. The political feeling runs very high. The elections in Pa. take place next week, & will tell the probable result to be expected in Novr. A collision between whites & blacks took place at Camilla in Ga. ten days ago in which ten blacks are said to have been killed & 40 wounded, 6 or 8 whites wounded. The negros were headed by two white radical (northern) candidates. They escaped early. [A Republican rally at Camilla turned violent when a drunk fired his pistol. In the ensuing panic seven blacks were killed, and others in the crowd were wounded.]

Our rolling mill is going cheerily, making cotton ties, in the hands of lessees, Capt Alvis & a firm in Montevallo. We have decided not to send Willie to N. O. this winter, but to prepare him here to enter at University Place.

Oct 11 (Sunday) [1868]   Ther 61°. We have had heavy rains in the early part of this month. On Thursday of last week (Oct. 1) I went down to Selma to see a large "barbecue" of the "democrats," white & black. The gathering was quite large, say 8 or 10 thousand people. There were speeches, after a procession, in a grove in the city, by Gen. [James Holt] Clanton, [former] Gov [Thomas H.] Watts, & Col. [Joseph W.] Taylor of Eutaw, the last an eloquent speaker, the others good "campaign" speakers. I met a good many people whom I knew—Mr. Lyon, Gen. Clanton, [former] Gov. [John A.] Winston & I went to Gen. Hardee's house for a little lunch. There was a torch light procession after dark which I did not stay to see. The term "barbecue" is derived from the preparation of the meats for dinner. Whole sheep are laid over long trenches supported on cross sticks, with fires underneath. The tables were rough pine planks, under the shade of the trees. The dinner consisted of bread & roast meat, & some pickles, & a little confectionery at the ladies tables, not a very sumptuous "spread" certainly. Ma & Milly arrived here on Wednesday last, both looking very well. I have concluded not to send Willie back to N. Orleans, but to prepare him to enter Sewanee next February. I am still trying to get charcoal to put the Furnace in blast, & shall I suppose eventually succeed.

Oct 22d, [1868]   Ther 46. The weather is clear and beautiful. Tuesday Judge Walker made a speech to the men of the neighborhood on political topics, urging them especially to register, so that they can vote at the next election or at any time hereafter. I am laid up with a little sore on my leg, which is quite painful.

The disturbances continue at various points thro'out the country. Last week the Sheriff & Judge of Probate of Franklin La. were assassinated. This will produce great excitement at the north, & will help Grant.

The result of the October elections in the three great States of Pa. Ohio & Indiana rather depresses us, as all have gone for the radicals, despite the confident predictions of the democrats. Yet the majorities are not such that they may not be changed in November.

Our furnace work gets along slowly for want of wood choppers. Labor can be had for almost every purpose except to cut cord wood.

I am hearing Jessie & Willie every day some in a little lesson of French

& Latin; & Willie in arthmetic. Mamma is suffering from a severe cold, a prevalent disease just now.

Nov 26, [1868]   The weather has been cold earlier than usual, the thermometer has been as low as 28°. It is raining heavily to-day beginning last night.

I returned from Selma on Monday, having gone there on my way to attend court at Montgomery. News came [that] the Judge Busteed was not there.

The exit of Queen Isabella & the revolution in Spain excite a good deal of attention. The new form of government is not yet agreed on.

An eruption of Vesuvius has again taken place & heavy earthquakes in California & elsewhere are chronicled. At San Francisco many buildings were ruined & some lives lost.

The papers are filled with surmises as to Grants probable course. The radicals begin to repent of his election.

I met Mr. Lyon & Mr. Prout in Selma & we talked over the difficulties which beset our works here without coming to any conclusion. It is to be feared that our property will be sold & sacrificed by the first mortgagee (Mr. Walton). Sunday Evey we went to see Gen. [Edmund] Pettus [prominent Selma Democrat and later U.S. senator]. This little ancedote speaks highly of his notions as a lawyer. I give it in his words: "Mr. Lyon you will be surprised to hear that I had B. F. Saffold [Republican justice on the Alabama Supreme Court] for a client. He came into my office a few days ago, & said, 'Gen. you are surprised to see me in your office.' I assented. 'I come to you for professional assistance, & claim it under your advertisement. You offer your services to all as a lawyer, & I come as a client.' Putting it on such grounds, I told him I would undertake his case. He then stated his case, & I promised to look into it, as his professional adviser. On examination I found he was right; and I went to Brooks (Judg[e] Wm. H. [William M.] Brooks) who was on the other side, and showed him that Saffold was in the right, & in <u>half an hours interview Brooks & I settled the matter, without difficulty!</u>["] This is a high view of the calling of a lawyer.

The papers this morning chronicle the shooting of St. Reeves Pollard, brother of the historian (so-called) of the War [Edward A. Pollard]. He was shot by the brother of a lady whose name he had introduced unfavorably into his paper.

Decr 1, [1868]   Ther 27° at 7½ A.M., bright & sunshiny. My man of Charcoal came to the Furnace on Saturday, <u>but</u> no hands! I fear he will do me little good. It is very tedious work & <u>I</u> see no end to it.

Decr 8 [1868]   Went to Selma on Thursday last. Supped & stayed at Gen. Hardee's, & played whist with Col. [N. H. R.] Dawson,

Major Lewis, & Mr. [Richard M.] Nelson (who was at West Point in '59 to '61.) It rained Thursday night. Thermometer this morning 26° at 7¼ P.M. [A.M.]

Richie was taken with something like spasms last evening, & has this morning a good deal of fever. He seems to have a heavy cold.

There is nothing new in politics. Parties seem to have quieted down. The impression prevails that there will be a strong hand at the helm, after Mch 4th. We will see.

Gen. [Howell] Cobb [of Ga.] died suddenly on the Steps of the 5th Avenue hotel about the 20th of Nov. [October 9].

Cotton continues to bring 22 to 23 cts in Mobile & N.O. Gold stands at about 135 to 136.

The furnace prospects are improving a little but it will be spring time before we shall go into blast. Meantime I shall have a sorry time of it in meeting my expenditures, & if at last the furnace should fail we shall be beggars. Enough to make a man serious.

Decr 11, [1868]   Ther at 8 A. M. 18, bright & windy from north. Richie is still quite sick, the disease is pronounced by the doctor to be pleurisy.

Mr. Johnson's message is in the papers. It is denunciatory of the past legislation of Congress. In the Senate they refused to hear it, after the first few paragraphs. In the house it was laid on the table instead of referred as is usual.

Dr. McPherson told us yesterday of the death of old Dr. Broughton. A neighbor, Mr. Dan Prentiss died a few days ago.

Decr 21, [1868]   Ther 34° at 7½ A. M. Weather moist but sunshiny at sunrise. Our Rolling mill stands idle for want of coal. The charcoal at the furnace comes in slowly but still there is some progress made constantly, & I judge we will be able to go into blast by 1st of March. We will see.

Ritchie is recovering from his attack of pleurisy but looks very thin and is very cross, obstinate & wil[l]ful. He tries his mother's temper severely. The mutual devotion between him & Jessie is something remarkable. It had its counterpart many many years ago according to my mothers report, between my sister Eliza & myself, when our ages were about the same relatively as that of these two.

Christmas at our Sunday School is to be quite an event, & occupies the minds of pupils & teachers. Mamma (Genl Supdt!) is of course the center of hopes & of work. [Amelia's older sister] Sarah is expected here on Wednesday from Eutaw.

Decr 27 Sunday [1868]   Thursday the 24th was the coldest day of the season thus far, the thermometer standing at 13 at 9 A. M. Christmas day was clear & cold, a fine day. Unfortunately Mamma's boxes did not come, so that she had to put off her Sunday School celebration greatly to the chagrin of the pupils.

Sarah & [her daughter] Clara came on Thursday, with pretty presents for all the children, & even I got a pair of slippers. Then Jessie gives me ten dollars to buy a flute, & good Anne [the children's nurse] arranged secretly with Col. White while he stopped here over night to send me a 5 gal demijohn of good whiskey. The children were all very happy. We passed Christmas Eve at home, with an egg nogg, & a game of Euchre, the McMains being here. Christmas Evey the children had a dinner at the McMains & a little supper. We all went except <u>Ma</u> & Matt.

Decr 31, [1868]   Ther. 55° at 10 A. M. Another year gone. It is rainy & disagreeable. I have a sore throat for the first time in over two years, & stay in-doors to-day. Mamma's Sunday School celebration for Christmas took place on Tuesday, & had great success. There are about 70 children.

There is nothing startling in politics. The <u>silence</u> of Gen. Grant, the Presdt elect, seems to puzzle his friends, his political friends, somewhat. Still there is no reasonable doubt, that he will carry out what seems to be the pet project of the radicals, viz: negro suffrage. A negro congressman from La (Leonard) seems to give the radicals in Congress some trouble. They don't want him but cant find a decent pretext to dispose of him.

The Presdt published a <u>general amnesty</u> on Christmas day. This disposes no doubt of the prosecution of Mr. Davis.

Jany 4 [18]69   During the holidays we had a succession of rains, hindering our work at the Furnace very much. I have never before seen so much wet weather here in winter.

Jany 9, [1869]   Another day of rain. Ther. 56°.

We are so isolated down South that the movements at Washington seem to have little to do with us. There is still a good deal of speculation as to what Gen Grant will do.

The negros on the Ogechee [River] have driven off the white people & taken possession of the plantations. The military force has been directed to interfere. They carried away women & children, beat the whites, raided & burned houses, according to published reports. It is a little remarkable tho' & speaks well for the negro, that thus far no murders are reported.

The children went over to Capt. McMain's & danced until 11 o'clock. I was a good deal troubled with my throat.

[January] 15 [1869]   It rained on Monday. Tuesday & Wednesday were fair days. Yesterday it began to rain at 1 P. M. & rained heavily all night, & it is still raining.

[January] 16 [1869]   Fair. Ther 30 at 8 A. M.

[January] 18 [1869]   Fair. Ther 29 at 8 A. M., slight rain yesterday afternoon.

[January] 19 [1869]   Ther 25 at 8 A. M, sunshine. The rolling mill is going this morning, cheerful music. My charcoal at the furnace is coming in slowly.

Jany 20, [1869]   Ther 38° at ¼ 8 A. M. Weather cloudy. Rode yesterday nearly all day, besides walking a good deal to ascertain some of our boundary lines.

One of our mules died on Monday night, of colic it is supposed produced by botts [larvae of a species of gadfly attach to the stomach of horses or mules]. I rode thro the two coalings going on without finding much to my satisfaction. It seems impossible to get a steady set of woodchoppers. Our old acquaintance Mr. W. P. Browne, died suddenly a week ago in Talladega. Poor troubled spirit, he has found rest at last.

Jan 23, [1869]   Ther 28° at 8 A. M. clear sunshiny. Yesterday at 3 P. M. Ther at 58°. Two northern people Mr. English & Prof. Herring came here day before yesterday; & yesterday two more, Ostrander & Finney. They came from northern N. York.

[January] 24, [1869]   Ther 45° at 9 A. M. cloudy. Our Yankee visitors returned at 10 A M and left for Montevallo. They seemed to be pleased with the country. Rained at 6 P. M. with high wind.

[January] 26 [1869]   Ther 29 at 8 A. M. Our furnace work looked more hopeful yesterday. There seems to be a prospect of getting a sufficiency of wood cutters to keep our charcoal up to some extent when we go into blast. We must be able to see 800 to 900 bushels coming in per day else our blast will be a very short one.

Jan 27 [1869]   Ther 40, 8 A.M. Cloudy no wind.

[January] 29 [1869]   " 52 " Hail storm at 3 P.M.

[January] 30 [1869]   " 39 " at 7¼ A.M. Cloudy. Sarah Clara & Milly [Crawford] go away this morning, back to their present home at Eutaw. We rode out to the Furnace on the tram yesterday, Clara never having seen it. Mrs. McM[ain] got caught in the rain & hail & got wringing wet. There is nothing new in the political world. Grant seems to rise in public estimation thro his reticence.

Feby 1 [1869]   Ther 28 at 7½ A.M. Cloudy & heavy frost. Went to Montevallo on the train to see Judge Parker & other Northern men who are here to make purchases of coal and iron lands. Walked back in the rain near 5 miles. Mr. Lyon arrived by the evey train. It was raining heavily.

[February] 2 [1869]   Rained heavily since 5 P.M yesterday, & lightly from 12 M. before that. Poor prospects for charcoal. Had a letter from Bishop Quintard yesterday urging me to be at Sewanee on the 10th. I will try to do so.

[February] 3d [1869]   Cloudy & inclined to rain. Went to Selma & returned in the evening.

[February] 5 [1869]   Ther 24° at 7½ A.M. Clear & bright with heavy frost. Mr. Lyon is much in the humor of finishing our nail works, & making nails. I should be glad to have it done, but doubt whether we can sell nails enough to warrant the outlay. The Furnace is getting on to the point of preparing for blast! I fear old Mr. Kline is too slow now that it becomes necessary to bestir ourselves to make the final preparations.

XIII

"I am now daily teaching"

Feby 28 [1869]   Ther 20°. Clear & wind North W. I went to Sewanee on the 7th, & was present at the opening of the school on the 10th. I left there on the 20th & got home last Sunday at noon.

I found but little progress on the Furnace. Still the getting of charcoal goes on which is the main point. On Friday the thimble was being lowered into its place, when the rope slipped out from a fastening & the thimble fell thro' to the bottom of the furnace, doing however little damage, which was repd yesterday. Work begins on the engine to-morrow, & probably also on the hearth.

At Washington Grant continues to be the great problem for radical Study. The radical Senators are generally unwilling to repeal the "Tenure-of-office" act which Grant wants done.

Willie and I are progressing in Latin Algebra & French. He is very apt at algebra & does very well in Latin & French, but is not as quick as Jessie in French, <but doesn't lack perseverance.>

The girls are growing up wonderfully, and Jessie will soon be a young woman. On their accounts I desire to transfer myself to Sewanee where there would be less objectionable society for them.

Mch 2 [1869]   The Ther yesterday was 21 to 22, to day 26 to 27. I leave to morrow morning for Sewanee to be absent 10 days. I hope to find the hearth in the Furnace, & a good deal done at the machinery by the time I return, tho I have little hope of starting the furnace before the middle of April, & I very much fear my means will give out before that time. I rode out on the tram yesterday, stayed out all day & walked back by 6 P.M., heard Willie's lessons until after 8 P.M. & then wrote 4 business letters.

[March] 19 [1869]   Returned from Sewanee last Sunday. I found the weather quite cold there for the first three days but after that quite mild & pleasant. The boys were getting on very well. There were 38 when I left & more expected.

I found the furnace getting on very well tho' not as far advanced as I expected. The hearth is not quite half in, and it will take all of next week I expect to complete that. I fear it will be after the first of April before we are ready to put the furnace in blast. Gen Grants new cabinet are Hamilton Fish of N.Y. Secy of State, Gov Boutwell of Mass, Secy of Treas (vice A. T. Stewart of N.Y. who had to resign, on acct of an old law which forbade the Secy of Treas from doing business while holding the office), Adolphe Bore of Phila Secy of Navy, Mr. [E. R.] Hoar of Mass, Atty Genl, Gov [Jacob B.] Cox of Ohio, Secy of Interior, Mr. [John A.] Creswell of Md. P.M. Genl, Gen [John A.] Rawlins (Grant's chief of Staff) Secy of War. These seem to give satisfaction, altho' little known to fame.

Gen. Breckinridge has just returned from abroad to Ky. Mr. Davis' persecution has been abandoned, & his sureties released. Gen. Longstreet is nominated as Surveyor of Customs at N.O., as being the most thoroughly reconstructed "rebel" in the South, a bad elevation for a distinguished soldier of the South.

Apl 10, [1869]   The weather is pleasant & rather warm. Frost has somewhat reduced the prospect for peaches, but still the crop will be pretty good. We put fire into our furnace the day before yesterday & expect to put the blast on on Monday. It has been a most tedious work, but I hope we shall yet be successful.

Apl 20, [1869]   Disappointment attends all my efforts with the Furnace. We put the blast on at 10 A.M. on Monday the 12th & thus far have made nothing but "Rolling Mill" iron. To-day I quietly displaced Mr. Kline, poor old man, & put in a young active man (Mr. Babbington) as founder. I hope he will do better. He takes hold as tho' he meant business. I have also discharged my Engineer on acct of insobriety, and put in a sober man who had run the same Engine. The machinery gives us trouble, & we have to stop frequently on account of it.

Our spring is a cold one & most of our fruit is destroyed by the frosts. I have just rec'd a letter from Sewanee urging me to come there. I hope to go in two weeks if all goes on well here. Johnny [John Marshall Gayle, one of Amelia's half brothers] came over from Greensboro on a visit to his mother & left to-day.

Nov 5 [1869]   At University Place Tenn. The Furnace operations detailed above proved a serious loss to me. We have to go out of blast the day after the above entry, & take everything out of the furnace, the hearth having proved entirely worthless.

I continued on however, got a new hearth at very heavy expense, & went into blast again about the 20th of June. In less than 30 days we had run out all our ore, & our charcoal was nearly out. I put the furnace out of blast & turned all the stock & material on hand over to Capt. Alvis, who has just again gone into blast. My losses in running the furnace are about two thousand dollars: if Capt Alvis cannot pay me for the stock turned over to him, my losses will be fully four thousand dollars. In fact all I had. The iron property is now offered for sale on the 13th of Decr., & if the money loaned to the Company is also lost, as I fear it will be, we shall be literally penniless. To increase the trouble my brother Solomon declines to pay me the bal. due me by him which is about $1500.

I came here to take permanent charge on the 1st of July. The number of pupils has increased to 100 matriculations tho there are only 89 present. Our present term closes on the 20th of this month, & I shall then go on to Brierfield to be present at the funeral obsequies of the past four years. I trust when that is over I shall settle down quietly to work here, perhaps for the remainder of my life. I must work now just to support my family, having by bad investments lost the little property I had.

May 3d 1870   Our school is doing well, has 110 pupils, & is going on very well. The School broke up for its winter vacation on the 20th of Nov & re-assembled for the Spring Term on the 24th of Feby. I found everything in great disorder on the 15th of Feby when I came up here. The Halls had not been repaired nor cleaned up, and nothing was in order for the reception of the boys. Besides the snow was lying on the ground & alternately melting & freezing made the roads very wet. Altogether the times were most disheartening. But I have lived thro' them & will forget them. There has been a good deal of light sickness among the boys and three very serious cases—Typhoid fever, Typhoid pneumonia and Erysipelas [a skin disease], all well again. Of the boys who were here at the opening of the School three have gone away, 2 called away by illness of their fathers, & 1 gone on acct. of threatened consumption. I am much occupied in trying to get up a house for my own family. The University has very little money, & it will not do to go in debt much. All I can hope to do at present is to put up a small inexpensive house.

May 5, morning [1870].   The weather for a week past has been most charming, & the woods about us are springing into leaf. Mamma writes that she longs for the home here which is to be ours for life. I shall be glad when we are all settled down together here, and have no further prospect of change for years to come, I hope for all our lives. Mamma says if this life suits me she will be contented here, altho' I know she longs for a far different life, a life less monotonous. Well, Well, it will not be for very long now. But the life is a peaceful one, a fit period to prepare for the great change which must soon come.

May 21, [1870]   The weather has been very hot for the past 4 or 5 days. Vegetation has fully developed, and the woods are again full of undergrowth and the little torments red-bugs. Yesterday, two more boys arrived from Fla. At least 10 have come in this month. I propose now to erect little frame cabins for them. The frames of our Schoolhouse, & my dormitory came also yesterday.

Jany 17 [18]71   About the 27th of June 1870 we reached Sewanee, bag & baggage, not to leave it permanently I hope for the rest of my natural life. Amelia was much fatigued by the labor of setting up the household gear when it arrived, & a good deal broken down by it. In consequence she became very ill with inflammation of the intestines, so that her life was in danger. Happily the disease took a favorable turn, & she recovered as rapidly as the attack had been sudden.

Our School prospered quite beyond expectation during the past year. Our receipts for tuition from 187 boys were [$]16,008. Our expenses for tuition & incidentals were less than $13,500.

The close of the year 1870 was marked by very cold weather, the mercury standing at $-5°$ on Friday night & Saturday morning 23d & 24th Dec.

I am now daily teaching in the Winter School which embraces the Vacation. I should prefer to have all my time to devote to organization, but cannot afford to let the little emolument ($225) pass by. It will take all I can earn to support my family.

The great events of the last half of the year just closed are the great War of France & Prussia in which Louis Napoleon has lost his empire. Nothing could be more astounding than the total & utter defeat of the French forces. At Sedan over 85,000 men were surrendered, & at Metz over 100,000. In about 60 days after the first shock of arms the French armies of nearly 300,000 men were utterly annihilated. (4¼ P.M—the bell rings for Chapel.)

[January] 22d, [1871]   Yesterday we had our first funeral on the Mountain, Irene Polk. The weather was beautiful & to-day balmy. Bishop Green preached an appropriate Sermon for us to-day. His venerable looks added to the effect of the Solemn theme. The news from France does not change the aspect of affairs. Bombaski is said to have been defeated, while Faidhebs is progressing in the North. The King of Prussia was formally proclaimed Emperor of Germany. (Eddie's [one of Amelia's half brothers] bill to Bayne $278.64)

[January] 28, [1871]   Rainy & heavy mist. The news from Paris seems to indicate an early surrender, & we need not be suprised to hear of it any day now. The winter since Jan 1st has been quite mild, the Thermometer not going below 20°.

May 1, [1871]   Paris fell in due time, and was partially occupied by the Prussians. One of the terms of peace was the payment of 5000,000,000 francs. [Louis Adolphe] Thiers was placed at the head of the French government. The Red Republicans in Paris have since repudiated the authority of the Thiers' Govt, called now the govt of Versailles, on points connected with the administration of Paris, and fighting has been going on for the last six weeks or more between Paris & the Versailles troops. Poor Paris must be utterly ruined.

Our School opened on the 16th of March, & we have now 173 boys present. I hope we shall get on thro' the Term smoothly, but we are by no means without financial troubles.

The Spring elections in several of the States North indicate decay in the strength of the Republican party. It is a sign perhaps of a better government in the future.

Last week we moved into our new home, & are now domiciled there. It promises to be quite comfortable.

Aug 20, [1871]   We are now comfortably settled in our new home, and have had plenty of room to entertain our friends during the summer. We have not been without guests since the 1st of July.

Bishop Wilmer of Ala, Rev. Mr. [A. Toomer] Porter [of S.C.] & Gen. [J. B.] Kershaw [of S.C.] were our guests of the Board of Trustees; Col Robertson of New Iberia La. & his wife, Mr. Woods of Nashville, Com. [Isaac N.] Brown (of the Ram "Arkansas" of Conf. memory) & others have been with us. Mary [Gayle Aiken] with her two children is here since about the middle of July. Amelia is a good deal troubled with her housekeeping, as we have 18 boys here, & the servants are very unsteady & not handy. She is just now trying two young Swiss. Ma is still on a visit to her nephew Jas. Wemyss at Gallatin Tenn. Willie has turned student since nearly a year ago, and is perhaps the first scholar here. The medal for Scholarship from Alabama was awarded to him. It is a very beautiful gold medal. His mother & sisters are very proud of it & him, to say nothing of my feelings on the subject. Since the middle of July the weather has been quite warm, tho' the nights continue cool. A very respectable number of visitors continue to crowd the several houses, & make us pray for the building of a hotel to relieve us from this influx.

I have been severely poisoned & confined for two weeks to the house by it. Last night we went to hear a Miss Patterson read in the Grammar School (Gray Hall). She is a girl of 18 or 19 & read very well.

I should have recorded the marriage of our good friend Gen. Shoup [professor of mathematics] to Miss Hessie Elliott, which happened about the middle of June in St. Augustine's Chapel [at Sewanee] at 6 o'clock in the evening.

Novr 14, [1871] The first snow of the year fell last night. To-day has been very cold & blustering, & to night as I write there is a high wind, & the mercury must be a good deal below freezing. Fires all over the house hardly keep us warm. Up to this the weather has been so very mild that this sudden access of cold takes us by surprise.

I took Jessie & Mamie to [Columbia Female Institute] their first boarding school at Columbia Tenn. on Saturday, the 16th of Sept. The poor girls were very home-sick when I left them on Monday night to return home.

We are all looking forward eagerly to the close of the School on the 20th of December. Willie is going to Texas to spend his vacation in hunting with his friend Duncan Gordon who lives not far from Matagorda [Tex.].

Decr 28, [1871] Ther. last night at 10 P.M. 19°, now 10 A.M. 35°. The Sunday Schools of the valleys about us (coves) were assembled here yesterday about a Xmas tree. It was the first time of such a celebration here, & will do good by making these people know us better.

[December] 31 [1871] Sunday Ther at 9 A.M. 62, cloudy but pleasant. Went to morning services at 9 A.M. Had letters from Jessie & Mamie last night. The letters of the latter surprise us all. She is developing so rapidly. Jessie has always been advanced, & therefore her excellent letters do not surprise us.

Jany 2, 1872 Ther 44° at 9 A.M. Our good gentlemen & some of the boys observed the time honored custom of calls on New-Year's Day. Where we had 4 houses open 2 years ago we have now 18 houses to call at. We have two bride[s] on the Mtn. Mrs. Phelan [wife of Judge John D. Phelan of Ala.] & Mrs. [W. H.] Tomlinson [wife of the local postmaster], the latter was handsomely dressed & looked very beautiful. The weather has cleared off, it was foggy yesterday, & is very fine. We played a game of whist for the first time on the Mtn in our home, last night. Mr. & Mrs. Caldwell & Mr. Gibson.

[January] 6, [1872] Ther 41 at 8½ A.M. We dined at the Caldwell's yesterday. An excellent dinner cooked by Mrs. C. & all placed on the table at once, soup & all, for want of servants. We had soup, venison steaks, roast duck, & dessert. The weather is very fine.

[January] 21, [1872] Sunday, Ther 28°, Minnie [their twelve-year-old daughter] & I leave for N.O. to-morrow morning, I to be absent 3 weeks, she to come home with Willie, perhaps. Mamma has been quite ill with tooth-ache & a swelled face, & has suffered a good deal. The winter has thus far been singularly pleasant. This morning there is a sprinkling of snow, but the sun is now shining out occasionally thro' the heavy mist clouds, & will soon melt the snow.

Mch 3d & 4th, [1872]   Snow fell on Friday night, the 1st of March to the depth of 9 inches average, & there is now some lying after 3 days. Monday 4th, the Mercury stood at 37° at 8 A.M.

I went to N. Orleans as above & returned Saturday two weeks ago, stopping a[t] Mobile 5 days on my way back. I succeeded only very partially in my object of getting subscriptions to our University bonds. I went up to Mt Vernon to see Matt who is almost helpless, & must be nursed like a little child. He cannot even carry his food to his mouth. I looked at the Arsenal, the place to which I brought your mother as a bride, with mournful interest. It is very little changed. Most of the things I placed there are still there. The water works which I put up in 1855, are still in good order, & the sun dial still marks the hours. Many of my men are still living near there & received me very cordially. Amelia takes chloroform to-day to have her teeth taken out for a new sett, & we are all a little uneasy about it, & dread it. [Family anxiety about oral surgery resulted from the memory that Amelia's mother, Sarah H. Gayle, had died in 1835 with lockjaw following oral surgery.]

Oct 18 Friday [1872]   Bishop Quintard arrived yesterday & according to promise made to the boys last Summer I have given them a holiday to-day. The weather is very beautiful, & they enjoy it to the full, playing foot ball, going chestnut hunting & on excursion to Tracy City & into the valley. Willie has gone down into the valley hunting, with several of the boys.

Bayne & his family have been here for six weeks, & seem to enjoy the beautiful weather & the country very much. They leave for N. Orleans on Monday. I heartily wish they could settle down here. Our house holds, besides our own family of 9, Ma, Helen, baby & nurse, Bayne, Maria, [four of their children] Mamie, T. L., Minna & Edith. Mother has been quite indisposed this week, with cold settling in her face, & headache. She is pretty well again to-day.

Our School life goes on regularly & pleasantly enough, with about 200 pupils. We have our financial troubles, and rub along with difficulty. Bishop Quintard goes out now on a tour of collection, hoping to get a large endowment for the University.

Novr 16, [1872]   The first snow is falling fast. Mercury down to 24° last night and the night before down to 20°.

The election of Grant [as president] for another four years is decided, Greeley receiving but about 60 electoral votes. This result is ascribed a good deal to the corrupt influence of money.

As I write the snow ceases & the sun looks out over it; but I suppose, as the clouds look heavy it will snow again, the mercury being now at 23°.

XIV

"*I was not well pleased with the action of the Board of Trustees*"

Feby 4, [1873] The death of Mr. Greeley which occurred some time in Decr last is the chief event of the past year, unless it were the death of the Emperor Napoleon which occurred at Chiselhurst soon after Mr. Greeleys death. The winter thus far has been unusually severe here; and the coldest that has been known in the North West for many years. Many deaths have been occasioned there by the cold & the driving snow, it is said over 700 in the country west of Chicago. People were overtaken close to their homes, blinded by the driving snow, & frozen almost in sight of their houses.

Mamma left for N. Orleans on the 30th ult & will stay away quite 5 weeks. We are all very lonely without her. Bishop Quintard is succeeding pretty well in his mission, & will materially assist us in maintaining the financial credit of the University. Our Mr. [William P.] DuBose [Sewanee chaplain] takes his sick wife off to-morrow to a more genial clime. God grant it may restore her to her little children.

The weather is now quite warm, but the skies cloudy. Mercury at 12 M. 61°.

Mch 26, [1873] Ther 22° at 7¼ A.M. with a little snow on the ground. We had beautiful weather for the opening of the School, Mch 13, & it has been mild since then; but it changed last evening & fell from 56° yesterday at noon, a change of 34° in about 12 or 15 hours.

Mamma returned from N.O. the day before the School opened, & has had a very pleasant visit, especially to her old friends at Mobile, where she had not been since July 1856, when Jessie was a baby, & we started thence for Augusta Maine.

The School opens under good auspices & has about 165 present. I think we shall have 250 by the 1st of August.

Apl 6, [1873]   The weather has been delightful for the past 5 or 6 days, the mercury yesterday & day before up to 82° in the Shade! Rev. Telfair Hodgson [rector of Trinity Church in Hoboken, N.J.] & his wife have been here during the past week. He will probably be one of our Professors next Fall. [Hodgson joined the Sewanee faculty and purchased the Gorgas's home.] A terrible accident happened a week ago to the Steamer Atlantic from Liverpool, which ran on a rocky island (Prospect) & drowned 550 of her passengers, chiefly immigrants, not a woman nor child saved. The news from poor Dick makes us fear that he cannot live long. [Richard H. Gayle died on April 9, 1873, in New Orleans.] Our School is filling up rapidly, there are about 182 present, and many more are likely to come. We shall have 250 I think by the 1st of July. The Hodgsons dined with us yesterday, with Mrs. Quintard Dr. & Mrs. [H. M.] Anderson, Mr. [Robert] Dabney [professor of metaphysics], Gen. Shoup & Aunt Mary [Gayle Aiken], a pleasant dinner.

A week from to-day will be Easter Sunday.

June 22, Sunday [1873]   Ther 74°, 7¼ A.M. Have just returned with Mamma [and] Minnie from morning service. On these beautiful summer mornings the Service is additionally attractive. Jessie & Mamie are both at Fairmont at school [near Monteagle, Tenn.]. They come down every few weeks to spend Sunday. This is a great improvement on [their school at] Columbia. No political news of importance. The "Modoc" [Indian] War was ended by the surrender of Capt Pack [Kintpuash, known to whites as Captain Jack], & the question then was what to do with the prisoners. They are to be tried by mil. commission. [Kintpuash and three other Indians were hanged.] The cholera is prevailing terribly in Nashville & some other places. Deaths reported there yesterday 72, worse than it was in 1866. People are flying in all directions to places of refuge. The School numbers about 200 now, some are coming in still & some are going. Our Board of Trustees are expected here on the 9th of July, but owing to an error in the Calendar they may not be here until the 16th which is the day prescribed by the Statutes—6½ P.M.—83°.

Nov 20 [1873]   Ther 10° at 7 A.M. Snow yesterday & very cold.

Decr 1 [1873]   Ther 60°.

[December] 3d [1873]   ″ 63 Rainy from the S.E.

The sensation for the past three weeks has been the capture of the Virginius off the coast of Cuba, and the execution of her Captain ([Joseph] Fry) and about 54 of her passengers & crew. Spain accepts the demands of the U.S. to surrender the vessel & the Survivors, to salute the flag, to punish the offenders & to indemnify the families of the slain.

The School which has had as many as 225 present this Term is to close just two weeks from to day.

Decr 11, [1873]   Ther 68 at 1 P.M. The weather is warm & beautiful—almost too warm for out-of-door exertion.

The examinations are going on & doing very well, better than any previous year.

[December] 13, [1873]   Dormitory burned.

[December] 27, [1873]   Snow fell last night to the depth of 4 inches.

[December] 28, [1873]   Ther 22° & snow lying firmly on the ground.

Mamma spent last night with Mrs. DuBose['s] sick baby, after having a dance for the children of the Mtn. until after 9 P.M. She thinks the baby is fast sinking.

Jany 1 1874   Made calls on our neighbors. 17 of the houses did not receive, 7 were open. A vast change from 4 years ago when I came up here from home to see how things were going on, when there were but 5 or 6 families on the Mountain.

Decades.

In 1824 on this day I was a little boy running about the streets of a village in the interior of Pa., called Myerstown in Lebanon Co.

In 1834 I was the youngest apprentice in a printing office in Lyons, N.Y., probably I was distributing the "Carrier's Address" for it was the duty of the youngest to carry about the papers of the village subscribers.

In 1844 I was on this day a Lieut in the U.S. Army, having gone thro' West Point, stationed at a little hamlet where there was an Arsenal, Dearbornville, about 18 miles west of Detroit.

In 1854 on this day I was a happy bridegroom at Mt Vernon, my darling wife, a bride of 3 days, with me. Two years ago, after an absence of 17 years, I went back to see the house to which I had taken her as a young wife. What a history between now & then, passed thro' my mind. I saw the same walks we had trodden together, the same trees we had looked on. What indescribable emotion, to think of those happy, happy days, when life seemed without a care & the whole world was joy.

In 1864, on this day, I was in Richmond, chief of the Ordn Dept of a great young nation which had received its death wound, & was slowly lapsing to destruction. But we were even then still hopeful. Like the victim of consumption we mistook every little success for recovery from that certain death toward which we were hastening & from which there was no earthly power to save us.

In 1874 I am here turned pedagogue & living on the recollections of the past, a past which is fast verging to its close for me. I may yet hope to see another Decade, 1884, but after that——.

He who has chronicled 5 Decades, & has but one more left to look forward to ought to think more of the future beyond this life, than of the past in this, unless the retrospection furnish him with a text for a better future in this life.

Apl 29, [1874]   The snow covered the fences and piazzas this morning with a cold N.W. wind.

The last month has been one of continued rains, causing general overflow of the Miss & Red Rivers, & others of the Rivers flowing into the Gulf. There is much suffering & destitution in consequence and the Federal Govt has ordered distribution of ½ million of rations.

There is a conflict of Governors at Little Rock, & there has been slight bloodshed, but the presence of Federal troops prevents more extended collision. [Liberal Republican Joseph Brooks and Republican Elisha Baxter claimed to be governor, and both had armed supporters. U.S. troops attempted to keep peace, but violence left one dead and one wounded. When the two groups clashed near Pine Bluff, nine died and twenty were wounded before President Grant recognized Baxter as Arkansas governor.] Would that the collision could come—it were better for the final rest of the country.

June 28 Sunday [1874]   The weather is extremely warm & has been so for a week past. The Therm at 10 last night stood at 80°, & is now 9 A.M. a little above 80°.

Bayne's babies came here 3 weeks ago and are enjoying the country. Charley [one of Bayne's sons] has a pony which Willie selected for him upon which he canters about all the time.

The visitors are coming together for their summer holiday, and our Chapel which has just been enlarged is filling up. If we had one good hotel it would soon be filled.

The political news is unchanged. The character of the General Government is as common as ever. Much distress exists at the South, consequent on the overflows of April, which were unprecedented. The Genl Govt authorized the issue of some 50,000 rations per day, which is still going on.

Mamie came down from her school at Moffat yesterday morning. She succeeds admirably at School, is good looking, & will make a fine woman.

Octr 19, Monday, [1874]   The day is most beautiful, the Therm. standing at 65 in the shade & the sky without a cloud. This month has been exceptionally beautiful. Bayne & I took a stroll together this morning, thro the woods about "Tremlett" [one of the student residences]. He with [his wife] Maria [and daughters] Mamie & Edith came here about the 5th of October. Maria is recovering from a low fever she had at Mobile, & is still unable to walk out much.

The School was filled to its number last year & a few more. I was not well pleased with the action of the Board of Trustees which met here Aug 6. I hope they will do something more for us next year.

In politics the current of success sits against this corrupt administration, the majorities whose elections have been held clearly indicate this.

A brief attempt to overthrow the infamous [W. P.] Kellogg [Republican] government in La. was entirely successful; but Grant interfered & replaced it. So blood was shed apparently in vain, only apparently we hope.

April 17, 1875   It is quite cold to-day & we had freezing weather last night, destroying all our peaches & pears of which we had good promise. The Lord hath given & He taketh away, blessed be His name. It is a hard lesson to learn.

I have been severely afflicted with a pain in my right arm this past winter. The disease was pronounced atrophy, or wasting of the muscle of the arm, by Drs. [Montgomery] Brown & [Daniel W.] Brickell of N.O. whither I went early in March. They say the pain will cease with the disappearance of the substance of the muscle. I have slept but 3 nights since the middle of December last, except under the effects of medicine. I get up & warm my arm by the fire several times during the night. The paroxysms of pain recur about every 2 hours at night & are very severe. In the daytime I am less troubled. This cold weather is unfavorable.

The School opened on the 18th of March, & has its usual numbers of about 200 pupils. Gen. Shoup left us last winter, and I have to teach the Calculus in that Dept. We are also without a Master of the Gr. School which throws some additional duty on me.

April 20, [1875]   I suffered much with the pain, in my arm last night, & do not see either how I am to be relieved, or how I am to bear it.

We had yesterday a poor boy one of our students, before two magistrates on the charge of shooting another student in an altercation, with a small pistol. Turpin, of Bastrop La, was the boy, McCune of Columbus O. the boy shot, both are over 18. The wound tho serious is not supposed to be dangerous.

The trees are still devoid of foliage. Mamma & I constantly long for a climate where we shall have less of winter, & more of green, altho' this climate can hardly be called cold. The winter at the North & West has been an unusually severe one, tho' here it has been rather an open winter with not even an inch of snow. My sister Eliza (Mrs. Chapman) died at

Lyons N.Y. about 6 weeks ago or more (Feby 6th perhaps). There are now four sons & 1 daughter left of the family of 10. The first death occurred about 20 years ago. Thomas the oldest living child was 75 last January. He lives at Greentown Ohio.

Oct 13, [1875]   I went to the Warm Springs in N.C. about the 1st of June hoping to derive benefit from the baths there, but returned in 10 or 12 days without relief, except that my general health was restored from the injury inflicted by the use of opiates, chiefly injections of morphine under the skin.

Willie's majority was celebrated by a handsome dinner to his friends. He is still ardently prosecuting the pursuit of a cadetship at West Point, & I am doing all I can to help him, tho' it grieves me to see him so infatuated about West Point, & so opposed to the law, in which he would have so capital an opportunity with his Uncle Bayne.

The weather is very beautiful & sunny. We had our first decided frost on the night of the 11th. The children are all going out chestnut hunting, lured by the beautiful weather, except myself, who still suffers severely from the pains in my arm. We have all been well this year.

October 29, 1876, Sunday   Over a year since my last entry in this book. I am still afflicted with the severe pains in my shoulders referred to before. I am now somewhat alarmed at the numbness which I have felt the last few days in my left arm, & also in my left leg, extending up to my left cheek, it looks a little like threatened paralysis. I hope to be spared such an affliction, but have feared it for some time past. Many things have occurred in the last year. Willie went to New York in Sept. to begin the study of medicine. He exhausted himself, trying to get to West Point, & attended several competitive examinations, until on the 3d of this month he passed beyond the prescribed age (22). I am quite satisfied with his choice of a profession, and am quite sure he will succeed (D.V.) [Deo volente, God willing]. Prof Dabney died here on the 1st of April of pneumonia. He came here with me in Sept. 1868 to open the School, & had been here ever since. Two months after died Col A. M. Rutledge, a graduate of West Point of the class of '37 who had settled here, hoping to spend the quiet evening of his days here. Two months later his son, Joe, died here. He was one of our most promising students.

In the outside world the presidential election, which takes place on the 7th of Novr. absorbs all interest. Should [Samuel] Tilden [of N.Y.] be elected the South will feel renewed hope in her future. The affairs of Turkey attract the attention of the European world. Whether peace is to be kept, or whether Russia goes to war, with the notion of getting Constantinople is the question. At present the chances are still for peace.

Our weather is truly beautiful. This day is as balmy as summer with all the tints of Fall. On the mountain the leaves are fast falling from the trees. Our School is not as full this year as usual.

Monday, Jany 1, 1877.   My ink is frozen & I take to the pencil. A snow storm of great violence has been raging for the past 24 hours & in fact since Saturday evening. The snow is over a foot in depth on a level & has drifted to the depth of 18 inches in many places. I got to my office with some difficulty this morning. There will be no New Year's callers to-day I suspect.

The country is still in a state of the deepest anxiety & uncertainty over the Presidential struggle [the disputed 1876 election, then still unresolved]. People cannot certainly foresee that there will not be war. People however begin to think there will be no appeal to arms. This will be due to the calmness of the South, which refuses to be violent. It declares its resolution to appeal only to the laws. But even thus far all can see that this form of government has its weak points, & is not yet proved to be the "best government in the world."

Willie is apparently satisfied with his choice of profession, & I feel assured he will succeed in it. I shall feel easy as soon as he is established in his profession.

July 16 [1878]   Over a year since my last entry into this journal, & I have now completed sixty years of my life. A little fleeting remnant is all that is left to me. <The past year has been one of the quietest of my life. But this year opens with a bitter outlook. The very unkind and undeserved action of the Board of Trustees at the last session, determined that this would not be our future home. They will I believe find that in dispensing with my services they have made a mistake.> [After months of friction between Gorgas and the clerical leaders of Sewanee, the trustees decided that the post of vice-chancellor should be held by a cleric.] I shall resign here on the 27th inst., on the meeting of the Board, and go to look after my new place of duty at Tuscaloosa, where I have been elected President of the Univy of Ala. <a most opportune and unlooked for promotion, which completely deprives the action of the Board toward me of its sting.> I owe this to the personal friendship of Col N. H. R. Dawson of Selma, a member of the Board of Trustees of the Univ. of Ala. Strange to say that I am no sooner provided with a place which I longed for, than I get a telegram from N. Orleans offering me the Chair of Mechanics in the Univy of La. I will not move our household to Tuscaloosa before Decr, but shall go there myself by the middle of Septr. I spent the month of Feby in Washington, simply to look about me, & possibly see something to which I could apply myself. The Russo-Turkish War has ended in the treaty of San Stefano, Turkey having been completely beaten, which treaty has just undergone the revision of the Great

Powers at Berlin, & a definitive arrangement reached. England has occupied the Island of Cyprus by Treaty with Turkey, an important military post for her. Willie is still hopefully prosecuting his studies in New York. If he lives, I hope his life will be one of usefulness, and of distinction. Our children, thanks to a kind Providence, are all that parents could ask for. Mamie Bayne [the oldest daughter of Maria and T. L. Bayne] was married at the close of Novr to Mr. Geo[rge] Behn, a well-to-do young business man of N.O. of French descent. Bayne has dissolved his business connexion with [his law partner] Mr. [Thomas A.] Clarke, much to his own satisfaction. The most noted invention of many years has been the phonograph, & the telephone, kindred developments of science; Edison, a merely ingenious telegraphist, the inventor.

"July 1st 1877 [1878]   Another melancholy birthday—my sixtieth. How do people learn to grow old contentedly & gracefully. I think if I had the very moderate competency which I have lost by mistakes since the War, I could grow old with more serenity. My mode of life here is very irksome to me, the charge of boys, especially those at my house is very disagreeable; & yet I must submit to it in order that our children may be educated & placed in life. When that is accomplished I pray the good God to let me go from my work here.

Fifty nine years accomplished & in my sixtieth; incredible! I hope Willie at that age will be an honored member of his high profession, & will have attained a competency, without which old age is not honored & may become a burden.

The Russo-Turkish war is the great theme of interest. The Russians are pressing back the Turks in Asia, & have crossed the Danube in Europe. Victory will of course be with them unless England interferes, in order to prevent the occupation of Constantinople."

The above copied from my Father's journal.

J. G. [Jessie Gorgas]

Epilogue

The fall of 1878 was one of the few tranquil periods in Josiah's life after the Civil War. If poor health had not plagued him, life could not have been better. With the pain on the left side of his body steadily worsening and his nerves frayed, he sought relief at Blount Springs, Alabama, in August because his suffering so distressed his family. As he said to Amelia, he "ran away" to be by himself. "I can bear it better in solitude."[1] Unfortunately, his health did not improve, as pain kept him awake so that a full night's sleep became rare.

In September while Amelia, Anne, Mary Aiken and her family, and the Gorgas children remained at Sewanee, Josiah met The University of Alabama faculty; they welcomed him warmly. In October Josiah moved into the President's Mansion on The University of Alabama campus, and the next month sons Willie and Richie arrived for a visit. Willie, then a student at Bellevue Medical College in New York, grew deeply concerned about his father's health as Josiah now suffered with severe headaches; Willie communicated his alarm to his mother before he returned to medical school. A few days after Christmas Amelia, Anne, and the Gorgas children moved to Tuscaloosa and settled into their handsome new home. Tuscaloosa residents received the family as one of their own come home; many older Tuscaloosa residents remembered Amelia as a little girl when her father had been Alabama governor. A roof over their heads (and a magnificent one at that) and Josiah's fine income from a dignified job as head of a school whose faculty respected him made past worries of near bankruptcy, no place to live, and ungrateful associates seem distant problems. As for Sewanee, Josiah wrote Amelia, "I don't want to see it again—never."[2]

However, despite his peaceful presidency at the university symptoms of his health problems grew ominous. He sporadically found himself in a state of "bewilderment," unable to speak, to read, or to connect ideas to words. The headaches increased if he stooped or sneezed.[3] Pain grew particularly severe at night, and he could not endure being cold.[4] Earlier, he had sought relief with opium, quinine, morphine, chloral with a shot of gin, a pill containing an extract of Indian hemp ("the best sleeping potion I have yet had"), and phosphorous pills.[5] But to no avail. "I lose patience with all medicine," he wrote Amelia, "and want to throw it to the dogs."[6] Now the medical profession recommended more remedies: chloral, chloroform liniment, cod liver oil, phosphorous pills, phosphoric acid, sulphur water baths, and "electricity."[7] For months he had carried a piece of sheep skin to warm his feet wherever he went. Yet, he found a swallow of whiskey as effective (if not more so) as medical prescriptions to secure relief from his pain.[8]

In an instant the new-found serenity and security was threatened when Josiah suffered a severe stroke on February 23, 1879, while Amelia was at Sewanee nursing her sister, Mary Aiken, who had fallen ill. Immediately, Amelia returned to Tuscaloosa and found Josiah's speech, vision, and thoughts greatly impaired.[9] The cumulative effects of the medical prescriptions were enough to depress or kill him if the stroke did not: "nitrate of silver, a little opium and rheubarb."[10] In March Mary Aiken and her children moved in with Josiah and Amelia in Tuscaloosa while Mary continued her recovery from illness.[11] During the weeks that followed, Josiah's condition improved slightly, and in April he was able to travel to Mobile to consult Dr. James F. Heustis (son of Amelia's father's cousin and her mother's best friend, Elizabeth Swepstone Gayle). In July Amelia's sister Maria died, and the now recovered Mary Aiken moved into the Bayne household in New Orleans to care for the Bayne children.[12]

By summer Josiah's health failed to improve, and he determined to resign the presidency of The University of Alabama. Instead, in July 1879 the board of trustees, more sympathetic than those at Sewanee earlier, granted him a year's leave of absence, but in September Amelia and Josiah concluded that indeed he should resign. The board accepted his resignation, appointed him university librarian, and provided the family with The University of Alabama's steward's hall as their new residence.[13] Such good fortune was beyond the family's expectations. They had another fine place to live and income from a job that Amelia and the daughters could ghost for Josiah when necessary. Responsibility for the library gradually passed to Amelia's hands.[14]

In February 1880 Josiah was able to travel with his son Richie to New Orleans to visit T. L. Bayne. In June of that year Willie was appointed a surgeon in the U.S. Army after graduation from medical school in 1879.

The following year, 1881, the family excitedly planned the wedding of daughter Minnie to George Palfrey of St. Mary's Parish, Louisiana, on December 29, the twenty-eighth anniversary of her parents' wedding. Six weeks later in February 1882 the family's beloved Anne Kavanaugh died of complications from consumption.[15]

Josiah's health steadily worsened in 1882 and 1883. Periods of improvement were increasingly brief. Amelia's letters in these weeks suggest that he suffered additional strokes leading to partial paralysis. On the evening of May 14, 1883, Josiah grew rapidly weaker. After administration of a hypodermic of morphine the patient was "perfectly quiet" until midnight when "stertorous breathing returned." At daylight Amelia sent again for the doctor, and his examination convinced her that her "darling" was beyond medical help. Amelia described the deathbed scene to her older sister: "the professors gathered round their old chief never leaving him until his faint breath expired with the last rays of the setting sun. At the last it was the gentle breathing of an infant & not a sound disturbed the stillness of the room as we knelt beside his bed, his dear hand in mine & my hot cheek pressed to his cold forehead" while a family friend "read for me in her clear, sweet voice the parting prayer beginning 'Go forth Christian soul.'"[16]

Josiah died on May 15, 1883, in the Gorgas house on The University of Alabama campus. After a funeral at Christ Episcopal Church in Tuscaloosa, Josiah joined Anne in the Gorgas family plot in Evergreen Cemetery in Tuscaloosa.

Notes

1. This epilogue is drawn from Vandiver, *Ploughshares into Swords;* Johnston, *AG,* 101, 104; Wiggins, "A Victorian Father," 249–52; JG to AG, August 2, 1878, GFP.

2. JG to AG, February 2, 1879, GFP; JG to George R. Fairbanks, November 25, 1878, George R. Fairbanks Papers, University of the South Archives, Sewanee, Tenn.; Johnston, *AG,* 104–05; Vandiver, *Ploughshares into Swords,* 308–11.

3. JG to AG, no month 27, [1878], September, 15, 1878, GFP.

4. Ibid., [late 1868–1869?], December 23, 27, 1878.

5. Gorgas Journals, June 9, [1864], October 13, 1875; JG to AG, January 17, 18, [24], 26, February 5, 7, 1876, June 16, [1878?], GFP.

6. JG to AG, January 17, 1876, GFP.

7. Ibid., June 16, [1878], September 25, October 4, 6, 13, 30, 31, 1878, no month 27, [1878]. These medications were sedatives, a local anesthetic, laxatives, and pain killers.

8. Ibid., August 30, October 31, 1878, February 17, 1879.

9. AG to WCG, February 27, 1879, ibid.

10. Ibid., March 8, 1879.

11. M[ary Gayle Aiken] to Maria [Gayle Bayne], March 19, 1879, ibid.

12. Sarah Gayle Crawford to Amelia Gorgas, Sarah Gayle Crawford Papers, Perkins Library, Duke University, Durham, N.C.; Hugh A. Bayne Memoirs, microfilm typescript, p. 118, Bayne-Gayle Papers; Johnston, *AG,* 107–08; Vandiver, *Ploughshares into Swords,* 311–12.

13. AG to WCG, December 28, [1879], GFP.

14. AG to [T. L.] Bayne, January 12, 1881, ibid.; Johnston, *AG*, 108–10; Wiggins, "A Victorian Father," 249–50; Vandiver, *Ploughshares into Swords,* 312–13.

15. Johnston, *AG*, 110–11.

16. AG to Sarah [Gayle Crawford], May 17, 1883, GFP.

Biographical Directory

FAMILY AND FRIENDS OF JOSIAH GORGAS

Hugh Kerr Aiken (1822–1865) was born July 5, 1822, in Winnsboro, South Carolina, the sixth child and third son of Nancy Kerr and David Aiken. Educated first at Mount Zion Academy, he entered South Carolina College as a sophomore in 1842. After graduating from college with distinction, he occupied himself as a planter until 1856, when he moved to Charleston, South Carolina, where he became a cotton factor, founding H. K. Aiken and Company. He continued in business there until the opening of the Civil War. As a young man he was interested in military affairs and was active in state militia organizations. In 1850 he was promoted to brigadier general and later succeeded his friend and classmate P. M. Nelson to the position of major general. On December 15, 1852, in Mobile, Alabama, he married Mary Rees Gayle, daughter of Alabama Governor John Gayle. The children of Mary Gayle and Hugh Kerr Aiken were Nancy Kerr ("Nannie") Aiken (1855–1857), John Gayle Aiken (1859–1935), Carolina Margaret ("Carrie") Aiken (1863–1911), and Mary Gayle Aiken (1864). When South Carolina seceded in December 1860, Aiken joined the Confederate Army and remained on the coast until promoted to colonel of the 6th South Carolina Cavalry. After guarding the Charleston and Savannah Railroad for several months, the unit was ordered to Virginia. On June 11, 1864, at the battle at Trivillian Station, Aiken was shot while leading a charge, fell from his horse, was taken prisoner, and then left to die. Friends found Aiken and nursed him back to health. When he returned to service, he was dispatched to South Carolina to harass Sherman's march through the Carolinas. On February 27, 1865, Aiken's cavalry unit suddenly encountered federal troops near Darlington. Aiken was shot and killed, dying in the arms of a nephew who buried him at Mount Elon Church, Darlington County, South Carolina. After the war his remains were moved to the Presbyterian churchyard in Winnsboro, South Carolina. His younger brother Wyatt Aiken served in the Confederate Army and in the postwar era as a representative from South Carolina in the U.S. House of Representatives.

Mary Rees Gayle Aiken (1829–1910), the fourth child and third daughter of Sarah Haynsworth and John Gayle, was born in Greensboro, Alabama, September 23, 1829. After the death of her mother in 1835, Mary and her younger brother Dick lived in Mobile with their father's cousin, Billups Gayle, and his family until John Gayle remarried in 1837. When her father was a congressman in Washington, Mary accompanied him and received much attention from young army officers there, including an army lieutenant named William Tecumseh Sherman. As a young girl, she was known as the family coquette. One of her suitors was a handsome, dashing young man who gambled and drank, and Governor Gayle refused to consent to a marriage. The family thought that she married Hugh Aiken (1822–1865) on the rebound on December 15, 1852, in Mobile. Aiken, of Winnsboro, South Carolina, came from a wealthy family prominent in South Carolina politics. Aiken met Mary on a business trip to Mobile. The couple were introduced by James Crawford, brother of William B. Crawford, husband of Sarah Gayle. The Crawfords originally had lived in Winnsboro. After their marriage the Aikens lived on one of his family's plantations in South Carolina until 1856. At that time they moved to Charleston, where Hugh Aiken went into business as a cotton factor. When the Civil War began, Aiken enlisted in the 6th South Carolina Cavalry. As Sherman made his "March to the Sea," his army passed near the Aiken home in Winnsboro. Sherman called to pay his respects and offered to place a guard around the house to protect the family from the irregular bands who accompanied his army, robbing the local inhabitants. Unwilling to receive Sherman in her home, Mary met her old friend on the steps of the front porch, where they reminisced about happy times in Washington. Sherman then spoke with regret of the suffering that the war had brought to the South. "But," he added, "it can't be avoided, for War is Hell." After Sherman left, Mary realized that for the last moments of their conversation, he had held one of her hands in both of his. A short time thereafter Hugh Aiken was killed in February 1865 in an ambush near Cheraw, South Carolina. Federal soldiers removed all papers from the body to check for possible useful information. Among his papers was a letter addressed to his wife. Fifteen years later General Sherman, through his brother U.S. Senator John Sherman, delivered the letter to Congressman Wyatt Aiken, Mary's brother-in-law, to be delivered to her. The children of Mary and Hugh

Mary Rees Gayle Aiken (Courtesy of Hoole Special Collections, University of Alabama, Tuscaloosa, Alabama)

Aiken were Nancy Kerr ("Nannie") Aiken (1855–1857), John Gayle Aiken (1859–1935), Carolina Margaret ("Carrie") Aiken (1863–1911), and Mary Gayle Aiken (1864). After the death of her husband Mary Aiken was left penniless, as her husband had invested heavily in Confederate bonds. (The family remembered that Mary had a trunk full of such worthless paper.) Mary spent extended periods with her sister, Amelia Gayle Gorgas, and her family. In 1871 Mary moved to Sewanee, Tennessee, where she became the matron at Tremlett Hall at The University of the South. When the Gorgas family moved to Tuscaloosa, Alabama, Mary moved into the Gorgas home in Sewanee. With her came her two children, Gayle and Carrie, and her sister-in-law, Miss Carrie Aiken. In

March 1879 she moved to Tuscaloosa to join the Gorgas household. Mary had promised her sister, Maria Gayle Bayne, that if Maria died, she would take care of the Bayne children. After the death of Maria in July 1879, Mary Aiken moved to New Orleans and assumed responsibility for managing the Bayne household and rearing the Bayne children still at home. She never remarried. She died in New Orleans on December 20, 1910, and is buried in the Holcombe-Aiken plot in the Metairie Cemetery in New Orleans.

Anna Maria Gayle Bayne (1835–1879), the sixth child and fourth daughter of Sarah Haynsworth and John Gayle, was born on February 19, 1835, in Tuscaloosa, Alabama. As a girl she attended a school in Mobile conducted by a French count and countess, émigrés from France during the Revolution of 1830. They taught Maria to speak French with a perfect accent and instructed her in the doctrines of their faith, Roman Catholicism. At about the time of her marriage to Thomas Levingston Bayne (1824–1891), a successful New Orleans attorney, on December 22, 1853, in Mobile, she became a Roman Catholic. Maria and T. L. had met when he came to call on the Gayle family in Mobile in 1852. All of the Bayne children were reared in the Roman Catholic faith. In late April 1862 as the U.S. Navy threatened New Orleans from the south, Bayne was in New Orleans recovering from a wound received at Shiloh. He determined to move his family out of the city, and they went to Jackson and Meridian, Mississippi, and Mobile, Alabama. After remaining in Mobile a few days Bayne moved the family again, this time to Winnsboro, South Carolina, to the home of Maria's sister, Mary Aiken. Bayne soon settled the family into a cottage in Winnsboro, while he went to Richmond to report for active military service. Later that year the family moved to Richmond. At the end of the Civil War Bayne left Richmond with the Confederate government. He sent word to Maria that he would join her in Baltimore, Maryland, but could not fix a date. Her brother, Dick, recently released from federal prison, moved Maria, who was then pregnant, and her children and then her sister, Amelia, and her children to Baltimore. There the elderly father of Bayne's Yale roommate (John Donnell Smith) took them into his home, and Maria gave birth to a son, Thomas Levingston Bayne, Jr., in July 1865 at the Smith's country home in Dorchester County, Maryland. Later that summer Bayne moved his family from Maryland back to New Orleans. In the 1870s Maria suffered from ill health and traveled extensively in the North, seeking medical advice. In 1879 the family traveled to Denver, and Maria died in a hotel in Chicago on July 11, 1879, before the family could return home. She is buried in the Gayle plot in Magnolia Cemetery, Mobile. Their children were Mary Aiken ("Mamie") Bayne (1855–1921), an unnamed stillborn son, John Gayle Bayne (1858–1864), twins Edward Bowen and Thomas

Anna Maria Gayle Bayne, 1853 (Courtesy of Dr. David Aiken and George Denègre)

Levingston Bayne (1860), Charles Bowen Bayne (1861–1884), Edith Bayne (1863–1936), Thomas Levingston Bayne, Jr., (1865–1934), Amelia Elizabeth ("Minna") Bayne (1867–1893), Hugh Aiken Bayne (1870–1954), and Joseph Denègre Bayne (1871–1873).

Thomas Levingston Bayne (1824–1891), New Orleans attorney, son of Eliza Bowen and Charles Bayne, was born August 4, 1824, in Clinton, Georgia. When his mother died a year later, the child remained with his father for a time. Thereafter, he lived in the care of first one relative and then another. In 1834 after his father remarried, Bayne went to live with his uncle Edward Bowen on a large plantation in Butler County, Alabama. Bowen considered Bayne as his son and planned to will considerable property to the young man. There he was tutored for two years in Latin and Greek by a Mr. Lowry, a graduate of Dublin University, Ireland, who had been a tutor at South Carolina College. Bayne attended Yale University, 1843–1847. When he reached Yale, he was clad from hat to shoes in garments made on the Alabama plantation; he described himself as looking "unusually countrified." After encountering amusement from his classmates, he adopted the prevailing local style of dress. His college roommate and devoted friend was John Donnell Smith, son of a wealthy Baltimorian. Bayne achieved great success as a student at Yale, where he became a member of Skull and Bones. After graduation he returned to Butler County, Alabama, although his uncle wished him to study law at Harvard. He began to read law in Camden, Alabama. The contrast between this quiet, dull country village and his exciting college life was too much, and after a month he persuaded his uncle to allow him to seek a position in New Orleans. In January 1848 he began work in the law office of Thomas Slidell and Thomas A. Clarke in New Orleans and became a partner in the renamed firm of Clarke and Bayne. On December 22, 1853, in Mobile, he married Anna Maria Gayle (1835–1879), daughter of Alabama Governor John Gayle. Edward Bowen had intended that T. L. should marry Bowen's daughter; when T. L. announced his intention to marry Maria Gayle, Bowen disinherited his nephew. T. L. felt honor-bound to write Maria of his reduced financial prospects. She misinterpreted his letter, thinking that he had changed his mind about marriage, and replied that they should consider the engagement broken. Her sister, Mary Aiken, served as intermediary to reunite the couple. The children of T. L. and Maria Bayne were Mary Aiken ("Mamie") Bayne (1855–1921), an unnamed stillborn son, John Gayle Bayne (1858–1864), twins Edward Bowen and Thomas Levingston Bayne (1860), Charles Bowen Bayne (1861–1884), Edith Bayne (1863–1936), Thomas Levingston Bayne, Jr., (1865–1934), Amelia Elizabeth ("Minna") Bayne (1867–1893), Hugh Aiken Bayne (1870–1954), and Joseph Denègre Bayne (1871–1873). An opponent of secession, Bayne enlisted in the 5th Company of the Washington Artillery in 1861 and was wounded in the shoulder at Shiloh. Commissioned captain, then major, then lieutenant colonel, he was appointed in 1864 as chief of the Bureau of Foreign Supplies after serving in the Ordnance Department for two years. As Confederate currency depreciated, Bayne sold his possessions or bartered as he tried to provide for his family. After the Civil War he returned to his law practice in New Orleans, where he became one of the city's most distinguished attorneys. President U. S. Grant offered Bayne a

Thomas Levingston Bayne, 1853 (Courtesy of George Denègre)

judgeship on the U.S. Circuit Court if he would declare himself a Republican. Bayne refused the offer. In 1888 he was elected vice-president of the American Bar Association. After the death of his wife in 1879, he never remarried. When he resumed practicing law in 1865, he had only $5,000 left from his prewar fortune. During the next twenty-five years he supported a family of eight, lived well, entertained generously, sent his children to boarding school and to college, and gave a home to each daughter on her marriage. When he died in New Orleans, December 10, 1891, he left an estate of nearly $500,000. Although the Bayne family in Georgia and Alabama had been Baptist, he encouraged his children to follow the Roman Catholic faith of their mother. On his deathbed Bayne was baptized by a Roman Catholic priest and given the sacrament of Extreme Unction. He is buried in the Gayle plot in Magnolia Cemetery in Mobile.

John Archibald Campbell (1811–1889), attorney, justice on the U.S. Supreme Court, was born in Washington, Georgia, June 24, 1811. He graduated from Franklin College (later University of Georgia) in 1826 and then attended the U.S. Military Academy, 1826–1829. After the death of his father he abandoned his military career because of the poor condition of his father's estate. Back in Georgia, he studied law and was admitted to the bar in 1830. Within a year he moved to Alabama, first to Montgomery and then Mobile, and opened a law practice. He served in the Alabama House of Representatives, 1836–1838. Twice he declined appointment to the Alabama Supreme Court. He returned to the Alabama House of Representatives, 1842–1844, and attended the Nashville Convention in 1850. In 1853 he was appointed as an associate justice on the U.S. Supreme Court and served until his resignation in May 1861. Although opposed to secession, he supported the Confederacy. While T. L. Bayne was away in the army from his family in New Orleans during the first year of the Civil War, Campbell looked after the Bayne family and took a room in the house next door so that Maria Bayne could feel that a friend was nearby. In April 1862 T. L. Bayne returned to New Orleans after being wounded at Shiloh. As the U.S. Navy threatened the city, Bayne moved his family to a safer place, and Campbell left the city with them, traveling to Jackson and Meridian, Mississippi, Mobile, Alabama, and Winnsboro, South Carolina, the home of Mary and Hugh Aiken. Bayne went on to Richmond to report for active military service. At the home of Confederate Secretary of War G. W. Randolph, Mrs. Randolph asked Bayne if he knew anyone from New Orleans who could assist the overworked Randolph in the Confederate War Department. Bayne and his brother-in-law, Josiah Gorgas, suggested Campbell, who became assistant secretary of war in October 1862. In February 1865 he was one of the southern representatives to the Hampton Roads Peace Conference to confer with U.S. President Abraham Lincoln and U.S. Secretary of State William H. Seward. After the Confederate evacuation of Richmond, Campbell remained and obtained an interview with President Lincoln in which Campbell obtained from Lincoln permission for the Virginia legislature to convene to consider Lincoln's plan of Reconstruction. Within a few days Lee surrendered, Lincoln withdrew his sanction of the meeting, and Lincoln was assassinated. In the subsequent excitement Campbell was charged with having misrepresented to the U.S. commander in Richmond Lincoln's purpose in assembling the legislature. Campbell was arrested, and for six months he was imprisoned at Fort

Pulaski, Georgia. When he was released by President Andrew Johnson, his property in Mobile had been destroyed, and in 1866 he resumed his law practice in New Orleans. He died on March 13, 1889, in Baltimore, Maryland.

Sarah Ann Gayle Crawford (1824–1895), the second child and first daughter of Sarah Haynsworth and John Gayle, was born March 24, 1824, in Claiborne, Alabama. After the death of Sarah Haynsworth Gayle in 1835, daughters Sarah and Amelia remained in Tuscaloosa for two years under the care of their mother's friend, Mrs. Alva Woods. Sarah boarded at schools in Tuscaloosa. In June 1839 at the age of fifteen she enrolled in Madame Adele Canda's boarding school in Brooklyn, New York. She remained there for two years and returned to Mobile in 1841. On December 6, 1842, she married Dr. William Bones Crawford (1810–1853), a distinguished physician from Winnsboro, South Carolina. Dr. Crawford graduated from South Carolina College, where he was a classmate and close friend of John B. Floyd, U.S. Secretary of War, 1859–1860. Crawford received his medical training in Paris, France, 1832–1833. After his marriage to Sarah, Dr. Crawford practiced medicine in Mobile until his health declined in the late 1840s. He and his wife left their children with the Gayle family and traveled to the Northeast and to Europe, seeking to improve his health. In 1853 they settled in Malaga, Spain, where he died at the Fonda de la Alameda, Malaga, on December 28, 1853. His wife returned to Mobile in February 1854. Their children were Clara Jane Crawford (1843–1875), Amelia Gayle ("Millie") Crawford (1845–1908), William Bones ("Billy") Crawford (1847–   ), and Sarah ("Sallie") Crawford (1852–   ). During the Civil War Sarah resided in Mobile and in 1864 moved to Eutaw, Alabama. Colonel James Crawford, brother of her late husband, owned a plantation near Eutaw and assisted Sarah in this period. By January 1876 Sarah had returned to Mobile, where she was taking boarders to augment her meager resources. As she aged, she suffered from severe arthritis, and from 1884 to 1894 she lived with her daughter Sallie Crawford Hughes in Edgefield, South Carolina. In 1894 she returned to Alabama to stay with her sister, Amelia Gayle Gorgas, for more than a year. Late in October 1895 Sarah's granddaughter, Sarah Crawford Hughes, was burned to death, and Sarah Gayle Crawford was devastated. A month later she died in Tuscaloosa, Alabama, at the Gorgas home on November 29, 1895, and is buried in the Gayle plot in Magnolia Cemetery in Mobile.

Nathaniel Henry Rhodes Dawson (1829–1895), U.S. Commissioner of Education, was born in Charleston, South Carolina, February 17, 1829. The family moved to Carlowville in Dallas County, Alabama, in 1842.

Educated at St. Joseph College (now Spring Hill College) in Mobile, Alabama, Dawson read law under George R. Evans at Cahawba and was admitted to the bar in 1851. He moved to Selma in 1858. By that time he was a prosperous aristocrat whose property included fifty-one slaves and 2,129 acres of land. He was a delegate to the 1860 Democratic conventions at Charleston and Baltimore. He was a captain in the Confederate Army and was elected to the Alabama House of Representatives in 1863. After completion of one term in the legislature he returned to the army. After the civil war he resumed his law practice in Selma. He served as a presidential elector in 1872, as a trustee of The University of the South, Sewanee, Tennessee, 1870–1881, and as a trustee of The University of Alabama, 1876–1894. He was a Sewanee trustee when the trustees decided that the post of vice-chancellor should be held by a cleric, a decision that provoked Josiah Gorgas's resignation. Dawson was simultaneously a University of Alabama trustee, and he was instrumental in the selection of Gorgas as University of Alabama president. Dawson was a member of the Alabama State Democratic Executive Committee, 1876–1886, and chaired that committee, 1885–1886. He returned to the Alabama House of Representatives, 1880–1881, and was chosen speaker. Although an active contender for governor in 1882, he failed to receive the Democratic nomination. In 1884 Dawson became president of the Alabama Bar Association, and in 1886 President Grover Cleveland appointed Dawson U.S. Commissioner of Education. Columbia University awarded him an honorary doctorate of letters in 1887. Dawson resigned as commissioner of education after the election of Republican Benjamin Harrison as president and returned to his Selma law practice. In 1892 he was elected again to the Alabama House of Representatives. He died in Selma on February 1, 1895.

William Edward Dorsheimer (1832–1888), lawyer, New York lieutenant governor, was born on February 5, 1832, in Lyons, New York, the son of Philip Dorsheimer and Sarah Gorgas (the older sister of Josiah Gorgas). Educated at Andover Academy and Harvard College, Dorsheimer was admitted to the bar in 1854 and practiced law in Buffalo, New York. During the Civil War he served on the staff of John C. Fremont in the summer of 1861 before returning to Buffalo to practice law. In 1867 President Andrew Johnson appointed him federal district attorney for southern New York, a post that he held until he resigned in 1871 to support the presidential efforts of Horace Greeley. He attended the Liberal Republican convention in 1872 and was elected lieutenant governor of New York in 1874 and 1876. In 1882 he was elected to the U.S. House of Representatives, where he served on the judiciary committee. An active supporter of Grover Cleveland, Dorsheimer was appointed again as federal district attorney for southern New York in 1885. He soon resigned to operate the New York *Star,* an unsuccessful newspaper venture. In ill health in 1887 he moved to Savannah, Georgia, where he died on March 26, 1888.

John Buchanan Floyd (1806–1863), Virginia governor, U.S. Secretary of War, was born in Smithfield, Virginia, on June 1, 1806. He graduated in 1829 from South Carolina College, where he was a classmate and friend of William Bones Crawford, later the husband of Sarah Ann Gayle. Floyd returned to Virginia to practice law in Wytheville and soon moved to Arkansas to practice law and plant cotton. Bankrupt and in poor health, Floyd returned to Virginia in 1837 to practice law in Abingdon and was able to pay off his debts in a few years. In 1847 he was elected to the House of Burgesses, where he served until elected governor in 1849. He served in that post for four years and was a Democratic presidential elector in 1852. President James Buchanan appointed him secretary of war in 1859. Floyd opposed secession but resigned his post in December 1860 and joined the Confederate Army. Assigned to Fort Donelson, he withdrew and left command of the fort to Simon B. Buckner. Thereafter, the Virginia legislature made him a major general. In ill health by 1863 Floyd died at his daughter's home in Abingdon, Virginia, on August 26, 1863.

Clarissa Stedman ("Ma" or "Clara") Peck Gayle (1815–1881), wife of Judge John Gayle, was born November 30, 1815, in Alabama. She received an excellent education for her time, studying two years in New York before she married John Gayle on November 1, 1837, at Gaston, Alabama. The Gayles settled at Toulminville near Mobile. Their children were Frederick Peck Gayle (1844–   ), Helen Eliza Gayle (1846–1919), John Marshall Gayle (1850–1895), and Edmund Dargan Gayle (1853–   ). After the death of her husband in 1859 Clarissa Gayle lived in Mobile. In 1865 she was living in Greensboro, Alabama, with her four children and her eldest stepson Matthew, who had suffered a nervous breakdown and thereafter made his home with her. She moved with the Gorgas family to Sewanee, Tennessee, in June 1870, and after the marriage of her daughter Helen in December 1871 she returned to live in Greensboro. She died December 22, 1881, in Greensboro, Alabama, and is buried in the Gayle plot in Magnolia Cemetery in Mobile.

John Gayle (1792–1859), U.S. Congressman, Alabama governor and jurist, was born September 11, 1792, in Sumter District, South Carolina. Educated at South Carolina College, he graduated in 1813 and came to Alabama, where he read law with Judge Abner S. Lipscomb at St. Stephens. He opened a law practice at Claiborne, Alabama, in 1818. He served in the Territorial Legislature in 1817, was solicitor of the First Judicial Circuit in Alabama, was elected to the Alabama Supreme Court in 1823 and the Alabama House of Representatives in 1829, where he was speaker. He served as Alabama governor, 1831–1835, and as a Whig presidential elector in 1836 and in 1840. After the expiration of his term as governor he returned to his law practice in Mobile. In 1847 he was elected to the U.S. House of Representatives and in 1849 was appointed judge of the U.S. District Court in Alabama. He continued as district judge until his death on July 21, 1859, in Mobile. He had only one eye and wore a glass eye so perfectly matched that few knew of his limited vision. He is buried in the Gayle plot in Magnolia Cemetery in Mobile. He married twice. He first married on November 14, 1819, near Claiborne, Alabama, Sarah Ann Haynsworth (1804–1835), the daughter of a prominent South Carolina family recently moved to Alabama. Their children were Matthew Gayle (1820–1875), an unnamed stillborn son (1822), Sarah Ann Gayle (1824–1895), Amelia Ross Gayle (1826–1913), Helen Louisa Gayle (1828), Mary Rees Gayle (1829–1910), Richard Haynsworth Gayle (1832–1873), and Anna Maria Gayle (1835–1879). After the death of Sarah Haynsworth Gayle in July 1835, Judge Gayle married Clarissa Stedman Peck (1815–1881) in Gaston, Alabama, on November 1, 1837. Their children were Frederick Peck Gayle (1844–   ), Helen Eliza Gayle (1846–1919), John Marshall Gayle (1850–1895), and Edmund Dargan Gayle (1853–   ).

Matthew Gayle (1820–1875), physician, was born December 24, 1820, in Claiborne, Alabama, the eldest child of Sarah Ann Haynsworth and John Gayle. He attended The University of Alabama, 1834–1836, and received the M.D. degree from the Jefferson Medical School in Philadelphia in 1842. He was a civilian contract physician at Mount Vernon Arsenal near Mobile from May 1844 to October 1845 and from December 1852 to April 1858. Appointed a first lieutenant and military storekeeper in the Confederate artillery on November 16, 1861, at the behest of his brother-in-law, Josiah Gorgas, Gayle was posted again to the Mount Vernon Arsenal. After the fall of New Orleans in 1862 the arsenal moved to Selma, although Gayle remained at the Mount Vernon Arsenal as late as the end of February 1863. He was in Selma during the federal attack on that city in April 1865, was captured, and was paroled in Demopolis on June 3, 1865. He signed his own parole and about that time suffered a nervous breakdown from which he never recovered. His stepmother, Clarissa Gayle, provided a home and care for him for the remainder of his life. He was totally dependent upon her and could not feed himself. His brothers-in-law, Josiah Gorgas and Thomas L. Bayne, gave money to Mrs. Gayle for his care. Matt Gayle died unmarried in Mount Vernon on July 10, 1875, and is buried in the Gayle plot in Magnolia Cemetery in Mobile.

Flora Levy Gayle (Courtesy of Hoole Special Collections, University of Alabama, Tuscaloosa, Alabama)

Richard Haynsworth ("Dick") Gayle (1832–1873), Confederate blockade runner, was born February 26, 1832, in Greensboro, Alabama, the fifth child and second son of Sarah Haynsworth and John Gayle. His childhood was spent in Mobile, Alabama. In 1851 he was appointed a midshipman at the U.S. Naval Academy. He returned to Mobile in 1853 to complete his education at Spring Hill College. From May through December 1856 he embarked on a trip on a steamer to South America, ultimately arriving in Peru. There he obtained command of a damaged vessel, the *Rodmond*. Gayle arranged for the repair of the ship, sailed around Cape Horn, and landed in Genoa, Italy. Next he sailed to Sicily, arriving in March 1857. He was again at sea from March 1857 to August 1858, when he traveled as a passenger from Boston to Buenos Aires. In April 1859 he became U.S. consul at Montevideo, Uruguay. During the first two years of the Civil War he was an independent blockade runner for the Confederacy. In 1863 he became a lieutenant in the Confederate Navy assigned to the blockade runner *Cornubia* at Bermuda. On November 9 the U.S. Navy captured the ship returning from Bermuda loaded with supplies. Imprisoned at Fort Warren near Boston, Richard corresponded regularly with Julia Gardiner Tyler, widow of President John Tyler, then residing in New York. One of Mrs. Tyler's stepdaughters lived near Montgomery, Alabama. Gayle was exchanged on October 20, 1864, and joined the Gorgas family in Richmond. In early December he was assigned to the *Stag* at Wilmington, North Carolina. Returning from Bermuda with arms and ammunition for the Confederacy, he was captured a second time on January 20, 1865, and again imprisoned at Fort Warren on February 7. He resumed his correspondence with Julia Tyler and was exchanged in June 1865. After the war he operated a sawmill near Mobile and in the late 1860s moved to New Orleans, Louisiana, where he married Flora Levy (1839–1889) on November 17, 1866. The couple had no children. His health was never strong after his wartime imprisonments, and he died in New Orleans on April 9, 1873. Funeral services were held at his residence at 6 St. Peter Street, Pontalba Building, New Orleans, on April 11. He is buried in the Gayle plot in Magnolia Cemetery, Mobile.

Amelia Ross ("Minnie") Gayle Gorgas (1826–1913), wife of Josiah Gorgas and University of Alabama librarian, was born on June 1, 1826, in Greensboro, Alabama, the third child and second daughter of Sarah Haynsworth and John Gayle. The family moved to Tuscaloosa in March 1833, while Gayle served as Alabama governor. Here her mother's closest friend was Mrs. Alva Woods, wife of the president of The University of Alabama. When Amelia was almost seven, she was caught riding a pony into the halls of the state capitol. Her mother characterized Amelia as being of very different temperament from her older sister Sarah. Returning from a walk, Sarah moved slowly with a feeling of joy and hid her face when her mother kissed her. Amelia was wild, running to her mother and throwing herself into her mother's arms. Tragically, Amelia's mother died suddenly on July 30, 1835, of lockjaw following a tooth extraction, leaving six children ranging in age from fourteen years to five months. The Gayle children were separated into the care of friends and relatives, and Amelia remained in Tuscaloosa to live with Mrs. Alva Woods for two years after John Gayle moved to Mobile a few months after the death of his wife. In 1837 Dr. Woods resigned the presidency of The University of Alabama and moved to Rhode Island, and John Gayle remarried, now to Clarissa Stedman Peck of Greensboro on November 1, 1837. The Gayles settled at Toulminville near Mobile and reunited the scattered Gayle children. Gayle practiced law in Mobile, and his wife endeared herself to her six stepchildren. In 1841 Amelia was sent to Columbia Female Institute in Columbia, Tennessee, for one year. When John Gayle was elected to the U.S. House of Representatives in 1847, the family decided that Clarissa Gayle would remain in Mobile with their children and that Amelia would accompany her father to Washington. There father and daughter took rooms at a boarding house also occupied by John C. Calhoun of South Carolina and his family. Apparently, Calhoun doted on Amelia and treated her like a daughter, and the two regularly took early morning walks. In 1848 Calhoun invited Amelia to sit on the platform to witness the laying of the cornerstone of the Washington Monument. At the end of the summer Amelia and John Gayle

Amelia Ross Gayle Gorgas and William Crawford Gorgas, Tuscaloosa,
circa 1908 (Courtesy of Hoole Special Collections, University of Alabama,
Tuscaloosa, Alabama)

returned to Mobile, Amelia traveling as far as Richmond with Secretary of Navy John Y. Mason. Amelia discussed with Mason her brother Dick's hopes of an appointment to Annapolis, and subsequently Mason wrote to her that arrangements had been made for Dick to be examined for admission to the academy. When John Gayle returned to Washington in 1848, Amelia remained at home because he could not afford to bring her with him. In Mobile Amelia was a favorite of the children of relatives, and in early 1849 she assumed full responsibility for the three children of her sister, Sarah, while Sarah and her husband traveled, hoping to improve his failing health. In early 1853 Amelia visited in New York and in Providence, Rhode Island, where she saw Dr. and Mrs. Alva Woods. When she returned to Mobile, she found the family distraught over Dr. Crawford's worsening health. The Crawfords left on another extended trip, leaving their children with Amelia. Yellow fever struck Mobile by midsummer 1853, and Amelia moved the children to the healthy high ground of the Mount Vernon Arsenal north of Mobile, where her brother Matt was post surgeon. Matt's quarters were next door to those of the arsenal's commander, Josiah Gorgas. Daily, Amelia read to the children on Matt's porch, and Josiah always maintained that he fell in love with Amelia's voice before he met her. Amelia and Josiah were married at Christ Episcopal Church in Mobile on December 29, 1853, a week after her sister Maria had married Thomas Levingston Bayne of New Orleans. Josiah's army assignments took them to Kennebec Arsenal in Augusta, Maine (1856–1858), Charleston Arsenal in Charleston, South Carolina (1858–1860), and Frankford Arsenal near Philadelphia (1860–1861). Josiah resigned from the U.S. Army in March 1861, accepted a commission in the Confederate Army in April, and moved the family back to Charleston, South Carolina. The family rejoined him in October 1861 in Richmond, Virginia, where they lived at the Virginia State Armory during most of the Civil War until the city's evacuation in April 1865. The Gorgas children were William Crawford ("Willie") Gorgas (1854–1920), Jessie Gorgas (1856–1925), Mary Gayle ("Mamie") Gorgas (1857–1944), Christine Amelia ("Minnie") Gorgas (1859–1953), Maria Bayne ("Ria") Gorgas (1861–1953), and Richard Haynsworth ("Richie") Gorgas (1864–1935). After the war Amelia and the children lived in Cambridge, Maryland, for a year until Josiah moved them in 1866 to Brierfield, Alabama, where he operated an ironworks. The family moved again in June 1870, this time to Sewanee, Tennessee, where Josiah was vice-chancellor of The University of the South. In July 1878 Josiah left Sewanee to become president of The University of Alabama in Tuscaloosa. Amelia and the family remained at Sewanee until late December 1878, when they moved to Tuscaloosa. Josiah suffered a severe stroke in February 1879, and he resigned as university president in September of that year. The trustees appointed Josiah librarian, a position that Amelia and her older daughters could ghost for Josiah. By this time the eldest son was in medical school in New York, while the other five children remained at home. Josiah never fully recovered, and he died on May 15, 1883. Amelia then became university librarian in name as well as fact. In March 1886 Amelia added the position of university postmistress to her other duties. At commencement exercises in 1905 university alumni presented her with a silver loving cup, and she permitted her photograph to be taken on one of the rare occasions of her life. In January 1907 she retired from her duties at the university at the age of eighty. She continued to live in the Gorgas home on the campus of The University of Alabama until her death on January 3, 1913. Her funeral was held in the auditorium in Morgan Hall next door to the Gorgas home, and she is buried in the Gorgas plot in Evergreen Cemetery in Tuscaloosa.

Jessie Gorgas (1856–1925), the second child and first daughter of Amelia Gayle and Josiah Gorgas, was born March 17, 1856, at Mount Vernon, Alabama. A few months later the family moved to Kennebec Arsenal in Augusta, Maine, where her father was assigned for two years before being sent to Charleston, South Carolina, in the summer of 1858. In July 1860 Gorgas was assigned to Frankford Arsenal near Philadelphia, Pennsylvania. In March 1861 Gorgas resigned from the U.S. Army, moved his family back to Charleston, South Carolina, and accepted a commission in the Confederate Army. His family rejoined him in October 1861 in Richmond, Virginia. When the federal army threatened the city in 1862, the family refugeed south, and Jessie went with Amelia to Greensboro, North Carolina. The family was reunited in Richmond later that year and remained there for the duration of the Civil War. After the war Amelia and the children lived in Cambridge, Maryland, for a year until Gorgas moved them in 1866 to Brierfield, Alabama, where he operated an ironworks. The family moved again in June 1870, this time to Sewanee, Tennessee, where Gorgas was vice-chancellor of The University of the South. In September 1871 Jessie and her younger sister Mary were sent to the same boarding school in Columbia, Tennessee, that their mother had attended as a young girl. In 1873 the girls were enrolled in a new school at Monteagle near Sewanee. As a young woman Jessie steadily assumed increasing responsibilities within the Gorgas household. By spring 1878 she was operating a little school at Sewanee and at home maintained a garden and assisted with housekeeping. When Gorgas became president of The University of Alabama, the family moved to Tuscaloosa, Alabama, in the fall of 1878. Now at age twenty-two Jessie was described as shy, retiring, and the most practical member of the family. After Gorgas suffered a severe stroke in 1879, Jessie became the family's business manager, a role she continued after the death of her father in 1883. She lived at home and never married. After several years of fragile health, she died on September 13, 1925, in the Gorgas home in Tuscaloosa and is buried in the Gorgas plot in Evergreen Cemetery in Tuscaloosa.

Maria Bayne ("Ria") Gorgas (1861–1953), the fifth child and fourth daughter of Amelia Gayle and Josiah Gorgas, was born August 4, 1861, in Charleston, South Carolina. A Confederate officer, Gorgas moved his family to join him in October 1861 in Richmond, Virginia. When the federal army threatened the city in 1862, the family refugeed south, and Ria went with Amelia to Greensboro, North Carolina. The family was reunited in Richmond later that year and remained there for the duration of the Civil War. After the war Amelia and the children lived in Cambridge, Maryland, for a year until Gorgas moved them in 1866 to Brierfield, Alabama, where he operated an ironworks. The family moved again in June 1870, this time to Sewanee, Tennessee, where Gorgas was vice-chancellor of The University of the South. By 1878 Ria was attending boarding school, and in 1880 she was studying in Cincinnati. By 1886 Ria was teaching at Fairmount Female College, Monteagle, Tennessee. In 1889 she abandoned her teaching career, moved to New York, and entered nursing school. After graduation she remained in New York to care for Amelia Lyon, a daughter of Francis Strother Lyon, one of Josiah's friends and business partners. Her next position was that of nurse-companion to Mary Leroy King, daughter of Mrs. Edward King of Newport, Rhode Island. A semi-invalid whose doctors recommended European travel to improve her health, Miss King toured health spas with her mother and her nurse. Ria lived in an exciting world of wealth and privilege during those years. She remained with Miss King until her death in 1904. On one visit to Tuscaloosa during those years she helped to plan a program of study for the care of the mentally ill for the nurses at Bryce Hospital (Alabama Insane Hospital) in Tuscaloosa. She never married, and by 1906 she had retired to live in the Gorgas home in Tuscaloosa. There she died on June 11, 1953, and is buried in the Gorgas plot in Evergreen Cemetery in Tuscaloosa.

Mary Gayle ("Mamie") Gorgas (1857–1944), the third child and second daughter of Amelia Gayle and Josiah Gorgas, was born October 28, 1857, at Augusta, Maine. The family moved to Charleston, South Carolina, in the summer of 1858. In July 1860 Gorgas was assigned to Frankford Arsenal near Philadelphia, Pennsylvania. In March 1861 he resigned from the U.S. Army, moved his family to Charleston, South Carolina, and accepted a commission in the Confederate Army. His family rejoined him in October 1861 in Richmond, Virginia. When the federal army threatened the city in 1862, the family refugeed south, and Mamie went with Amelia to Greensboro, North Carolina. The family was reunited in Richmond later that year and remained there for the duration of the Civil War. After the war Amelia and the children lived in Cambridge, Maryland, for a year until Gorgas moved them in 1866 to Brierfield, Alabama, where he operated an ironworks. The family moved again in June 1870, this time to Sewanee, Tennessee, where Gorgas was vice-chancellor of The University of the South. In September 1871 Mamie and her older sister Jessie were sent to the same boarding school in Columbia, Tennessee, that their mother had attended. In 1873 the girls were enrolled in a new school at Monteagle near Sewanee. In 1877 Mamie lived for several months with the Baynes in New Orleans. As Josiah's health declined by 1878, Amelia relied increasingly on her daughters to run the Gorgas household. She described Mamie as assisting her greatly as a successful seamstress and housekeeper. By 1880 Mamie had taken a teaching position in Talladega, Alabama, and by 1886 she had returned home to assist her mother in The University of Alabama library. After Amelia retired as university librarian in 1906, Mamie continued on the library staff as assistant librarian. She never married. She lived in the Gorgas home until her death, December 27, 1944, and is buried in the Gorgas plot in Evergreen Cemetery in Tuscaloosa.

Richard Haynsworth Gorgas, 1878 (Courtesy of Hoole Special Collections, University of Alabama, Tuscaloosa, Alabama)

Richard Haynsworth ("Richie") Gorgas (1864–1935), the sixth child and second son of Amelia Gayle and Josiah Gorgas, was born in Richmond, Virginia, November 3, 1864. At the end of the Civil War in 1865 the family moved to Cambridge, Maryland, for a year and then to Brierfield, Alabama, where his father operated an ironworks. From 1870 to 1878 the family lived at Sewanee, Tennessee, where his father was vicechancellor of The University of the South. There Richard attended the Sewanee grammar school. When Gorgas became president of The University of Alabama in 1878, Richard joined his father in November 1878 in Tuscaloosa, Alabama, where he attended Verner Academy. Others in the family followed a month later. He received the A.B. degree in 1884 from The University of Alabama. After briefly studying medicine he turned to law, receiving the LL.B. degree in 1890 from The University of Alabama and then practicing law in Florence, Alabama. From 1886 to 1889 he was a clerk in the U.S. Bureau of Education in Washington while his father's friend, N. H. R. Dawson of Selma, Alabama, was U.S. Commissioner of Education. (As a University of Alabama trustee Dawson had been instrumental in the selection of Josiah Gorgas as university president.) In 1901 Richard was a clerk in the Engineering Department in Montgomery, Alabama. During World War I he volunteered for service and was commissioned a captain in the Sanitary Corps stationed at Camp McClellan near Anniston, Alabama. After the war he returned to Washington as an assistant attorney with the Veterans Bureau. He continued in government service from 1918 until he retired in 1931 to live in Tuscaloosa in the Gorgas home with his sisters, Mary and Maria Gorgas. He never married, and one family member recalled that he was deeply in love with his cousin, Minna Bayne, one of the daughters of Maria and T. L. Bayne. After a lengthy illness he entered a Birmingham hospital on September 22, underwent a major operation on September 28, and died on September 29, 1935. He is buried in the Gorgas plot in Evergreen Cemetery, Tuscaloosa.

William Crawford ("Willie") Gorgas (1854–1920), sanitarian and surgeon general of the U.S. Army, was born on October 3, 1854, at Toulminville near Mobile, Alabama, the eldest child of Amelia Gayle and Josiah Gorgas. His father was a career officer in the U.S. Army, and the family moved from post to post as assignments changed: Kennebec Arsenal in Augusta, Maine (1856–1858), Charleston Arsenal in Charleston, South Carolina (1858–1860), Frankford Arsenal near Philadelphia (1860–1861). In March 1861 Josiah resigned from the U.S. Army, moved the family back to Charleston, South Carolina, and accepted a commission in the Confederate Army. The family rejoined him in October 1861 in Richmond, Virginia, where they lived in the Virginia State Armory. In 1862 when the federal army threatened Richmond, the family refugeed south, and William Crawford went to live with the Aikens in Winnsboro, South Carolina. The family was reunited in Richmond later that year and remained there until the city's evacuation in April 1865. After the war Amelia and the children lived in Cambridge, Maryland, for a year until Josiah moved them in 1866 to Brierfield, Alabama, where he operated an ironworks. The family moved again in June 1870, this time to Sewanee, Tennessee, where Josiah was vice-chancellor of The University of the South. William Crawford's education was irregular until the move to Sewanee, where he graduated from The University of the South in 1875. For a year he worked in the law office of his uncle, T. L. Bayne, in New Orleans, although he hoped to pursue a military career like that of his father. Leaving New Orleans for personal reasons and unable to get into West Point, he entered Bellevue Hospital Medical College in New York in 1876. Despite financial difficulties, he graduated in 1879, spent a year's internship at Bellevue Hospital, and was appointed to the Medical Corps of the U.S. Army in June 1880. His tours of duty took him to army posts in Texas, North Dakota, and Florida. While serving at Fort Brown, Texas, he contracted yellow fever in 1882 and recovered after having a mild case. During the epidemic he met Marie Doughty (1864–1929) of Cincinnati who fell victim to the

William Crawford Gorgas, 1883 (Courtesy of Hoole Special Collections, University of Alabama, Tuscaloosa, Alabama)

disease while visiting her sister at the fort. The pair remained in touch after she returned home, and in the summer of 1884 Marie visited Tuscaloosa. The couple were married in September 1885 in Cincinnati and came to Tuscaloosa after their wedding. They had one child, Aileen Lyster Gorgas (1889–   ). During the Spanish-American War he was appointed chief sanitary officer of Havana, and his success in controlling yellow fever in Cuba by eliminating the breeding places of the *Aedes aegypti* mosquito brought him an international reputation. Gorgas was stationed in Washington, D.C., 1902–1904, and promoted to colonel. In June 1904 he was assigned to the Panama Canal Zone, where his efforts to improve sanitation received support after an outbreak of yellow fever struck in November 1904. Progress in Panama was slow, and efforts were made to discredit Gorgas's work and to replace him. The endorsement of President Theodore Roosevelt saved Gorgas, who became a member of the canal commission. For two years Gorgas had virtually a free hand until the arrival in 1908 of Colonel George W. Goethals as commission chairman and chief engineer. Goethals ruled the canal project with an iron hand, undermined sanitation efforts, and treated Gorgas with contempt. Nevertheless, Gorgas succeeded in ridding the Canal Zone of yellow fever and making the cities of Colon and Panama into models of good health. He was the only associate of the canal project to remain with the project throughout American involvement. In 1913 he traveled to South Africa to advise on the control of pneumonia among black miners. In January 1914 he was appointed surgeon general of the U.S. Army and promoted to brigadier general. He returned to the United States in April 1914, assumed his new post, and was promoted to major general in 1915. In 1916 the International Health Board enlisted him to tour Central and South America to advise on control of yellow fever. During World War I he headed the medical service of the army until the armistice; on his retirement from service in 1918 he returned to public health work. In 1920 the International Health Board asked him to investigate yellow fever on the west coast of Africa. He and his staff went to London and on to a meeting of the International Hygiene Congress in Brussels. Returning to London, he suffered a severe stroke on May 30 and was taken to Queen Alexandria Military Hospital, Millbank. While Gorgas lay ill, King George V came to the hospital to present him the insignia of the Order of St. Michael and St. George. Gorgas died on July 4, 1920. An elaborate funeral was held in St. Paul's Cathedral in London, and the body was returned to the United States for a funeral at the Church of the Epiphany in Washington, D.C., on August 6. He is buried in Arlington National Cemetery.

Anne ("Nana") Kavanaugh (–1882), Irish housekeeper in the Gorgas family, was born in Newry, Ireland. She came to the United States to marry her sweetheart who was working in Maine but found that he had died before she arrived. On the recommendation of a Roman Catholic priest the Gorgas family, then living in Augusta, Maine, hired her as a nurse for their children, who became deeply attached to her. In April 1858 Anne left the family to join her brother in Portland, Maine, a separation that distressed the Gorgas children. Josiah Gorgas went ahead to his assignment in Charleston, South Carolina, to prepare a home for the family while Amelia and their eldest son recovered from typhoid fever. In June Anne visited Amelia and the children in Augusta before they left for Charleston, and before the family left Maine, Anne agreed to return to the family on a more or less permanent basis. She remained with the Gorgases for the rest of her life, considered as a family member as one would an unmarried aunt who made her home with them. She accompanied Amelia and the children to Richmond, Virginia, in 1861, refugeed to Greensboro, North Carolina, in 1862, and returned to Richmond for the duration of the Civil War. In 1865 she accompanied Amelia Gorgas and Maria Bayne when they settled in Maryland. She moved with the Gorgases in April 1866 to their home at Brierfield, Alabama, in 1870 to Sewanee, Tennessee, and in 1878 to Tuscaloosa, Alabama. Thereafter, her health grew increasingly fragile as she suffered from consumption. On December 29, 1881, escorted by William Crawford Gorgas, she attended the wedding of Christine Amelia "Minnie" Gorgas to George Palfrey of St. Mary's Parish, Louisiana. A few months later she died quietly on February 22, 1882, at the Gorgas home in Tuscaloosa and is buried in the Gorgas plot in Evergreen Cemetery in Tuscaloosa.

Francis Strother Lyon (1800–1882), representative from Alabama to the First and Second Confederate Congress, was born on February 25, 1800, in Danbury, North Carolina. He attended school in North Carolina, before moving to St. Stephens, Alabama, near Mobile. After employment in a bank and then in the office of the clerk of the county court, he read law at St. Stephens with Abner S. Lipscomb. Three years earlier John Gayle also had read law under Lipscomb. Lyon was admitted to the bar in 1821 and opened a law practice in Demopolis. He served as secretary of the Alabama Senate, 1822–1830. In 1833 he was elected to the state Senate and in 1834 was chosen Senate president while John Gayle was governor of Alabama. A Whig, he served in the U.S. House of Representatives, 1835–1839. A secessionist, he was chairman of the 1860 state Democratic convention and was a delegate to the 1860 national Democratic convention, where he walked out with William L. Yancey. In 1861 he served in the Alabama House of Representatives and although elected to the Provisional Confederate Congress declined to serve. Elected to the First and Second Confederate House of Representatives, he served until the end of the war. He supported President Jefferson Davis and served on the Ways and Means, Currency, War Tax, and other committees. Lyon invested heavily in the Confederacy, and the war destroyed him financially. During Reconstruction he joined Josiah Gorgas in the unsuccessful Brierfield Iron Works near Montevallo. A delegate to the 1875 Alabama Constitutional Convention, he was elected to the Alabama Senate in 1876. Lyon died in retirement on December 31, 1882, in Demopolis, Alabama. He married Sarah Serena Glover on March 4, 1824, in Demopolis. Their children were Mary Amanda Lyon (married William H. Ross, Mobile merchant), Sarah Norwood Lyon, Helen Gaines Lyon (married General Zachariah C. Deas, C.S.A.), Amelia Lyon, Eugenia Lyon, Frank Glover Lyon, and Ida Lyon (married Dr. William M. Polk, son of General Leonidas Polk, C.S.A., and friend of William Crawford Gorgas). Lyon's niece was Mary Henry Lyon (Mrs. James Alfred Jones), close friend of Amelia Gorgas in Richmond during the Civil War and godmother to Richard Haynsworth Gorgas.

John William Mallet (1832–1912), professor of chemistry, was born on October 10, 1832, in Dublin, Ireland. He received the A.B. degree from Trinity College, Dublin, in 1853 and the Ph.D. from the University of Gottingen in 1852. He came to the United States in 1853, taught chemistry at Amherst College, Massachusetts, in 1854, was chemist to the geological survey of Alabama, 1855–1856, and professor of chemistry at The University of Alabama, 1855–1860. In 1861 he served on the staff of Confederate General R. E. Rodes until he transferred to the artillery in 1862. Thereafter, he was given responsibility for the Confederate ordnance laboratories and left the army at the end of the war as a lieutenant colonel. In May 1866 he joined Josiah Gorgas at the Brierfield Iron Works before returning to the academic world to teach chemistry at the University of Virginia, 1868–1883. In 1883–1884 he was professor of chemistry and physics and chairman of the faculty at the University of Texas and in 1884–1885 professor of chemistry at the Jefferson Medical College in Philadelphia. In 1885 he returned to the University of Virginia and remained until 1908. Widely honored as a leader in the sciences, Mallet received numerous awards and honorary degrees during his academic career. Mallet is one of many scientists associated with the Confederate Ordnance Department who became the next generation's chemistry and physics professors at southern colleges and universities. He married Mary E. Ormond of Tuscaloosa in 1857 and after her death Josephine Burthe of New Orleans in 1888. He died in Charlottesville, Virginia, on November 6, 1912.

Christine Amelia ("Minnie") Gorgas Palfrey (1859–1953), the fourth child and third daughter of Amelia Gayle and Josiah Gorgas, was born June 4, 1859, in Charleston, South Carolina. In July 1860 Gorgas was assigned to Frankford Arsenal near Philadelphia, Pennsylvania. In March 1861 Gorgas resigned from the U.S. Army, moved his family back to Charleston, South Carolina, and accepted a commission in the Confederate Army. His family rejoined him in October 1861 in Richmond, Virginia. When the U.S. Army threatened the city in 1862, the family refugeed south, and Minnie went with Amelia to Greensboro, North Carolina. The family was reunited in Richmond later that year and remained there for the duration of the Civil War. At the age of five Minnie was honored when a steamboat on the James River Canal was named for her. Apparently, Amelia did not consider Minnie to be as attractive as the other Gorgas children, for she described the child in 1864 as "poor little Minnie [whom] they say inherits my appearance as well as name." After the war Amelia and the children lived in Cambridge, Maryland, for a year until Gorgas moved them in 1866 to Brierfield, Alabama, where he operated an ironworks. The family moved again in June 1870, this time to Sewanee, Tennessee, where Gorgas was vice-chancellor of The University of the South. In 1872 Minnie enjoyed a winter season with the Thomas L. Bayne family in New Orleans. Minnie returned to New Orleans in 1877 for the wedding of Mamie, the eldest child of the Baynes, to George Behn of New Orleans. Minnie remained for the winter social season and became reacquainted with George deClouet Palfrey of St. Mary's Parish, Louisiana, a friend of Sewanee years. On December 29, 1881, Minnie married George Palfrey (1858–1930) on the twenty-eighth anniversary of her parents' wedding. The Palfreys lived in Franklin, Louisiana. Their children were Jessie Gorgas Palfrey (1883–1971), William Taylor Palfrey (1885–1957), and Amelia Gayle ("Minnie") Palfrey (1888–1971). George Palfrey died in 1930. In 1947 Minnie Palfrey returned to Tuscaloosa to live with her sister, Ria, in the Gorgas home in Tuscaloosa. Minnie died on February 3, 1953, and is buried with her husband in the Gorgas family plot in Evergreen Cemetery in Tuscaloosa.

George Wythe Randolph (1818–1867), attorney, Confederate Secretary of War, was born on March 10, 1818, at Monticello, the home of his grandfather, Thomas Jefferson. After his grandfather's death he went to live with a relative in Boston, Massachusetts, where he was educated. At the age of thirteen he was appointed a midshipman in the U.S. Navy and was at sea for the next six years. He entered the University of Virginia at the age of nineteen and remained two years. He then resigned from the navy to study law. He practiced law briefly in Albemarle County before moving in 1850 to Richmond, Virginia, where he developed a successful practice. He was said to read a Latin or Greek author before breakfast every morning. About 1852 he married a young widow, Mary E. Adams Pope. During Mrs. Randolph's first marriage she had resided in Mobile. In 1861 Randolph was one of the peace commissioners from Virginia to the U.S. government. A secessionist, he was elected to the Virginia convention. He was an early advocate of a stringent conscription law. He joined the Confederate Army and was promoted to brigadier general. On March 22, 1862, he was appointed Confederate Secretary of War, a position that took a great toll on his health. He resigned on November 15, 1862, applied for a field position, but soon resigned. By this time he was suffering with tuberculosis and went to France for his health. He returned to Virginia after the war as his health continued to fail, and he died on April 3, 1867, at Edgehill, a family estate.

Bibliography

Manuscript Sources

Alabama Department of Archives and History, Montgomery, Alabama

Compiled Service Records of Richard H. Gayle: career summaries
Sydenham Moore Papers: letters of Sarah Haynsworth Gayle (1833–1834)
Daniel J. Prout Papers: Brierfield correspondence

Cemetery Records

Evergreen Cemetery, Tuscaloosa, Alabama, Gorgas Lot; Magnolia Cemetery, Mobile, Alabama, John Gayle Lot; Metairie Cemetery, Metairie, Louisiana, Aiken-Holcombe Lot; birth and death records for four generations of Gayle, Gorgas, Bayne, Aiken families

Hoole Special Collections Library, The University of Alabama, Tuscaloosa, Alabama

Brierfield Ironworks Papers: ledgers and business correspondence of Brierfield Ironworks (1864–1897)
Sarah Gayle and William B. Crawford Papers: Sarah Gayle Crawford scrapbooks and photograph albums; Sarah Gayle Crawford journal (1839–1840, 1849, 1853–1854); William B. Crawford journal (1833); correspondence of Gayle and Crawford families (1842–1978); portraits of Sarah Gayle and William B. Crawford
Gorgas Family Papers: correspondence of Gayle and Gorgas families (1810–1953); Josiah Gorgas European travel journal (1845–1846); Josiah Gorgas Mexican War journal (1846); original and three typescript copies of Josiah Gorgas journal (1857–1878); Josiah Gorgas daybook (1877–1878); Josiah Gorgas account books (1857–1875); Gorgas, Gayle, Bayne, Aiken

family photograph albums; original and two typescript copies of Sarah Haynsworth Gayle journal (1827–1835); typescript copy of Solomon A. Gorgas
journal (1876–1888); Gayle and Gorgas family Bibles; Josiah Gorgas sketchbook and watercolor paintings; Richard Haynsworth Gayle journal
(1856–1865)
William Crawford Gorgas Papers: correspondence of Gorgas and Gayle families
(1880–1920); W. C. Gorgas account books and appointment calendar
(1877–1879, 1910–1919)

Manuscript Department, Perkins Library, Duke University, Durham, North Carolina

Sarah Gayle Crawford Papers: correspondence of Sarah Gayle Crawford
(1835–1895); William B. Crawford journal (1832–1833)

Manuscript Division, Library of Congress, Washington, D.C.

William Crawford Gorgas Papers: correspondence of Gayle and Gorgas families
(1880–1920); W. C. Gorgas account books and appointment calendar
(1880–1910), 1899–1910 volume contains commentary by W. C. Gorgas;
typescript copy of Josiah Gorgas journal (1857–1878); watercolor painting by
Josiah Gorgas; photographs associated with construction of Panama Canal;
W. C. Gorgas speeches, articles, pamphlets

National Archives, Washington, D.C.

Compiled Service Record of John L. Hardee, E193, General and Staff Officers
Papers, RG109: correspondence (1861)
Compiled Service Record of Matt Gayle, E193, General and Staff Officers Papers,
RG109: correspondence, time cards (1861–1865)
Compiled Service Record of Richard H. Gayle, E193, General and Staff Officers
Papers, RG109: correspondence (1862)
Summary Data Cards relating to posts and stations of medical officers, Office of
the Surgeon General (Army), RG112: assignment list for Mount Vernon Arse-
nal (1829–1860)

National Library of Medicine, National Institutes of Health, Bethesda, Maryland

Stanhope Bayne-Jones Papers: typescript copy of Thomas L. Bayne Autobiography (1870) contains information on Bayne, Gayle, Gorgas families for three
generations; correspondence and photographs of Bayne and Gorgas families
(1899–1918); W. C. Gorgas speeches, articles, pamphlets

South Caroliniana Library, University of South Carolina, Columbia, South Carolina

Aiken Family Papers: Mary Gayle Aiken day calendar (1865, 1874–1888)

Southern Historical Collection, University of North Carolina, Chapel Hill, North Carolina

Bayne-Gayle Papers: correspondence of Bayne, Gayle, Gorgas families (1821–1880); microfilm of typescript of Solomon Gorgas journal (1850–1851); microfilm of handwritten and typed copies of parts of Sarah Haynsworth Gayle journal (1827–1835); microfilm of typescript copy of Hugh A. Bayne memoirs (1917–1940), includes family information for three older generations; genealogical charts of Gayle, Gorgas, Aiken, Bayne families

Gayle and Crawford Papers: microfilm copy of Sarah Gayle Crawford journal (1839–1840, 1849, 1853–1854), and William B. Crawford journal (1852)

Special Collections, Tulane University Library, New Orleans, Louisiana

Thomas Bayne Denègre Papers: correspondence and photographs of Bayne family (1893–1967); typescript copy of Sarah Haynsworth Gayle journal (1828–1835)

Stanhope Bayne-Jones Papers: correspondence of Bayne family (1914–1930); preliminary work toward biography of Dr. Joseph Jones

University of the South Archives, The University of the South, Sewanee, Tennessee

Robert Dabney Papers: correspondence related to University of the South (1868)

George R. Fairbanks Papers: correspondence related to University of the South (1869–1888)

Josiah Gorgas Papers: correspondence of Mary Gayle Aiken (1878) and Josiah Gorgas (1869–1881)

C. T. Quintard Papers: correspondence related to University of the South (1869–1875)

Printed Sources

Acts of the Session of 1866–67, of the General Assembly of Alabama. Montgomery: Reid and Screws, 1867.

Adams, George Worthington. *Doctors in Blue: The Medical History of the Union Army in the Civil War.* New York: Henry Schuman, 1952.

Alexander, Edward Porter. *Fighting for the Confederacy: The Personal Recollections of General Edward Porter Alexander,* ed. by Gary W. Gallagher. Chapel Hill and London: University of North Carolina Press, 1989.

Amos, Harriet E. "Religious Reconstruction in Microcosm at Faunsdale Plantation." *Alabama Review,* XLIII (October 1989), 243–69.

Armes, Ethel. *The Story of Coal and Iron in Alabama.* 1910, reprint ed., Leeds, Ala.: Beechwood Books, 1987.

Arnet, Ethel Stephens. *Greensboro North Carolina: The County Seat of Guilford.* Chapel Hill: University of North Carolina Press, 1955.

Baldwin, Thomas, and J. Thomas. *A New and Complete Gazetteer of the United States; Giving a Full and Comprehensive Review of the Present Condition,*

Industry, and Resources of the American Confederacy; . . . . Philadelphia: Lippincott, Grambo & Co., 1854.

Biographical and Historical Memoirs of Louisiana . . . . 2 vols., Chicago: Goodspeed Publishing Co., 1892.

Boatner, Mark M. III. *The Civil War Dictionary.* New York: David McKay Co., 1959.

Bridges, Hal. *Lee's Maverick General: Daniel Harvey Hill.* 1961, reprint ed., Lincoln and London: University of Nebraska Press, 1991.

Buel, Clarence C., and Robert U. Johnson, eds. *Battles and Leaders of the Civil War.* 4 vols., New York: American Heritage Publishing Co., 1888.

Charleston [S.C.] *Mercury,* 1859.

The Church Almanac For the Year of Our Lord 1859. New York: Protestant Episcopal Tract Society, 1859.

Connelly, Owen, ed. *Historical Dictionary of Napoleonic France, 1799–1815.* Westport, Conn.: Greenwood Press, 1985.

Cook, James F. "The 1863 Raid of Abel D. Streight: Why It Failed." *Alabama Review,* XXII (October 1969), 254–69.

Cote, Richard N., ed. *Dictionary of South Carolina Biography.* Easley, S.C.: Southern Historical Press, 1985.

Cunningham, H. H. *Doctors in Gray: The Confederate Medical Service.* Baton Rouge: Louisiana State University Press, 1958.

Durkin, Joseph T. *Stephen R. Mallory: Confederate Navy Chief.* Chapel Hill: University of North Carolina Press, 1954.

Dyer, John P. *The Gallant Hood.* Indianapolis and New York: Bobbs-Merrill Co., 1950.

Echard, William E., ed. *Historical Dictionary of the French Second Empire, 1852–1870.* Westport, Conn.: Greenwood Press, 1985.

Fairbanks, George R. *History of the University of the South.* Jacksonville, Fla.: H. & W. B. Drew Co., 1905.

Faust, Patricia L., ed. *Historical Times Illustrated Encyclopedia of the Civil War.* New York: Harper and Row, 1986.

Fitzgerald, Michael W. *The Union League Movement in the Deep South: Politics and Agricultural Change During Reconstruction.* Baton Rouge and London: Louisiana State University Press, 1989.

Fleming, Walter L. *Civil War and Reconstruction in Alabama.* New York: Columbia University Press, 1905.

Foner, Eric. *Reconstruction: 1863–1877.* New York: Harper & Row, 1988.

Foote, Shelby. *The Civil War: A Narrative.* 3 vols., New York: Random House, 1958, 1963, 1974.

Foscue, Virginia O. *Place Names in Alabama.* Tuscaloosa: University of Alabama Press, 1989.

Furniss, Norman F. *The Mormon Conflict, 1850–1859.* New Haven: Yale University Press, 1960.

Gardner, Charles, comp. *Gardner's New Orleans Directory for 1861,* . . . . New Orleans: Charles Gardner, 1861.

Gates, John D. *The Astor Family.* Garden City, N.Y.: Doubleday, 1981.

Gibson, John M. *Physician to the World: The Life of General William C. Gorgas.* 1950, reprint ed., Tuscaloosa: University of Alabama Press, 1989.

Gorgas, Mary Gayle. "Captain Richard H. Gayle." *Tyler's Quarterly Historical and Genealogical Magazine*, XXX (January 1949), 206–07.

Gorgas, Josiah, and John Hillhouse. "Epistolary Gossipings of Travel, and Its Reminiscences." *Russell's Magazine*, V, VI (Charleston, 1859–1860).

Hamersly, Thomas H. S., comp. *Complete Army and Navy Register of the United States of America, From 1776 to 1887*. New York: T. H. S. Hamersly Publishers, 1888.

Hancock, J. M., and J. E. Baker, comp. *Charleston City Directory, 1875–6*. Charleston, S.C.: Walker, Evans & Cogswell, 1875.

Hardy, John. *Selma: Her Institutions and Her Men*. 1879, reprint ed., Selma: Bert Neville and Clarence DeBray, 1957.

Harris, W. Stuart. *Alabama Place-Names*. Huntsville, Ala.: Strode Publishers, 1982.

Henry, Robert Selph. *"First With the Most" Forrest*. Indianapolis and New York: Bobbs-Merrill, 1944.

Holland, Cecil Fletcher. *Morgan and His Raiders: A Biography of the Confederate General*. New York: Macmillan, 1942.

Hoole, W. Stanley. "Captain Richard H. Gayle of Alabama and the Voyage of the *Rodmond*, 1856." *American Neptune*, II (January 1951), 42–58.

Jackson, Walter M. *The Story of Selma*. Birmingham: Birmingham Printing Co., 1954.

Johnson, Bradley T., ed. *A Memoir of the Life and Public Service of Joseph E. Johnston, ...* Baltimore: R. H. Woodward & Co., 1891.

Johnston, Mary Tabb. *Amelia Gayle Gorgas: A Biography*. University, Ala.: University of Alabama Press, 1978.

Jordan, David M. *Winfield Scott Hancock: A Soldier's Life*. Bloomington and Indianapolis: Indiana University Press, 1988.

Journal of the Proceedings of the Sixty-Seventh Annual Convention of the Protestant Episcopal Church in South Carolina, Held in St. Philip's Church, Charleston, On the 13th, 14th and 15th of February, 1856 . . . . Charleston, S.C.: A. E. Miller, 1856.

Journal of the Congress of the Confederate States of America, 1861–1865. 7 vols., Washington, D.C.: Government Printing Office, 1904–1905.

Lancaster, Clay. *Eutaw: The Builders and Architecture of an Ante-Bellum Southern Town*. Eutaw, Ala.: Greene County Historical Society, 1979.

"Letters From a Tyler Collection." *Tyler's Quarterly Historical and Genealogical Magazine*, XXX (October 1948), 93–114; (January 1949), 184–206.

McFeely, William S. *Grant: A Biography*. New York and London: W. W. Norton, 1981.

McKenzie, Robert H. "Horace Ware: Alabama Iron Pioneer." *Alabama Review*, XXVI (July 1973), 157–72.

McMillan, Malcolm C. *The Alabama Confederate Reader*. University, Ala.: University of Alabama Press, 1963.

McPherson, James. *Battle Cry of Freedom*. New York: Oxford University Press, 1988.

Mack Smith, Denis. *Garibaldi: A Great Life in Brief*. New York: Alfred A. Knopf, 1956.

Malone, Dumas, ed. *Dictionary of American Biography*. 22 vols., New York: Charles Scribner's Sons, 1928–1944.

Mears & Turnbull, comp. *The Charleston Directory . . . [1859]*. Charleston, S.C.: Walker, Evans & Co., 1859.

Myers, William Starr. *A Study in Personality: General George Brinton Mc-Clellan*. New York and London: D. Appleton-Century Co., 1934.

Nathans, Elizabeth Studley. *Losing the Peace: Georgia Republicans and Reconstruction, 1865–1871*. Baton Rouge: Louisiana State University Press, 1968.

Oates, Stephen B. *To Purge This Land With Blood: A Biography of John Brown*. New York: Harper & Row, 1970.

O'Connor, Richard. *The Cactus Throne: The Tragedy of Maximilian and Carlotta*. New York: G. P. Putnam's Sons, 1971.

The Official Atlas of the Civil War. New York and London: Thomas Yoseloff, 1954.

Owen, Thomas McAdory. *History of Alabama and Dictionary of Alabama Biography*. 4 vols., Chicago: S. J. Clarke Publishing Co., 1921.

Palmer, Thomas Waverly, comp. *A Register of the Officers and Students of the University of Alabama 1831–1900*. Tuscaloosa: University of Alabama, 1901.

Pearce, Haywood J., Jr. *Benjamin H. Hill: Secession and Reconstruction*. Chicago: University of Chicago Press, 1928.

Proceedings of a Court Martial for the Trial of Surgeon B. M. Byrne Held at Fort Moultrie, S.C. on March 24th, 1859. Charleston, S.C.: Walker, Evans & Co., 1859.

The Protestant Episcopal Almanac, for the Year of Our Lord 1868. New York: John A. Gray & Green, 1868.

Rable, George C. *But There Was No Peace: The Role of Violence in the Politics of Reconstruction*. Athens: University of Georgia Press, 1984.

Ramsdell, Charles William. *Reconstruction in Texas*. New York: Longmans, Green & Co., 1910.

Roland, Charles P. *Albert Sidney Johnston: Soldier of Three Republics*. Austin: University of Texas Press, 1964.

Rosengarten, Frederic, Jr. *Freebooters Must Die! The Life and Death of William Walker, the Most Notorious Filibuster of the Nineteenth Century*. Wayne, Pa.: Haverford House, 1976.

Scharf, J. Thomas. *History of the Confederate States Navy . . . .* New York: Rogers & Sherwood, 1887.

Sears, Stephen W., ed. *The Civil War Papers of George B. McClellan: Selected Correspondence 1860–1865*. New York: Ticknor & Fields, 1989.

Sellers, James B. *History of the University of Alabama*, Volume I. University, Ala.: University of Alabama Press, 1953.

Soard's New Orleans City Directory for 1874 . . . . New Orleans: L. Soards & Co., [1874].

Sparks, Jared, ed. *A Collection of the Familiar Letters and Miscellaneous Papers of Benjamin Franklin; Now for the First Time Published*. Boston: C. Bowen, 1833.

Still, William N., Jr. *Iron Afloat: The Story of the Confederate Armorclads*. Nashville: Vanderbilt University Press, 1971.

Strode, Hudson. *Jefferson Davis: Tragic Hero. The Last Twenty-Five Years 1864–1889.* New York: Harcourt, Brace & World, 1964.

Summersell, Charles G. "Introduction," Peter J. Hamilton, *Colonial Mobile.* 1910, reprint ed., University, Ala.: University of Alabama Press, 1976.

Sutherland, Daniel E. *The Confederate Carpetbaggers.* Baton Rouge: Louisiana State University Press, 1988.

Trefousse, Hans L. *Andrew Johnson: A Biography.* New York and London: W. W. Norton, 1989.

Truran, W. *The Iron Manufacture of Great Britain, Theoretically and Practically Considered;* . . . . London: E. and F. N. Spon, 1865.

Vandiver, Frank E. "Josiah Gorgas and The Brierfield Iron Works." *Alabama Review,* III (January 1950), 6–21.

——. *Ploughshares into Swords: Josiah Gorgas and Confederate Ordnance.* Austin: University of Texas Press, 1952.

Vandiver, Frank E., ed. "The Capture of a Confederate Blockade Runner: Extracts From the Journal of a Confederate Naval Officer." *North Carolina Historical Review,* XXI (April 1944), 136–38.

——. *The Civil War Diary of General Josiah Gorgas.* University, Ala.: University of Alabama Press, 1947.

——. "Extracts From the Diary of Richard H. Gayle, Confederate States Navy." *Tyler's Quarterly Historical and Genealogical Magazine,* XXX (October 1948), 86–92.

Varney, George J. *A Brief History of Maine.* Portland, Me.: McLellan, Mosher & Co., 1888.

von Breton, Robin. *Miss Aiken's School.* New Orleans: Trinity Episcopal School, 1991.

Wakelyn, Jon L., ed. *Biographical Dictionary of the Confederacy.* Westport, Conn.: Greenwood Press, 1977.

Walsh, J. H. *The Horse, In The Stable and The Fields:* . . . . London: George Routledge and Sons, 1873.

War of the Rebellion: Official Records of the Union and Confederate Armies, Series I. 128 vols., Washington, D.C.: Government Printing Office, 1880–1901.

Warner, Ezra J. *Generals in Gray: Lives of the Confederate Commanders.* Baton Rouge: Louisiana State University Press, 1959.

——. *Generals in Blue: Lives of the Union Commanders.* Baton Rouge: Louisiana State University Press, 1964.

Wiggins, Sarah Woolfolk. "Amelia Gayle Gorgas: A Victorian Mother," in *Stepping Out of the Shadows: Alabama Women, 1819–1990,* ed. by Mary Martha Thomas. Tuscaloosa: University of Alabama Press, 1995.

——. "Introduction," to *Physician to the World: The Life of General William C. Gorgas,* by John M. Gibson. 1950, reprint ed., Tuscaloosa: University of Alabama Press, 1989.

——. "The 'Pig Iron' Kelley Riot in Mobile, May 14, 1867." *Alabama Review,* XXIII (January 1970), 45–55.

——. "Press Reaction in Alabama to the Attempted Assassination of Judge Richard Busteed." *Alabama Review,* XXI (July 1968), 211–19.

————. "A Victorian Father: Josiah Gorgas and His Family," in *In Joy and In Sorrow: Women, Family, and Marriage in the Victorian Era*, ed. by Carol Bleser. New York: Oxford University Press, 1991.

Wilson, James Grant, and John Fiske, eds. *Appleton's Cyclopaedia of American Biography*. 7 vols., New York: D. Appleton and Co., 1888.

Wright, Marcus J. *General Officers of the Confederate Army: . . . .* New York: Neale Publishing Co., 1911.

Index